For my grandmother

WHEN YOU AND YOUR MOTHER CAN'T BE FRIENDS

RESOLVING THE MOST COMPLICATED RELATIONSHIP OF YOUR LIFE

VICTORIA SECUNDA

Delta

A Delta Book
Published by
Dell Publishing
a division of
Bantam Doubleday Dell Publishing Group, Inc.
666 Fifth Avenue
New York, New York 10103

Contents

The more we idealize the past . . . and refuse to acknowledge our childhood sufferings, the more we pass them on unconsciously to the next generation.

—Alice Miller, Ph.D.

Acknowledgments

Many authors say that writing is a lonely profession. In my experience, it is anything but. This book could not have been accomplished without the help and involvement—intellectually, professionally, and personally—of others.

I owe an enormous intellectual debt to those researchers, social scientists, and clinicians who have studied patterns in how and why people behave as they do. These authorities include:

Alexander Thomas, M.D., and Stella Chess, M.D., professors of psychiatry at New York University Medical Center, who have studied temperament in children since the 1950s and who coined the terms "easy child," "difficult child" and "slow-to-warm-up child";

Virginia Satir, a pioneer in family therapy who, in her book *Peoplemaking*, cited patterns in how people deal with rejection;

Sharon Wegscheider, whose landmark book about the impact of alcoholism on families, *Another Chance: Hope and Health for the Alcoholic Family*, brought the terms "Enabler," "Hero," "Scapegoat," "Lost Child," and "Mascot" into the lexicon;

Lucy Rose Fischer, Ph.D., who described patterns of mother–daughter relationships in her book *Linked Lives: Adult Daughters and Their Mothers*;

Tessa Albert Warschaw, Ph.D., who described styles of behavior in her book *Winning by Negotiation*, and with whom I collaborated for *Winning with Kids*, which discussed behavioral styles in children as well as in their parents.

Inspired by their work, and drawing from my own journalistic experience, I discovered constellations of behavior in the hundred women I interviewed for this book. I found these women through

xi

two sources: first, through friends who graciously and enthusiastically gave me dozens of names. Second, through an ad I placed in the *Pennysaver,* a publication of classified advertisements that is delivered to most of the homes of people in Westchester and Putnam counties in New York.

The ad—which said, "Author seeks interview subjects for a book on difficult mother–daughter relationships"—drew more than 150 responses, many from women in other states whose friends or relatives had sent it to them. There was no dearth of interview subjects: indeed, I was still receiving calls from women eager to describe their relationships with their mothers and/or with their grown daughters and sons long after my research was complete.

Through these sources, I was able to find a cross section of women, aged twenty-two to seventy-nine, from every socioeconomic level. There is no way to thank them adequately or to convey how deeply they all moved me. Their candor was stunning, sometimes shattering. The trust they placed in an author they had never met was extraordinary, and I will eternally be grateful to them. To protect their identities, I have changed their names and identifying characteristics.

I am grateful also to these authorities who generously and patiently shared their expertise in interviews:

Jane B. Abramson, Ph.D., psychologist, faculty member of the National College of Education in Evanston, Illinois; Jill Cannon, A.C.S.W., C.A.C., addictions family specialist; Ann F. Caron, EE.D., developmental psychologist who conducts mother–daughter workshops; Christina Crawford; Adele Faber, coauthor of *Siblings Without Rivalry;* Judith M. Fox, psychoanalyst; Elizabeth Fishel, author of *Sisters: Love and Rivalry Inside the Family and Beyond;*

James Garbarino, Ph.D., president of the Erikson Institute for Advanced Study in Child Development in Chicago; Judith Gerberg, M.A., art therapist and authority on change management and career development; Marianne Goodman, M.D., psychiatrist and associate clinical instructor in adult psychiatry at Mount Sinai Medical Center in New York; Ann Gordon, M.A., psychotherapist who conducts mother–daughter workshops; Michael D. Kahn, Ph.D., professor of psychology, University of Hartford; Michael Kerr, M.D., psychiatrist, Director of Training, Georgetown University Family Center; Harriet Goldhor Lerner, Ph.D., clinical psychologist and psychotherapist at the Menninger Clinic in Topeka, Kansas; Elaine Mazlish, coauthor, *Siblings Without Rivalry;* Lilly Singer, director of the

Bereavement Center of Westchester Jewish Community Services;
Allan Stempler, M.D., psychiatrist, instructor in clinical psychiatry,
Cornell University at Northshore University Hospital and adjunct
instructor at New York College of Osteopathic Medicine.

For research help and valuable leads, I wish to thank Liz Smith;
Stephen L. Isaacs, director of the Development Law & Policy
Program at the Center for Population and Family Health at Colum-
bia University; Danielle Clarke, director, Lee Stark, reference li-
brarian, and the staff of the North Castle Public Library, Armonk,
New York.

I am grateful also to Lazarus Secunda, M.D., psychiatrist, assist-
ant professor of psychiatry at UCLA (retired), for his careful reading
of the manuscript and for his knowledge.

The encouragement and support of my friends were incalculable.
These people cheered me on in the long months of my hibernation,
clucked over the snags and occasional hairpulling that accompanied
it, and gave me extremely helpful suggestions. I wish to thank
especially Kathleen Beckett-Young, Judy Chriss, Barbara Coats, Sherry
Suib Cohen, Eileen Prescott Drape, Janet Elder, Ava Swartz Isaacs,
Mary Alice Kellogg, Enid Moore, Laurie Nadel, Margaret B. Parkinson,
Jane Bryant Quinn, Nancy Rubin, Ann McGovern Scheiner, Peggy
Schmidt, Jane Snowday, Judy Tobias, and Stephanie von Hirschberg.

My thanks go also to Mary Anne Sacco of Delacorte for her
unflagging patience, intelligence, and good will.

However, there are six people who were of particular and immea-
surable help to me, and to whom I owe the greatest debt:

Donna Jackson, editor-at-large of *New Woman*, is the godmother of
this book. It is she who first gave me the courage and impetus to
write about mother–daughter disaffection, and who assigned me the
article "Should You Divorce Your Mother?" that ran in *New Woman*,
parts of which appear in this book. Donna has been my professional—
and in many ways, personal—mentor since we met in 1984; she is a
woman of consummate editing skill, insight, brilliance, and compassion, whose friendship I cherish and count upon.

Janet H. Gardner, another treasured, talented, and admirable
writer, editor, and friend, read the manuscript and gave me invalu-
able comments in countless meetings. Janet saved me from my
hapless penchant for mixing metaphors, among other egregious editorial atrocities (including an excess of alliteration). Her part in the
smoothing of the manuscript, to say nothing of her hand-holding,
cannot be overstated.

Bob Miller, editorial director of Delacorte and my editor on this book, is its godfather. He has—in his solicitousness, availability, enthusiastic and immediate responses to chunks of manuscript and phone calls, professionalism, good humor, and sensitivity—spoiled me forever. His belief in this project and gentle and extraordinary guidance were boundless. He is a gentleman of the old editorial school, and I cannot thank him enough for his advocacy and confidence in me.

My agent, Elaine Markson, and her associate, Geri Thoma, have, from beginning to end, been enthusiastic and supportive. Elaine is a woman of uncommon understanding, intelligence, and generosity. I am lucky indeed to be represented by so kindred a soul.

My daughter, Jennifer Heller, not only patiently endured my ungraceful crankiness under pressure and my work schedule, which banished her from what was once the family room and is now my office, but also contributed enormously in her courageous willingness to be discussed in print. It was she who encouraged me to describe in detail our connection, its highs and lows, and who enjoined me not to soften its occasional painfulness. This book had a profound impact on each of us, separately and together. Our relationship, mother and daughter, evolved with this project, and is essential to it. If I have taught her, so, too, has she taught me. Being a mother, and having this specific and amazing young woman as my daughter, is the most profound, complex, and rewarding experience of my life. Because of it, I was able, finally, to grow up.

Finally, I wish to thank my husband, Shel Secunda, who is the kindest person I ever met, and whose support of my writing over the years, in spite of its attendant setbacks and frustrations, has never been less than wholehearted. He is my rousing champion, partner, friend, and fearless editorial critic. His reading of everything I write has had the deepest impact on my work, and I am grateful to him beyond counting. But for him, I would not be a writer today.

—VICTORIA SECUNDA

Introduction

There is something about the painful mother–daughter relationship that can linger, for many adult daughters, with punishing tenacity. These daughters may be bright, sensitive, competent women who are valiantly trying to overcome their troubled beginnings—yet they are haunted by them, as though they had flunked childhood.

These women—tempered by stormy or chilly attachments to their mothers, survivors of emotional want, strong by any other measure—grow weak in the knees, or are choked with sadness, or are shaken with rage, when recalling their childhoods. Their mothers may be long dead, or white-haired and infirm, but still they have a profound hold on their daughters, who talk of them as though they were about to be sent to their rooms.

How is this reign of terror by little old ladies possible? Because when these adult daughters speak of their mothers, the daughters are once again rebuked children, and the mothers are again young parents with the power to break a child's heart with a look. Recollection strips away the years and smooths the wrinkles, as though the family album abruptly ended decades ago and there are no recent photographs. Time may have moved on, but not childhood feelings and fears, trapped in the emulsion of a grown daughter's memory.

But to do battle against an outdated—and, perhaps, distorted—image of one's mother is, in a sense, like flailing away at someone who, by holding you at arm's length, does not allow you in close enough to land a punch. The mother who is feared or despised is no longer there—only a pale and aging trace of her remains—and so the struggle is moot.

Yet the struggle often continues with anguishing zeal. Why? And what can be done about it?

The odyssey of transcending a painful and seemingly hopeless mother–daughter relationship is what this book addresses. It is written for that group of women whose extremely painful childhood relationships with their mothers skew their adulthoods in ways they may not even recognize. These daughters are often unaware that it is possible not only to resolve an unhappy mother–daughter connection, but also to understand their mothers, and even to feel empathy for them.

But to achieve that resolution, the daughters must have the courage to examine the relationship with a desire to make sense of it and to heal, rather than overreact to it, either through supplication or rage. They need to see their mothers not as falling short of mythical maternal perfection, but as women of human proportion who are products of their times and experiences.

For when a difficult mother–daughter relationship is unresolved, it has the potential of jeopardizing, even destroying all our other attachments—to friends, lovers, spouses, colleagues, children, grandchildren.

That lack of resolution can keep us tethered to our mothers, or to an image of them, like a disoriented whale that cannot be coaxed out into the open sea but instead keeps returning to unsafe shore. And it can distort our perceptions—trust comes hard, or far too easily, and our instincts become muffled.

For example: *We may befriend people who have many of our mother's most destructive characteristics.* One woman told me, "I am always drawn to strong, forceful, controlling women, and I always end up being intimidated by them. It's as though I'm trying to tame a kind of tiger—they remind me of my mother, so if I can get them to like me by taking their advice, or never disagreeing with them, it's like getting her to like me."

For example: *We may impulsively, and unfairly, reject or hurt people who remind us of our mothers.* "Sometimes I see my mother where she doesn't exist," says another woman. "If a friend corrects my grammar, for instance, I lash out, because it feels as though she's trying to humiliate me, the way my mother always did. I'm learning to say to myself 'Take a beat—the person *reminds* you of Mom, but she *isn't* Mom. Don't overreact.' "

For example: *We may marry people who are very like our mothers.* Said a third woman, "I married my mother's psychic twin—a man who needed me to 'mother' him, to make all his decisions for him. Fortunately, I realized what I had done, got some therapy, and eventually got out."

For example: *We may try to create in our children the loving mothers we never had, rather than being a source of parental strength and nurturing to those children.* Says a fourth woman, "My daughter was my 'pal.' For the first ten years of her life she was the center of mine, which almost destroyed my marriage. I was going to have fun with her in a way I never did with my mother. I would tell her all my problems. The upshot is that today she has no friends and is afraid to go to school; she doesn't know how to get along with kids her own age."

For example: *We may be unable to draw the line with our mothers and set limits, repeatedly subjecting ourselves and our families to inappropriate behavior.* "My mother gets unbelievably nasty and ugly," says a fifth woman, "but I can't help worrying about her. Recently she had a cold, and my five-year-old son and I went to visit her. He accidentally dropped a glass of milk on the floor; she flew into a rage and threw us out of the house. Even so, I still feel this obligation to call her all the time."

The biggest challenge for the daughters in these examples is to separate from their mothers so that they can gain a healthy perspective not only about those mothers, but also about themselves, their relationships, and their choices.

Separation does not mean firing one's mother from the family (although, as we will see, in extreme cases it may mean either not seeing her for a time, or making a permanent break); rather, separation means not having one's self-esteem *depend* on her approval but, instead, learning how to approve of, and understand, oneself.

The goal of this book is to help readers achieve that separation so that they can either find a way to be friends with their mothers, or at least recognize and accept that their mothers did the best they could—even if it wasn't "good enough"—and to stop blaming them.

Among the issues to be covered:

• To understand how a daughter's attachment to her mother—more so than her relationship with her father—colors all her other relationships, and to analyze why it is more difficult for daughters than sons to separate from their mothers, as well as why daughters are more subject than sons to a mother's manipulation;

• To recognize the difference between a healthy and a destructive mother–daughter connection, and to define clearly the "bad mommy," in order to help readers who have trouble acknowledging their childhood losses to begin to comprehend them;

• To conjugate what I call the "Bad Mommy Taboo"—why our culture is more eager to protect the sanctity of maternity than it is to protect emotionally abused daughters;

• To describe the evolution of the "unpleasable" mother—in all likelihood, she was bereft of maternal love as a child—and to recognize the huge, and often poignant, stake she has in keeping her grown daughter dependent and off-balance;

• To illustrate the consequent controlling behavior—in some cases, cloaked in fragility or good intentions—of such mothers, which falls into general patterns, including:

> the Doormat
> the Critic
> the Smotherer
> the Avenger
> the Deserter

• To understand that the daughter has a similar stake in either being a slave to or hating her mother—the two sides of her dependency and immaturity;

• To illustrate the responsive behavior—and survival mechanisms —of daughters, which is determined in part by such variables as birth rank, family history, and temperament, and which also falls into patterns, including:

> the Angel
> the Superachiever
> the Cipher
> the Troublemaker
> the Defector

• To show how to redefine the mother–daughter relationship, so that each can learn to see and accept the other as she is today, appreciating each other's good qualities and not being snared by the bad;

• Finally, to demonstrate that a redefined relationship with one's mother—adult to adult—frees you from the past, whether that redefinition ultimately results in real friendship, affectionate truce, or divorce.

Learning to abide one's mother—hence, oneself—embraces two leitmotivs: generosity and self-preservation. Both are difficult to achieve when you haven't discovered your separate identity.

I interviewed one hundred women between the ages of twenty-two and seventy-nine who have or had difficult relationships with their mothers, and who are in varying stages of resolving their unhappy childhoods. They are caught somewhere between the twin imperatives of longing for an *ideal* relationship with their mothers and becoming reconciled with what is *possible;* between childlike fantasy and measured, adult perspective.

Many of these women struggle to be good enough mothers to their own children and anxiously attempt to avoid repeating the mistakes their mothers made. But they have a tandem struggle—learning to accept themselves as good enough daughters and getting beyond blame.

These mother–daughter connections run the gamut of expectation and resolution, from murderous rage to loving respect for each other's differences. There is the eighty-five-year-old mother living with her sixty-two-year-old-daughter, each with a padlock on her bedroom door to prevent intrusion and theft by the other.

In contrast to that ferocious attachment, there is the thirty-eight-year-old woman who said of her mother, "I have never for one moment doubted that she loves me. At the same time, she overrates me, believing that I am capable of extraordinary things. I've never been able to live up to that expectation."

Then there's the forty-one-year-old woman who sees her mother only at weddings and funerals. "She hates me because my father and I have a closer relationship than she and I ever did. He only calls me when she's out of the house—if she's there and she finds him talking to me, she makes him hang up. I can understand why she is the way she is—her father died when she was a little girl—but I'll never forgive her for shutting me out."

And there is the twenty-nine-year-old woman who describes her extremely critical mother as "never being hurtful to me out of a need to destroy me, but out of a need to protect herself. Once I realized that, she could no longer harm me." She and her mother have resolved their differences, and formed a friendship that in ways is sturdier and more tempered than most because of its rocky beginnings. (*Note:* Such mothers are often able to make up for their past parenting mistakes by becoming wonderful grandmothers.)

Admitting that you are among the group of "unacceptable" daughters described in this book—if indeed you are—is to feel, in the deepest reaches of the soul, permanently abandoned by the one person who is *supposed* to love you, *no matter what.* You never completely get over it. But you can learn to make sense of it and to recognize the cost, so that healing can begin.

One cost that many of these daughters share is that while in childhood they craved affection, they nevertheless often grow up to be adults who unconsciously sabotage themselves by not allowing others to love them, and by not knowing how to love. The child who constantly tried to please her unpleasable mother can become an adult who doesn't recognize or trust healthy love when it comes her way because she's never experienced it. She only recognizes it if it resembles the "love" she got at home. And so the truly loving man may be perceived as weak and manipulable, even as she was "weak and manipulable"; *she treats him as she was treated, knowing no other way.* "Love" gets skewed.

Compounding that cost is the Bad Mommy Taboo, the cultural mandate to put a good face on your childhood and not expose the wounds, to camouflage the grief and rage, never to say "My mother could not demonstrate love for me." For some women this is a simple truth—but they express it at their peril. And so they learn to hate themselves—and, later, perhaps, their children—instead.

The Bad Mommy Taboo appears in many forms, including the view that *any* criticism of mothers amounts to so much "mommy bashing." Such a position equates saying that one's mother was unpleasable with a campaign to keep women down. The real fault—so the argument goes—rests in not holding fathers, whose parental role is minimal (compared to the mother's), equally responsible for how their kids turn out.

Women, say these critics, are not only not allowed a position equal to men in the culture and in the family, they are also, and unfairly, held responsible for acting out their consequent frustrations with their children.

It is true that many mothers reared in the 1920s and 1930s were incalculably frustrated at being the sole and unsung arbiters of their children's souls and bowels, while fathers got the cultural power and glory. But that ineffable division of gender-based labor and social worth doesn't make it right that certain of those mothers—not *all* of them—overreacted to that inequity by wielding inappropriate power over powerless children.

Obviously, there are times when a daughter will jump track and the mother is not responsible—such variables as certain forms of severe psychological and physical illness are beyond a mother's control. And there are times when a mother will, when her daughter is grown, try to make amends, and the daughter, refusing to grow up, will have none of it.

But if a mother has an unhealthy need to dominate her children—which she demonstrates by bullying, terrifying, neglecting, suffocating, indulging, humiliating, overprotecting, or abusing them—those children must come to the recognition that such treatment is wrong in order to begin the long process of recovery and ultimate understanding.

At the same time, the daughters, in adulthood, must also make the effort to really *know* their mothers—which many daughters do not—in order to understand what forces shaped those mothers. These daughters need to discover what torment may have unwittingly informed their mothers' parental choices, and to see their mothers as composites of strengths and weaknesses, rather than as all good or all bad.

We forget in order to survive our childhoods, when we are totally dependent on our parents' goodwill; but to recover from such childhoods, we must begin by remembering—the bad and the good.

The first step toward recovery, then, is recollection—a complicated process, as we will see in Chapter Three. Often it requires the help of a skilled, empathetic therapist to make such recollection safe.

The second step is to allow the feelings of loss to surface rather than be unconsciously rerouted and bubble up in other relationships. When we can recognize that we are not responsible for our childhood deprivations, and that we are entitled to *feel* anger (but not to act on it—awareness is not a license to kill), then we are able to *let go of that anger* and not be controlled by it.

It is then possible to begin to relinquish childish expectations, which persist in our need in adulthood either to continue to try to win the approval of one's mother, or to continue to hate her. Most of the time this means making changes in oneself so that a healthy relationship with one's mother on *some* basis can be established.

But in extreme and rare cases it means dealing with her in absentia, either temporarily or permanently. For some daughters—for their sanity and salvation and hope of any kind of loving future—it may never be safe to go home again.

But always those daughters must, if only in anguished memory, learn to accept their mothers—who could not get past their own demons—in order not to be imprisoned by lifelong, highly charged reactions of either fury or unconditional surrender. Only then can the daughters find answers to the questions that haunt them: Am I an emotional cripple? Will I visit upon my children the sins that were visited upon me? Am I unlovable?

The process of healing includes seeing one's mother as *other* than oneself; recognizing that she is the legatee of *her* mother's behavior; acknowledging how terribly limited her choices may have been; realizing that such mothers are more to be pitied; and being freed from, as psychoanalyst Alice Miller puts it, the "prison of childhood."

Out of that effort, it is possible to forge an understanding of, sometimes even a close friendship with, one's mother. By resolving our feelings toward our mothers, we can learn to accept them and, in so doing, gain a deeper understanding and acceptance of ourselves.

Most important, we can finally grow up so that we do not perpetuate the historical imperative of unpleasable mothers, one generation after another, each too wounded to allow love in or out. The "cure" comes in being able to become a loving mother to oneself—and to one's children—in spite of having a poor role model upon which to pattern our maternity. The victory is in choosing not to be victims of the past but, instead, in *breaking the cycle of unhappy mother–daughter connections* as they echo in all our attachments.

We cannot rewrite history, but we can redirect the future, by not becoming unloving mothers—or uncaring friends, or lovers, or colleagues—ourselves. We can learn to see our mothers as women of human proportion. And we can become a generation of transitional daughters through whom the legacy of unacceptability got rerouted, and with whom the metaphorical parental buck stopped.

No daughter ever wants to feel like an unloved child; no young woman wants to feel that she could never be a good mother; and no mother wants to believe that she has failed as a parent. When mother and adult daughter can get beyond their wariness, their catalogue of grievances, their losses, hesitations and hurts—when they can get beyond *blame*—the potential for healing is enormous.

"Nothing, ever, wipes out childhood," wrote Simone de Beauvoir. With sympathy for both sides of the generation gap, *When You and Your Mother Can't Be Friends* explores the difficult mother–daughter connection and the importance of resolving the most intimate and complex relationship—the first one—in a woman's life.

Part One
Ghosts in the Nursery

1
Natural Allies, Natural Enemies

I have always tried to be all the things my mother wanted me to be: ever the lady, always polite, never inconsiderate. I run my business the way my mother ran our house—everything just so. In some ways I am my mother—full of life when I'm happy, very cold when I'm angry. People say I look just like her.

I'll tell you a secret: Every time I pass a mirror, I gasp. I wonder if there's more here than meets the eye.

—Karen, thirty-nine

Few comments strike as much terror in the female heart, or more rapidly raise a lovers' tiff to the boiling point, than the comment "You're getting more like your mother every day."

You may love your mother. You may even *like* her. Nevertheless, there resides within each daughter the need to be different, to improve on the old model, to be a composite of all your own unique goodness and take total credit for it. Woven into the mother–daughter tie is a built-in and unavoidable tension that goes with the territory of being someone's child.

And so the suggestion that you are your mother's clone cuts to the very heart of independence; it suggests not only that you are still a child and incapable of standing on your own but, worse, that you may be a composite only of her flaws—*all of which you know intimately and in excruciating detail.*

At the same time, there is a genetic booby trap in trying to carve out your identity when your mother shares much of that identity.

3

For a daughter to withdraw entirely from her mother is to reject her role model, her mentor, her template; love-hate is the natural order of things—we can separate, but only so far.

There is for daughters a limit to how different from Mom we realistically can be because, damn it, in many ways we simply *are* like her, ways that we cannot change—and when we're feeling good and able to see her as a whole person, might not even want to. Besides, who has known us longer than she has?

The truth is, in moments of crisis or tearful self-doubt, we need her—somehow, magically, we want to believe she is capable of making it all better, there, there. So we *don't* want to hurt her feelings and we *don't* want to risk her disapproval. On some level, rejecting Mama feels like shooting yourself in the foot.

And yet she can make us crazy.

I am standing in the sun-splashed kitchen of Martha, a friend since college, sipping a cup of coffee. While she is momentarily out of the room, her twenty-five-year-old daughter, Debby, visiting for the weekend, pads in for breakfast, her face shrouded in gloom. She pulls a mug from the cabinet, pours herself a cup of coffee, and says with a sigh,

> Mom sure is "off" today. Every time I ask her what's wrong, she says, "Nothing." I've spent the whole morning making nice, wondering if she's mad at me. My brother's much smarter than me. He sees her in a snit, asks himself, "Did I do something wrong?" decides he didn't and that it's her problem, gives her a big kiss, and goes about his business.
>
> Why can't I be like him? I *know* I didn't do anything, but still, I *feel* as if I did.

We do, still, very much want our mothers to love us; indeed, our mood, even our well-being, often depends on it.

So much so that we sometimes think we've erred *even when we haven't.*

So much so that she can shatter our day with a single phrase: "Nothing's wrong."

And she can do it, whether she is a saint or a monster.

Like Mother, Like Daughter

Mothers and daughters—they are, as journalist Liz Smith puts it, "natural allies [and] natural enemies." Loving your mother represents the best and the worst of times.

I remember once remarking to my mother, when I was in elementary school, that a friend of the family reminded me of Miss Havisham in Dickens's *Great Expectations.*

"That's very well put," she said.

Set aside, if you will, the fact that I had plucked the analogy from something I had read because it sounded good to me, too. The fact is, I have never forgotten the compliment—indeed, it was the moment at which my ambition to become a writer first began to take shape.

But I have also never forgotten the time when, at sixteen and, no doubt, in high adolescent dudgeon, I disagreed with her in front of guests about something. My mother, as though struck, whirled around and snapped, "Sit down in front of your elders and your betters." Even in decades-old recollection, the rebuke still stings, like a raw sunburn.

No relationship is as highly charged as that between mother and daughter, or as riddled with expectations that could, like a land mine, detonate with a single misstep, a solitary stray word that, without warning, wounds or enrages. And no relationship is as bursting with possibilities of goodwill and understanding.

What is it about the attachment that gives it such *power?* Why is it so different from the relationship between mothers and sons, or fathers and sons, for that matter?

For one thing, there is no human being who is, literally, as similar to us—indeed, mothers and daughters mirror each other right down to genes and sexual engineering. We may even look like her. Like mother, we have breasts, can bear children, and feminist revisionism notwithstanding, are usually our family's, or partner's, emotional caretaker. And like her, we are vulnerable to sexism and rape.

Nor is any relationship as competitive: like Mother, we compete for Dad's attention. And, both spawned in female vanity, we are encouraged to be vain, vying for a favorable report from the mirror on the wall and the bathroom scale on the floor. We try to tailor ourselves to at least keep pace with her—if not best her—on the work path or in our choice of mates.

She is the yardstick against which we measure ourselves: have we done "it"—education, career, sexuality, marriage, thinness, popularity, chic, motherhood, the gentle arts of homemaking—as well as she has? Better? Differently?

Because if we have done "it" both well *and* differently, we are then prepared to survive without her. We have completed the course.

But there's a hitch in the mother–daughter separation process: We want to survive, but not entirely without her. We want to detach, but not defect. Because, like it or not, we are still very much bound up with her.

Whether our relationship is strained or easy, hostile or amiable, we need her, if only in memory or fantasy, to conjugate our history, validate our femaleness, and guide our way; we need to know she's there if we stumble, to love us *no matter what*, to nurture the child that resides within us even now without infantilizing us. It is a need that never leaves us in the best of mother–daughter attachments and, in the worst, yawns wider than the heart can bear.

A mother sets the tone for her daughter's life, provides a road map and role model, continues through the daughter's middle and old age to be her example, particularly her genetic and emotional example. So we ask her: When did she menstruate? Begin menopause? How did she feel about and deal with love? Friendship? Work? Sexual longing? Loneliness?

But if mother and daughter have no connection, we cannot ask the one person whose psyche and body have programmed our own. That's why the loss is incalculable when a daughter has to figure it out for herself, trailblaze rather than follow her mother's example or learn from it. Such a daughter has to discover herself, alone.

"Women may define themselves . . . in terms of their work roles, but the pull in the opposite direction, to merge blissfully and symbiotically with the mother, is as strong as ever," writes Dr. Jane B. Abramson in *Mothermania: A Psychological Study of Mother–Daughter Conflict.* "It is inherent in the human condition."

That merging becomes evident in ways that are expected and very much conscious, as well as at the most unexpected and surprising moments.

Joan is by any measure an independent, achieving woman. President of an advertising agency, she is the pride of her physician husband and her two grown sons, who adore her. She is invited to give speeches and to receive awards all over the country. But at forty-nine, Joan still calls her mother for advice at least once, sometimes twice, every day, no matter where she is. Says Joan,

I can't be with my mother five minutes without wanting to kill her. And yet I really believe in my heart of hearts that I would be nothing without her.

She has always said, "In the end, no matter what happens—you could murder, you could steal, you could be a disgrace—no matter what happens *only your mother really loves you. Your mother will never, never turn her back on you. You can't trust anybody but your mother.*" And I believe it.

Angela, thirty-nine, a divorced elementary school teacher in a small town, feels her mother's presence in other ways:

My mother influences my choices even though she's not here to see what they are. I know what she *thinks*. I hear her voice when I clean my house, telling me where to put this and where to put that and not to sweep anything under the rug.

I've always wanted to become a lawyer. But I hear my mother again, saying, "How could you give up your job and abandon your family? How could you *be away from me* for two whole years?"

No matter what I do, I always hear her voice. So I don't clean my house so well—my rebellion. But I also don't go to law school.

These "messages," these "voices," are repeated over a daughter's lifetime in a maternal litany that shapes the contours of our lives. They begin with the first breath we draw as infants, our physical connection to our mother abruptly severed, and our first step in the journey toward independence as abruptly begun.

Infancy is a time of wondrous sorcery when we have no sense of ourselves as a thing apart from mother. The infant cries and is picked up, its body shudders in relief, unaware of where it ends and the mother begins—they are, as far as the child is concerned, still one. It is the most perfect of unions, every need met—shelter, protection, love, food—all suffused by physical closeness to mother, the warmth and comfort of her skin, the smell and taste of her milk, the soothing reassurance of her voice, her adoring smile and touch.

Unless, of course, the infant cries and is *not* picked up. Or is yelled at. At that awful moment, the baby, her body tensing, begins to be aware of something missing, even if she does not understand cause and effect; she continues to howl for some *thing* to ease the panic, the anguish of *not* being held, or fed, or tended to.

And if mother, or her surrogate, does not "rescue" the child, the world begins to be a dangerous place.

One reason it is vital to respond to an infant's needs is that the baby feels it is the cause of its own neglect, although this is not a conscious thought. Such narcissistic feelings pave the road to an infant's psychological and physical growth; since the baby senses no boundaries between herself and her mother, she "believes" that her cries cause the mother to tend to her.

And if the mother does *not* tend to her, the baby believes that she created her own rejection by not being lovable, not worthy of care. It is a belief that haunts one's life. (Eventually, if repeatedly ignored for long periods of time or abandoned, the baby shuts down all feeling, all hope, all awareness, all appetite, and loses its will to live.) The absence of "Mommy"—or of whoever the caregiver is—becomes terrifying, even life-threatening.

But if, as is usually the case, its mother does give love and attention and nurturing, the baby begins to learn that the world *is* a safe place, and she eagerly runs to explore it. For as much as the infant longs for the protective warmth of its mother's arms, so too does it yearn for a wider world—and the wider world is where the baby finds her "self."

Watch the toddler, her face wreathed in smiles, triumphantly stomp behind a chair, out of her mother's sight; and watch also the instant she realizes she cannot see her mother and, her face now frozen in fear, drops like a stone to the floor and frantically scuttles back to her mother's side.

The baby can "leave"—if, at first, only for a few moments—because, in a sense, she takes her mother with her. Because the mother has, time after time, been there for the baby, the baby becomes acquainted with trust. She internalizes the loving mother, incorporating her in her memory, and so is fueled to withstand longer and longer absences from her. (In adulthood, the internalized mother ultimately blends with the daughter's sense of self-esteem—she *becomes* a good mommy to herself and to others. But she can also internalize a *bad* mommy, as we shall see.)

The internalized, loving mother is the bedrock upon which a

sense of self is built, and that sense occurs only when the child feels secure about being *separate*. All later attachments reflect whether or not a mother has given loving permission to the child to be a "self"—even if that self is very different in temperament, goals, and timetables from the mother's.

Integral to being emotionally healthy is to have a mother who has the ability to respect her child's differences and not perceive them as betrayals. Separation presupposes that the mother feels good about herself, and, by recalling her own childhood, that she can both sympathize with her child's ambivalence about separation *and* give her a gentle push toward independence.

Such maternal love embraces both intimacy *and* separation: if she can lovingly let go, you can "leave" and become a confident, loving self, able to survive alone. And if she cannot, you will do anything in your power to *stay*—in childhood, by figuring out exactly what it is that she wants and delivering it (a "false self"), and in adulthood, by becoming excessively needy and inept or by constantly fighting with her. Anger binds us as tightly to our mothers as does surrender to them.

Until you can internalize a good mommy, you cannot trust a wider world.

And so life begins with a balance between the amazing grace of physical closeness to one's mother and the anguish of being apart from her. Because leaving her is *also* inherent in the human condition.

For infant boys and girls, separation means approximately the same thing, with minor differences—they are equally helpless. But once the baby reaches the age of eighteen months or so, the girl baby begins to become aware that she's *different* from boys. The world underscores that distinction: Boys are encouraged to take risks, to move as far and freely as possible without harming themselves, to hoard their feelings, to succeed on a solitary course, to be more like Daddy. And girls are encouraged to be cautious, to stay close to home, to wait to be invited to dance, to tell Mommy everything, to be generous, to be sensitive to the feelings of others, to pattern themselves after their mothers.

For these and other reasons, it's harder for girls to separate from their mothers than it is for boys.

Lucy Rose Fischer, who has studied mother–daughter relationships, writes,

The daughter's process of separation takes place against a background of mother–daughter intimacy: Mothers (much more than fathers) are argued against, withdrawn from, and rebuffed—while at the same time daughters continue to rely on their mothers' nurturance. For most of the daughters, it is the stability of their mothers' attachment to them that allows them to go through the process of separation and develop a sense of independence.

And even if the mother *cannot* give her daughter that kind of stable love, it is nevertheless more socially acceptable for a daughter than for a son to remain dependent and *not* strike out on her own.

"During adolescence," writes psychologist Louise J. Kaplan, "the emotional dissension between mothers and daughters can assume wild proportions. The struggle . . . is always exacerbated by the subtle social message that *girls are better off if they remain childlike*" (emphasis added).

Or, as this bit of nineteenth-century doggerel puts it, "Oh, my son's my son till he gets him a wife/But my daughter's my daughter all her life."

Boys Will Be Boys

How different it is for sons. A boy is born separate from his mother in an incalculably important way: having a penis, he is her sexual antithesis. Biology is very much destiny in the nursery; while the culture may smile benignly at the dependent daughter, it recoils at the first inkling that a son may be a "mama's boy."

If, according to social and psychological dictates, it is perilous for mothers and daughters to separate entirely, it is *as perilous* for mothers and sons not to. And the traditional method of preventing either dire eventuality, according to several feminist psychologists—who take issue with the double standard under which children are brought up—is to raise daughters within a framework of attachment, and to raise sons within a framework of separation.

Integral to that double standard, as Nancy Chodorow discusses it in *The Reproduction of Mothering*, is the fact that child-rearing, especially in the first three years of life, falls almost entirely to women, even when they work full-time. By contrast, most fathers are—and are socially sanctioned to be—relatively detached from the parenting process.

Put in the simplest terms, Chodorow's theory is this: Boys are encouraged to be separate and autonomous and are considered emotionally handicapped if they are dependent on other people, including mother, father, and siblings. Because they are in childhood usually more in the company of mother, who is the primary caregiver, than of father, sons learn to be "men" by keeping a certain emotional distance from her. And they identify with Dad not through intimacy with him but, as Chodorow puts it, in terms of being "not-mothers." She writes, "A boy, in order to feel himself adequately masculine . . . must categorize himself as someone apart . . . and learn the masculine role in the absence of a continuous and ongoing personal relationship to his father."

For sons, then, there is no great mystery about separation. All they have to do is watch what Mom does and do the opposite—wear pants, not a dress; be a tough guy, don't cry; choose the tires for a new car, not its color.

As for daughters, they are accustomed to intimate relationships, and are considered emotionally handicapped if they cannot form attachments. Identification with Mom is a natural and inevitable outgrowth of their ongoing connection and—relative to mothers and sons or daughters and fathers—greater time together. The identification process works both ways: a mother's daughter is an extension of herself in ways that her son can never be, so Mom expects more of her—more closeness, more understanding, more allegiance.

While such emotional stereotyping handicaps both sexes, it is much harder on girls, who are damned if they remain too attached to mother, because they risk becoming emotionally engulfed, and damned if they reject her entirely, because they risk both devaluing their ability to connect and inviting social derision.

If, in addition to this division of emotional labor, you factor in the mother–son incest taboo—heavy with sexual implications, fraught with the danger of son–father jealousies—it becomes even more urgent for Mom to establish boundaries between herself and her son.

Mother cannot risk causing a rift between father and son, nor can she jeopardize her role as wife by making her son Dad's rival, and so she sees to it that neither occurs by encouraging the son to be "manly"—to play rough-and-tumble games, to be outdoors, to not be "wimpy," to be less earth- and hearthbound than her daughter. And, of course, by not becoming too attached to him.

Says Dr. Marianne Goodman, a psychiatrist and associate clinical instructor in adult psychiatry at the Mount Sinai Medical Center in New York,

The whole myth of Oedipus is about a certain natural inborn taboo to the closeness between mothers and sons. Little boys become young adolescents, and when they do, they instinctively are attracted to their mothers—as well as their sisters—because they are the females who are available. But at the same time they are repulsed. And so in order to maintain a boundary between sons and mothers, sons have to push their mothers away. It's more difficult for daughters to separate from their mothers because girls are not only like mother in sex, but they are like mother in activity.

So if daughters reject mother, they're made to feel that there's something wrong with them. But if sons *don't* reject mother, there's something wrong with *them*.

Society smiles on this tacit agreement that a son ricochet from his mother in almost every way—*with mother's help* (save, of course, from being her eventual protector and, perhaps, source of financial support) —and, indeed, frets if he does not. It is mothers, then—even more so than fathers—who are the "builders of men."

"The Sainted Son"

The result is that, in general, Mom not only has fewer expectations of her son than of her daughter, but, because she feels less ambivalently tied to him, she may even prefer him to her daughter, or so it seems—it's what I call the "Sainted Son Syndrome."

The mothers I interviewed who have sons *and* daughters all confess to treating their sons with greater leniency—and if there is any perceived favoritism, it takes the form of mothers staying off their sons' backs.

Moreover, mothers can frequently be looser with sons, in part because they don't expect the same kind of devotion they do of a daughter. The mother of a twenty-four-year-old son put it this way: "There's not that urgency with him that I have with my daughter, that trying to make up for my childhood, to have a closeness that I didn't have with my mother. With my son, I have nothing to prove. So he and I can just horse around."

The inequities of this dynamic are not lost on daughters, who often writhe in prolonged sibling rivalry with a favored brother. "My brother can do no wrong," says Johanna, thirty-two. "If he calls my mother up, she thinks he's God almighty; if he doesn't call, she says, 'Oh, he's busy.' But if *I* don't call, I catch hell—she says, 'I never hear from you.' "

Favoritism toward sons is particularly noticeable when there is an illness in the family—daughters are called upon to be their mothers' surrogates to help with the "woman's work" of caregiving. Says Jessica, twenty-nine,

> My mom expects so much of me, but she never asks anything of my brother, David. Last year my dad was in the hospital for open-heart surgery, and I left my kids and went down there every day to visit him. One day my son was sick and I couldn't make it, so I said, "Tell David he has to go." She said, "He doesn't want to, he hates seeing Daddy like that." I said, "And you think I like it?"

A Word About Fathers

Just as maternal favoritism toward sons can erode a daughter's relationship with her mother, so, too, can a father's favoritism toward his daughter. Which is not to say that a father does not have a critically important role to play in his daughter's emotional and psychological well-being.

Under normal circumstances, a girl's father epitomizes freedom from her mother, an escape from maternal enmeshing. His primary psychological value to his daughter is in providing a sense of separateness from her mother—a function that is less urgent, for the reasons just discussed, with sons.

And, as a buffer between them, he can take the heat off the mother–daughter relationship. He does not use his daughter to fight his marital battles for him, nor does he allow himself to be a conduit for the mother's or the daughter's unresolved issues with each other. Instead, he encourages them to sort it out together.

Dr. Louise J. Kaplan, in *Oneness and Separateness*, argues that while daughters may mirror their mothers, when they are with their fathers they "begin to experience the possibilities of feminine identity outside the exclusive relationship with the mother. Being feminine doesn't mean being mommy."

Dad can supply a lap of understanding when Mom is absent, or blue, or out of sorts; his is another voice—indeed, a much *deeper* voice—that offers a different point of view and that also interprets for his daughter something of what it means to be loved by a man. And if he is closely involved with his daughter in a supportive, sympathetic way, it becomes easier for her to see her mother in a more objective light.

At his best, then, Dad—without being disloyal to his wife or undercutting her authority—becomes his daughter's safety valve, her male mentor, her port in the storm.

All too often, however, fathers can contribute to mother–daughter hostility. They do so in two ways: by becoming a nearly invisible presence within the family—avoiding upset at all costs and not coming to the daughter's defense when she is being mistreated; and by making their daughter "Daddy's Little Girl" and, hence, mother's rival. Neither course of action augers well for the mother–daughter relationship, as we will see in Chapter Four.

Sorting It Out

For these and other reasons, the mother–daughter relationship is, of all human attachments, the most intense, the most complex, and the most wrenching. *And part of why that is so is because the role of mother is the most difficult there is.* Women who are mothers are judged more by their parenting "successes" or "failures" than by any other area of their lives, and are held much more accountable for them than fathers are: for mothers, everything, it sometimes seems, is riding on how the kids turn out.

At the same time, women for whom having children means righting previous wrongs from their own childhoods, or ameliorating a bad marriage, may feel shortchanged by the mothering process. Because ultimately, your children, whether sons or daughters, are really only yours in that brief, vibrant, tender moment of their infancy—from the instant they are born to the first time they say no. Which, since "no" can be expressed by a face puckered in rage or spinach spat across a table, can be a matter of weeks or months.

If motherhood is the only identity a woman has, and if that woman was unloved by *her* mother, a "no" from her child feels like a blow.

All of which is understandable. But it can be an unbearable legacy for the daughters of such mothers, who inherit a double load of angst—their mother's doomed expectations, and their own. Daughters, more than sons, are stuck with the residue of their mothers' unmet needs and unrealized dreams.

Striking the delicate balance between longing to merge with mother and wanting to be a self is a lifelong process for both mother and child—the child is trying to create a separate identity, and if the mother did not create such an identity for herself, she may feel like a still-dependent child.

But motherhood is, in a sense, a one-way street; we give to and love our children not so they can love us back *in the same way*, but so that they will give to and love *their* children, *their* partners, *their* friends. The love they give back to us, child to parent, is unique; it cannot be the same, because being someone's child, regardless of age, is a thing apart.

We do not have the same loving agendas, nor can we, for when we do, the daughter cannot mature, cannot come into her own.

The unhappy mother–daughter bond that remains unresolved threatens all our attachments. When a daughter cannot separate from her mother, and when she *will not* or *is unable to* examine why, her unresolved feelings turn up in all her other relationships—what she could not get from her mother surfaces as an unrealistic need and expectation. She becomes all want, little give; all disappointment, little optimism; all appetite, little confidence. And so she may, in the saddest sense, indeed become more like her mother every day.

According to Dr. Kaplan and other therapists, people often go into therapy because of problems arising out of an inability to separate from their parents, to define themselves and stop trying to win parental approval.

Friendship between two people, even when they are mother and daughter, depends on clear boundaries between where you leave off and I begin; anything else is domination.

And so coming to terms with your mother begins with the hardest step of all: recognizing that all may not be well between you, and realizing that it's not only okay to reach that awareness, but that it may be imperative to your own mental health and to the potential health of your connection with your mother to do so.

But coming to terms also means acknowledging where your relationship is good and where your mother has honestly done her best. Because, since you and she are natural allies, the potential is there for a loving relationship and deepening understanding. The special bond you have, through shared biology and experience together, can nourish your ability to love and respect and support and learn from each other, cherishing your similarities and your differences. You can enlarge and enrich each other's worlds.

As Ruthann, forty-two, put it,

> Even though we were quite different in personality—she was shy and rather old-fashioned, I was an outspoken kid—it was my mother's pleasure to see me rebel and be alive. She didn't want me to be her clone—if anything, she wanted to be more like me, to be more a part of the world. I helped her to do that, but the help was reciprocal—she softened my sharp edges. I never questioned her love for me, never questioned that she would be there to support me in any circumstances. I felt that way until the day she died. I miss her terribly. And in the missing, I realize how very lucky I was that she was my mother.

And since you are also natural enemies, the potential for enmity—sometimes harrowing—is there as well.

Resolving the relationship by treasuring what is good, changing what can be changed, and accepting what cannot, can spell the difference between fulfilling your hopes for yourself or having none, between having a rich future or simply repeating the past, between believing that you are worthy and lovable and loving and believing that you are not and cannot be.

The difficult mother–daughter relationship is a time bomb, set to go off in the next generation. It is inherited as surely as are blue eyes or brown. Curing it is painful; it means shedding light on the dark places of your history to discover where you can look for love and where you must give up looking for it.

But it is not nearly so deadly as pretending that there is no problem.

2
Good Mommy/Bad Mommy

My mother was always beautifully dressed, compulsively thin, perfectly made up. And I was always big and clumsy. She was constantly taking me to plastic surgeons and saying to them, "What's wrong with her?" So I grew up with this tremendous inferiority complex about my appearance.

Once when I was ten and at my most awkward, she said, "If you don't get your nose fixed, people will stare at you. It's grotesque."

"What does 'grotesque' mean?" I asked. She said, "Something sickening."

I wanted to die.

—Lisa, thirty-one

One Saturday evening, in the early stages of researching this book, I went to a large dinner party where there were seven couples present. Over coffee, the topic of conversation turned to children, and I asked, "How many women here have a good relationship with their mothers?" Not one hand went up. The results were unanimous, a fact that was not lost on the women, who, laughing nervously and swiveling their heads to compare responses, looked immensely relieved to discover the mutuality of their melancholy experiences.

The cautious journalist in me dismissed as a fluke the result of my totally unscientific poll. But as the weeks and months went by, I met more and more women to whom I described my project, all but a handful of whom eagerly said, "You've *got* to interview me," as though about to reveal for the first time a deep and burning secret.

17

Could it be, I wondered, that there are *so* many terrible mothers? That many daughters, harboring dark memories, are bereft of loving attachments to their mothers? And why are daughters so embarrassed to discuss it, except, perhaps, privately, and not always then?

According to a study conducted by social scientists Grace Baruch and Rosalind Barnett, the findings of which were the basis of *Lifeprints: New Patterns of Love and Work for Today's Women,* approximately 25 percent of women have a "low rapport" with their mothers, and another approximate 25 percent rate the relationship as "somewhat rewarding." But the numbers may in fact be much higher—a great deal depends on one's willingness, or ability, to go on record on the subject, or even to acknowledge the possibility. It is virtually impossible to quantify so subjective a matter. Much also depends on the daughters' perception of what constitutes a "bad mother."

Few daughters want to admit either that they have a Bad Mommy or that their mothers have serious parenting flaws. To confess that one's mother hasn't got the right maternal stuff is, perforce, to be an emotional foundling. There is short-term solace—albeit long-term torment—in a child's, or an adult's, denial.

Awareness is no less tormenting (although the pain is briefer, because it is the key to dealing with the legacy of that denial). Vivian Gornick, in *Fierce Attachments: A Memoir,* her extraordinary chronicle of her relationship with her mother, describes what it was like to feel like a disappointment to her mother and to believe that the consequent tension between them was an ineluctible, immutable fact of her life:

> She could not see that her insistent unhappiness was an accusation and a judgment. "You?" it said with each resentful sigh. "You're not the right one. You cannot deliver up comfort, pleasure, amelioration. But you are my dearest of dears. Your appointed task is to understand, your destiny to live with the daily knowledge that you are insufficient to cure my life of its deprivation."

Children make this kind of parental mandate manageable by volunteering for blame, a coping mechanism that is perversely constructive. If it is *your fault* that your mother is miserable, it becomes a potentially *fixable* affront. Taking blame means that at least the hope of love is still there—all you have to do is deserve it.

Awareness, then, that something is wrong with Mom, and not

with you, is in childhood assiduously to be shunned, and once dismissed, recedes deeper in a girl's—and later, a woman's—consciousness.

And so, many daughters live out their lives avoiding or abiding or arguing with their mothers—burying the long-ago injury or insult of childhood deprivation under a blanket of forgetfulness—and not confronting it head-on. It's humiliating to remember the ways in which one demeaned oneself in order to prevent being in a mother's bad graces, the willingness to do *anything* in order not to be rejected, when rejection felt like death.

Another reason it is dangerous to acknowledge that you were unloved is that it implies the possibility that your mother may have been *right*—you *are* unlovable. This is especially true in families where you are alone in your feelings of anger and longing. You feel isolated—your siblings don't have the same thorniness with Mom, having had a different experience of her, and may think you are deranged or crassly disloyal, or you may be a reminder of a past they'd prefer to escape.

Unless you have something other than your own experience as a basis for comparison—such as getting to know other families intimately and observing up close another way of *being* in a family—you may *believe* the parental judgment of your unworthiness. It is a belief most people try to dilute or deflect.

And so in adulthood, denial picks up steam, fueled by sophisticated rationalizations and lubricated with "fairness." You leap over your confused feelings of inadequacy to automatic, socially acceptable responses and artful aphorisms.

"Do you love your mother?" someone asks. Your stomach convulses into knots. But your lips say "Of *course* I love her—she's my *mother*." The relationship may not give you what you want, you may even add, *she* does not give you what you want, but what else is new, maybe you don't satisfy her *either*, she's getting on in years, nobody's perfect.

All of which is fine and circumspect and evenhanded. But it doesn't explain the knot in your stomach that doesn't go away. And it doesn't explain why every time you hear her voice on the phone you stiffen, alert to possible attack.

Your words and mind muffle your real feelings, but your body interrupts with nonverbal messages: *Something is very wrong here and I'm working as hard as I can to keep it hidden,* like sitting on an overstuffed trunk to prevent the lid from flying open. The trouble is, you can never let up in your efforts, and in time the denial threatens your mental and physical health and begins to erode your relationships.

Women who feel they must "keep a lid" on their real feelings about their mothers may not realize that two things contribute to their resistance. The first is that they do not feel entitled to their awareness; they have nothing with which to replace it—better an unloving mother than *no* mother. The second is that we live in a culture that forbids that awareness.

What muzzles the daughter and drives her instincts underground is the Bad Mommy Taboo, the cultural repugnance to and denial of maternal imperfection, which will be the focus of Chapter Three.

But for the purposes of this chapter, it's important to recognize that we are entitled to our awareness *as adults* that our relationship may not be normal, not adequate, not loving, because now we can deal with it—we are no longer helpless children. And if we can deal with it, we can begin to see our mothers, and ourselves, in a different, more accepting, light.

To begin sorting out our true feelings, it's useful to define our terms. How do Good Mothers differ from Bad Mothers?

The Good Mommy

One definition of a good mother is that she "does not inflict on the child [her] own needs at the expense of the child's." Another is that the good mother is neither upset by her child's occasional aggressiveness nor threatened by the child's individuality and independence; she does not require that her child try constantly to please her.

A good mother can understand that her child may harbor both bad *and* good feelings about her. At the same time, a good mother can tolerate her *own* good and bad feelings toward her child. She forgives herself for the occasional maternal glitch—such as a dark, unforgiving mood or loss of temper—and is able to control those lapses by acknowledging them and figuring out what she has done to contribute to her own frustration.

"Her less-than-perfect responses demonstrate to the child that he can possess his mother's love without having to be a perfect, all-good extension of her self," writes Dr. Louise J. Kaplan. "By not relinquishing the space that rightfully belongs to her, the mother lets her child go and eases him into the space that rightfully belongs to him."

And so she can allow her child to be less-than-perfect as well.

Monica, a thirty-five-year-old travel agent, is the mother of Angela, a seventeen-year-old daughter whose pubescent sensitivities and snarlings would stress Mister Rogers. And yet Monica—whose own mother used to read her mail, listen in on her phone calls, and otherwise invade her privacy—has made a concerted effort to see her daughter as a separate person, different from her, in need of working through her own adolescent demons rather than a kid bent on breaking her mother's heart. Says Monica,

> Angie's been going through the pushing-Mom-away stage. So when she screams, "*I hate you!*" I just never take it to heart. You can't. I remember that I hated my mother too. I even wrote it in my diary, and she read it, and she never let me forget it. So when Angie says that, I don't take it seriously. Instead, I just watch for mood changes to see that they're appropriate, so I'll know that something is wrong and deal with it.
>
> Also, I *know* her; she's never been one to sit and talk—why should it be different now? So I don't push it.

Susan, forty-five, is also able to respect the differences between her daughter Amy, twenty-three, and herself, because she's able to see both sides of the generation gap, and both sides of her own maternal ambivalence. She says,

> Amy has a much easier time separating from me than I do letting her go. This has been true ever since the first time she took the school bus to nursery school—the kid's ready for separation and, especially if it's your first child, you don't know what to expect. Each step of the way has been something new for me to adjust to as a mother and to understand.
>
> So I felt sad and happy during her growing-up years—sad that I was losing something by her leaving more and more, but happy that she *was able* to leave.
>
> That's always been my endeavor for her, to help her leave, even though it isn't always easy for me. Isn't that every parent's endeavor, to prepare their children to go out into the world?

The good mother is one who loves you unconditionally and can let you go; who can allow you to be yourself, different from her, and celebrate and learn from that difference; who can, if asked, lovingly tell you the truth but knows when what you really need is a hug; who can allow you to make reasonable mistakes and learn from their consequences; who can allow you appropriate responsibility and decision making; who can admit when she's wrong; who can encourage your risk taking and be there at the finish line of your efforts, cheering you on no matter where you place; who allows you occasionally to go home again without swallowing you whole; who can nurture your autonomy by helping you to find choices.

The bad mother is unable to give her daughter this kind of loving freedom.

The Bad Mommy

"Good mothers" are fairly easy to spot and to define. Not so the "Bad Mommy," whose badness is a matter of degree and therefore subject to argument.

There is no argument about what constitutes an *evil mother*—one who is truly malicious and even sadistic in her maternal behavior—except, perhaps, among such mothers themselves, who do not see it as such. There are unspoken cultural rules regarding the treatment of children, prohibitions to child brutality, exploiting an innocent, defenseless being, a collective morality about which most people agree. We agree that

incest is wrong;
physically torturing and mutilating a child is wrong;
starving or abandoning a child is wrong.

What happened to Roberta, thirty-three, is wrong. She recalls,

> When I was five, my father raped me. And when I said, "I'll tell Mommy," he stabbed me with a knife—the only reason I didn't bleed to death is because he knew a doctor who would treat me and hush things up, for a fee. No one knew. I went mute about it for the rest of my childhood. I never said a word, never shed a tear until I had had six years of therapy.
>
> When at thirty I finally did tell my mother, and said

that I felt like killing my father, she said, "You're awful. It never happened." I showed her my gynecologist's records that documented my internal wounds from when I had been a child. She said, "You must have provoked it."

What happened to Eleanor, forty-six, is also, by any measure, wrong:

My mother was a falling-down alcoholic. When she was on a tear, you ran for your life. Once when I was seven, she heard me say "damn." She held me up in the air by my feet, put my head in the toilet, and flushed it over and over, saying, "This will teach you not to use filthy words."

These are unpardonable outrages to the human spirit, so abhorrent that they are horrifying to hear or read about. And it is against that moral absolute that we humbly compare our childhood experiences, often believing either that our childhoods were perfectly normal—when they may not have been—or hardly worth discussing compared, say, to Roberta's and Eleanor's.

It is the gray areas of "bad mothering" that are much more pervasive—and much harder to define as harmful to children. When, for instance, does a spanking become an attack? When does character building become degradation? When does obedience become enslavement? When does affection become seduction?

Here the definitions become a matter of interpretation because they fall outside the normally accepted notion of child abuse. Most people believe that if their parents never slugged them, never sexually molested them, never starved them or failed to provide for their bodily needs, they had "normal" childhoods—when in fact they may have been *psychologically* abused.

Nancy, a forty-two-year-old librarian and mother of two teenagers, sits in her living room, gazing pensively out the window, collecting her thoughts; she struggles with a memory as though poised on a high diving board, deciding whether or not to leap into space. She is reluctant to appear to be critical of her mother, and prefaces her responses to my questions with such comments as "but I love her, please don't misunderstand," and otherwise trying not to seem disloyal. At length she says in a rush, her voice breaking,

When I was a little girl and I misbehaved, my mother would tell me she was leaving me, and that when Daddy got home, I was to explain to him where she went and why she had left. I still vividly remember begging her, "No, Mommy, please don't leave me, don't leave me, you can't leave me, please don't leave me, I'll be good, I'll be good." I didn't know that what she was doing was wrong.

Nancy is a victim of psychological maltreatment—a form of child abuse. One way to define such abuse is by the child's reaction to it: as one authority puts it, "In almost all cases, it is the psychological consequences of an act that define that act as abusive," whether that act is sexual or physical abuse, or merely an assault on the spirit.

A child who believes she is *to blame* for the fact that her mother does not love her, or cannot demonstrate love for her—*and that she deserves the harsh or cruel or indifferent treatment she receives*—is a psychologically maltreated child.

Even though it does not draw blood or leave scars, psychological maltreatment is not only a form of child abuse—like physical battering or sexual assault—it may be the most damaging of the three. What makes it so is the question of emotional intent, which may be unconscious, behind a parental act.

If, for instance, a mother accidentally knocks down her child while trying to open a recalcitrant kitchen cabinet door, the child would not take it as an offense, because it was not deliberate. If, on the other hand, the mother shoves the child to the floor in a fury because the door wouldn't open, the child would be emotionally wounded. It isn't the physical injury per se that is so harmful to a child; it is *the reason why* that injury was inflicted.

And so Roberta, whose father raped her—he was later institutionalized for insanity—has been able to forgive him because he was mentally ill. She cannot forgive her mother, who never touched her. Says Roberta,

What my father did wasn't even the worst part. The most painful thing is that I still have not lost the feeling of humiliation, the part of me that suffers from the damaged-goods syndrome because of a mother who re-

fused to believe me, who didn't care that all this stuff
happened to me. My mother could sit there with a face
of stone and say, "You asked for it."

Dr. James Garbarino, president of the Erikson Institute for Advanced Study in Child Development and coauthor of *The Psychologically Battered Child*, told me, "What matters is that the view you have of the world reflects the quality of your family experience. It's like what happens in wartime; who do people hate more, the enemy, or the traitors in their own camp? Psychological maltreatment of one's child is a betrayal. And that's why I think it's the most important form of child abuse."

And parents who psychologically maltreat their children, he says, are accountable. "To call something abuse and neglect is a statement saying, 'You should have known this is not a good way to treat children.' If someone says, 'I didn't know that hitting a child with a two-by-four would hurt them,' or 'I didn't know having sex with an eight-year-old was bad for them,' you say, 'You should have known.' There is a collective judgment that you should know this is not something you do to kids."

The same yardstick applies to psychological maltreatment.

Dr. Garbarino and his coauthors define psychological maltreatment as "a concerted attack by an adult on a child's development of self and social competence, a *pattern* of psychically destructive behavior." This behavior, they write, takes five forms:

Rejecting (the adult refuses to acknowledge the child's worth and the legitimacy of the child's needs).
Isolating (the adult cuts the child off from normal social experiences . . . and makes the child believe that he or she is alone in the world).
Terrorizing (the adult verbally assaults the child, creates a climate of fear, bullies or frightens the child . . .).
Ignoring (the adult deprives the child of essential stimulation and responsiveness, stifling emotional growth and intellectual development).
Corrupting (the adult . . . stimulates the child to engage in destructive anti-social behavior, reinforces that deviance, and makes the child unfit for normal social experience).

Some authorities consider emotional smothering a form of child abuse. If your mother lived your life as though it were her own—

never allowing you a moment of distress or frustration, routinely sleeping in your bed when you had a bad dream, never setting limits or establishing boundaries, seldom or never letting you out of her sight, excusing and failing to provide consequences for your negative or hurtful behavior, insisting on a daily chronicle of *every detail of your life*, all in the name of maternal love—then you never had to grow up and take responsibility for your actions. You remain a child.

The process of becoming an empathetic, autonomous adult— through all the wondrous and exhilarating and challenging, even painful, transitions of emotional growth in childhood—is not unlike learning how to walk; each step makes you stronger for the next one. But if your parent is doing the walking for you, you do not have the muscles even to support your own emotional weight. You cannot stand alone.

Such children often become narcissists in adulthood, craving constant praise, unable to give love, unable to accept the consequences of their actions, unable to do anything but manipulate people and to blame them for their own losses.

Child maltreatment that leaves no physical scars does not carry the public relations weight that sexual or physical abuse do—hence, it is easy to deny and to trivialize. *But it is profoundly harmful* because, say authorities on psychologically battered children, it is the crux of *all* maltreatment. It is not physical or sexual cruelty alone that so ravages a child's ability to trust; what hurts is that the one person who is supposed to protect you at all costs can deem acceptable— even morally uplifting—behavior that terrorizes a powerless, vulnerable child.

Too often, mothers perceive a child's opposing point of view, or grimace, or personality, or appearance, as a stake in the heart. Some parents get the vapors, for instance, when a child pierces his or her ear in a neat row of dots. Such behavior feels to the mother as though she has flunked parenting. Worse, it feels as though the child is rejecting her.

Some mothers are so involved with their child, or so involved with themselves, that the child seems to reflect the mother's worth *as a human being*, when in fact the child is simply trying to get a sense of *her own worth*. As a result, the mother will behave—especially toward a daughter—in ways that will deflect those wretched feelings of failure and rejection. Even when that daughter is an adult.

The best way to avoid feelings of wretchedness is to be more powerful than the daughter—and power has many faces, some of them friendly, some righteous. The older the daughter is, the more elaborate are the mother's attempts to wield that power.

In my interviews I discovered eight patterns of manipulating behavior by mothers toward their adult daughters. These ploys are symptoms of strained mother–daughter relationships:

> Raising the stakes
> No-win situations
> Divide and conquer
> Tyranny of illness
> Ancient history
> Wrestling for control
> Skewed priorities
> Never-never land

Let's examine them one at a time.

Raising the Stakes

The main feature of this behavioral pattern is that the mother's needs are insatiable—whatever you do, no matter how painstakingly you strive for perfection, she finds a flaw; however much you think you've pleased her, she wants more. The minute you clear a jump, she raises the bar and you must vault it again.

Jackie, fifty-one, is an award-winning New York filmmaker whose three Emmys do not seem to appease her mother's appetite for her daughter's achievements. Says Jackie,

> Whatever I do, I always hear, "But now, why don't you do something else." My mother will, unbidden, give me a running commentary on my career. Lately, it's "Well, they're only TV shows—why don't you get into feature films?" It's never enough—she wants more, more.

Anita, twenty-four, who is studying computer programming in adult education, has learned that a compliment from her mother is a sign of trouble:

> She'll praise me, then *whack*. Every big accomplish-
> ment that happens in my life somehow becomes a
> failure. For example, I'm trying to develop a line of
> software for hospitals. It's very important to me that I
> picked an area that will help people. She said, "Good
> for you. But is there any money in it?"
>
> She keeps changing the rules. She tells me I spend too
> much time on work and that I should relax occasionally.
> But when I ease up on my work, she accuses me of laziness.
>
> Or she'll tell me I should take such and such a course,
> so I take it, and then she says, "Why did you take it on
> weekends instead of at night?"

No-win Situations

In this category, mothers overtly—or subtly—attempt to sabotage
a daughter's happiness, and sometimes even set the daughter up for
that sabotage.

Barbara, thirty-four, has always had a weight problem; like her
mother, she tends to be twenty to thirty pounds too heavy.

> I've been on so many diets, and I can't seem to keep
> the weight off. But it doesn't help to hear my mother—
> who is hardly an example—constantly telling me I
> should be on a diet. Once she said, "If you don't
> lose weight, no man will ever be able to put his arm
> around you."
>
> So I start a diet, full of resolve, and she changes
> her tune. She says, "How can you eat so little? You'll get
> sick—eat this, eat this," trying to shove food into me.

Sometimes no-win situations reach bizarre proportions. Rachel,
forty-four, was raised with very high expectations—academic achievement was, as she puts it, "a given in my house." So she got on the
honor roll throughout her education. But she never got parental
praise. She recalls,

> Once I asked my mother why she had never praised me
> when I was a child. She said, "Oh, no, no, I couldn't
> possibly have done that." I asked her why. She said,
> "Because you might have had expectations of yourself

that would be destroyed when you grew up and found
out that you couldn't meet them. You would have thought
that I had deceived you."

Divide and Conquer

These mothers seek allies, usually from within the family, in an
unconscious effort to place their daughters, or keep them, in the
wrong. This dynamic often pits siblings against one another well
into their adulthood, fighting over who does more for Mom or gets
more from her, when the real issue is how each child is or is not
dominated and manipulated by her.

Elizabeth Fishel, author of *Sisters: Love and Rivalry Inside the
Family and Beyond*, writes that a daughter's relationship with her
mother is the child's first model of intimacy and thus sets the tone
for the daughter's sibling attachments:

> Parents . . . drive sisters apart by talking about one behind her
> back to the other, by fomenting rumors or repeating confidences,
> by making a "son" out of one sister and a cuddly "daughter" out
> of another, by holding one up too often and insistently as a model
> to the other—and even by encouraging sisters to be friends too
> emphatically. . . . Again and again, the rivalry we see between
> sisters is, at least in part, an expression of the rivalry girls experi-
> ence with their mothers, in a more manageable, less threatening
> form.

Patty, forty-four, and her sister Karen, thirty-nine, were willing to
be interviewed together on the subject of their relationship even
though, as Patty puts it, "we are not friends." The two women are
polar opposites in personality and in their life-styles. Patty lives in a
twenty-two-room mansion in Beverly Hills, and her sister lives in
Los Angeles in an attractive, but far less opulent, three-bedroom
ranch house. Patty's husband is an executive of a film company to
which he is chauffeured each day; Karen's husband owns a plumb-
ing supply store.

Patty doesn't get riled by their mother; Karen, to use her words,
hates her mother's guts.

During the interview, the rhythm of conversation mirrors the
sisters' temperaments. Karen interrupts, weeps, and sighs; Patty

listens in stony silence or tries to ameliorate the harshness of her sister's comments about their mother.

Curiously, each sister has adopted certain characteristics—which they both loathe—of their mother, as though they had divvied them up. Karen is moralistic and judgmental, Patty is materialistic and easily dominated.

Karen: "My mother's always calling me and saying, 'Patty got a new couch. Maybe you can get one just like it.' But she never visits me, because she can't tell her friends how royally my husband and I entertain her and how much money we have, because we don't. My sister is a snob, just like my mother—she never has us over—we're too common."

Patty: "I like having money, I like the freedom it brings, and I'm not going to apologize for wanting to marry a rich man. And I have asked Karen and her husband over—but she disapproves of the fact that we smoke. One sniff and she's gone. She acts like our mother— she tries to control my life. So I back off."

Indeed, *together* Patty and Karen *are* their mother; separately, they maintain a cool detachment from each other. It is a detachment their mother has always encouraged.

The four Martin girls grew up hardly knowing each other, belying the myth that siblings are built-in friends. Says Barbara, thirty-three, the firstborn, "We were strangers under the same roof. My sisters and I were no comfort to each other. We were clambering for the same bit of warmth, fighting over the same maternal crust. My mother saw to it that we hated each other; whoever wasn't there had her most glaring flaws exposed in detail, over and over. You dared not turn your back."

But as adults, the women have learned not to allow their mother to drive wedges between them and will not be drawn into a discussion with her about each other. Their solidarity drives their mother crazy. Barbara recalls,

> One year my sisters and my parents were staying at my house. It was the night before Christmas, an annual event at my place that my grandmother had always helped me to prepare. That morning, Grandma had a stroke and was in the hospital. We were all terribly worried, and didn't get home until around midnight, exhausted. To unwind, my sisters and I had a few drinks and started kidding around and laughing.

My mother, her face buried in her handkerchief of grief, heard our laughter, looked up, and growled, "Grandma is in the hospital, and you don't even care." Then, looking straight at me, because she always hated me the most, she added, "She wouldn't even *be* there if it weren't for you—you made her cook all this food, and it may just kill her."

Tyranny of Illness

This is a particularly effective means of controlling a child's behavior because *there is always the chance that your mother is really sick.*

Often, however, "illness" flares up in a mother primarily when her daughter defies her, or seems to. Defiance can include your being the center of attention and removing the spotlight from her, and her consequent envy can reach cruel proportions.

When Enid got pregnant for the first time, she had difficulty carrying the child, and spent the last two months of the pregnancy in bed. During that time her mother, with whom she usually spoke every day, became unavailable to her. Says Enid,

> I can't tell you how hurt I was. But somehow my mother can always top the hurt—she can top you at anything, especially illness. So when I went into the hospital, she pleaded sickness; I had a hideous delivery and long hospitalization. She never visited. And when I got home, I was incredibly weak. She called me up and never asked how I was—instead, she said, "I'm fading; I think I'm dying." There was absolutely nothing wrong with her. The fact that I almost died freaked her out, not because she'd lose me, but because I was getting all this attention and she wasn't.

A mother's pretending to "die" was particularly wrenching for Rachel, whose father was killed in an automobile accident when she was four. Now fifty-one, she says,

> It was a wonderful ploy, her dying. At first, I was sucked in by it—I was terrified that I'd be left all alone. But then I caught on—she'd stage her heart attacks whenever I did something she didn't like. I remember once

when I was twenty stepping over her body to go out with my boyfriend—whom I later married—because she had faked yet another seizure.

Today she's eighty-four years old, and still going strong. She's never going to die, *never*.

Ancient History

Some mothers seem to keep a running count of offenses committed by their daughters, neatly catalogued according to subject, and when the daughter commits a new one, she hears about a lifetime of similar breaches. At those moments the daughter's "ancient" history is hauled out and used as evidence against her.

When Irene, twenty-four, told her mother that she was leaving her husband, she assumed that her mother, who herself had been divorced in her early twenties, would be supportive of her decision.

Did she sympathize? Are you kidding? What she did was tell me that she never liked the guy in the first place, that I had always had terrible taste in men. She reminded me of Tom in high school, the one who dumped me, and later of Dave, who got busted for drugs. She reminded me of every unhappy romance I had ever had. It was as though she was *waiting* for me to screw up again so she could add something fresh to the list—and it seemed to make her day when I did.

Sometimes this technique is used to deflect one issue, replacing it with another. Wendy, thirty-five, has a seven-year-old son who has a learning disability. Her mother had once offered to pay for private school for the boy; Wendy had demurred, believing that mainstreaming him in a less rarified public school system would be good for him. But his handicap became untenable, since he required much more attention than the school could provide.

I called my mother and said, "I think I'll take you up on your offer." She turned to ice. She said, "I'm not surprised he's having trouble; you were never a good student, and you've obviously never taught him good study habits. There's nothing wrong with him that low-ering the boom won't cure. What he needs is discipline—you certainly never had any."

Wrestling for Control

Some mothers feel disenfranchised once their daughters are grown, because they are no longer consulted on routine matters. These mothers attempt to maintain maternal control by undermining the daughter's decisions and confidence, or, in extreme cases, by going head to head in competition with her.

The most bizarre case that I encountered in my interviews was that between Janet and her mother. Janet had always been a quiet and deferential child—at thirty-two, she still seems almost fragile—easily cowed by her outspoken mother. But when Janet reached her twenties, she corraled enough courage to move out of their Boston apartment, get her own place, and start a small catering business, which she called "Leave It to Us." Says Janet,

> My mother pleaded with me to let her get involved in the business, so I told her she could try to get corporate accounts—I figured that would keep her busy, and I was more interested in doing private parties anyhow. And besides, I still wanted her approval—I desperately wanted to be close to her, something we had never been—and anyhow, I was new at all this. But as time went on, she began making more and more business decisions and gradually started taking over the whole enterprise. Since business was booming, I let her get away with it. But finally I couldn't take it anymore, because she was treating me like a slave in my own shop.
>
> I reminded her that this was my business, and that I'd be glad to discuss decisions with her, but that the final say had to be mine. All hell broke loose—she was so enraged and out of control that I thought she'd have a stroke. She stormed out and I didn't see her for weeks.
>
> The next thing I knew, she had opened up her own catering business a few blocks away. And she called it "Leave It to Me."

Skewed Priorities

Mothers in this category make it clear that they expect their daughters to place them first in their list of concerns. One way that expectation is met is when a daughter continues in adulthood to include her mother in most of her domestic decision-making, such as menu planning or child-rearing advice.

One woman told me, "When I was married, I went to buy furniture. Who went with me? Not my husband—my mother did. It was simply understood: I was not to buy anything for my own home without her approval. My husband's only role in all this was to pay the bills."

Few things can skew a daughter's priorities as effectively as the promise of a parental bequest. When an inheritance is at stake, many daughters make some hard—even absurd—choices. As one woman put it ruefully, "She'd say 'jump'; I'd say 'How high?' "

Joan and Carolyn have been best friends for thirty years. But Carolyn was not invited to either of Joan's daughters' weddings, nor to her twenty-fifth anniversary party. Why?

> Because my mother doesn't like Carolyn, and never has. She once told me that if I continued to be friends with Carolyn, she'd cut me out of her will. So here we are, two fifty-year-old women, sneaking around to have lunch or go shopping, as though we were having a clandestine affair.

Never-never Land

The power of an impoverished mother–daughter bond is potentially so great that it can, in the most extreme cases, cause a daughter to suspend disbelief in the interests of accommodating her mother's ravenous ego. Unless the daughter realizes her mother may have a serious problem—whether psychological, medical, or alcohol-or drug-related—she can be swept into a kind of twilight zone wherein she may think that she is the one who is crazy.

When Samantha was five years old, she was sexually molested by her mother's brother. She told her mother about the incident, and her mother said, "Oh, he's just being friendly." The molestation continued, and only after Samantha told her father, from whom her mother was divorced, did the molestation stop. Her mother was threatened with a custody suit, and her uncle was threatened with physical violence—he moved away.

But the damage done to Samantha lingered, with punishing persistence, in her nightmares and in her inability to form romantic attachments. When she was in her thirties, she went into therapy to deal both with the childhood trauma and with her mother's refusal to take her complaint seriously and her mother's choice, instead, to protect her brother. "I've never gotten over the fact that I was betrayed by my own mother," Samantha says.

Fear is another controlling mechanism that has similar long-lasting psychological consequences.

I interviewed a woman who worries constantly that her daughter, who is thirty, will be killed in an automobile crash, or will contract AIDS, or isn't eating right. She regales her daughter with chilling cautionary tales, culled in lugubrious detail from television news programs or gathered from neighbors in the lobby of their Chicago apartment building, about young women who have been deceived, or raped, or maimed.

Such "concern" can be emotionally crippling. Indeed, it *has* crippled her daughter, who, although she has a good job in a bank, cannot summon up the courage to move out of her parents' apartment and into her own.

Dr. Ann F. Caron, an educational psychologist who runs mother–daughter workshops, describes the true nature of excessive and chronic maternal fretting: "Worry is a long lead chain. The mother who worries a great deal about her daughter may seem to do it in a very loving way—but by constantly expressing her concerns, she's making sure that her daughter stays very close."

Too Far to Go

Taken one at a time, most of these examples do not indicate an unrepentant and viciously destructive mother with not a single redeeming virtue. But when these symptoms are multiple or chronic—and when they are seldom offset by loving moments—the daughter may reach this conclusion: *That her mother's happiness depends on her unhappiness and lack of ego strength.*

The price of these eight methods of controlling a daughter's behavior, and of undermining her self-esteem, is that it can stunt her emotionally; while she may feel enormous rage at being mistreated in these ways, she also finds it harder and harder to break away—until and unless the day comes when she realizes that her mother is, however unintentionally, inflicting a psychic wound.

"She has done the worst thing," one woman said. "She has made me doubt myself."

When a mother attempts to bind a grown daughter to her, whether by fear or neediness or illness or rage, the consequences can be devastating. To continue trying to please an unpleasable mother threatens an adult daughter's mental health and all her relationships. And yet such daughters often keep coming back to their mothers, without the daughters' altering that relationship and their bitter or anguished reactions to it. (How to repair and redefine the painful mother-daughter bond will be explored in detail in Part Four).

These daughters remain stuck in a psychic limbo, shuttling between the fear of being emotionally ensnared by maternal invasiveness and the terror of being set adrift with no maternal moorings.

Lilly Singer, a clinician and coauthor of *Beyond Loss: A Practical Guide Through Grief to a Meaningful Life*, explained in an interview why some adult daughters continue to be dependent, one way or another, on an unloving mother, and why that dependence is a consequence of their mothers' emotional abusiveness:

If you are told from the time you are one month that you're no good and you're not smart and you can't do it and you don't have an opinion of your own and you pick the wrong friends and you don't study the right way and you don't wear the right clothes and you don't look nice, at some point you're going to start believing it. And if you believe it, you're going to need a mommy to tell you what to do.

And that's abuse. Not to let your child grow up to be an independent, respected human being.

What are these adult daughters to do about their painful entanglements with their mothers? They can begin to disengage by becoming aware that their mothers, usually without any conscious desire to harm their daughters, may simply *not* have had the right maternal stuff—for reasons we shall explain—when those daughters were young, and that their childhoods weren't normal.

And the best way to get a sense that your experience may not have been normal? "You have to compare your expectations about life and people with other people's," says Dr. Garbarino. "That's where you begin to get a perspective about your own experience. And that's very hard to do if your only intimate contacts are your own family."

Another step is that daughters can learn to monitor their own feelings and instincts by saying, "I feel uncomfortable [angry, dominated, usurped, inadequate, guilty, furious] with my mother more often than I do not. I have to pay attention to that, because it shows in how I treat my friends [lover, spouse, kids, colleagues]. There is validity here. I don't have to blame or excuse my mother—I just have to *see* her so I can *see* myself."

If unloving mothers were able to see their behavior as abusive, they either would stop behaving that way or they would get help for their dysfunction. But many cannot: instead, they deny it, to themselves, their families, and the world at large, in order to avoid a sense of guilt, to avoid having to make changes in their lives, or to avoid the bruising awareness that they, too, were unloved children.

As psychoanalyst Alice Miller writes,

We punish our children for the arbitrary actions of our parents that we were not able to defend ourselves against. . . . Those who were permitted to react appropriately throughout their childhood —i.e., with anger—to the pains, wrongs, and denial inflicted upon them either consciously or unconsciously will retain this ability to react appropriately in later life too . . . they will not feel the need to lash out in response.

But what the child sees is not a mother's fears and subconscious reactions to her childhood; what the child sees is *the anger—the mother's defense against the fear.*

"The problem is that you tend to do what was done to you because it's what you know," says Dr. Marianne Goodman. "If you're very lucky, and you picked the right mother, chances are you'll be a pretty good mother yourself. If you didn't, you're going to have a much harder time of it because it just doesn't come naturally."

According to a study conducted at Vanderbilt University Medical School, the greatest predictor that a child will become an abusive parent is the feeling of being "unloved and unwanted by one's parents."

*   *   *

To be freed from her unhappy past, the inadequately loved daughter must accept the possibility that there is something profoundly wrong with her relationship to her mother. Unfortunately, we live in a culture that does not encourage such awareness.

3

The Bad Mommy Taboo

It's interesting how people react when you tell them you don't talk to your mother. I happened to mention it over dinner one night to a guy I was dating. He said, "Is she alive?" I said, "Yes." He just stared at me. Then he said, "What do you mean you don't talk to her?" I said, "We don't speak on the phone, and I don't see her."

"At all?"

"At all."

"How long?"

"Six years."

He started cutting the rice on his plate. He didn't say anything more, he just kept absently cutting his rice, like he couldn't process all this. Finally, I said, "Let's change the subject." We stopped going out after that.

—Erin, forty-two

"Mother." To most of us, the word conjures up cozy visions of homespun family life—mother with an infant at her breast, mother making cookies, mother tenderly tending to a feverish child, mother sympathetically listening to our tragedies, mother as our champion. That's what "mother" is supposed to be—either in how we experience her, or pretend she is, or long for her to be.

But to some of us, "mother" carries with it more sobering visions—mother as degrader, mother as critic, mother as martyr, mother as withholder of sanction and sanctuary. This is not the mother of anyone's wistful reverie—this is the mother of painful, sometimes intimidating, even frightening experience.

39

People who have good mommies chorus that fact; people who don't, often keep it a secret.

Sometimes, they even tell lies.

When Kate was seven, her mother served her oatmeal for breakfast one day, and Kate refused to eat the lumpy mess because it nauseated her. Her mother would not permit a substitute; Kate was obdurate. So her mother upended the bowl of uneaten cereal onto her daughter's head and made her go to school without washing it off.

Such battles were routine in Kate's family—but they weren't in her friends', and she knew it:

> It was pretty obvious that my mother didn't like me. But I pretended she did. When my friends would say that their mothers expected them home by six o'clock— dinnertime—I would say, "Oh, my mom wants me home at five-thirty." I had no curfew. I just wanted them to think that I did, that I had a mother who would worry about where I was and who would be overprotective. So I made up rules that didn't exist in my family: *My* mother wanted me home earlier than anybody's— which made it sound like she loved me more.

Like Erin, Kate, who is in her fifties, no longer sees her mother. And, like Erin, she no longer tells people that she doesn't like her mother. Oh, sometimes she'll open up about it, but only when she's very sure the person with whom she shares the information has had a similar experience, or if she's had a little too much to drink. It's just too exhausting—too embarrassing, too discouraging—to try to explain.

Most people shrink from "mother stories." No matter how damning the facts, if you go public with them, in general the reaction is one of the following:

- "She can't be *all* bad." (Variation: "She couldn't help it.")
- "You can't go through your life blaming your mother." (Variation: "You've got to pull yourself up by your bootstraps.")
- "How can you say that about your mother?" (Variation: "Shame on you.")

And all three possibilities serve one purpose: to keep you from sullying the image of the All-Good Mother. Even if you are thoroughly justified in your reasons for disliking her, few people want to hear them. It puts people on the spot: if they sympathize, it feels as though they were betraying Motherhood in general, hence their *own* mothers. They feel guilty for listening. The result is de facto censorship; daughters quickly learn to keep the facts to themselves.

These daughters seldom get the empathy and understanding they often seek when stating that their relationships with their mothers are either strained, or destructive, or nonexistent. As one woman said with a sigh, "I gave up trying to explain my mother a long time ago. It's like explaining the color red to a blind person. If it wasn't their experience, people don't get it."

What keeps people from "getting it" is the Bad Mommy Taboo.

The Bad Mommy Taboo is an outgrowth of the biblical commandment "Thou shalt honor thy father and thy mother." By its unwritten rules, one neither discusses nor describes the ways in which one's mother was cruel or demeaning or unavailable. Because to do so is to violate a sacred trust that goes back as far as time—you do not say anything negative about the woman who gave you life. "And he that curseth his father, or his mother, shall surely be put to death," warns the Book of Exodus.

"There is one taboo that has withstood all the recent efforts at demystification: the idealization of mother love," writes Alice Miller in *The Drama of the Gifted Child*.

Our culture is far more eager to protect the image of the Good Mother than to deal with the reality of the neglected or mistreated child.

The sanctity of motherhood in spite of compelling contradictory evidence was at work in the outraged reaction to Christina Crawford's book *Mommie Dearest*, which chronicled in chilling detail the beatings and banishments to boarding school of Joan Crawford's adopted daughter. Shortly after the book was published, and partly in reaction to the indignation it ignited—in outraged letters to editors and elsewhere—Christina had a stroke.

Today fully recovered, she recalled for me the angry reaction to her book and its troublesome aftermath a decade ago: "I was totally unprepared for the kind of depth of emotion that spewed forth. There was nobody to turn to for help, because nobody had been there before. And that was very, very hard on me and for my family."

Christina laid bare her mother's private life—and that was to many people more socially reprehensible than anything her mother did to her. In our culture, the idea of home as refuge is supreme—and when a family's privacy is invaded, the concept of domestic sanctuary is shaken.

It is that privacy that may keep the invader out—but it also keeps a child's maltreatment, and her family secrets, locked in, hidden from public view and exposure. The inviolability of family privacy eclipses all other values—and distorts our perceptions.

For as much as social progress over the centuries has resulted in child labor laws, mandatory universal education, and other legislation designed to protect and nurture children, that protection almost always stops at a child's doorstep.

For a mother to be declared unfit to keep custody of her child— or for a father's visitation rights to be withheld—in a court of law, is, with some exceptions, virtually impossible. According to a 1989 article in *People* about mothers and children on the run from sexually abusive fathers, "Because judges are generally reluctant to accept the testimony of very young victims, offending parents often escape conviction and retain custody of visitation rights. Too often, say angry child advocates, inconclusive criminal and civil court proceedings leave the victim at the mercy of his or her molester."

As journalist John Crewdson puts it in *By Silence Betrayed: Sexual Abuse of Children in America*, "The real reason for the lack of public discussion [about sexual abuse] is the notion, still widely held, that what goes on inside the home and within the family ought somehow to be exempt from public scrutiny."

That "exemption from public scrutiny" is occasionally challenged, at least in the press. Since the headline-grabbing white-collar case in 1987 of disbarred New York lawyer Joel Steinberg, who was convicted of killing his "adoptive" daughter, Lisa, the public has become more sensitized to the issue of child abuse.

But where that abuse is not life-threatening—where it involves only the humiliation or death of the spirit—the public is less inclined to be sympathetic to the child who is simply ignored or browbeaten or emotionally smothered or degraded. The culture is even less understanding toward the adult whose life reflects the residue of self-doubt that is the legacy of those childhood deprivations.

The Roots of the Taboo

The Bad Mommy Taboo comes from three sources: the culture, the parents, and the child herself.

Motherhood as the sacred and exclusive child-rearing role for women is a fairly recent phenomenon in the United States. According to anthropologist Maxine L. Margolis and others, it wasn't until the early nineteenth century that mothers were expected to make children the focus of their lives, and that child-rearing excluded fathers, who left the land to work in factories while mothers toiled at home, raising children alone.

By the early twentieth century, motherhood was a celestial mandate. In a speech before the National Congress of Mothers in 1905, President Theodore Roosevelt said reverentially, "As for the mother, her very name stands for loving unselfishness and self-abnegation and in any society fit to exist, it is fraught with associations which render it holy."

It was made the solemn duty of women to raise their children into law-abiding, God-fearing citizens for the good of family and a nation growing in wealth and might. Her constant maternal vigilance was urgent—even a minor lapse could scar the child for life. This was mother as saint; later, as we shall see, she would be reprimanded for coddling her children. But throughout, whether idealized or vilified, she was still *the* parent who was held most accountable for how her children turned out.

With all that pressure, it is small wonder that mothers angrily or tearfully retaliated when their children talked back or disagreed with them.

Even though her image has occasionally been buffeted, the All-Good Mother, celebrated each year on Mother's Day, has become historical Holy Writ. To say otherwise, at least in company, is a conversation-killer.

Mother as the embodiment of purity, mother as keeper of the moral flame while Daddy puts food on the table, is a daunting responsibility. So to say "I hate my mother" is to violate a revered canon, as though you had slapped a nun.

The Bad Seed

But if mother is a paragon of virtue, or is expected to be, and is above public reproach, why do some kids go bad? It must be because they were *born* that way.

Fanning the moral flame of maternity is the idea of the child as essentially wicked. This view is tied to the Christian concept of original sin, which baptism washes away. In fundamentalist religions, children are deemed to be born into sin, which must be purged from them. The theme of child as evil agent is reflected in such films as *The Exorcist* and *The Omen*.

And so beating of children, for example, can be justified by some people as a controlling device or as a method of spiritual cleansing. That high moral purpose is at work in the laws in thirty-one states that allow corporal punishment of children in the school.

What is considered appropriate child-rearing practice is bound up with a sense of communal acceptability and collective social sanction. That which is perceived by the majority of people to be helpful in forming morally correct children who obey authority is considered acceptable. One cannot, then, say categorically that all corporal punishment fits the social and clinical definition of child abuse, because many people think it *is* acceptable. But, says Dr. James Garbarino, a leading authority on child maltreatment, "It's entirely appropriate to say that it should be *considered* child abuse."

Historically, the use of physical force to purify the child was not only justified but recommended. In *For Your Own Good*, Alice Miller includes these quotations from two advice-giving books by German child-rearing pedagogists of the early 1900s:

> Even truly Christian pedagogy, which takes a person as he is, not as he should be, cannot in principle renounce every form of corporal chastisement, for it is exactly the proper punishment for certain kinds of delinquency: it humiliates and upsets the child, affirms the necessity of bowing to a higher order and at the same time reveals paternal love in all its vigor . . .

> Willfulness must be broken "at an early age by making the child feel the adult's unquestionable superiority." Later on, shaming the child has a more lasting effect, especially on vigorous natures.

While beating a child is losing some—although not all—of its social probity, nonviolent use of parental power to demean or frighten children is not. Guilt has always been a useful tool in controlling children ("if you wear that low-cut dress, you'll give your father a heart attack"). But recent research into human behavior indicates the use of shame—in which one's dignity is stripped—is a far more effective, and savaging, controlling device; indeed, it is now considered a "master emotion."

In a 1987 *New York Times* article, Daniel Goleman defined guilt as an emotional reaction to an act that does not *necessarily* lead to self-loathing. On the other hand, shame, he wrote, "goes to one's basic sense of self and is most often experienced as . . . humiliation."

This is not to say that guilt cannot cause us to writhe with embarrassment or even self-hatred. But parental shaming, in the form of humiliating a child, sears into the memory the most painful moments in one's childhood. Having to be sent to school with cereal in your hair is one example of shame that can lead to self-loathing.

And shame bolsters the Bad Mommy Taboo. Family therapist Marilyn Mason, coauthor of *Facing Shame: Families in Recovery*, told Mr. Goleman, "The family's implicit rule becomes not to talk about painful life experiences of all kinds. The sense of shame leads them to become emotionally controlled and set demanding standards for themselves."

The idea of child as evil agent and the parent as source of all that is good is a division of moral labor that has had disastrous consequences in the field of psychiatry. Sigmund Freud's "oedipal theory"—in which the child unconsciously desires sexual involvement with the parent of the opposite sex, suppresses that desire, and later transfers it to a relationship outside the family—was his way of making "sense" of the confessions by his female patients of incest abuse by their fathers and other male relatives. He interpreted these confessions as fantasies of sexual desire for the patients' fathers because the daughters had not worked through their oedipal yearnings. His theory "explained" for his time and for his analytic followers why children would say that an uncle, or a friend of the family, or Daddy himself, might touch them in a sexual way.

What Freud did in the psychiatric literature, in terms of sanitizing or denying the truth children see and experience, some mothers have done at home. According to John Crewdson, incest is the least reported form of child abuse because mothers do not want to hear about it. And so children learn that they must not bring Mommy this particular bad news, because she wants to maintain the status quo within the family—she dare not jeopardize her marriage. He writes, "When incest victims finally decide to tell someone, it's no accident that most of them choose a teacher, a school counselor, a neighbor, a girlfriend—anybody but their mothers."

Many children of abuse, whether sexual or physical or emotional, hold their passive mothers more accountable than their abusing fathers because the mothers could have done something to protect them and *didn't*. Emily, thirty-three, recalls the following incident from her adolescence:

When I finally worked up the nerve to talk to my mother about my father's alcoholism and volcanic temper, she said, "Well, you know how he is at the end of the day—he gets tired. He wants to relax. But he's no alcoholic." My father was known to tear doors off their hinges and the next day wonder what had happened. It was surreal. Denial was my mother's major way of handling life with father. He could have burned the house down and she would have said he was innocent, even if he was caught holding the match.

And so the Bad Mommy on a cultural level gets protected. Or she protects herself. Or she is protected by her husband, who cannot bring himself to acknowledge even to his children that their mother errs.

Fathers often reinforce the Bad Mommy Taboo. As we will see in the next chapter, these fathers tend to ignore any unpleasantness between mother and daughter; by taking the emotional low road, they maintain a status quo with the family that, although often stormy, is nevertheless manageable in its predictability.

Says Sandy, forty-three, "Occasionally my father would say these wonderful words: 'Beatrice, leave Sandy alone.' It was so seldom it was not to be relied upon. But it was something—I remember all five times he said it."

The daughters of domineering mothers often idealize their unassertive fathers. Marietta, sixty-eight, recalls wistfully, "I realize now that I loved my father as much as I did chiefly because he didn't humiliate me. It was a very negative love. He was pleasant, but he had no strength. The one time I tried to talk to him about my mother he said, 'I just don't want any trouble,' and I never mentioned it again."

Other daughters had their passive fathers accountable. Gloria's mother was a tyrant whose hair-trigger temper and scathing admonitions kept everyone in line, including Gloria's father. Today Gloria's anger at her mother has devolved to an apparent indifference, a kind of numbness. But her anger toward her father is as fresh as when she was a child. Why? Because her father would not protect her from her mother—instead, he protected his wife. Gloria says,

I just wish he weren't so damned meek. And that he had gone to bat for me. As a child, I think that was the biggest hurt, not her constantly berating me so much as his allowing her to treat me the way she did. He knew what she was like. Yet he would say, "You have to show respect for your mother," whenever I'd complain to him.

I knew that if they ever broke up, she would make it very hard for him to see me, and he would just give up out of weakness. I wouldn't be able to count on him. That's how he is. And that hurt me terribly. It still does.

Deceiving Ourselves

The Bad Mommy Taboo has a powerful ally—children themselves. When children are born they are totally dependent upon their mothers for food and warmth and protection. As we discussed in an earlier chapter, Mommy as giver of life and sustenance is also the giver of our good feelings about ourselves.

A child plays with her toys, looks back, and locks eyes with her mother's adoring gaze and—fortified by her love and approval—keeps on playing. But if the mother should glance away in disapproval or disgust, the child stops playing and tries to crawl onto Mommy's lap in the belief that she is to blame for some unnamed crime; Mommy doesn't like her. Rather than see herself as innocent, the child sees herself as consummately "wrong." It is the only explanation the child can imagine—and it works, because it clears up a mystery.

"No matter how bad mother is," says Dr. Marianne Goodman, "she's all you've got. A three-year-old can't go out and get an apartment, get her own food, take care of herself. No matter how bad mommy is, you have to make her 'good' for your own world. Your world has to be predicated on something solid, something substantial that you can count on."

And so children will distort—themselves, their parents, their grasp of the environment. Since they cannot conceive of a "bad mommy," they do what psychiatrists call "splitting."

By the time a child is around three, she has gone through specific stages of what psychoanalyst Margaret Mahler called "separation and individuation." She is beginning to feel her psychic oats, her boundaries, her sense of herself as separate from her mother. But she is not yet so emotionally mature, so savvy, that she can see that Mom can have her "off" moods and still be a good mommy. Mother, without whom we would die, is *only* good.

The child cannot afford to see her mother as "bad," because her survival depends upon seeing her as good. This person who is yelling at me or shaking me must be someone else—a good mommy, my good mommy, wouldn't do this to me. So the mother is seen as *two* mothers—good and bad. In the same way, the child sees herself as perfect or awful. This is "splitting."

All children at first settle this ambiguous hash with a kind of double vision—the child perceives her mother, and herself, as two entirely separate people, one moment the "good" self, another moment the "bad" self.

But even if the mother is altogether "bad" and the child can't avoid that conclusion, she explains it to herself by believing *she is a bad girl and deserves her mother's anger and rejection.* At the same time, the child, in her normal, egocentric way, believes that her anger has the power to annihilate. And so the child guards against her own bad feelings, because she doesn't want to hurt Mommy. Either way, the child has "caused" her mommy to be "bad."

Eventually, if the child has received sustained and predictable love and attention, and if that loving mother is more "good" than "bad," the two images blend into one, and the child can see her mother as a whole human being, with mostly good qualities and a few not-so-good qualities, but altogether "good enough."

And the child can view herself the same way, knowing that even if she incurs her mother's anger on occasion, Mommy won't abandon her. Because of the dependability of such mothering, the child internalizes those good feelings as reflected by Mom's approval and love; the child internalizes the Good Mommy. It is the internalized Good Mommy that makes it possible for the child to separate.

In time, the mommy's love for us becomes love for ourselves, approval of ourselves, self-confidence and self-respect. A setback or rejection will not kill us, because the internalized good mommy protects us from crippling self-doubt, protects us from the awful feelings that we will die without her because, on a deeply subconscious level, we are never without her goodwill.

But if the child has not had that sustained nurturing and affection, if she instead has internalized a Bad Mommy, she begins to see the world in absolutes—all good *or* all bad, all white *or* all black. While she is still a child, however, she dares not see her mom as all bad; so much does she defend the all-good fantasy of her mother that she blocks out any other information in her memory. It is this defense that makes it so difficult to recognize and resolve in therapy our feeling unloved—this is the heart of our resistance.

Blocking is a common way of dealing with unhappy memories. But for two of the women I interviewed, blocking eliminated their entire childhoods. One of them could not remember the first eight years of her life; the other could not remember the first twelve years. Not the name of a teacher or a friend. Not playing, nor crying. Nothing.

But blocking can work in another way. Some daughters go to the opposite extreme: they *only* see their mothers as all bad, unable to recognize any of their mothers' good qualities. Holding their mothers wholly responsible for all the ills in their lives becomes their excuse for not taking responsibility for them.

So in adulthood, unloved daughters often see their relationships as all good or all bad with no gradations in between. The dear friend becomes the "perfect" kindred spirit, idealized out of all proportion—until that friend forgets a lunch date or is unavailable to return a favor. Then the friend, no matter how good her track record as a true and generous and otherwise loyal mate, becomes the unforgiven archenemy.

But these daughters do not let themselves off the hook with such puritanical thinking; they exalt and hate themselves with as much, and as severe, judgmental vigor. The grown daughter becomes her own harshest critic. Any lapse, any failure, feels like an execution—she cannot forgive herself because the mistakes, pooled in an overflowing reservoir of self-doubt, all flood her thoughts with every new blunder. The lost job renders her irredeemably incompetent—she has been "discovered" for the fraud she is. The lost lover has proven her undesirability once again, suffusing her with distraught feelings—if not with actual memories of the long-ago source of her unacceptability—of being the bad, unlovable child.

And, if they become mothers, these daughters see their children—especially their daughters—in the same harsh, exacting light and darkness. The cycle is complete.

This, too, is splitting—but long after it should have been resolved, long after emotional maturing should have caused us to outgrow such polar thinking.

The adult who needs to explain the world in terms of cops and robbers is an adult who is being true to her memory of her mother, the internalized mother; she is not being true to herself. That is because she is unsure of who that "self" is.

The False Self

Diane, thirty-seven, is office manager of a personnel agency in Chicago and the divorced mother of a teenage daughter. Her demeanor is no-nonsense; she is an efficient worker, and she brooks no sexism from the men she dates.

But when it comes to her child, she is mush. The hardest thing for her to do as a parent, she says, is to set limits; she's especially devoted to her teenage daughter, who treats her mother alternately with consideration and with adolescent surliness. It's the surliness that Diane cannot bear—it seems to break her heart, as though her life were at stake. She's convinced that she's a bad mommy, a bad person—she is unable to forgive herself when occasionally she loses her temper with her daughter.

When you talk to Diane about her childhood, you get the sense that only an act of will keeps her from bursting into tears. She says,

> We kids were not allowed feelings. You spoke only when spoken to. If you didn't do what you were told, you got spanked with a hairbrush.
>
> I never wanted to get punished, and I rarely was, because I always managed to do the right thing. I'd think it out very carefully in order to avoid getting into trouble. I'd think, "What do I have to do so she won't get mad?" and I would do it. I became the best little girl in the world.
>
> So I am incredibly hard on myself. And when I screw up—especially with my daughter—I want to kill myself. It feels like I'm five years old again, trying desperately to get back in her good graces.

Diane is a good example of what happens when a child tries so hard to win her parent's love that she loses her self. And in its place, creates what D. W. Winnicott, a pediatrician and psychoanalyst, calls the "false self personality."

By its dictates, the child figures out what her mother wants her to be, wants her to do, wants her to feel, *wants her to want*, and acts as though she wants them for herself, instead of—as they are—what her mother expects of her. The child senses, correctly, that her survival depends on this trade-off: "If I am everything my mother wants me to be, she might love me. If I am everything I feel or want to be, she won't." She figures out what her mother wants—and delivers.

As we shall see in later chapters, the false self can sabotage all the child's natural inclinations; Mom wants an angelic daughter, or an achieving one, or a scapegoat, or a slave, and so the child, depending on her temperament, ignores her own instincts and feelings and becomes one or more of those things.

Alice Miller describes the false self this way:

[The child] cannot develop and differentiate his "true self" because he is unable to live it. . . . A process of emptying, impoverishment, and partial killing of his potential actually took place when all that was alive and spontaneous in him was cut off. . . .

[The child] cannot rely on his own emotions, has not come to experience them through trial and error, has no sense of his own real needs, and is alienated from himself to the highest degree. Under these circumstances he cannot separate from his parents. . . . Instead, he develops *something the mother needs, and this certainly saves his life (the mother's or the father's love) at the time, but it nevertheless may prevent him, throughout his life, from being himself* [emphasis added].

The mother may sincerely believe that she loves her child with all her heart. But she sends out messages, subtle or obvious—or even, sometimes, bizarre—of how she wishes her child to respond to, and demonstrate gratitude for, that love. And so the child gives her what she wants—which may not necessarily reflect what the child wants and desperately needs: *to be loved and accepted for herself, as she is.*

The false self shores up a child's insecurities and self-doubt. Since the child's existence requires her mother's goodwill, she blames herself when she does not get it. She thinks, "It's my fault my mother doesn't love me because, since she's perfect and all-knowing, clearly she would love me if I were a better person."

And where reality becomes unbearable, children augment the false self with fantasies. They idealize other people's mothers. They imagine that they were adopted. As one woman put it,

I convinced myself that my real mother had left me in an orphanage and that this awful other mother was raising me. I was absolutely sure of this, because I had blue eyes and blond hair, while my mother was a brunette. I was sure that one day my real mommy would realize she had made a terrible mistake and she would come and find me and take me away and make up for everything.

Other children dream of having an all-good mother substitute who will rescue them. Sometimes it's a grandmother or an aunt or a teacher. For Laura, who was raised as a Roman Catholic, it was the Virgin Mary.

Laura was the seventh of eight children who were raised in one of the poorest counties of Appalachia. There were days when the children went to school with no food in their stomachs and came home to a house with no food. Sometimes they went barefoot because there were no hand-me-down shoes that fit. A shy child who tried to be perfect so her mother would not beat her, her life was as bleak as any I found in my interviews.

Now forty-two, Laura recalls,

> I had this special tree in the backyard, and when I was a little girl, I used to sit under that tree and wait for the Blessed Virgin to come down from heaven and save me from my mother. I thought, "This is the perfect spot; if she were going to appear anywhere, it would be here." And I would go there and sit and wait for her.

Half in jest, she adds, "The bitch never came."

To this day Laura cannot bring herself to get angry with her mother or with the circumstances that created her sense of terror and abandonment. Instead, she blames herself for everything that causes her pain. If somebody's car veers over the center line and sideswipes hers, it's because she was "driving carelessly"; if a man rejects her, it's because she's "a loser."

Laura cannot separate who she is from the child she had to be in order to survive. She still sees herself as a bad girl. Why does she cling so desperately to a reality that's unreal? Says Dr. Jane B. Abrahamson, a psychologist and author of a study on mother–daughter relationships, "If you can feel any emotion, you're going to feel something beyond nothing, which is dead, and that's how the connection to mother is kept going. It's the awful deadness which is terrifying, tantamount to nonexistence. So anything is better than that, even the most negative emotion."

"The sad thing," says Dr. Marianne Goodman,

> is that there are daughters who keep trying. They keep banging their heads against the same bloodied wall over and over again, not only in their relationships with their mothers, but with everybody else as well. They end up choosing exactly the same people, seeking out the same situation in an attempt to change the outcome. But what they are really doing is recapitulating the old outcome because they are still protecting their parents. They are still trying to keep their parent "correct," and so they are willing to be the bad ones. They won't admit that their mothers didn't love them—instead they blame themselves. They say, "I was unlovable. I was a terrible child." They make excuses for their mothers.

The false self is the Bad Mommy Taboo turned inward. And since you tend to repeat all through your life what you learned in childhood— unless you get some professional help—when you continue to operate as a false self, you continue to be a child. You learn *that* your mother cannot let you feel good about yourself; you don't learn *why* she is unpleasable.

So you take the internalized Bad Mommy message with you, a message that, like time-release pills, keeps sending out signals that you are a bad girl and that Mommy, the all-good, all-wise, all-pure, and all-powerful molder of souls, is always right. Like a phobia, that message keeps getting reinforced—until the time comes when it becomes automatic, and the false self wins.

In adulthood, those distortions take a terrible toll. Says Dr. Garbarino, "It would not be surprising to me that kids who think it was their fault would have the hardest time getting over abuse. The principal aim of many of the therapeutic interventions for children is to get this message across: To define the reality and say the adult's responsible, and children should not be held accountable."

Children are so conditioned to believe that their parents are right that if those parents are manipulative and if they mistreat their children "for their own good," those children learn to extinguish their uncannily honest and straightforward ability to "see." So when they are grown, they sometimes cannot believe their senses. Says Jennifer, thirty-one,

I have certain blind spots. I just lose my sense of identity because I was so overpowered by a mother who said, "But darling, I was just trying to help." Instincts get labeled as sickness. I started labeling my intuition very young as sick—there was something wrong with me.

Enduring Legacies

Unacceptable daughters stumble through life, stopping, starting, trying to break free, even to get angry, but only getting as far as the metaphorical door. They hold on to an illusion of independence— temperamental outbursts, moving far away, attempting to fill in their feelings of emptiness with an unending and unsatisfying round of achievements or failures—but still, unaccountably, they do not feel good about themselves. They are uncomfortable in their own skins. And—confused, angry, depressed, bereft—they don't know why.

Such women are connected to their mothers by the fantasy that somehow, miraculously, it will be different, the relationship will change, the mother will change. They are emotional orphans, adrift in a kind of purgatory: they are estranged in the guilt and rage they feel, and abandoned by a social order that punishes the offended child for disloyalty if that child says, "Enough. I cannot put any more of myself into this relationship the way it is."

In her book *An Unknown Woman*, Alice Koller eloquently describes what it means to be so estranged, an alien to oneself:

I haven't really lived this life that's lasted thirty-seven years. I've only played at living it, pretending I've been alive, saying and doing things to let other people believe I'm alive. But the joke's on me. Because now that I've stopped playing the game, there isn't anything real to take its place. . . . I failed because the things I set myself to do weren't things I *chose* to do. There was no real "I" to do the choosing.

These are the terrible bargains that are made when a child, now an adult, either is not able to see her mother as anything but good, or anything but bad. This is the anguishing cost of the Bad Mommy Taboo. And it is a cost that gets handed down generation after generation, unless the adult daughter determines to stop the cycle—of anger, of blame, of false expectations, crushed hopes, and serial disappointments—with her own generation. With herself.

Coming to terms with that legacy in the face of the Bad Mommy Taboo, then, is a feat of incalculable courage and risk; and for many daughters it takes an act of desperation to render them willing, finally, to address it. Because of the hazards of social and psychic censure, many of them cannot. They become the taboo's ultimate, and tragic, casualties. The cycle continues.

But within it there is a supreme, sad irony: one victim of the Bad Mommy Taboo may be Mommy herself.

Part Two
Behind the Curtain

4

The Evolution of
the Unpleasable Mother

*I am constantly comparing myself to my daughter when I was
her age, and her experience is light-years away from mine. I
grew up on a small farm in the Depression—there were eight
of us kids and we were dirt poor. When I was sixteen, I did
farm chores after school and on weekends I worked in a store.
But when my daughter was sixteen, she spent her afternoons
and weekends hanging out with her friends.*

*When I was twenty-five, I was married and raising three
kids full-time. Now she's twenty-five, and she's studying to be
a lawyer.*

*She's an alien to me. I have no way to identify with my
child. She has all these things I never had.*

—Margaret, fifty-five

A couple of years ago my husband and I attended the fortieth
birthday party of Leslie, one of my closest friends. Among the
guests was Leslie's mother, Rose. I knew in detail the ways in
which Leslie hates and fears her mother—for years I had heard
about Rose the fault-finder, Rose the whiner, Rose for whom nothing and no one is good enough—"Rosie the Riveter," Leslie calls
her.

But the Rose I was meeting for the first time was a tiny, soft-
spoken, gray-haired woman in her late seventies. With a mixture of
keen interest and charming shyness, Rose asked me about my work
and my family, and spoke with loving pride of Leslie, who is an
English professor. I was beguiled.

59

Later, I sat down next to Leslie and jokingly remarked, "*This* is Rose? What did she do, get a lobotomy?"

"You don't know her," Leslie hissed, twisting a cocktail napkin in her hands. "Guess what she gave me for my birthday: *The Oxford Book of Death*. What does that tell you? She knows I use reference books—but *c'mon*."

The gift could be taken two ways: It could mean that Rose, seventy-one and in precarious health, has death very much on her mind. But to Leslie, there is only one message: Her mother wishes her dead.

So, too, could Rose be taken two ways—the mother Leslie experienced growing up is not the frail, self-effacing woman that other people see at a party, graciously declining a second piece of birthday cake.

Like Leslie and her mother—and Margaret and her daughter—in many ways mothers and daughters *are* aliens, each regarding the other as an extraterrestrial. The chasm that separates them often seems very nearly unbridgeable.

Most mothers of the senior generation did the best job they could in raising their children. But even a parent's best efforts are no guarantee that a child will turn out well: unforeseen events and unfortunate breaks can uncouple the most enlightened mother–daughter connection—the child's congenital physical or mental handicap, the death of a spouse, the runaway bus that plows into a school, the mother's incapacitating illness.

The mother herself could not control the immutable facts of her own history: perhaps all her siblings were girls, or she was an only child; or one of her siblings was retarded; or her parents were divorced; or Grandma lived with them; or they were rich, or poor.

A thousand variables create the whole of a child, and the whole of her mother. It is these variables that can cloud their relationship and help to explain—although not necessarily excuse—why some mothers seem so unpleasant.

The Generation Gap

That mothers and daughters have different views of the world is a notion that is as old as time. Twenty-five years ago, Simone de Beauvoir wrote of her mother,

She had appetites in plenty: she spent all her strength in repressing them and underwent this denial in anger. In her childhood her body, her heart and her mind had been squeezed into an armor of principles and prohibitions. She had been taught to pull the laces hard and tight herself. A full-bodied, spirited woman lived on inside her, but a stranger to herself, deformed and mutilated.

But women who today are in their thirties and forties probably have even *less* in common with their mothers than any two generations of women in history.

For one thing, these daughters are part of the largest generation in history, and its demographic bulge has bullied the culture that fed it—and fed from it—every step of the way. The Baby Boom generation, the seventy-six million men and women born between 1946 and 1964, changed the face of America, monopolizing media attention and advertising dollars, which were targeted *just for the kids*. It was the first generation of children to be coddled and wooed for its profitability—they were an economic *gold mine*.

For the first time the senior generation was upstaged—and outnumbered—by its progeny, instead of the other way around. "We ain't never, never gonna grow up!" shouted Yippie Jerry Rubin. "We're gonna be adolescents *forever*!"

Changes for women in this generation were staggering. No longer were women going to be defined solely by spouses and children. No longer would they unblinkingly accept pay unequal to their male peers'. There is virtually no field that growing numbers of women have not invaded, working as lawyers, builders, pilots, clergy, police, and even army generals—the whole range of careers that were once male-only bastions.

Even on the elementary and high school playing fields, girls—their bodies swollen by football gear—sweatily scrimmage alongside the boys.

The whole notion of what it means to be a woman has been stood on its head. This generation of women cut its pubescent teeth on the Pill. They made it more acceptable to be never-married mothers. Through artificial insemination, they reduced "father" to his anonymous semen, unsentimentally deposited into a sperm bank. They eschewed love and marriage in favor of career and cash flow, putting their personal goals over collective altruism.

And this was the generation for whom sex could be a casual expression of transient chumminess, rather than a marital and procreational obligation. By the time most young women graduated from college, they had lost their virginity. And they didn't want just *any* sex—they wanted *great* sex. But this was also the generation that, thanks to the ravages of AIDS, found that sex could be lethal.

The concept of manhood changed too: the father of the 1940s was considered a milquetoast if he hauled out a vacuum cleaner or touched a dish. Many of today's fathers change diapers and can be found in the veggie section of the supermarket, discussing the fine nutritional points of alfalfa sprouts.

The ideal family of the 1950s—Daddy as breadwinner and Mommy as bread baker and home-based childbearer—has, like the bustle, faded into history; by 1989, this family constellation characterized a scant 10 percent of all American households. In 1940, only 9 percent of mothers of young children worked outside the home; by 1987, 64 percent of women with children under the age of six worked. And the fertility rate has plummeted: in 1960, 13 percent of women between the ages of twenty-five and twenty-nine were childless; today the figure has more than doubled.

Fold into this statistical stew the stark reality that half of all marriages end in divorce, a social disgrace forty years ago; that 60 percent of all children born in 1984 will live in a single-parent home before they reach eighteen; that women headed 11.5 percent of families in 1970, a figure that today is 23 percent.

And when they hit the emotional rapids, Mom is not their only source of solace. With the widespread phenomenon of myriad therapies and self-help groups, daughters relieve their emotional bends in a stranger's office: Mom has in many cases been replaced by the fifty-minute hour.

As for the love sweepstakes: Where once mother influenced, even determined, her daughter's choice of mates, now she is often replaced by the personal ad and the dating service. The American dream for many young women is epitomized by television news superstar Diane Sawyer, who didn't marry until she was rich, famous, and in her forties.

Consider the world of our mothers as they gaze, aghast, upon the unfamiliar terrain of their daughters' lives: cloistered into the confines of nursery, matrimony, and weekly allowance, our mothers *began* life at a disadvantage.

By virtue of their sex alone, they were considered a handicap at birth *even by their mothers*, upon whom the culture smiled only if they produced *sons* (and ignorant at that time of the all-important fact that gender is determined by the father).

The preference for male progeny goes back to biblical times—but that preference has lingered well into this century. As recently as 1976, when women were asked which sex they favored, they chose boys over girls by a ratio of two to one (for husbands, the ratio was between three and four to one). It is a bias that seems to be obsolete for most of today's young women, even as it colored their childhoods. Several demographers have told me that no figures about current gender preference are available; the question is simply not asked, because for young women, who can support themselves, it is no longer an issue.

When the mothers of today's adult women were growing up, they were not favored by the niceties of therapy, self-expression, and "letting it all hang out." These women were to be seen and not heard, to address their parents as "ma'am" and "sir." With the exception of the most enlightened families, they could not speak of their longings, their sexual yearnings, their dreams.

Quarantined by gender, their very femininity equated with lifelong dependence, how could they easily understand their daughters, whose lives were so very different? How could they absorb the great feminist premise and promise that they could "have it all" when they had so little?

The Cultural Gap

This senior generation of women, now in their 60s and 70s, finds the world of their daughters alien in other ways—the traditions, even the language, with which they were raised are often obsolete, like a key that won't fit a lock.

Many were immigrants or first-generation Americans whose parents brought them up with foreign values and foreign accents.

"My parents were from Italy, and my father and my brother were the family chieftains," says Cristina, thirty-four.

> My mother was an unwanted child because she was a girl; hence, her daughter was unimportant to her. I was "less than"—not as important as—my brother. She never shouted at my father—that was too threatening. Her son was not to be tampered with. So I took the brunt of her frustration.
>
> The only thing she could contribute to life was food. It was important for a good Italian mother to cook, and

to have a family eat *a lot*. And, because mothers did not force husbands or sons to do anything, let alone eat, you especially needed a *fat* girl to show that you were a successful mother. I looked like I had rickets. My mother tried to force me to eat; we had monumental fights over food. So from her point of view, she was a failure.

Then there were the mothers who had been raised in Old World affluence and manners. Marta's mother grew up in prewar Austria and was weaned on stiff social protocol, governesses, and noblesse oblige. Along came Marta, who was weaned on anti-Vietnam War demonstrations, sex, drugs, and rock and roll. She says,

My mother wanted me to live up to her background by having a husband from a fine family and good breeding. She wanted me to be a perfect model of what she was. Instead, I married a carpenter's son who never finished high school. That was the worst. She's still crying over it.

Even when a family is assimilated, the cultural strands of the past tug down through the generations. Dr. James Garbarino recalls a friend who was teaching a college course on cultural and ethnic differences between people. He says,

A student said, "I think this ethnic business is a crock." The instructor turned to the class and said, "Okay. Let's check this out. How often do you call your parents?" One group said, "every week," and another group said, "once every few months." The instructor said, "How many of you are Italian or Jewish?"—most of these were the students who called every week. Then she asked, "How many are WASPs?" and that was mostly the group that called every few months.

Folkways of other cultures cling to very traditional families and provide fodder for mother–daughter disaffection. Among many Jewish families, for example, you disparage a bit of good luck or a favorable turn of furtune—as in, "We'll pick up your father's bonus tomorrow, I should live so long"—so as not to draw the attention of God, who might, in the interests of providing a lesson in humility, change the outcome.

Some Jewish mothers even follow the Eastern European tradition of slapping their daughters upon their menstrual debuts in order to ward off evil spirits.

Many of the daughters of these women react to these echoes of their mothers' cultural histories with confusion and rage, taking them altogether personally (a conclusion it's hard to avoid), even though that wasn't the intention.

The Historic Gap

Many of the mothers of the women interviewed for this book came of age during the Great Depression of the 1930s. It is impossible to overstate how this event sent their generation reeling—it marked the end of unlimited dreams and unalloyed faith in American prosperity.

Unlike the "crash" of 1987, the Depression sent tentacles of despair and poverty to the far reaches of all levels of society. It had a particularly devastating effect on women. Most mothers of the Depression could not afford large families, so the choice to have fewer children took away a huge piece of their cultural value.

Many of today's women are also not having children. But this time it's because they want more money, more freedom, more options than their mothers had. Not having children *enhances* their chances of grabbing the financial and professional brass rings. The record for the lowest fertility rate was set not by Depression-era mothers but by Baby Boomers.

The historical gap that divides mothers and daughters includes attitudes toward child-rearing. The yardstick by which a mother is judged is very much a measure of her time.

Just as there are fashions in clothing, so, too, are there fashions in mothering, and God help the mother who deviates from them.

As we saw in Chapter Three, Mother at the turn of the century was a corseted paragon of powdered virtue and modesty—who better to be assigned the hallowed task of purifying her children and rendering them into dutiful, patriotic, and God-fearing citizens?

But by the 1920s and 1930s, Mother was considered by the still fledgling psychological profession to be unequal to the high moral purpose of her task.

Mother as madonna suddenly was considered a hazard to her children because of her zealous, naive, and sentimental love for them. The culture that swept mothers into idealized ghettos of domestic grace now chided them for their lack of worldly wisdom. They were unceremoniously demoted from their revered position at the very time that many of the mothers described in this book were growing up.

The daughters of these debunked mothers suffered the harsh consequences. The leading child-rearing guru of the 1920s and 1930s was psychologist John B. Watson, who believed that mothers were "dangerous." Mothers, in their unsullied adoration of their children, were considered to be the instruments of their children's weakness and dependency, their lack of spine and character. At risk were their children, who might not be able to tough out the daunting demands of a capitalistic society.

Dr. Watson came to the rescue, ready to save mothers from their weak-willed, ignorant selves. His was a stern, no-frills canon: Treat your children like young adults. "Never hug and kiss them," he cautioned, "never let them sit on your lap." If a mother, unable to check her misguided neediness, were to succumb to "smother love" and actually *kiss* her child, she was to do so only at bedtime; in the morning (presumably, having pulled herself together and restored her dignity), she was to shake her child's hand.

Most children of this period were to be raised with military, scientific precision: feeding and toilet training followed a strict schedule. Discipline and emotional restraint were the hallmarks of the well-bred child.

If mothers were not allowed to show affection to their children, how could those children—half of whom are the mothers of today's young women—come to believe that the mother was anything but uncaring? And what would it mean if that mother herself craved affection? She would shamefacedly turn herself and her children off, like a spigot. She would keep her feelings to herself, like yellowing love letters on some psychic shelf.

One cannot imagine that all mothers followed the good Dr. Watson's advice. Some women simply ignored it and relied instead on their own horse sense and emotional instincts. But since women were not *encouraged* to do so, the ones who did were unusual in their maternal confidence and independent spirit.

When the young girls bred on such rigidity were themselves mothers, theirs was a vastly different maternity, one of post–World War II plenty and a child-rearing pendulum that swung in the opposite direction—to child-rearing permissiveness.

The country, burgeoning with a skyrocketing birthrate and postwar wealth, revolted from the austerity of the Watson era and instead embraced the more gentle, sensible rubrics of Dr. Benjamin Spock. Now we had an era of consumer excess, and the generation raised with Depression-era penuriousness and pinched emotions welcomed the new, open permissiveness as much for themselves as for their children.

But these mothers of the 1940s and 1950s—whose maternity reflected the twin messages of Watsonian rigidity and Spockian flexibility—hadn't forgotten their own childhoods. It must have seemed unimaginable to them that they would produce the self-absorbed children who would one day be termed the "Me Generation." Just as they had been taught to respect their elders, they expected no less from their children.

For mothers of Baby Boomers to find themselves denigrated—subtly or blatantly—for putting their children first, ranked with filial mutiny and betrayal. *Especially* if that denigration came from a daughter. It would feel like a renunciation of everything the mother had been taught to hold dear—nurturing, feeding, cleaning, cooking, caring for child and husband, sacrificing for them her own ambitions and needs.

How could the mother avoid thinking, Is this the thanks I get? I did as I was told, as my mother did, as did her mother before her—my daughter is rejecting her heritage.

No wonder mothers and daughters seem alien to each other—one raised on emotional and financial austerity, the other on choice and plenty. Each is a citizen of her own vastly dissimilar childhood context, struggling to decode the other's messages.

The Temperamental Gap

The cultural and historic differences that separate mothers and adult daughters serve as an overlay of their *temperamental* mix. Then and now, their intrinsic personalities governed how mothers would respond to those differences.

It is here that we see how mothers can vary in the treatment of each of their children. Many siblings often wonder if they grew up in the same household, so different was each of their experiences of Mom.

Temperament is a profound barometer of how people behave, as countless researchers have discovered. Stella Chess, M.D., and

Alexander Thomas, M.D., of New York University Medical Center, for example, in their longitudinal study of children, have written of the "easy," "difficult," and "slow-to-warm-up" child. Mothers are simply grown-up versions of the same temperamental categories.

Behavior has many sources.

Genes. According to studies of twins, genes account for more than half of personality traits—the balance, less than half, are shaped by family and experience. A shy child, for instance, cannot be made to be aggressive but can be encouraged to be less timid. Leadership and languidness, obedience and vulnerability, even certain psychological pathologies, are to a large degree also inherited. You can witness these differences in a hospital nursery: some babies scream, others sleep peacefully, one fidgets, another stares into space.

Intimacy needs also seem to be heritable—such needs separate born loners from born huggers. "[The need for intimacy] is one trait that can be greatly strengthened by the quality of interactions in a family," Dr. David Lykken told a *New York Times* reporter.

A person's general way of looking at life is her own. Like a musical chord, it may go into a minor key, its tempo may vary, but eventually it resolves itself. How she views herself and the world is established in the early years, a combination of her inherited and experienced childhood. She can't change her basic self, but she can adapt, learning to be at ease with herself and to respect people's differences, especially if she has parents who understand that "being different" is not necessarily "being wrong."

But the mothers described here themselves had parents who had practically no knowledge of these things.

"Fit." Mothers often tailor the prevailing parenting advice to their own tastes and personalities, likes and dislikes, and children fall into roles that reflect their unique and innate reactions to their mothers' behavior. How they "fit" together, as Drs. Chess and Thomas have discovered, depends on the temperaments of each.

Says Dr. Marianne Goodman,

If you get dissimilarity between mother and child, it's like fingernails on a chalkboard. You see this with infants. A mother may be very energetic and vivacious, and have a sensitive baby who gets overstimulated and cries—then you have a real mismatch. When the mother does her normal high energy stuff, she is distressing the more placid child. They're both being themselves, but they do not work together.

What happens when the daughter is older? If the daughter isn't providing mother with what she wants, the mother may become a passive and bitter victim.

This lack of similarity was the case in Norma's family. Norma, forty-one, was slow-moving and easygoing in contrast to her mother's more exacting and impatient personality, and they lived in a state of constant friction. But Norma's youngest sister, Adele, was in many ways a temperamental echo of their mother. Says Norma, "Sometimes my sister will hear me talk about how I don't like my mother, and she'll get very upset. She just doesn't *see* Mom that way. She just doesn't understand why I feel the way I do."

Sometimes sisters can divvy up their mother's characteristics, rather like choosing from a menu of traits, depending on their own temperaments. Molly, thirty-nine, and her sister Chloe, thirty-five, also have entirely different reactions to their mother. Says Molly,

> My mom's much closer to my sister, because she was terribly formal and my sister was like her, ladylike and "refined." I was considered unrefined; I was a go-getter, I hung out with the rough kids, I was a jock. Chloe and Mom spend a lot of time together; I do my own thing.

Because of temperamental hitches between mothers and daughters, one mother's "joy" can be another's "problem child."

And so, as we will see in the next five chapters, mothers fall into certain *general* behavioral categories. So, too, do their daughters adopt certain roles, rooted in their temperaments, which will be explored in Part Three. Sometimes their temperaments grate against each other—and, as we shall see, build up so much friction that they can cause a kind of earthquake within the family.

The Emotional Gap

Tension is demonstrated in how mothers and daughters express—or restrain—their feelings for each other. The contextual and temperamental differences that keep mother and daughter at odds with each other seep into their emotional expectations. History notwithstanding, many daughters feel that no matter what they do, their mothers will remain forever unpleasable.

Most mothers do love their daughters. So why can't some of those mothers express it? A major reason is that since they were raised to respect their elders at their own expense, and to restrict their feelings and needs, they weren't allowed to address their differences of opinion.

Since the emotional survival of those mothers required their unquestioning obedience and the invention of a "false self" (see Chapter Three), they had to repress their anger and instead believe that mother was always right, always knew best. Caught between memories of their rigid childhoods and the new wave of parental permissiveness, they are often torn by ambivalence.

Ideally, a daughter can express a feeling without acting upon it, and a mother can hear a feeling without overreacting to it. That's not what happens in unhappy mother–daughter relationships. Mothers who cannot bear to listen uncritically to their daughters respond with long-denied anger or sadness, hearing the duet of their childhood deprivations and their adult frustrations rather than the conversation they are having.

Patricia, sixty, is tortured by her mixed feelings for her daughter, Debby, who is thirty-six. Says Patricia,

> There's always this tension, this monitoring. I feel I have to be always on guard. I have a very, very difficult time opening up with her. I can talk to you, I can talk to a friend, but I'll be goddamned if I can talk to her. The overriding feeling I have is that I'm not a good mother, that I am not open and honest and capable of baring myself and allowing her to see the hurt. I wasn't raised that way. I feel so vulnerable with her—she can hurt me so much. It's like stripping yourself naked in front of another human being.

As psychologist Jane B. Abramson, who conducted a study of difficult mother–daughter relationships, told me,

> I think that one of the major distinctions between my generation and my mother's generation was that hers was told what to do by some higher authority, such as a parent or child-rearing expert, instead of having faith in themselves. These women had to distort themselves in order to please somebody instead of being naturally true to themselves and their feelings. The need to be phony in

this way—a "false self"—is one reason why some people go into psychoanalysis; it's the reason people mess up themselves and their children.

Child psychologist Bruno Bettelheim describes the cost of a mother's denial of her needs and emotions. He writes,

This mother unconsciously fears that her child's happy play would arouse her repressed feelings of unhappiness and anger, to the degree that they can no longer remain repressed but break out into the open. . . . So to keep the repression going, she may either see to it that her child is not too happy and thus does not rouse jealousy in her, or she may distance herself emotionally from her child, so that what he does will not make so strong an impact on her that it would break down her repressions.

A mother who has not resolved her relationship with her parents—and certainly the elder generation had no cultural permission to do so—projects that dissonance onto her children. She may favor the child who gives her "no trouble" and come down hard on the child who reminds her of her insecure self—the "unreliable" or "ungrateful" child—whatever it is about her that once made *her* mother frown at her in disapproval.

Triangling. The child who is the scapegoat gets the mother's harshest feelings. But that child in an insidious way serves that mother's purpose. Writes Dr. Harriet Goldhor Lerner, "Focusing on a 'problem child' can work like magic to deflect awareness away from a potentially troubled marriage or a difficult emotional issue with a parent or grandparent."

The mechanics of this dynamic is called "triangling." Dr. Murray Bowen of Georgetown University developed the Bowen Family Systems Therapy, which (among other things) looks at how the family unit operates, and in particular the ways in which difficulties between two members involve a third.

When a mother finds *excessive* fault with a child, for example, often she is "triangling"—siphoning off her unhappy feelings about her husband, or about her mother, about which she is unable or unwilling to do anything, and placing them instead on her child (we shall discuss "detriangling" in Chapter Seventeen).

Her behavior is the legacy of generations of such triangles. She may raise her hand to spank, or to cover her face in anguish, and generations of maternal reactions are echoed in her gesture. She is demonstrating "learned" behavior that speaks to her mother's and grandmother's childhoods, when their mothers struck or sobbed. Reactions to conflict or pain are refracted down the generations of one family—great-grandmother to grandmother to mother to child.

Triangles work in a variety of ways; the mother who hates confrontations, for instance, may not directly curb one child's temper but instead may align with a more passive child to persuade the angry child to behave more civilly.

This is the heart of dividing and conquering—of such stuff are favoritism and intense sibling rivalry born. The "splitting" of which we spoke in Chapter Three finds its way to the varying treatment by mothers of each of their children. When the immature mother has not separated from her mother—when she still divides the world into good guys and bad—she will often "split" the good parts in herself and project them onto her children, who become the "good kid" or the "bad kid."

As Stephen P. Bank writes in *Siblings in Therapy: Life Span and Clinical Issues,*

> The unending adoration lavished on one child accompanied by the regular devaluation of another says that the disfavored one is worthless or worth less than a brother or sister. . . . The unfavored sibling often cannot face the parents' dislike and prefers to focus the anger at the favored brother or sister.

Triangling fuels mother–daughter enmity by pitting one child against the other, dancing around the true source of conflict. Triangling is also used to *exploit* a daughter to keep her mother's marriage afloat.

When the daughter matures and leaves her first family, her parents' loveless or dull marriage fills up the void. Now there is an unobstructed view across a silent dinner table. Denied a third member to take the triangular heat, mother and father face each other and their strained relationship. What better way to keep unspoken conflicts between mother and father at bay than to make a daughter the continued repository of spillover recriminations, the unwilling taker of sides?

The Father Factor

Mother may have been shut out of other roles, but in her own house she was the doyenne of domesticity. Her marriage, home, and children were *her turf*—anything that threatened that, including a daughter, could shake apart her only foundation. She may have reacted like a tigress when her cubs were in danger—but she guarded her husband's affections and her place in his bed no less jealously.

It is against this cultural, temperamental, and emotional background that fathers loom in importance.

If these women, so culturally sequestered within the wifely and motherly definition of women's work, perceived that their daughters garnered too much of his charmed attention, the daughter was in for a bumpy ride.

Passive fathers. The father who was head of the family in the 1940s and 1950s often gave up power, willingly, in the nursery. A disproportionate percentage of the daughters I interviewed—at least half—described their fathers as "browbeaten" or "dominated" or "weak" on the home front. These fathers tended to duck any unpleasantness between mother and daughter; by keeping a low profile within the family, they maintained a status quo that, although often punctuated by heated exchanges or chilly silence, was nevertheless manageable in its predictability.

Fathers often were the quiet centers of their daughters' storms and, by putting themselves in the "eye"—that is, by not intervening on the daughter's behalf or by clandestinely siding with her—stoked the turmoil that surrounded them. In an effort not to "make waves," in their passiveness they nevertheless often created emotional hurricanes.

In frustrated response, their wives frequently vented their feelings of redundancy onto the only people over whom they were allowed total control: their children, *especially* their daughters. Since these husbands seldom objected to their wives' hostilities toward their children, and even defended it ("Oh, she doesn't mean it"), they were by default approving of it.

And so their daughters often felt bereft of *any* parental protection. Says Enid, thirty-two,

> I know my Dad loves me, but I feel he has a lot of trouble controlling his own life. My mom's really jealous because he and I have always been close. So when I

have an argument with her and I don't talk to her for a while, *I don't hear from him*—it's like I died. I call him up and say, "Hey, you're a grown-up, you can do anything you damn well please. If you want to see me, you can come and see me." And he doesn't.

Daddy's Little Girl. Many other fathers allow themselves to become entangled in a web of female jealousies, caught between two females—mother and daughter—who are fighting for his favor. It is here that mothers and daughters are, or can be, "natural enemies."

Their rivalry is particularly painful if the daughter is a firstborn girl. Says Dr. Goodman,

> She is the usurper of the mother's special relationship with her husband. Even though it's her baby, it immediately sets up a triangular situation, particularly when the mother is insecure. Now mother has to share daddy. The child is no longer a part of her—she's daddy's little girl, daddy's prize, all those things that Mom may have wanted to be, and may have been, especially in a superior/inferior relationship between husband and wife. All of a sudden, there's another inferior female, a lot more adoring, a lot more cuddly, and mother is kicked out of the box. You depend upon mommy to recognize this, not to feel threatened, and to enjoy the fact that her daughter is growing up; she can bide her time and later on she'll get a friend in her daughter. But if the mother is insecure about herself or her marriage, she will begin to compete with this little girl.

Such triangles can be devastating for daughters, both destroying their attachment to their mothers *and* distorting their connections to their fathers, and to men in general. Says Diane, twenty-six, "Mom doesn't like Dad paying too much attention to me. I have one foot on a banana peel for just being a girl."

Some fathers—especially if they are in an unhappy marriage that they have no intention of leaving—unwittingly or deliberately put a wedge between mother and daughter. In the name of being a haven from mother's wrath, Daddy becomes the daughter's gallant rescuer. He may, in forming a bond that excludes Mom, even treat his daughter "like a son."

Alexandra, thirty-eight, is head of the chemistry department of a leading university. She says,

> I was Daddy's Little Girl because my mother and I never got along. Mom wanted me to be a secretary— she wasn't particularly interested in anything I did. But Dad used to say to people, "When Alex graduates from college she's going to go to law school and then she's going to become the first female president of the United States." He meant it.
>
> I would love to have had a mother I could talk to or laugh with or get advice from. But she wasn't that kind of mother. So I learned not to need her and not to listen to her. And we have absolutely no relationship today.

In the worst cases, Dad will abuse his authority and will go head to head in a power struggle with Mommy—whom he ignores or humiliates or rejects—wooing the daughter into siding with him.

In the Phillips family, one would never surmise from its California image of wholesome, outdoorsy togetherness that Lauren, twenty-nine, is paying dearly for being Daddy's Little Girl. Her father, unwilling to confront his marital difficulties with her mother directly, instead uses them to create in his daughter an adoring "mate."

> My father thinks I'm perfect. He's always on my side when my Mom and I fight, he doesn't even have to hear what the argument's *about*. That's caused no end of arguments between them.
>
> I confide in my dad—he knows a lot more about me than she does because she just finds fault with whatever I do. He feels stuck in his marriage; it's something we talk about all the time, how he's going to survive living with my mother.
>
> My dad's the sweetest, most even-tempered, calmest man. But my mom just nags and nags and nags, and finally he'll blow up; he has to resort to her tactics to make her stop arguing. Sometimes he has to just slap her. And yet he's such a gentleman and would never do those things if she didn't drive him to it.
>
> I don't know who to feel sorry for. Intellectually, I'm on my father's side, but emotionally I'm on my mom's side. I see her crying and I know she's in pain and I see my father getting so mad, and I tell him to stop.

The cost of being a father's favorite is high. Such daughters, because Mom has been shunted aside, idealize their father, the only parent left on whom to rely for affectionate counsel, and approval. But in a real sense, the daughter loses *both* parents; choosing Dad casts her into a psychological twilight zone, unable to identify with either parent.

When the mother is excluded, the daughter suddenly, and inappropriately, rises in family rank in a giddy ascent. She becomes the vehicle by which her father rationalizes either his remoteness from, or hostility for, her mother, or she becomes his excuse for "not making trouble" or for losing control in the name of "rescue." Far from shielding his daughter, he sets her up by stoking his wife's jealousy of her.

And so Dad, rather than serve as buffer, may instead widen mother–daughter rifts—and his daughter, denied a healthy family role may, emotionally, be stranded.

The Disenfranchised Mother

Mothers of adult daughters have had to maneuver within the lack of cultural prestige and choice that has haunted their generation. Bereft of social value and sometimes redundant within her own family, there was but one place left for her to bleed off her anger: her daughter, whom she might "punish" for all the options that had been denied her. And since much of this skewed redressing of losses was unconscious, she either felt little remorse for her behavior—or she vigorously, even righteously, defended it.

Before daughters can begin to unravel the real source of their mother's wrenching—albeit sometimes unfairly and inappropriately resolved—discontent, they often have to be grown and, in many cases, veterans of lengthy therapy. Says Hillary, a forty-two-year-old stockbroker,

> When I was a freshman in college, I came home for Christmas vacation, and the first day I showed my mother some of my textbooks; I was so proud that I'd gotten them secondhand. She picked them up and threw them to the floor with such violence, some of the spines broke.
>
> "You and your books!" she screamed. "That's the problem. I never should have allowed you to learn how

to read. All these damn books talk about is how everything is your mother's fault."

It was a non sequitur. You'd have thought I had said, "Look at this—'Freud on Mothers.' " Something clicked in my brain and I thought, "Don't react to this." At that moment I realized that most of the time there was no connection between what my mother was angry about and anything I had actually *done*.

I later understood what was behind her rages: The real reason is she never went to college. She never had a chance to prove herself through a rewarding career. She was trapped in a horrible marriage. She could not escape.

And I am all the things she will never be.

To say, then, that today's adult daughter is in varying ways a threat to her mother is, if anything, to understate; the chief variable is *degree*. Mom looked to the narrow context of her family, especially her children, for a sense of satisfaction. Her daughter, brought up on 1960s music and mores, looked to herself in the wider context of choice and economic self-determination.

The Depression-era generation of mothers, reared on the values of flag, mom, and apple pie, believed in self-sacrifice and commitment to others. For them, the worst fate was to be *independent*: a spinster, or married to a man who couldn't support his family on his salary alone, and *have* to work.

Their daughters, jolted by Vietnam, the sexual revolution, and feminism, were largely committed to themselves. For them, the worst fate was to be *dependent*.

In many ways, these mothers—blinded by their histories, blinded by an envy that they would never become what their daughters are or have options to be, blinded by buried childhood feelings of unacceptability—did not even *see* their daughters. Rather, those mothers had expectations of themselves *through* their daughters, mirroring their own mothers' expectations and values of another era.

Isolated from adult sources of affection, sexual fulfillment, and intellectual stimulation, these women looked to their daughters to make up for all that, binding their female children ever closer to them. A girl's early childhood was prime time for these mothers; and when that girl began to separate, and later to play out the goals of another, newer, revolutionary role—not following her mother's example but setting her own—the mother often felt utterly abandoned.

How would she respond? She would either attack or become clinging and helpless—or become emotionally detached.

As psychologist Louise J. Kaplan writes in *Oneness and Separateness: From Infant to Individual,*

> An ordinary devoted mother cannot flourish in a society where women are humiliated by a self-definition as helplessly dependent. Like a helpless child who strives to be as powerful and dangerous as his all-powerful oppressors, an oppressed woman will protect herself from humiliation and the terror of aloneness by trying to become as dangerous and tyrannical as her oppressors. . . . The cycle of female oppression will be reinforced as the mother turns away from her daughter when she does not embody the attributes the mother wished to have but never acquired. Should the daughter strive to acquire such envied attributes, her mother will subtly undermine her ambition.

When, for all the reasons we have discussed, a mother feels unworthy, unappreciated, and shut out of avenues for finding herself and for expressing unhappy feelings in a healthy way, she may be emotionally unable to accept her daughter's independence, or her sexuality, or her individual ways of being a wife and/or mother, or her freewheeling life-style.

That mother, in every sense but literal, may try to cut her daughter "down to size." Herself unseparated from her mother, and having only her motherly role, she will have a poignant and devastating stake in her daughter's failures.

And so she may attempt to sabotage the envied daughter's happiness or treat her in a demeaning way. As Dr. Harriet Goldhor Lerner writes, "as long as an object is devalued it need not be envied." Mothers who were brought up to be "nice," "ladylike," "yielding," "feminine," will find circuitous ways to release their not nice and unladylike feelings—and what safer way than upon their daughters? Says Dr. Abramson, "It's an absolutely natural dumping ground."

How could such mothers realistically evaluate and openly admire their daughters in the airless environment that was the legacy of their own constricted childhoods and marriages? For them—to whom motherhood was all, children were all, family was all—the empty nest becomes a tomb.

Like a caged hamster running endlessly on a wheel, many mothers remain trapped in their feelings of rejection. They protect their maternal flanks by living in the past and by engaging in countless arguments and sighing numberless sighs over the same thing: Why can't my daughter see things *my* way? Why can't she appreciate me more? I was a good girl—why isn't she?

These mothers desperately try to prolong their maternal power and clasp their daughters to them, unable to allow into the relationship the breath of fresh air of real separation and mutual respect. Their unhappiness is animated by the variables of their histories—temperament, genes, birth order, life experiences, and the "oughts" of their femininity. And because of their histories and fears of being abandoned on alien soil, many of them can *only* connect with their daughters by encouraging crippling dependency.

It is not that these mothers do not love their daughters; it is that they *dare* not.

The behavior of unpleasable mothers falls into certain general patterns. Such mothers "control"

> through neediness (Doormat);
> through rigidity and corrections (Critic);
> through enmeshing (Smotherer);
> through fear (Avenger);
> through silence (Deserter).

Many of these maternal roles overlap. Some mothers run the gamut of behaviors—critical at one time, mollified at another.

It isn't Mama *alone* who charts our course, for good or ill. And it isn't Mama *all the time and in all situations* who can be held responsible for the shifting currents of our self-confidence. She may have been one person at twenty-five and quite another at forty; too tense early in her maternity, too slack at its biological ebb; a Good Mommy to one child and a Bad Mommy to another; a confident parent with teenagers, an insecure one with toddlers.

Nevertheless, there is a major theme in how mothers treat their daughters that, allowing for these variables, has more impact on those daughters than any other single ingredient. "The development of self-esteem is always a social process," write psychiatrists Thomas and Chess.

Looking at these maternal roles is important for two reasons. First, it puts Mother into perspective so that we can understand her different experience and temperament. For some daughters, it may be enough to recognize that their tensions with their mothers are not so terrible that they cannot reach some kind of accommodation together.

But for other daughters, recognizing the depth of their differences—beyond generational explanations—helps them take the first step in deciding whether or not they are inimical to *any* kind of loving relationship.

In reading through these five maternal behaviors, certain factors must be kept in mind when applying them to your own experience.

1. These behaviors are the *extremes*.
2. These behaviors are *incessant*, not isolated incidents.
3. These behaviors can cause a daughter to feel a harrowing sense of *complicity*—that somehow she contributed to her own destruction because she was unable to prevent the outcome.

I did not interview a single daughter who had not been willing, at countless times in her childhood and adult life, to meet her mother more than halfway. But most reached a point at which they began to believe that the relationship might *never* get better.

For those caught in the limbo of that awareness, this question hung in the air: *Where do I go from here?*

That question raises three others, which are the heart of this book:

- How can we change the relationship to achieve a friendship that seems beyond our reach?
- Failing that, how can we at least reach a truce, and learn to respect and accept the differences that cannot be changed?
- When is the relationship so devastating and full of pain that we must bail out of it *and at the same time believe that there is hope for ourselves? How do we get past the anger and sadness?*

Understanding how a mother's life may have confounded or even destroyed her does not mean you have permission to use her behavior as a reason to be eternally unhappy and eager to assign blame. And so the first step to answering these three questions is to begin really to *see* your mother and not just to react to her.

The patterns of how mothers keep their adult daughters under their sway are the subjects of the next five chapters.

5

The Doormat

I love my mother. But I can't honestly say we've ever been what you would call "friends"—the concept of friendship was not even a consideration. That's because I always mothered her. My mother coped with life by being sickly. There was always something wrong with her, and she was never really sick. I remember as a child assuming responsibilities that were beyond her. Once my father was badly burned while he was barbecueing outside, and he told me to call an ambulance, because she couldn't handle it.

—Ann, thirty-nine

The Doormat is the ideal mother—but of another time. By the yardsticks of 1930s femininity, she would have been considered the epitome of womanhood, her demeanor summoning adjectives full of prefeminist praise: Yielding. Placating. Fragile. Soft. In need of protection by a big, strong man, she was all talcum, dimples, and demureness, enjoined not to worry her pretty little head about anything.

At this point in the closing years of the twentieth century, however, the Doormat seems, well, *embarrassing.* In her frailty, she may not have been out of place in her mother's time—when she followed her mother's and the culture's example of homespun meekness—but she is an anomaly in her daughter's. She is unable to make a suitably worthy contribution to a culture that is never so contemptuous as of the woman who says, "I'm just a housewife."

The Doormat is a woman of heartbreaking weakness and dependency who valiantly tries to do what her husband and children ask of her, if only she could muster the energy and will. There is not a trace of rancor in her—indeed, she gives the impression that she is a victim of life's inequities, a prey for the meanspirited, taking the blame for everyone.

Sweet Suffering

How can you hate someone who is all those things? How do you judge someone who is so defenseless? It's like kicking a puppy. But many of the daughters of Doormats *do* hate their mothers, but with an explanation. When talking with these daughters about their mothers, unlovely words crop up, over and over, in an ambivalent litany of sympathy and condemnation: Dependent. Depressed. Childlike. Terrified. *Pitiful.*

But the Doormat seems to *ask* for that condemnation. At the heart of her daughter's ambivalent feelings is the fact that she was simply too fragile ever to be relied on.

Here's how Marion, thirty-six, and Anita, forty-three, describe their Doormat mothers.

When Marion was growing up, she dreaded going home after school, because she knew her mother would be reading "serials" in magazines as the laundry piled up, or in bed with an illness—or simply exhaustion—wrapped in a tired bathrobe and cloaked in sadness. Says Marion,

> You know how some early, early memories stick with you, like a kind of beacon? My earliest memory of my mother was when I was three; she was sick with the flu for a couple of days. I had this sense that if I got too close, I would drown in her sorrows. She wanted endless nurturing, being cheered up, agreeing with her about everything. I knew even then that this was a person who needed taking care of. Forty years later, she still does.

Anita describes her Doormat mother this way:

> My mother is so sensitive, the smallest criticism reduces her to tears. So everything with her is sweetness and light. Any problems I ever had with her, if I tried

to talk about them, she'd just kind of go out of focus—
she would just space out or walk away. Once she said to
me with complete seriousness, "I wish I were you." I
didn't take it as approval. I took it as a warning that she
wanted me to fill the emptiness of her life. It scared the
hell out of me.

The Doormat is the least separated of all five maternal types
described in this book. Temperament plays a major part in the
Doormat's lack of spine; as mentioned earlier, timidity is often an
inherited trait.

Her history seems to diminish her even more—in many ways,
she is still stuck in childhood, unable to grow up. Many of the
Doormats described here were from large families where they got
lost in the shuffle, left in childhood to fend for themselves. Others
were raised in an atmosphere of sullen obedience.

Most were raised in households where the father was punitive and
demanding and the mother was a compliant puppet of his unreachable standards. But some were the products of a matriarchy.

Paula's grandmother ruled her Baltimore roost. When her daughter, Willa—Paula's mother—got married, she and her husband moved
into the grandmother's sprawling brownstone. Willa's marriage was
the stepchild of her mother's suffocating demands. Says Paula,
forty-two,

> My grandmother demanded stuff from my mother that
> was beyond what one person should ask from another.
> She would not let my mother go on vacation without her.
> To this day my mother claims she can't cook, be-
> cause Grandma always prepared the meal. I would get
> these fits at dinner—I would be gasping for breath.
> They were anxiety attacks because I felt the tension
> between my mother and grandmother. As soon as you
> finished your food, my grandmother would jump up
> and start doing the dishes. My mom would say, "Mother,
> I want to have a cigarette and just relax. Wait." My
> grandmother could wait for nothing. And my mother
> was her slave.

Paula describes her mother as a "pathetic victim." Always friendly,
using such terms of endearment as "sweetie" and "honey" and

"darling," Willa would spend hours on the phone in the afternoon, talking to female friends. But she seemed to get no sustenance from those attachments.

"As soon as she would hang up, her face would go blank," Paula says. "It was as if a door slammed. Once they hung up, people didn't exist for her anymore." Paula has the feeling that she doesn't exist for her mother either, not because her mother doesn't adore her, but because she seems utterly worn out.

"When I call her, she sighs. There's nothing I can do to cheer her up. She isn't a tough woman. I think she was always in a rage, and couldn't show it. My poor mother has this personality she can't help—she just can't deal with life."

Unable to compensate for their childhood losses with inner reserves of strength, Doormats instead coasted from childhood through adulthood and parenthood, uncertain of anything.

Doormats have little sense of self; it's as though they are cartoon characters, but the pen strokes that define them are a series of broken lines. They cave in under the weight of their own unhappiness, behaving as though one more wound would annihilate them.

To borrow from *New York Times* columnist William Safire, trying to pin them down is like nailing Jell-O to a tree. Like sponges, Doormats seem to suck up the moods, especially the criticism, of people who are around them. At the same time, if you ask something of them, they seem to be emotional hemophiliacs, in danger of "bleeding" to death at the tiniest pinprick of anyone's disfavor.

These women are what Dr. Murray Bowen describes as "deselfed," unable to defend themselves, obliterating their own needs and instead punishing themselves. They believe that anything that goes wrong in their lives or families is their fault—they sit as their own judge and jury, unable to mount any defense, and accept unquestioningly their own verdict of unworthiness.

The Doormat's tragic handicap is that she cannot display anger. This is not to say that she doesn't *feel* it—but she turns it against herself, rather than toward others. "The partner who is doing the most sacrificing of self stores up the most repressed anger and is especially vulnerable to becoming depressed and developing emotional problems," writes Dr. Lerner.

Indeed, of all motherly types, she may be the *angriest*. But constrained from ever being so unfeminine as actually to *act* on her anger, she instead implodes—the simmering rage, finding no release, may in extreme cases cause her to have a breakdown or suffer from serious physical illness (see Chapter Nine).

Staying in Your Place

The Doormat has a string of adversaries who keep her in her long-suffering place. Triangulating within the family helps shore up the Doormat's helplessness—the more she displays weakness, the more she attracts people who are eager to be her champion, to "overfunction" to her "underfunctioning," as Dr. Bowen puts it. But her rescuers often harbor a deeper wish—to bully her. She unwittingly accommodates them.

Unsurprisingly, Doormats are often married to men who are domineering. In her book *Intimate Partners: Patterns in Love and Marriage*, Maggie Scarf writes,

> If . . . I were a "never angry" person, I might see anger as coming *only* from my husband—and actually get him to collude in this by forcing him to lose his temper and *express my anger for me.* . . . When one person is always angry and the other is never angry, it can be presumed that the always angry spouse is carrying the anger for the pair of them.

The Doormat is a prime target for the alcoholic husband. Sharon Wegsheider, in *Another Chance: Hope and Health for the Alcoholic Family*, coined the term "Enabler," the role often played by the wife of an alcoholic. The Enabler is characterized by "pseudo-fragility, hypochondria, powerlessness, self-blame. These are all defensive postures by which an Enabler avoids looking honestly at her position and doing something about it."

And so it seems that the alcoholic is the *Doormat's* prime target as well. For as long as someone is assuming control of her, she is protected from having to face her own anger; you feel sorry for her, so wretched is her fate. And as long as she is so helpless, the alcoholic is protected as well—she acts out his helplessness rather than face her own.

Nancy, forty-three, vividly recalls a childhood in which she was constantly begging her mother to leave her alcoholic father. She says,

> I was always my mother's confidante, because she didn't have many friends. Once when I was a teenager, he was

on a rampage and threatened her with a gun, and she took us to a friend's house for a couple of days. But she'd always go back. I'd ask her why she wouldn't go to her parents for help. She'd say, "Oh, no, I don't want to get them involved." She was miserable and had no place to go; it wasn't until I was an adult that I realized that she should have made a choice to protect herself, and us, from all that unhappiness. She made a choice—to stay because she couldn't bear to be alone. She's been rejected so much in her life, maybe she just can't risk it.

Whether or not there is the problem of alcoholism in the family, the Doormat is not without power, even if it is of the most passive kind. By abrogating all dependability and strength, she gets her family to function for her. Her children are enlisted in the complex process of keeping her down. They, too, "know their place." Just when they most need emotional nourishment, their mother is drained and depleted, so they learn early on how to cope, relieving her of her parental responsibilities.

And so, from their earliest years, the Doormat's children are thrust into the position of saving her from her domineering husband, or saving her from herself, or saving themselves from her.

One characteristic of some psychologically abusing parents is that they are overly dependent on their children. They themselves were usually psychologically maltreated as children, and rely on their children to replenish the hollowness they felt as a consequence of having parents who were unable to meet their emotional needs.

But the Doormat's children have problems of their own, which they resolve either by huddling together for a warmth and guidance that mother is too defeated to summon, or by flailing at each other—and sometimes at her—with an unbridled anger that can erupt into flames.

In *The Sibling Bond*, Stephen P. Bank and Michael D. Kahn describe what happens in the family when parents are unable to express or tolerate any kind of anger: ". . . with heads firmly stuck in the sand, [they] fail to perceive obvious aggression. Ignorance of their children's fighting provides temporary bliss, as the parents label vindictiveness as 'teasing,' humiliation as 'kidding,' abuse as 'a little wrestling.' Hoping that the children's arguments will disappear, they salve old emotional injuries of their own by being unobservant."

And their children, fulfilling their triangular destinies, often act out the very anger the Doormat cannot bear to express.

As we shall see in Part Three, many daughters of Doormats become their devoted rescuers. But other daughters—depending on their temperaments, and faced with the bottomless pit of their mothers' emotional hunger, respond by pulling away. They may idealize and identify with their fathers and become bossy, like the daughter who told me, "I could always beat my mother up verbally, and she'd never lift a finger to defend herself." Others, like the daughter who at thirty-five still lives with her mother, imitate her in their own weakness and become increasingly more childlike.

It is women, far more than men, who adopt this kind of crippling need because they were raised to be second-stringers rather than major players in the family. Woman's work, especially for Doormats, is above all a process of validating their social inheritance of instability, of being insignificant outside relationships, and at all costs, even of the self, of preserving their attachments.

And how do they control their children? Through guilt—not the kind that other mothers coerce from them (see Chapter Seven), but of the pitying kind, the way we feel when our car accidentally runs over a disoriented rabbit that has darted onto the highway.

The Doormat's daughters are themselves trapped—caught in a double bind of sympathy and self-preservation, on the one hand denying themselves, on the other, denying her.

Says Hannah, thirty-seven,

> When I was a child, I used to have this recurring dream: I'm looking everywhere for my mother, only I can't find her. And I'm frightened—but not for me; *I'm frightened for her.* If I could just get to her and say, "I'm safe, it's all right," then everything would be fine. Just to tell her that I was okay—that's all I worry about in the dream. And I would wake up in a cold sweat.

Feeding the Soul

The Doormat is the perfect personality profile to be obsessed with food and to develop an eating disorder. She may be overweight— "feeding the hungry heart," as one expert on anorexia and bulimia put it. Eating mounds of food seems to be the Doormat's way of trying to fill up an emptiness and emotional need that cannot be satisfied. Alternatively, starving or purging reflect her self-abnegation and revulsion.

As we know, eating disorders have become epidemic, spawned by a generation of women who were taught to be helpless. Kim Chernin sees these disorders as "a profoundly political act." In *The Hungry Self*, she writes,

I am describing generations of women who suffer from guilt: women who cannot mother their daughters because their legitimate dreams and ambitions have not been recognized; mothers who know they have failed and cannot forgive themselves for their failure; daughters who blame themselves for needing more than the mother was able to provide, who saw and experienced the full extent of the older woman's crisis, who cannot let themselves feel rage at their mother because they know how much she needs them to forgive her.

More in Sorrow

And so Doormats often become utterly dependent on their daughters. When they are old, there is frequently a role reversal that was never *really* reversed at all—the daughter, as always, is still her mother's mother. The Doormat's exquisite neediness and sensitivity is often a running theme in a lifetime in which the child was *always* mother to the woman.

Many of those daughters—as Lucy Rose Fischer observes in *Linked Lives*, her study of adult daughters and mothers—resent their aged and infirm mothers' dependency, in part because they no longer have any hope of *being* daughters—they can never be the mother's "child."

There are many good and sound reasons to feel sorry for the Doormat, whose sense of self-esteem is like a cobweb that rips away at a touch. In a way, to say that Doormats are destructive seems unfair, even callous; but harm occurs when those mothers cannot allow their children to be *children*, cannot allow their daughters to exhibit their own anxiety, or insecurity, or neediness. Doormats have cornered the family market on those defeatist commodities.

Having such a mother feels like living with a wraith who could be blown away with any sudden gust of wind. These daughters become enraged at never having their own sanctuary—rather, they have always been asked to *provide* one for their mothers who are unable to handle any form of maternal responsibility.

The results are often disastrous.

Hear the response of this woman, who throughout her childhood always felt she had to keep one eye out for her mother:

> One thing I always knew, ever since I was a small child, was that something was wrong with her, but I couldn't put my finger on it. I was so sheltered, and I didn't have friends to play with, because she was afraid I would get hurt. So I had to stay in the house except when I went to school. I felt so confined because I wasn't allowed to play outdoors. And when I did, I would feel guilty for leaving her alone. On those rare occasions, she'd either watch from the window or sit outside.

And listen to this daughter:

> My mother was a "hear no evil" personality. She never wanted to engage in a discussion. I always had the feeling that she truly wasn't interested in me. My strongest impression of her is that she felt cheated by life, that life had somehow conspired against her. She did so many things to make herself helpless; she never learned how to put the blender together, for instance, because someone would come along eventually and do it for her, and if not, well . . .

Because they do not physically harm or belittle their children and are often gentle and affectionate, these women may believe they are "loving." But they are nearly incapable of *providing strength*, unless they can get some outside help. And so their daughters, acutely aware of how vulnerable their mothers are, remain mired in the frustration of being unable to express their *own* needs.

The bargain Doormats strike with their daughters seems to be this: If I give up myself, you will gain a self. But in fact what often happens is that the daughter simply becomes frightened or angry because she is forced to become self-reliant, long before she is ready for it—she does not get to *have* a self. At least, not an always healthy one.

Profile of a Doormat

Jeannette sits in my living room, sipping iced tea on a warm May afternoon. Beads of perspiration drift down her round face, which, with a tissue, she dabs with fleshy hands—she is at least thirty pounds overweight. Pushing a strand of blond hair away from her moist forehead, she tells me the reason she answered my ad: "My daughter refuses to see me at all, and I'm trying to figure out why. I thought maybe talking it through might help."

Jeannette, fifty-seven, is one of the most intelligent and articulate of the women I interviewed. Not a trace of self-pity flavors the candor she brings to a merciless assessment of her parenting flaws. I genuinely pity her, perhaps because she does not seem to ask for or demand pity—there is about her a crumpled dignity. She seems stunned to discover that all her intelligence, her keen appreciation for life's ironies, her ability to tolerate intellectual ambiguities, have somehow failed her as a mother.

But then, I am not her daughter.

When I define for Jeannette the Doormat personality, she instantly recognizes herself.

She grew up in the Midwest in a small farming community sixty miles from Kansas City, the eldest of two daughters and a son. Jeannette's mother had given up a teaching career to marry her husband, a physician, and to raise their children.

"My brother and I agree that she should not have had children," says Jeannette, gazing unseeing at a bird feeder outside the window. "She was not a cold person. But I don't think she was equipped to handle the demands of children. I resemble her in more ways than I ever thought possible, much against my wishes."

Her family was not wealthy—her father's services were often paid for in sacks of potatoes—but her mother took great pride in her impeccable manners and high social standing. "Not nice people" had a specific weight in family conversations about neighbors who did not behave "correctly."

Jeannette knew early on that being a good girl was expected of her, particularly since her more rebellious brother incurred their father's icy displeasure. Being "good" suited her compliant nature, and she easily adopted the role.

Jeannette's brother maintains a seething animosity toward their mother, but Jeannette counters with such hackneyed phrases as "If you can't say something good about someone, don't say anything at all."

It amuses her that she is unable to repress such banal expressions, learned at her mother's knee, because she *hates* clichés and excoriates any writer who employs them. "When it comes to literature, at least, I have *very* high standards," she says, laughing. But clichés were her mother's tool for keeping her children at bay. Jeannette recalls,

> She had an absolute abhorrence of people expressing anger. If I had a problem or complained, she'd say, "What do you want to worry your little head about that for?" or "Ah, ah, ah, the temper, never, never never." You couldn't show your temper. You just *couldn't*. My brother did, but I didn't. With me, it all got driven inward—what it did was make me a conciliatory person, to my detriment. I didn't push, because I was the sort who never made waves—that's my temperament. But those expressions were my mother's way of shutting me up. It was an absolute no-win situation, because I would never be anything but runner-up, she'd always win, I would be bested at every turn because I wasn't allowed to feel.

When Jeannette graduated from high school, she went to the University of Colorado on a full scholarship, bent on pursuing a career as a ballerina, a talent her mother had encouraged with dancing lessons because it was "refined" and would improve her daughter's "carriage." But not for her daughter was a dancing *career*, working nights.

After she graduated from college, Jeannette moved to Denver and got a small apartment, and continued her ballet studies. But her mother disapproved of her living alone in such a big city—and while Jeannette earned a salary as a part-time secretary and took dance classes at night, her mother's displeasure hounded her.

"My mother would come to visit me, but she'd always stay in a hotel. She would never visit my apartment—she always found some excuse not to."

The question I asked every women I interviewed I now pose to Jeannette. "What was the cost of your childhood?"

She pauses and a look of exhausted sadness shadows her soft features. "I didn't learn how to be assertive in relationships," she says at last. "It's had devastating consequences. It finally had its outcome in the person I chose to marry."

When at twenty-one she met Gary, a real estate broker, Jeannette was eager to find a role that would accommodate her shyness and her mother's urging to get married, stop working, give up dancing, and have children.

Gary's mother, whom Jeannette describes as a "victim," was very like Jeannette herself. Gary's father was cold and tyrannical. So, too, was Gary. Jeannette says,

> He had impossible notions, very fixed ideas on female behavior, particularly young females. He wanted daughters rather than sons because, he said, he had observed other families and found that girls were more obedient than sons. He said, "Girls are easier to love." What that meant was they are easier to manipulate. I never questioned it.

And Jeannette, as a "girl," was a target of much of that manipulation.

> He would never tolerate criticism of any kind. He would sulk, clam up for days. I would always be the one to give in and offer the olive branch. I knew all the time that this was happening—a little voice kept saying, "You are making a big mistake, this will not do you any good," but I persuaded myself that this was in the interest of preserving marital harmony and that at some level I could feel superior, so I could say, "Well, he's behaving like a child, so I will placate him as one placates a child." But it got out of hand because it centered on our daughter, whom he controlled with his rigid expectations.

Gary taught their only child, Rachel, how to ski when she was five, and soon the family's winters revolved around the sport. Each weekend, and for two weeks over Christmas, the family drove up into the

Rockies to Estes Park, where they rented a ski chalet. He'd enter Rachel in every ski meet, and soon she was "hotdogging" and winning speed races. But as she reached her late teens, she began to rebel against the demands of her training and competitions, which rendered their home life similar to boot camp. Says Jeannette,

> I'm embarrassed to tell you what it was like. He'd wake us up each morning with a whistle, and to my eternal chagrin and regret and great shame I participated in his schedules by not saying anything. He was absolutely the captain of our ship, and I was his first mate. He was totally in control. Rachel would literally have to roll out of bed and hit the slopes. She told me that she hated it, that if she never saw another ski it would be fine with her. But I said, "Well, you can't let down the team or your father." I was always putting out fires. I thought it was important for children not to witness conflict, that the worst thing you could do was to let a child see parents at odds with each other. You iron out your differences behind closed doors. But, of course, we never ironed anything out—I just went along with whatever he said, being the perfect wife. I would always acquiesce—in the beginning it was because I wanted to maintain a united front, and later I just felt very, very tired, too tired to intervene.

As time went on, Jeannette began to gain weight, and her housekeeping, as she puts it, became "indifferent. I was passive-aggressive, really trying to make a statement, because in the early years of our marriage I had been extremely neat."

Occasionally she'd raise weak objections to Gary's increasingly intrusive parenting. Gary would go into Rachel's room and search her drawers, read her diary, grill her about her activities after school. "He would justify it by saying, 'What's the matter with you? Don't you know about all the drugs these kids today buy in school? Don't you care about your own daughter?' "

And on those by now infrequent times when Rachel would turn to her mother for aid, Jeannette would sigh, "He's your Daddy, he really loves you." So Rachel began to retreat into herself, like a downhill racer at the starting line, concentrating all her energies and girding her loins for a fast getaway. She became a dutiful daughter, but walled off, never confiding in either parent—and being increasingly withdrawn.

Just as Jeannette had been when she was a child.

When Rachel turned eighteen, she left home. And she never looked back, except for occasional holidays with her parents. Those visits became fewer and fewer, and finally stopped altogether.

Jeannette has not seen her daughter in five years—Rachel stopped visiting around the time Gary left Jeannette for a woman in her early twenties, a woman who is very like Jeannette as she used to be—lithe, graceful, shy, attentive, in need of a man who would teach her about life. Jeannette and Gary are now divorced.

Rachel is still wrestling with the legacies of her childhood, trying to choreograph a life that so far seems to be an angry ricochet from those years when her father's exacting demands and her mother's supplicating silence left no room for her to grow.

Rachel has proven that she is strong enough to get away from home. But she has not yet been able to reconnect with Jeannette—perhaps because her own strength seems so tenuous, she is afraid of becoming *like* her mother. Or perhaps she feels that she cannot take care of her mother's emotional needs when her own are so confused.

Her mother has no way of knowing. "She's never forgiven me for not taking her part," says Jeannette, ruefully. "Maybe someday . . ."

And now Jeannette, burdened with advanced middle age, sabotaged by a cumbersome body that betrays her with chronic fatigue, anguished by a punishing awareness of her terrible bargains in the name of peace—as a child, as a wife, as a mother—faces her narrowing options.

Living on an inheritance from her parents and a small amount of alimony, she is trying to sort out her life. She is in therapy, and seems finally to have the courage to address her demons, the ones that pushed her down past her instincts, past her passions, past an awareness of a larger world that once beckoned her to dance upon its stage.

6
The Critic

My mother has a positive genius for finding ways to put me down. I am a very successful lawyer, and not long ago I lost a case for the first time in years. She immediately assumed that it was my fault, that I screwed up somehow. At around the same time, a well-known attorney who is a close friend also lost a case. I told my mother about it, and she was shocked. I said, "You know, Mother, it happens—occasionally you lose one. Look at me." And she said, "Oh, but this is different— she's famous!" Here's my mother, defending someone she barely knows. But I'm chopped liver.

—Cynthia, forty-two

Without the Critic, the stand-up comedian would have a shortage of material. "My mother gives me two shirts for Christmas," the joke goes. "I put one on. She says, 'So what's the matter? You don't like the other one?' "

And there is no dearth of Critics: this was the largest category of maternal personalities I found. It was the daughters of Critics who regaled me with stories that always get a laugh, stories that give comic spin to the Critic's carping.

"No matter what I do, my mother always finds a flaw," one woman says, chuckling. "I send her a heartfelt note, and she corrects my spelling. I buy her a bunch of flowers, and the next day she calls to tell me they died."

Another woman guffaws when she tells this story: "I am an only child. Every day I call my mother and each time I say, 'Hi, Ma.' And each time she says, *'Who is this?'* "

Giggles punctuate a third woman's story: "She's an accountant at heart—she always keeps score. If I use Brillo pads, she thinks I'm deliberately *not* using her brand, SOS, to *spite* her."

Great comedic stuff.

It is practically impossible to exaggerate—or not to find ridiculous—the Critic's unflagging capacity for grave remonstrances over minutiae. Take the Issue of the Beaded Curtains.

Penny is the thirty-two-year-old daughter of a Critic. Recently, Penny and her husband, who have two small children, moved out of their small Manhattan apartment and into their first house, which she is in the process of redecorating. Says Penny,

> My mother loves beaded curtains in bathrooms—you know, those Casbah things that were popular in the sixties? I *hate* beaded curtains. But I was trying to find ways to explain to her why I wasn't buying them, because I didn't want to hurt her feelings. So I told her I was afraid if I hung them in the guest bath or the kids', the children would eat the beads and choke to death. She agreed with the wisdom of that decision. But I couldn't think up an acceptable excuse for not buying them for my bathroom. So now I'm in the doghouse. When she visits, she always walks around muttering, "Three bathrooms, and no beaded curtains. . . ."

Critics come in many forms—some are Grande Dames, regally condemning people who are "not the right sort" and dismissing them with a condescending snort.

"My mother has a way of throwing verbal hand grenades and then leaving the room before you have a chance to explode," says Caroline, forty-one. "Once I made the mistake of telling her that my mother-in-law has plastic covers on her living room furniture. My mother said, 'Well, what can you *expect* from those people? They have no breeding,' and she stalked out of the room."

Other Critics are Queens of the Hard Luck Story: "You think you have it bad?" chides a Critic whose daughter has just reported that her dishwasher broke down. "In *my* youth, we didn't even have *running water*, let alone such luxuries as washing machines."

Still, laughs aplenty.

But when you delve into the histories of these daughters, the humor pales. Strip away the comical component of the Critic's often bizarre pronouncements, and you find a mother and daughter at perpetual loggerheads, no matter how hard the daughter tries to soften her mother's prickly implacability.

The Critic is often a woman of high energy, and her personality is no less intense. Depending on her own family history and temperament, she may be given to loud outbursts. Many daughters of Critics recall their mothers' "screaming" or "constantly fighting," either with the daughters themselves or with the man of the house.

Other Critics are able to wall themselves behind a curtain of silence. "My mother can go for weeks not speaking to me," says one woman, "refusing my calls, if she's angry with me."

It is the daughter's eagerness to please that can drive the Critic to raise the ante and keep her daughter at a loss. A child's winning ways become a weakness rather than an endearing quality that inspires warmth. That weakness becomes a window of Critical opportunity.

The Critic seems to be coiled for an opportunity to be disappointed in her daughter. One daughter I interviewed recalled that when she was recently laid up with the flu, her mother offered to go to the supermarket for her. "My mother called from the market and said, 'I'm about to leave. Are you sure you have everything you need?' I said, 'Well, I could use some paper towels.' My mother said, 'Well, that means I have to go back and stand in that long checkout line. You might have told me before.' "

Where's Poppa in all this? He's lurking behind a newspaper, or working late, or puttering in the garage. The Critic is usually careful to marry a passive man. Given his more malleable personality, the chances are good that he will succumb to her commands. He is no more inclined to defy her than are her children, and so she drafts him into supporting her domination. Often he is called upon to carry out a punishment the Critic has promised in a threat that begins "When your father gets home . . ." But he is not always up to the task.

Says Alberta, thirty-five:

> When I was five, I forgot to walk the dog, and it peed

on our brand-new living room rug. My mother screamed, "When your father gets home, I'm going to have him spank you!" So that night, the first thing he did was spank me, as ordered—but then he threw up, because it upset him so much. *That* never happened again.

When the daughter reaches adulthood, it is her mortified father who calls the daughter to say, "Your mother is upset. She wants to know why you haven't visited her."

The Critic is achingly insecure, as we shall see later in this chapter; the patient loads of psychotherapists are clogged with daughters who lament having mothers who never had anything good to say about them. Therapists know that behind the Critic's daunting demeanor is her low self-esteem.

But that doesn't help when daughters are caught in the snare of trying to ingratiate themselves to—or at least avoid the censure of—the Critic. Because no matter how artfully the daughter attempts to dodge her mother's displeasure, *the situation between them is win–lose, and the "winner" is always the Critic.*

That's because the Critic knows how to set her daughter up for failure. The ways she does varies, but according to my interviews, Critics share many of the same characteristics.

The Competitive Edge

The Critic's family is a horse race, and she will do whatever is necessary to stay on the inside track, operating with her own sense of sportsmanship, the rules of which shift with her moods.

Playing for Blood. Beatrice, sixty-seven, thinks she's a wonderful, nurturing sort who took part in endless marathons of Monopoly with her only child, Karen, when she was little.

"But when she played," Karen, twenty-nine, recalls, "you'd think that she was an Atlantic City high roller. *She had to win.* Even when I was seven years old, she took each game with deadly seriousness. She would set her jaw and play for blood. She couldn't have fun. And if she *lost*, there was no talking to her—she'd sulk for hours."

Divided Loyalties. When the Critic has more than one child, she will try to pit one against the other, so that both children are defused, unable to rally forces against her.

Kelly, thirty-five, and her sister Sally, thirty-one, both describe their mother as "impossible."

Says Kelly, "She has no sense of other people's privacy. When she visits my house, if she has something she wants to say, she'll say it, no matter what is going on. Once my husband and I were getting ready for bed, and he was stark naked. My mother barged in without knocking to tell me that she didn't like the brand of toothpaste in the bathroom. When I said, 'Ma, this is not the time to discuss it,' she glared at my husband and said, 'Big deal. I've seen it before,' and resumed her comments."

Says Sally, "She's unbelievably opinionated. Everything's a personal affront. When I was in high school, I quit cheerleading, and she got hysterical. She started screaming, 'You'll never be popular! You'll never get a date! How could you do this to me?' "

But Kelly is able to tolerate her mother, whereas Sally is not. The sisters' divided loyalties stem in part from their temperamental differences—Kelly is circumspect, and is of the two the more relaxed. Sally is volatile and easily hurt; tapping her temple with her index finger, she confesses, "I forget nothing—it's all up here."

Their personality differences have been fine-tuned over the years by their mother, who since they were small has always denigrated one to the other. To Sally, a high school history teacher, she says that Kelly is "stupid." "She always called me that, behind my back and to my face," Kelly says. "She hired four thousand tutors for me when I was in school and I barely graduated. I'm used to it."

To Kelly, a housewife, their mother rails about how "uptight" and "hypersensitive" Sally is. "How could I *not* be 'hypersensitive'?" Sally says archly. "All she ever does is tell me how fat I am—never mind that she's thirty pounds heavier than me."

And while both sisters tell me that they no longer allow their mother to "badmouth" the other, they also confess that today "we are not close." Their mother does not need to drive wedges between the women, because the wedges were in place years ago. So instead of arguing with their mother—Kelly "strokes" her mother, Sally refuses to spend time with her—they argue with each other.

Dr. Jane B. Abramson explains that when mothers create in their children the roles of "good kid" and "bad kid" it is because they are unable to accept any imperfection in themselves. Says Dr. Abramson, "Each of her children will embody the bad parts and the good parts of herself; there would be the child she would reject and the child she would adore."

The Critic not only drives her children apart, she also frequently "splits," both psychologically and literally, with her own siblings. Many Critics have running feuds with one or more of their brothers and sisters. Quick to take offense, and cataloguing every slight, they expect their children to align with them in their lifelong family vendettas.

One daughter recalled for me her "happiest moments—they were when I was with my mother's younger sister. She was always kind to me, always made me feel welcome to drop over and have a piece of pie and just chat about my day. But my mother hated her sister— she felt that her parents had always favored her. So my mother always found reasons why I shouldn't visit her. Eventually she stopped speaking to her altogether—and I was no longer allowed to visit."

In her quest to keep her daughter isolated from any separate sense of self-esteem, the Critic will often try to sabotage her daughter's friendships.

"I'm embarrassed by my mother because of the way she talks about me to other people," says Sandra, who has an older sister named Debby. "She seems to go out of her way to belittle me to my friends. It's very subtle. Once I was sick, and a friend came by to visit. My mother unexpectedly showed up at the door, and when my friend let her in, my mother introduced herself by saying, 'Hi. I'm Debby's mother.' Not, 'I'm Sandra's mother.' "

And Critics frequently inject themselves between their daughters and sons-in-law, attempting to generate turmoil between them. "My mother loves to tell my husband that I've been out shopping all afternoon," says one woman. "She's not just being chirpy; she says it in a voice dripping with sarcasm, implying that I am somehow neglecting my duties as wife and mother."

But then, when the husband is out of the room, the same mother turns around and tells her daughter, "*That man* runs you ragged; you let him take advantage of you. When is he going to get a decent-paying job?"

The "Best" Mother. Another way the Critic competes is through disapproval of other mothers, comparing herself to them in ways that are often capricious.

When Connie was ten, she played outdoors one day with a new friend named Nancy. At 6:00 P.M., Nancy announced that she had to get home for dinner—that was her curfew. But Connie, whose father worked late, didn't have to be home until 7:00, the family's supper-time. Says Connie, thirty-seven,

> That day there were no other kids around, so when Nancy left, I wandered back to my house. When I told my mother why I was in early, she said, "Oh, yeah? Well, you're not going to live by her mother's rules. If she has to be home at six, I want you home at five-thirty."

Calling the Shots

The Critic controls her daughter with a lengthy list of demands, a list that expands as the daughter moves into adulthood and her own home. And one demand that crops up often is The Phone Call. If you call her once a week, she feels slighted because you don't call every day; if you call her daily, she wants to know why you are too busy to stay on the line.

"The difference between my mother and me," says one woman, "is this: She considers her day a success if she hears from me. But I do not consider my day a success if my daughter calls me; it's just not an issue."

The imperative of the phone call becomes a numbers game, an arithmetic symbol of maternal power and worth. Of a mother's need to have her daughter constantly check in with her, psychiatrist Marianne Goodman says, "My question is, why is it that mom wants that? Why is it quantity and not the quality? What's mom looking for? She's looking for someone to make up for something that's missing from her life."

And what's missing is having her daughter still at home, under her sway. So the phone is the instrument by which she tries to control the daughter from afar, a metaphor for the um-bilical cord.

Getting the phone call from her daughter isn't enough to make the Critic happy; if it were, the daughter wouldn't resent so much having to make it. If those telephone exchanges were pleasant, if the mother were able to reach out and *really* touch, or be touched by, her daughter, their conversations would be a loving link between them.

Instead, the phone becomes a tool for Critical power. And control is the only way she knows to prolong her maternal authority. Unable to allow her daughter the *option* of loving her—which includes the option *not* to love her—the Critic skews the notion of true intimacy. She cannot risk a peer relationship of give and take, because she cannot bear the vulnerability of healthy distance; nor can she bear the "closeness" that revealing her vulnerabilities could engender. It's too chancy—it *might* go the other way, the daughter *might* try to manipulate *her* or, worse, reject her.

At Arm's Length

Many Critics complain that their daughters are not physically demonstrative—but it is the Critics who are seldom able to express physical affection, or to receive it; they tend not to like being touched.

"My mother held me when I was little," Cynthia recalls, "but I never felt that her touch was loving—it was harsh. When she bathed me, she scrubbed me until my skin was raw. But she treats herself the same way she treats me. She's not physically kind to herself— she picks the skin off her hands until they bleed. She's as hard on herself as she is on me. She can't separate the two of us."

Eleanor remembers that her mother would tense up when she tried to hug her.

> I'd move to embrace her, and she'd pull back; she'd find something to criticize—it's like she used her disapproval as a way of keeping me from coming too close. She would correct my grammar, even if I were in midsentence. Or she'd say, "Don't you have homework to do?" When I was little, I was always running and falling, and she wouldn't help me up. Instead, she'd say, "You're never going to have legs like a lady." Everything was a correction, never "Gee, that's great." Never a pat on the back. She never said, "I think you're terrific." What she said was "Don't embarrass me."

Just as power is used to keep her daughter close, so is guilt used to ensure that her daughter doesn't get *too* close. *Guilt* is the method by which she establishes and maintains her authority. Says a forty-three-year-old woman who lives in California, five minutes from where her mother lives,

> My mother never fails to remind me that the day I was born, my father lost his job. I was brought up with the fiction that he was emotionally and physically frail. If I got a bad grade on a report card, for instance, she would say, "I won't tell your father tonight; let him at least get a good night's sleep." When I went to graduate school in New York, she said, "I only hope your father lives out the year." Mind you, my father today is eighty, and has never spent a day in the hospital.

The Ultimate Authority

The Critic is like a minister without portfolio. She has all the correct answers, but often they are based on a need to be in charge rather than genuine expertise.

According to the daughters of Critics I interviewed, when they were small, their mothers would belittle their most banal needs and remarks. Says one woman, "When I was a child, if I said, 'I'm hungry,' she'd say, 'How could you be hungry? You just ate three hours ago.' If I said, 'I'm sleepy,' she'd say, 'How could you be sleepy? You had plenty of sleep last night.' If I said I didn't know something, she'd say, 'How could someone be so ignorant?' "

And when her daughters are adults, the Critic's circle of authority broadens.

If the daughter is single, the Critic frequently applies pressure on her to marry—but not just *any* marriage. She wants her daughter to marry the richest, smartest, handsomest man—preferably someone of *her* choosing rather than her daughter's. Says Lonnie, thirty, an elementary school teacher,

> My mother will not get off my back about my being single. She even ran a personals ad about me in a magazine, listing the qualifications *she* has in mind for a suitable mate for me. She isn't at all interested in my career goals. She keeps saying that if I were married to someone who's successful, then she could *really* be proud of me.

When the Critic's daughters do marry and have children, she includes her grandchildren in her purview. Now Grandma knows best, and she is seldom reluctant to provide a running commentary on her adult daughter's mothering.

Dinah has two young children and one teenager. On a recent visit, her mother said to the youngest grandchild, an energetic, inquisitive five-year-old, "You're only good when you're asleep." Says Dinah,

> My daughter came running into my room in tears and told me what had happened. I told my mother never to talk to my daughter that way again. Her response was to launch into my teenager. She said, "Her friends come over and eat everything in your refrigerator. Don't their mothers feed them? What is this, a restaurant?" So I said, "Ma, mind your own business." It's always something. She just never stops.

And when the Critic isn't providing unsolicited advice on her grandchildren, she questions her daughter's ability to run her own household. Says Frieda,

> Once I went to pick out carpeting, and my mother insisted on coming along—she said she wanted to make sure I was getting a good deal. She complained about every sample the salesman showed us, and she accused him of trying to cheat me. It was humiliating—she just took over. Finally we settled on a carpet, and when she was out of earshot, the man whispered to me, "Whatever you do, don't ever bring your mother back here." When we were finished, my mother was fine; but I was a wreck. Sometimes I get the feeling that she's only happy when she's got something to complain about.

No area of the daughter's life is safe from the Critic's demeaning comments. A thirty-three-year-old novelist told me that when she was working on her first novel, she made the mistake of mentioning to her mother that she was going through a dry spell.

Her mother retorted, "What could you possibly know that's worth writing about? Novelists have to be at least forty to have anything to say."

The Tyranny of the Little Old Lady

In his eloquent, unsentimental, and poetic book *The View from 80*, Malcolm Cowley writes unsparingly of curmudgeonly old people: "If they had always insisted on having their own way, in age they become masters or mistresses without servants—except perhaps a loving daughter—and tyrants without a toady. If they had always been dissatisfied, they become whiners and scolds, the terror of nursing homes."

Old age does not diminish the Critic's store of censoriousness.

Clara was born in Ireland sixty-one years ago and at the age of four moved with her parents and five brothers and sisters to the United States. When Clara's father died ten years ago, her mother, then seventy-five, moved in with her. Clara's siblings refused to take on the onerous—given their mother's sourness—task, so Clara, still the responsible firstborn daughter she was in her youth, volunteered for the job. It was, she says, "the biggest mistake of my life."

> My sisters and I were always expected to put her first, even when we were grown up—that we were married and had children made no difference.
>
> She'd never call my sisters; she'd say, "It's their duty—they're supposed to call me." And then when one of them did, she'd say, "Tell her I'm sleeping." Or she'd hang up on them. She'd complain that they never came to visit her, and I'd say, "If you were nicer to them, maybe they'd come." She'd scream, "Shame on you—you should stick up for me, not them!"
>
> She made my life a living hell. She'd sit up in her room, waiting for me to pass by. Then she'd say, "Get me a glass of water." I'd say, "Can't you get it?" And she'd say, "My legs can't take me." But when she wanted something, like to come downstairs to eavesdrop on a conversation, her legs could take her.
>
> I loved my mother and I took care of her until the day she died. I'm from the old country, and you're

supposed to love and care for your mother no matter
what. But if I were young today—if I knew then what I
know now—I'd never do it again.

What Makes Mommy Run?

From an outsider's point of view, all this seems so trans-
parent—how silly the daughters are to acquiesce to these impossible demands, and how patently absurd and infantile is their
mothers' behavior. But the problem is that the Critic has *no* idea
why she is so critical, so demanding, because her defenses are
impenetrable. She is nearly incapable of cutting through them
with the kind of introspection that leads to change.

And her daughters, toppled by her raids on their self-confidence,
often remain tangled in their thwarted efforts to win her approval.
Even in adulthood, they frequently don't see the insecurity that
spurs her sabotage—they see only her disdain.

Unable to recognize her mother's vulnerability, the Critic's
daughter is caught in the ruse the Critic presents: "Do it my
way. But even 'my way' won't be good enough." *The daughter
feels she has been duped*, and that she has conspired in her own
humiliation.

What the child—and later, the adult daughter whose merciless self-criticism and self-doubt reveal a child's heart—doesn't
know is that her mother, the Critic, was probably raised *exactly
the same way*.

The tragedy in this standoff is that by her inability to draw her
children into loving intimacy, the Critic keeps herself isolated from
the very thing she most yearns for: the comfort of being acceptable,
the serenity of being loved for herself alone.

The Critic is a once helpless little girl who, in adulthood,
still feels unworthy. Her own childhood memories of feeling rejected are covered by layers of denial, like geological strata, piled
up over the years to conceal the source of her insecurities: her
inability to satisfy *her* mother. The reasons for the Critic's churning, restless rebukes are long forgotten—but the agitated feelings
still run high.

Not that she wasn't a good girl: critics are often eldest children,
who helped to raise their siblings when they were small. Many
were overloaded with responsibilities. But they were not appreciated

for their dependability. Indeed, they may have been harshly punished when they inevitably fell short of impossible demands and towering expectations.

The Critic is a woman in a state of constant dread, like a fugitive on the run—she is terrified someone will discover that she is really as unworthy as she accuses everyone else of being. The zeal with which she demeans her children is a desperate attempt to salvage, by comparison, some small shard of self-esteem. She conceals her tremulousness behind a wall of barbs, and digs, and nagging.

This behavior is symptomatic of the psychologically battering mother. But it is also symptomatic of the psychologically battered child within the mother. Describing this kind of mother in her book *Mothermania*, Dr. Jane B. Abramson writes, "She hides her dependency, her deep need of people, under an independent, critical facade. She deprecates others to avoid revealing how much she needs them; such an admission would expose her once more to the danger of exploitation and/or abandonment."

Eventually, many daughters realize that the more they give her, the more she takes and the less easy it is to summon up the empathy she craves.

For the Critic, the trouble always lies elsewhere; never is it seen as stemming from within. She is unable or unwilling to break out of her controlling, critical mode; she is stuck in behavior that she knows no way of changing. Because to change is to leave her wide open to the very attack she metes out.

This is the heart of why the Critic cannot be pleased: *She cannot risk lowering her guard because her tiny, frightened self might be consumed.*

And so the Critic wins, but she also loses. Because her "victory" requires her children's defeat, her worst fears—that she will be discovered for the imposter she is, that she will be unloved—come true. Her daughters will defect; or they will be dutiful but will not confide in her; or they will cling, too weak to be relied on. The Critic loses the very thing she most requires: a sense of mutual emotional support.

Profile of the Critic

Amelia answers the door of her suburban condominium and invites me to sit down in her living room. As she goes to fetch coffee for us, I look around the room—it is filled with antiques, culled from many trips to Europe and the Far East. There is about it a tranquillity and appreciation for loveliness.

So I am startled, when she returns and I have an opportunity really to look at her, to find that hers is a seventy-six-year-old face that is top-heavy with vertical furrows; no laugh lines grace her prim, unsmiling lips.

Why did she answer my ad? "I thought I could give you some help in understanding what it means to be a mother," she says, crossing her slender legs at the ankles. "I have two daughters—one I'm close to, the other I'm not."

"Let's talk about your childhood," I say as she pours fragrant coffee into my cup. "What was life like when you were growing up?"

Amelia sips her coffee and thinks carefully about this question—as she does all my questions—which, as she told me on the phone when we scheduled this interview, she wants to answer as candidly as possible.

"It's hard," she says. "My memories really begin when I was fourteen. Everything before that is a total blank." She pieces together a collage of her origins from stories handed down to her by her family, attempting to fill in the long sleep of her youth.

Amelia's mother, Irma, was raised in Cleveland, the fourth of five children. Irma's father died when she was an infant, and her mother married a pharmacist. "My grandmother was a very introverted woman," says Amelia, "and her new husband was quite rigid. He didn't particularly like my mother, and treated her as though she were a second-class citizen. My grandmother didn't know anything about children and psychology when she got married. So when my mother was born, her mother wasn't very nice to her. My mother was an only child, and she kept to herself."

Irma married when she was nineteen, and in rapid succession had three children—two boys, then Amelia. "It was difficult for my mother to show affection," Amelia says. "She was kind of frozen. She said she wanted to be involved with my life, but she was busy raising three kids."

But Amelia recalls nothing of those early years. The memories begin with the death of her brother, who had polio. "I remember huddling with my other brother, crying; we weren't allowed to go to the funeral."

Another memory of Amelia's adolescence is of the incessant quarreling of her brothers. She blames her mother for those arguments.

My mother was the kind of person who would talk
about one of us behind our backs, something I vowed I
would never do. And she'd talk about my father, too.
He was a very gentle, quiet, kind sort of person. She
was disappointed that he didn't make much of himself
—he was a department store salesman—so she never
had much respect for him. When I was sad, he'd give
me a dime and say, "I don't want you to be unhappy."
But he'd never stand up for me to my mother.

Amelia describes herself as having been docile and frightened as a
girl, but adds an incongruous comment: "I wasn't afraid of my
mother. It was like I was watching a play I wasn't a part of. I was
very lonely. There was no emotional attachment between us, no
relationship. She was every inch the matriarch. When she died at
seventy-eight, I felt relieved."

"What is your strongest memory of her?" I ask. Her reply is
immediate: "She always taught me to be utterly honest. To tell the
truth, no matter what the consequences. And I've gotten in trouble
for it ever since. Everyone tells me I'm tactless, and they're right.
But I felt I had to live up to her standards of honesty."

When she was a teenager, Amelia went to business school and
studied bookkeeping. When she began working, at twenty, she met
her husband, a banker. "He was very handsome, and very reserved.
The only time he was loving was in bed. I'm a very dependent
woman—at least with men—and he took care of me as though I
were a child. I'm still dependent on men—I have lots of men friends
and very few female ones."

Their lovemaking produced two daughters, Veronica and Cindy,
who are forty and thirty-seven. What kind of mother was she?

I didn't have the patience to play with them. Cindy
says I was disappointed in her. She wanted me to be
Donna Reed. But I was busy with my charity work and
taking courses in adult education. Cindy says I favored
Veronica. She once said, "Veronica's the one you talk
to; I'm the one who gets things done." You cannot talk
to Cindy—she gets her dander up. She says that I'm too
critical of her and that I was never interested in her. I'm
not very diplomatic with her, and she doesn't like that
at all. She's too sensitive; she can't take any criticism.

But Veronica says, "You're my best friend. If I had to pick out a mother, you're the one I would pick." There was extreme sibling rivalry between them.

Her daughters both tell her that she was always complaining about them behind their backs. "When I'd say something to one of them about the other, they'd say 'Tell her; don't tell me.' "

Curiously, when the girls were growing up, it was Veronica who gave her mother the most problems—she hung out with "hoods," she smoked, she stayed out all night. "She was always in trouble, coming home drunk, getting terrible grades. Cindy became an overachiever: always on the honor roll."

Cindy and Veronica exemplify Amelia's contradictory qualities of independence and dependence. Veronica, who is married and works as a physical therapist, is spirited and talkative—she and her mother speak on the phone every day. She has a great many friends.

Cindy, who has few friends, does not have a career—she can afford to stay home and raise her two young children. She is extremely dependent on her husband, Frank, and is unable to make decisions without his advice.

"It worries me about her," says Amelia. "Here's this very intelligent woman who can't make up her mind about anything. If we go shopping and she sees a dress she likes, she says, 'I'll have to see what Frank says.' She never asks my advice. I think she's afraid I'll tell her what I really think. And I do—I can't help myself. It's my honesty."

And one of the things Amelia did tell Cindy in all honesty was that she didn't approve of her daughter's choice of a husband. "The biggest mistake I made was to say that I thought she shouldn't marry him—she's Catholic and he's Jewish. And he didn't have any money. And I told her she was headed for disaster."

Two years ago, Amelia's husband died. Since then she has acquired a number of male companions—her dance card is always full. But because she has no female intimates, she feels isolated.

"You remember how I told you I was lonely as a child? I still am. After my husband died, I went into therapy. My therapist tells me, 'You give the appearance of confidence, but deep down you feel inadequate.' Funny, his saying that; I feel I can talk about anything. But last week he said, 'Amelia, you talk and talk, but we never get to the core of who you are.' "

Amelia walks me to my car, saying she hopes she has given me all the information I need. "One last question," I say. "Would you be less lonely if you were closer to your daughters, particularly Cindy?" Amelia straightens her spine and replies,

> I don't want to be *that* close to them. I want to have my own life. I don't want to be a baby-sitter for their kids. I don't want to be too caught up in their lives, too involved with what they do. It's *very important* for me not to be involved.

As I drive away, I am struck by the emptiness of Amelia's days, and by the unhappy irony of her life. She has just chronicled for me four generations of women who all felt estranged both from their mothers and from at least one of their daughters; who grew up in houses that were divided against themselves, and yet who created them anew with their own children.

Like the women before her, and—unless her daughters are able to change the course of their family history—like the women who will outlive her, Amelia is carrying on a legacy of disaffection. She has inherited a family pattern that is in danger of moving, unimpeded, toward future generations.

And, for the life of her, she cannot fathom how it happened.

7
The Smotherer

If I overdo anything with my children, it is in my affection. When they were little, I'd say, "Come here, I want to chew on you." I still do, only now they're in their thirties. I devour my family, too much. I am the most vulnerable person—to this day I seek the world's favor, and I'm always being hurt by people. I unzip my chest and expose my heart. I am much better at giving than taking—I'm happiest being enslaved by my family. When we're together, all the kids and grandchildren, that's heaven. Filling their needs fills my needs.

—Nell, sixty-four

To women whose mothers are critical and severe, the Smotherer seems like a saint. She's the mother who sat up all night, typing her children's term papers. She's the mother who slaved for weeks, fashioning for her daughter an elaborate fairy costume for Halloween, encrusting it with sequins and spangles. She's the mother who always wrote a note if her child didn't finish her homework or didn't feel like going to school.

When I was a child, I boiled with envy over friends who had mothers like that. On rainy days, they'd be lined up outside my school, clutching umbrellas and slickers and small pairs of rubbers, poised to ambush any errant drop of water before it could moisten their precious children's bodies.

Waiting at their home would be plates piled high with sandwiches—the crusts neatly amputated—and just-baked cookies. "Tell me all about your day, darling," they'd croon, helping their children peel off their rain gear. "Don't leave *anything* out."

I hated those kids. Unlike them, I would have to slog home through the downpour, alone and morose, my saddle shoes squishing and my heart saturated with jealousy.

I didn't have a mother like that. My friend, Bess, *did*. When in our twenties we shared an apartment in New York, she'd recall her high school days, and I would hang on every word. She'd say,

> When I went out on a date, my mother waited up for me, no matter how late it was, with fresh-squeezed orange juice and a snack, to hear all the details about what a fabulous time I'd had. She remembers every name of every friend I ever had, the names of their boyfriends and what they all wore to my Sweet Sixteen party. She has kept scrapbooks that are filled with pictures and programs from school plays and dance recitals I was in.

But there's more to life with the Smotherer than scrapbooks and fresh-squeezed orange juice. Talk to Bess today as she reflects on her "idyllic" childhood through the prism of her adult circumspection, and you find another side to her adoring mother.

Because Smotherers do exactly what the word implies: To "smother," says *Webster's*, is "to destroy the life of by depriving of air; . . . to stop or prevent the growth or activity of . . ."

Just ask Bess. Now in her forties—a famous movie star, her age known only to a few—and swearing me to secrecy ("If you don't conceal my identity in your book, I'll break your legs"), she says this about her mother:

> She had a barren life because she sacrificed it for me. She and my father have the worst marriage known to man. The only thing she has in the whole world is me. She lives through my success, through every breath I draw, and goddammit, I don't want that. She thinks I'm the greatest actress who ever lived, and God knows, I'm not even close. I have never seen any of my films—I can't bear to, because I'm not nearly as good as she says. I am the center of her universe—it's horrible having that pressure. Horrible.

Maternal Martyrdom

Talk to any Smotherer and she will tell you: "My proudest achievement is my children." Some women long to have had a mother who feels that way—but not the Smotherer's daughters, because it is usually their mother's *only* achievement.

In their study of mother–daughter relationships, social scientists Grace Baruch and Rosalind Barnett divided the mothers into two subgroups—based the subjects' responses to questionnaires—one of which they call the "coupled cluster." These mothers live through their children, relying especially on their daughters to comfort them with the certain knowledge that they are the best mothers in the world.

By contrast, in the other group of mothers Drs. Baruch and Barnett studied, the "autonomous" cluster, mothers "focused on the children as separate people—on their individual qualities, rather than on their own connection to their children."

Such women do *not* live through their children.

It isn't just that Smotherers identify with their daughters—*all* mothers do that, to a degree. Rather, it is that their maternity is a mandate to coerce their daughters into the mother's image of what a "happy childhood" is all about, and to that end will sacrifice themselves with unsullied moral certainty and tireless stamina.

The Smotherer wants to boost the odds that her daughter will be carefree and popular, the happiest little girl in the world. That desire, shared by many parents, seems to be set in motion by normal maternal concern. But, like a zoom lens, the Smotherer lunges forward in her loving zeal, enlarging her role and narrowing her focus to the exclusion of a healthy perspective. She wants only the best for her daughter, and she alone can provide it. Whatever you want, I will give it to you. *Do as I say*, because I will never fail you, and no one loves you more. Give yourself up to me, and I'll make everything wonderful.

But it is the Smotherer who decides what the daughter wants. She defines her child's happiness in terms of her own needs and perceptions, rather than the child's: "I'm cold," she says, "put on a sweater." Blinded by "love," they "see" in their daughters what they themselves yearn to be.

Such mothers press their noses against the windows of what they believe to be their little girls' joyous, seamless lives and say, "There. I've done it. Her happiness fills my cup—it's all I ever really wanted, and it was worth everything."

In many ways, the Smotherer seems in her selfless devotion much like the Doormat described in Chapter Five. But unlike the Doormat, who sees her sacrifice as an expiation of her shameful weakness and unworthiness, the Smotherer hoists her generosity of easily wounded heart as though it were a bloodied banner of triumph. Like the Doormat, she has few boundaries between herself and her daughter; unlike the Doormat, she has no doubts about the rightness of her single-minded maternal crusade.

In the name of love, she does not relinquish her children in a cloud of heartrending sighs and self-abnegation, as does the Doormat—rather, she *grasps* them. Literally and figuratively, she cannot keep her hands off her daughter, always smoothing, caressing, kissing, fussing.

The Smotherer follows her daughter everywhere: into the bathroom, to see if her daughter has her period or to wash by hand her daughter's underwear; into her daughter's bedroom, to straighten the bureau drawers and perhaps find a diary or stack of love letters, which she promptly reads; into the den, where she sits down with her daughter's startled and abashed chums, to be "one of the gang."

At her daughter's school, she grills the faculty and staff. Does the guidance counselor know, she asks with wringing hands, how her child is doing? Does she have enough friends? Is the teacher particularly understanding of her daughter's special sensitivities? Will the principal fire the teacher who flunked her daughter for not handing in a single book report all year?

The Pursuit of Happiness

How bad can such a childhood really be? At least the mother pays *attention* to her daughter—at least she *cares*. It sure beats neglect. Is "smothering" really *destructive?*

The answer is yes.

Smotherers are what Dr. Harriet Goldhor Lerner describes as "pursuers"—they do the "feeling" work for the child, a role that comes naturally to such mothers, who were raised to pump all their energies into the family. In engineering their daughters' happiness, Smotherers deny their children the capacity to experience sadness or frustration or empathy—emotions that are necessary for healthy maturity—as well as the ability to solve their own problems, however minor. Their daughters learn that they dare not bring Mommy any bad news—to make her happy, they *must be happy.*

The degree of damage done by these mothers depends on what kind of Smothering is involved, and how it dovetails with the daughter's temperament. While daughters' personalities are heavily influenced by smothering (as well as other maternal styles, as we will see in Part Three), two personality types emerge most frequently in the case of the daughters of Smotherers.

The Spoiled Child. According to author-journalist John Crewdson, smothering is a form of child abuse. He writes, "The child who is emotionally 'smothered' by his parents is . . . likely to grow into a narcissistic adult. . . . A child who can do no wrong is equally denied the opportunity to discover a realistic sense of himself. He receives so much attention, affection, and praise that the narcissistic cord is not only never cut, it is never even stretched."

Michelle, thirty-five, is the youngest of her mother's four children. Only recently has she been able to address the notion that the expectations of her mother, who "loved me to bits," robbed her of reality. Says Michelle,

> Recently she told me, "I only wanted you to have a perfect life—but you always made the wrong decisions." She raised me to be a princess. She always told me I was perfect—so beautiful, so sweet, so kind, so good. You'd think that would make you a wonderfully well-adjusted person. It didn't. I always knew she was exaggerating.
>
> I felt I had the weight of the world on my shoulders. I was absolutely responsible for her happiness. Once or twice I did things that she didn't want me to do, like go out with a boy she didn't like. She would cry and say, "I love you so much that when you do something like that, it worries me sick." My punishment was that she would be miserably unhappy.
>
> I couldn't look at all this until now because of the guilt. Friends of mine complain that their mothers didn't love them, but my mother *worshiped* me—wasn't I lucky? How do you fight that?
>
> So I've had a hard time getting in touch with what I want, and what I believe—I always thought I wanted what *she* wanted for me. But it never felt *right*—I let people do things for me, I have this awful inertia in my work.

I didn't have any sense of who I was until two years ago, when my husband left me for someone else and I was forced to look at myself. The reality that I am not the most wonderful woman in the world with the most wonderful mother hit me like a ton of bricks.

The Fearful Child. Dr. James Garbarino does not define maternal hovering as "child abuse." But it is, he told me, "an unwise child-rearing strategy. There is psychological damage done when a mother wants too much closeness. Smothering can create a child who is unfit to live a normal life because he or she is so anxiety-ridden."

Such a daughter is Maria, a lab technician who, at thirty, still lives with her parents. Her mother and father were raised in a small village in Greece and came to the United States in 1946. Through years of hard work, her father was able to rise from busboy to owner of a Greek restaurant and to accumulate enough money to buy a house in Brooklyn. Says Maria,

This is America, but my parents still live as if they were back in their little village—their marriage was arranged. I was never allowed to date when I was in high school. My mother thinks every man is going to rape me. I've had a few boyfriends, but I can't sustain a relationship. I just get so flustered with men—I'm terrified of marriage, because it robs you of any shred of independence. I know, look who's talking!

She's so protective, she always tells me what to do, the smallest things. For instance, she has this obsession. She doesn't think it's healthy for people to shower and then go out right afterward—I hear it every day as I come out of the bathroom: "You'll catch your *death* of cold!" She can't bear that I have even *that* much control over my life.

I know she loves me, but it's a primitive kind of love. Sometimes she's so right about things, it's almost spooky—she's like a seer. So I'm afraid to do anything without her approval.

She says I'm not capable of living on my own. I'm beginning to think she's right, but I have hopes—I'm in therapy. I don't dare tell her—she'd have a heart attack.

Tough Love

The Smotherer is anything but passive; she will fight for her children's health and happiness—no matter what the daughter says, no matter what the daughter really wants, no matter what the cost in the child's embarrassment.

The Smotherer justifies her behavior with martyred superiority; she extols her virtues and underscores them to her children ("You always had *everything!*"). Certain buzzwords and phrases of sacrifice flavor her conversation: "I'm too trusting," and "I give and give and never get anything back," and—when her children defy her—*"How could you do this to me? After everything I've done for you?"*

"My mother is a master at the self-fulfilling prophecy," says one woman. "She can set up a situation where she would be the hurt one, and you absolutely cannot prevent it. In spite of yourself, you aid and abet her. My strongest childhood memory is of my mother saying to me, 'Did you wake up this morning and decide that today you're going to make your mother miserable?' "

The Smotherer's hug is one that stifles rather than warms, leaving no room for the child to turn around, or even breathe. Her embrace tightens as the child squirms, until the child can no longer move.

The last thing the Smotherer wants is a spouse who tells her what to do or eclipses her parental authority. While Smotherers often express exasperation at their passive, or chilly, or workaholic mates—their daughters often describe their mothers' marriages as "stormy"— such spouses serve a purpose: in their abdication of parenting tasks, which the mothers encourage by saying, "You do it all wrong— *I'll* do it"—these fathers leave a larger space to be filled by the Smotherer. Within the family, she is supreme, having cleared the field.

The Smotherer takes center stage in her daughter's life. Even when the daughter is grown, the Smotherer wants to be involved in her social life, her friendships, her shopping sprees, even her thought patterns. "Tell me what's wrong," she begs. "I *know* something's wrong. Just tell me."

I'm Just Trying to Help

Something is always wrong, even though the daughter may not know it until the Smotherer points it out. If, for instance, the daughter is single, the mother believes that her daughter must be lonely, bereft, depressed; the daughter may like being single, may even *prefer* it. But, given the mother's anxieties, the daughter may begin to develop the same anxieties. A tiny glitch becomes a monumental crisis.

The mother *needs something to fix* in order to feel a sense of indispensability. She just wants to help, even if help isn't required. Writes Georgetown University's Dr. Michael Kerr,

> People become overinvolved in trying to fix problems in the name of helping others and on the basis of a belief that what is happening should not be happening. Fixers try to "correct" the situation and put it on the "right" track. The fixer's Achilles heel is underestimating the resources of the people he intends to "help." In the process, he can create a dependence in others that undermines their functioning.

Rona is a well-paid graphic designer, the eldest daughter of a Smotherer. Her mother had wanted to be a dress designer in her youth, but gave up her dreams to marry Rona's father and to raise four children. In the alchemy of genes and environment, Rona inherited her mother's drive and artistic talent. But she also inherited a sense that she is a fraud, and that her career success is based on luck, rather than ability and true grit. She says,

> I have achieved everything my mother wanted, and that goes back to grade school, but she always stacked the deck. She wanted me to be president of the third grade, so she invited my entire class over, and took us all to movies and out for pizza. She literally "fixed" the election, and so I won. When I went to college, she pulled strings with the admissions office to get me in—she knew one of the trustees, a wealthy industrialist who had just donated a million dollars. So I was accepted, even though my grades were so-so.
>
> She's so pushy, she never lets up. She tells me when to ask for a raise and for how much; she tells me who in the office is "out to get" me. She tells me the only person in the whole world I can trust is her. I can't stand to be with her for longer than the one night a week I have dinner at her house. She thinks we're best friends. I promise you, we're not.

Prisoners of Love

The Smotherer's deepest wish is to have her daughter forever joined to her. And her daughter, caught between the tender trap of her mother's warmth and her own separate sense of worth and competence, swings like a pendulum between engulfment and escape.

Often, the Smotherer and her daughter appear to the outside world to be the closest of soulmates. Indeed, they often *are* close—too close for the daughter's comfort.

Lucy Rose Fischer, in her book *Linked Lives: Adult Daughters and Their Mothers*, describes what happens when a mother and adult daughter are shackled together in "mutual mothering," the most common pattern in the mother–daughter relationships she studied.

Writes Dr. Fischer, "These daughters . . . 'listen' to their mothers' advice more than most of the other daughters. In fact, they attribute a kind of magical power to their mothers. . . . Mutual mothering does not necessarily mean that relationships are harmonious or loving."

Their relationships are intense, but far from serene—shouting matches are routine. Locked in each other's embrace, they wrestle in alternating moves of one-up, one-down rather than break the hold they have on each other, and each struggles with her own separate, internal furies. The "love" they express for each other is a kind of kiss of death.

Breaking Away

What happens when the daughter tries to detach? As Dr. Louise J. Kaplan writes, "[The mother] falls apart at her child's no-saying. . . . She is ever-watchful—on guard lest her child make moves in unpredictable directions which she might not be able to control."

Gretchen, twenty-nine, is the only daughter of a Smotherer who in Gretchen's youth was extremely protective, seldom allowing her daughter outdoors to play. But occasionally, since Gretchen's father loved the ocean, the family would spend the day at the Jersey shore.

> We'd get to the beach, and my mother would be exhausted and irritable. She'd have spent the whole previous day frying chicken and making potato salad and baking pies, and she'd be a nervous wreck. I never liked

her cooking, so I wouldn't eat. She'd burst into tears. To this day she reminds me of those outings, and about how hard she worked to prepare those picnics. She says, "I always tried to prepare food you liked, to make it special, and you never appreciated it." And I scream, "But that was your obsession! That wasn't for us, that was for you. All I wanted was a hot dog!"

Joyce, forty-one, and her mother have always fought, and always about things that the mother does out of "concern" for her daughter. She recalls with a shudder her mother's invasiveness.

Even when I was in college—I'm embarrassed to tell you this—my mother would ask me every day if I'd "been to the bathroom." She was always asking about my bodily functions. So, naturally, I wouldn't tell her. Why was that so threatening to me? Because it feels like you're trapped and there's this person all over you. I wouldn't even characterize it as *loving* concern—it was more a matter of satisfying her sense of duty, to make sure that she was doing everything a mother should do. I didn't want her concern—I wanted her confidence in me. And I never got it. So I shut her out.

The more the daughter struggles to break free, the more the Smotherer is spurred on to even more Byzantine intrusions into her daughter's life.

Karen, twenty-seven, is the mother of newborn twins, and lives, with her husband, in Evanston, Illinois. Her mother lives in Chicago. "There are trains between Evanston and Chicago," Karen says somberly, "and my mother knows the schedule by heart."

During her pregnancy, Karen developed complications, and told her mother that she was seeing a doctor the next day. Her mother offered to go with her; Karen said, "Ma, I have a husband; he'll take me." Says Karen,

We get to the doctor's office, and there's my mother sitting in the waiting room—she had called up to find out what time my appointment was. The doctor says, "Well, since your mother's here, let's have her come in, too." Now he's asking my husband and me about our lovemaking, because he wants to make sure the fetuses weren't disturbed—he was afraid I'd miscarry. And my mother's sitting there, nodding her head, asking questions, like it's her pregnancy, and not mine. My husband is furious, because our sex life is none of her business.

That kind of thing is where my mother loses me. I refused to talk to her for a month after that.

Smotherers are not able to stop themselves when it comes to their hovering and worrying, because, they say, they do it out of love. Isn't it a mother's obligation to be like that?

"For those of us who believe it is our sacred calling to save other people and shape them up," writes Dr. Lerner in *The Dance of Anger*, "the hardest thing in the world is to *stop* trying to be helpful."

And so they persist, because they cannot let go.

Terms of Endearment

The Smotherer states her terms: Let me love you the way I want, and I will give you the world, providing also you love me the way I want.

But the terms are too stringent, the reins too tight, and ultimately the mother loses precisely what she has worked so hard to get—her daughter's unconditional love.

She loves as a child wishes to be loved; she does not love as *her child* wishes to be loved.

Ultimately, the daughter will recoil from the Smotherer's invasiveness. And if she does not—if the daughter becomes more dependent than the mother bargained for—the *mother* may recoil, just as her mother, in all probability, recoiled from her.

Says Dr. Kerr,

The mother may say, "I will give to this child so she will grow up to be a whole person." So she gives and gives, as she defines it, and the daughter grows up addicted to her love, and puts more pressure on her mother to provide it. Until the mother starts to withdraw. Then the daughter starts to feel cut off and unloved. And the mother feels guilty and angry.

No one is happy with this arrangement, least of all the Smotherer, who has no identity apart from her daughter. Both mother and daughter end up hungry for something else, something more, something less, something *other* than what they have together.

Profile of a Smotherer

Marcia, fifty-eight, shows me where to plug in my tape recorder in her spotless, shiny kitchen. The table is covered with a gaily colored tablecloth, and on it is a spread of buttery cookies, rich cakes, lush fruit, and a pot of steaming cinnamon coffee—enough for a crowd, although there are only the two of us.

Everything about her is ripe; her hips and breasts, her generous mouth, and wide, expressive eyes that are covered with deftly applied makeup, her denim jumpsuit that glitters with rhinestones set in circular designs. As soon as I finish my cake, she quickly cuts another piece and presses it on me—I do not demur, and gulp it down. "I can't resist," I murmur guiltily, between bites.

"My daughter can," she says, jerking her head toward a photograph on the wall of a lovely, slender young woman. "She's always yelling at me for serving too much food. She says, 'Haven't you ever heard the word "moderation"?' She's emaciated. Much too thin."

Marcia was born in Los Angeles, one of four children—a boy and three girls. Her father, who recently died, was a prosperous jeweler; her mother, a housewife.

Her parents did not have a good marriage, Marcia says. "My mother wiped up the floor with him, she treated him like dirt, even though he worked like a dog for her. She thought his parents were common. He wasn't good enough for her."

Her brother is a successful agent in the movie business—Marcia, however, has never worked. Well, not in a "real career," she says—she worked as a practical nurse until she married her husband, Jerry, a detective with the L.A.P.D., and, when her kids were in elementary school, did part-time private nursing.

I ask her about her mother.

My mother was the apple of her parents' eyes; she tells me that she was very spoiled and indulged, especially by her father. Her mother was a nervous woman, and was sickly. They always had the best of everything, until my grandfather lost everything in the crash of '29.

My mother has alway been selfish; nothing was ever too good for her son, the prince, but she treated me like garbage. I feel constantly hurt by her, because all she does is compare what I have to what my brother has. His house is a showplace. I try to make mine as attractive as possible, but I don't have unlimited funds. You know what's funny? I have her taste. I see myself in her all the time, and I appreciate her artistic sense. But I don't appreciate her nastiness.

When she was a teenager, Marcia was not allowed to wear anything her mother hadn't selected. "I remember we went shopping for winter coats, and I wanted this pale green one. 'Why do you want that coat?' she said in front of the saleswoman. 'You look like a melon in it.' "

"I have a temper," Marcia continues. "Once I talked back to my mother, and her hand went up and I went sailing across the room. I got up, ran over to her, and bit her on the shoulder. She never forgot it. Me either. It felt good."

Their fights have not lessened, she says, over the years. When Marcia got engaged, her fiancé bought her a ring with a modest-size diamond. "My mother thought it was the ugliest thing she ever saw. She had my father take Jerry down to the store to get me a bigger one, wholesale—they loaned him the money."

And yet, she says, her mother is not a generous or loving person. "She thinks I married beneath me. She makes fun of me, all the food I have, all the fussing I do over my husband's dinners, how much I worry about his cholesterol and how I get hysterical if he's late. I worry that he's been shot."

Marcia can laugh at the fact that she is, she says, "a worrywart." But she doesn't laugh when she discusses her children.

Marcia and her husband have two adopted daughters, Lucy, thirty, and Marie, twenty-eight. Lucy is married, and lives in San Diego, where she works for an insurance company. "They don't have kids," Marcia says ruefully. Marie, who is single, lives in Los Angeles and runs her grandfather's jewelry business.

How is she as a mother? Tears well up in Marcia's eyes and course down her cheeks. "I'm sorry," she apologizes, reaching for a tissue. "It's a touchy subject."

I'm like my mother in my feelings and I could be just like her if I don't watch out. I try to be her exact opposite.

I step on myself all the time with my children, because they think I'm nosy. They say I talk about them too much to my friends. It's hard for me, because I worry about them all the time, and I care a lot about them. Marie cuts me off like a knife. She didn't have a hard time separating—she says, "Remember, Ma, what will happen if you repeat this?" I say, "You won't talk to me." She says, "That's right." So she tells me things.

But Lucy doesn't talk to me about anything. She hides things from me, like I did from my mother—it causes me a lot of pain.

My children hurt me—they don't accept me as I am. I don't feel they're there for me. I think they're very selfish, interested in number one. I try hard to think only for me, and I find it very difficult. I did everything for those kids—*everything*. I worked carrying bedpans when they were children so they could have nice clothes.

When you're hurt so deeply, you can't let go of it because you can't allow anyone to hurt you like that again. I don't forgive anybody anything—except for my kids. I find it very hard to separate myself from my feelings for my children.

That's what I don't understand—when you have kids, it should be unconditional love for them. My mother never loved me unconditionally. And my kids don't love me unconditionally either.

I put in twenty-five years of caring and nurturing and supporting; it's a job that now is taken away from me, and it's very painful, even though you want independence for your children. It's very hard when you've been doing something for twenty-five years and then are rejected for doing the very thing you've been doing all along.

Marcia suddenly stops talking, breathless from crying and from her outpouring of sadness. We sit in silence for several minutes; the only sound is the dull *clunk* of the icemaker in the refrigerator.

She wipes her eyes and mouth, gets up to put the mound of crumpled tissues into the wastebasket under the sink. She sits down again with a sigh and says in a flat voice, "My biggest problem is that I'm a failure as a mother, and there's nothing I can do to change it. I always thought I was doing the right thing."

Marcia pauses—with her makeup gone, suddenly she looks like a child. Gazing at me, she adds, her lips trembling, "I guess I didn't."

8
The Avenger

My mother had this unpredictable mean streak that only her kids saw. I remember once, when I was a child, cutting my foot on a broken bottle while playing outside a friend's house, and being terrified of going home. The fear was unbearable—the glass had cut clean through my shoe, and even though blood was gushing all over the place, I didn't feel any pain. All I could think of was what she might do to me for hurting myself and making a mess. I was conditioned not to feel anything but fear.

—Olivia, thirty-four

You've seen her, or heard about her, a hundred times.

She's the woman in the supermarket, yanking her toddler by the arm and screaming, "I told you never to touch things! One more time, and I'm going to leave you here!"

She's the woman in the restaurant, haranguing her sheepish teenager: "You've been rotten since the day you were born. Everyone knows how you sneak around behind my back, deliberately trying to make a fool of me."

Next to the Deserter (see the next chapter), this form of maternalism is the most ravaging: here is where a mother's behavior toward her children crosses the thin line—honored by most parents—that separates civility and deliberate cruelty.

This is the Avenger, brimming with a harvest of shame to be vented upon her children. She does not merely want to hobble her daughter, by nagging or engulfing or leaning too heavily on her: she

127

tries to crush her in a domination beyond that of any of the other mothers described in this book.

Avengers are like rockets spinning out of control—they are rarely able to put the brakes on their behavior. Whatever detonates their vindictiveness or rage and propels it in shock waves through the family can seldom be foreseen.

The arsenal of weapons the Avenger uses against her daughter includes exploitation, shunning, degrading, terror, and beatings; the most frequent triggering devices are the mother's perceptions of her daughter's disobedience or sexual perverseness, and the mother's own vanity and jealousy.

Unfortunately, lots of children in our society get beaten, but it is not always considered a criminal offense. Strictly speaking, few of the mothers described in this chapter would be diagnosed as being criminally or pathologically insane. None of them were child batterers, mutilators or murderers—rather, theirs was a subtler mayhem. As we will see, many of them suffer from what is called by the psychological community a "narcissistic personality disorder."

Says Dr. James Garbarino, "There clearly are lots of people who are not crazy who get involved in psychological maltreatment. They may *appear* crazy when you read about the situation because they've gotten entrapped into a coercive cycle with the child, or they've built up an idiosyncratic system with the child that to the outside world looks crazy. If you could imagine running a video of their life backward to the beginning, you could see reasonably normal people who get caught up in a crazy way of relating to their children."

The Avenger has not lost her mind—but it often seems as though she were born without a heart.

One daughter, the veteran of many years of psychoanalysis and herself a psychiatrist, neatly summed up the garden variety Avenger:

> Their total lack of reality *is* their mental illness. Mothers like mine have a brilliant defense mechanism—they justify all the ghastly things they do by saying their children deserve it. My mother's perceptions are so distorted that what goes in as an innocent remark comes out as an attack. When my father died, I said to her, "I never really knew him." Her response: "How can you say that? After all he did for you?" It was a non sequitur.
>
> Once I asked her why she was always such a bully. She said, "I have this thing inside me that drives me,

and I can't stop it." It's the only time she ever came close to any awareness of her treatment of me. She was able to function normally in the world outside our home. But inside it, she caused nothing but havoc.

The unifying theme for the Avenger is retribution for crimes of the heart from her long-forgotten childhood, which is discussed later in this chapter. She seeks to settle scores beyond her children's imagining, and they pay the price for her childhood. So acute is the Avenger's need to wield power in the family—greater than any of the other maternal types—that the delicate balance between reason and rage can be upset by the smallest breeze of dissent.

Beginning in her marriage.

Marital Chaos

The Avenger is addicted to creating discord; one fight blends into another in a long crescendo and diminuendo of domestic disharmony. Her first victim is her spouse, who, for psychological reasons of his own, seems to be equally addicted to the friction between them. Frequently his marriage is a repetition of his relationship to another Avenger—his mother, or father.

Curiously, in the majority of Avengers' marriages I learned about in my interviews, the husbands did not leave, in spite of the Avengers' volatile personalities. Many of these husbands were initially attracted by the Avenger's vivacity and attractiveness—the daughters I talked with often described their Avenger mothers as being good-looking, intelligent, and animated. But in private, the Avenger lowers the mask of her often charming public face and reveals another face—one contorted in anger.

The Avenger's marriage is an unending clash of wills, with the Avenger usually emerging the winner. When she senses that her spouse might retaliate with commensurate force (although they were a minority, some of the husbands of the Avengers in my sample did in fact bolt), she belittles him. Dr. Louise J. Kaplan writes about husbands who are male versions of the Avenger, but she might easily be describing the Avenger herself: "The safer course is to make sure the frustrator is emptied of all power. It's easier to denigrate [his wife], to see her as a worthless nothing, a nobody who has no value at all."

"My mother absolutely castrated my father," one woman recalls. "I remember once, when I was little, seeing my doll go flying through a window, because she had thrown it at him. They fought constantly, and it was always my mother who would start a fight. To this day when people raise their voices, I shake, because all I think about are those horrible words in my childhood, the fighting and screaming and yelling."

Baby Makes Three

The birth of a child takes the Avenger's retaliatory strikes onto a new, more compelling front. Where, in the interests of survival, she *might* be inclined to curb her lashing out at her husband, she has no such compunctions with her children, who are totally dependent on her. And if one of those children is a daughter, that child is usually in for her cruelest treatment. Because a daughter, even if she is a little girl, is always "the other woman."

A daughter often serves for the Avenger's husband, as an oasis of sweetness and need; it is understandable that he would have a special place in his heart for her, because she may provide him with the adoration he cannot find with his wife. But theirs is at best a clandestine attachment. Avengers do not suffer gladly father-daughter affection, and do their best to sabotage it.

When there is more than one daughter, the girl who seems closest to the father often becomes the Avenger's scapegoat, freeing up the other to become her acolyte, as we shall see in Part Three. A number of daughters told me that they were cast into the scapegoat role and that their sisters were drafted into being the mother's favorite, the loyal child.

It is the "disloyal" child who evokes the Avenger's special ruthlessness, and when that child is grown, she is sometimes evicted from the family.

Eileen, twenty-six, has not seen her mother for three years—by her mother's choice. All through Eileen's childhood, her mother tried to destroy Eileen's relationship with her father. "She once told me that from the moment I was born, she was sorry she'd had me—that when she saw my father cradle me in his arms, it reminded her of her father, who had never been loving to her. My father adored me, but he was intimidated by her. So I was not to be loved, just as she had not been loved."

And to that end, Eileen's mother set about isolating her daughter from her father's affection. The summer she was six, she was sent to sleep-away camp, "even though I would cry and cry and beg to be taken home." At ten, she was shipped off to boarding school.

When she was home on vacation, her mother would not tolerate any evidence of father–daughter affinity. During Eileen's adolescence, the fashion fad among teenage girls was oversize men's jackets, and her father gave her his worn-out and frayed blazer. When Eileen's mother discovered the gift, she put it in the garbage.

Eileen was married when she was twenty-one—the marriage broke up five years later, after the birth of her son. Says Eileen,

> After my divorce, my mother decided she didn't ever want to see me again, because I was available to spend more time with my father. She refused to let him have any contact with me or my son. The pretext for my expulsion was that I was "sexually unregenerate"—she made up stories that I was a whore and promiscuous, trying to get him not to like me. I would write her letters, begging her to see me, and she wouldn't answer them. I would run into her on the street and she'd walk right past me.

Most Avengers do not resort to this degree of shunning their daughters, because they do not want to relinquish their maternal control—an absent daughter is beyond the mother's coercive reach. Besides, as one Avenger put it to her daughter, "The only reason I had you is so that I'd have someone to take care of me in my old age."

And, in the meantime, someone to serve her. For many Avengers, their controlling device is a steady application of pressure to perform in an obsequious manner, or wearing down their daughters with an unending stream of directives.

"I had to constantly wait on my mother," one woman recalls. "I couldn't walk across the room without her asking me to do something—get her a cigarette, or fetch a cup of coffee, or bring her a magazine. I was never allowed to relax—she could not just let me be. It was like a conditioned response: I'd move, she'd order. So I learned to sit very, very still."

By demolishing a child's sense of self, the Avenger ensures that the child will not abandon her. She has this trump card: her daughter's unsatisfied hunger to be loved by her role model. Unless the daughter can summon some miraculous inner strength, or find elsewhere the supportive affection that will help her to feel good about herself—which some daughters manage to do—she will not have the will to extricate herself from her mother's tyranny. (Mentors play an important role in these children's survival—see Chapter Ten).

Center Ring

The most striking feature of the Avenger's personality is her need to be the center of attention; she will do whatever is necessary to keep the spotlight on herself.

Avengers are frequently extremely vain; they often go to extraordinary lengths to appear youthful, slim, carefully coiffed and made up, and well dressed. It is not unusual for women to be preoccupied with their looks—but in the case of the Avenger, it is carried to extremes.

When Sada was eighteen, her mother stopped introducing her to people as "my daughter." Says Sada,

> After I graduated from high school, my mother went back to work and told people she had no children. The stated reason to me was that she didn't want them to know how old she was, because then she'd lose her job. But for many years she developed friendships with people outside work who didn't know I existed. She completely denied me. Now, if I'm with my son and she's with one of her friends, she'll say, "This is my niece, Sada." She doesn't want anyone to know that she's a mother, let alone a grandmother.

If the Avenger's daughter is more attractive than she is, the daughter's loveliness will be degraded.

Vivian is an extraordinarily beautiful woman of thirty. On the morning of her wedding two years ago, she went to the hairdresser's to have her hair piled high on her head in a graceful upsweep reminiscent of Edwardian ladies; the hairdo was in the romantic mood of her high-collared antique wedding dress. Says Vivian,

> When I got home, my mother took one look at me and said, "You look ugly—what have you done to yourself?" All my life, whenever I've gotten some attention, she's done something to take it away from me. Once she even said that a former boyfriend of mine was secretly attracted to her. My cousin said at the reception, "Your mother has to have the center ring—there's no room for you, even on your wedding day." She was right.

The Avenger's insatiable need to be the star attraction spills over into other areas of her daughter's life.

Joanne grew up in Michigan. Her lifelong ambition was to become an artist—she had always been gifted, and spent hours after school, sculpting. Once she brought home a statue of a pregnant nude figure she had worked on for months. "My mother threw it out—she said it was disgusting and she wasn't going to have such 'pornography' in her house."

Joanne got into the Boston Museum School of Fine Arts on a scholarship and enrolled over the strenuous objections of her mother, who said, "You'll only meet queers there." During her freshman year, Joanne's father died. She flew home to help with the funeral arrangements, and during that visit her mother extracted from her the promise that if she ever decided to sell the house and move into a condominium, Joanne would come back and help her.

In her sophomore year, Joanne arranged to spend the following year studying in Italy. A month before she was scheduled to leave, her mother called her and said that she had decided to get rid of the house. Honoring her promise, Joanne canceled her trip to Italy and returned home to help ready the house for realtors.

Two weeks later, while she was washing windows, her mother announced, "I've taken the house off the market. Having you here reminds me of how wonderful it is to have all this room." Says Joanne,

> She confessed that she had never intended to sell. It was the breaking point, and I did something I've never done in my life—I went berserk. I threw things out the window, smashed mirrors, destroyed everything in my room. I just totally lost it. She had always stepped on my dreams, but this time I just felt shattered. Everything I had worked so hard for was just dismissed with a wave of her hand.

Loretta had a similar experience with her mother. When she was twelve, her father, an airline pilot, divorced her mother. Says Loretta, "I became my mother's surrogate husband. She told me it was my duty to help her raise my younger brothers, and I did it all, because she wouldn't, the cooking, shopping, cleaning."

When Loretta was in high school, she got an afternoon job in the public library. "It changed my life. I began to read everything I could get my hands on. The director of the library took me under her wing, and we would talk for hours about great works of literature. She encouraged me to become a writer."

Loretta's mother tried to force her to quit her job.

> She said, "That woman wants to take you away from me. What are you trying to do—leave your mother behind?" Every creative thing I ever wanted she blocked—no music or dance lessons, belittling my writing on the school newspaper. She scorned everything that mattered to me. I knew I had to get out.
>
> So I got a second job, working nights, and saved enough money to go to a local community college. When I graduated, I was offered a job in New York, and my mother went nuts. She said, "You can't leave your brothers and me. I forbid you to go." It was only her way of keeping me around. I was so desperate to be important to her on any terms that her "needing" me eroded my ability to break away. I didn't know I had a right to have my own life. I didn't know I had a right to say no. These were not my children. I should have said, "I'm leaving." But I stayed for another five years.

"Sex Is Dirty"

Several of the Avengers' daughters I interviewed described their mothers' unaccountable interest in and encouragement of their daughters' sexuality and—in apparent contradiction—accusations of sexual wickedness.

Not surprisingly, many of these daughters had (or have) sexual problems in their adulthood—and often they can trace their conflicts to a mother who not only charged them with sexual promiscuity but also harbored a peculiar and invasive curiosity about their bodies and love lives.

One woman recalls that when she was in high school, she was going steady with a boy named Tom, who one night was invited for dinner. She winces as she recalls,

> The kitchen in our house was an L-shaped addition, and my mother could see into it from her bedroom. Tom and I were doing the dishes, and at one point he

took me in his arms and kissed me. When he went home, my mother came tearing out of her room and bellowed. "You tramp, I was watching you, the way you swayed back and forth, it's disgusting. You'll end up in the gutter—he will never respect you. What will the neighbors think! This family's reputation is ruined, thanks to you!" I was hysterical—something so natural, so loving and innocent, she turned into dirt.

When Maryann was seven, on summer days her mother would put a large washtub outside so that Maryann and her friends could fill it with water and play. "At one point, my mother came out and took off my bathing suit. She said, 'Why don't you skinny dip?' I screamed bloody murder. She literally exposed me in front of my friends."

When she was a teenager, Maryann hated to go shopping with her mother because she was always commenting about her figure to the sales people or other customers. "Once I tried on a strapless prom dress in the dressing room. My mother came in and shoved me out onto the selling floor, saying to a man who walked by, 'She's all grown up—look how she fills out the bust of the dress.' "

Her mother's voyeurism had a counter melody of cautionary tales about the unscrupulousness of men. Says Maryann, "She always told me, 'Men are only interested in one thing—sex. Once they get it, they leave.' "

Some Avengers seek to purify their daughters of imagined moral corruption. When Dinah was six, she loved going to her friend Peggy's house "because her mother was nice to me." One afternoon, they decided to take off their underpants and "play doctor." At that moment the friend's mother came into the room, and angrily sent Dinah home.

Her mother met her at the door and began screaming at her: "Peggy's mother called and told me what you did, you filthy girl!" Says Dinah,

> My mother took down my pants and spanked me, screaming, "Don't you ever do anything like that again," and sent me to my room. She wouldn't talk to me for a week. That was the worst moment of my life—I felt so degraded, so shamed.

Reign of Terror

Virtually all of the daughters of Avengers say that they have always been afraid of their mothers, a fear that began in childhood. Many Avengers are able to frighten their daughters without ever raising their hands—they do so through terror.

When Sonya was little, her mother loved taking her to horror movies. Says Sonya,

> I hated them, but she made me go with her. It was a way of controlling me—fear kept me in line. I was terrified of coming home to our apartment building. I always imagined there were monsters everywhere—in the elevator, or in my closet. My mother kept all these fears in place by saying, "If you aren't good, the boogyman will get you."

Laura's earliest image of her mother is an open, screaming mouth. When she was little, playing with her sister, her mother would rush into the room yelling, "Why can't you kids be quiet!" When she was a teenager, her mother would shriek at her for being home from a date ten minutes late.

Now she tells me of her most recent contact with her mother.

> I was laid up with pneumonia, and my mother dropped by my apartment. I let her in and stumbled back to bed, and fell sound asleep. All of a sudden I heard this banging, and then the roar of the vacuum cleaner. I staggered into the living room and she started this tirade: "How can you be such a slob? How dare you let your house get in this condition!" I said, "You know, Mom, I'm forty years old. I pay the rent here. I think it's time you finally stopped bullying me." She looked startled for a second. And then she stormed out of the apartment.

Linda's mother does not allow her any contentment—she haunts Linda in daily phone calls that catalogue a list of gruesome accusations. Says Linda, twenty-eight,

> The last big fight I had with her, she called me to make some point about how I was killing my baby by giving

him the wrong food. It isn't that she was just being concerned or even a nag—it was beyond the normal realm of behavior. What struck me was her relentlessness. She carried on and on, and wouldn't let up. There was a poisonous way in which she kept saying the same things over and over—that my son was in danger, that I was an unfit mother. She just wouldn't stop ramming me.

"Surprise Attack"

In the most extreme cases, Avengers used physical force to ensure that they would be obeyed. Almost anything could tip them over the edge.

Evelyn grew up with her Avenger mother and her playful and passive father, who both worked in their small grocery store. Evelyn's widowed grandmother lived with them, making it possible for them to run their business. Says Evelyn,

> My mother would come home from work and my grandmother would fill her head with tales about how lazy my brother and I were. Then my mother would come into the living room and beat us. The last time she hit me was a surprise attack when I was sixteen. I was standing in the bathroom putting on lipstick, and I ran into my room for five seconds to get something. She had a mania about turning lights off. In that five seconds, she saw the light was on and exploded. I went back in, and she slapped me across the face so hard, my glasses flew into the bathtub.
>
> I said, "Okay, you bitch, if it makes you feel good to beat up your daughter, you better do it right. Because the next time you try, I'm going to kill you." I had nothing left to lose, and she knew it. She walked away, I picked up my glasses, and she never laid a finger on me again.

For many daughters, such childhood treatment gets buried deep within the unconscious, too painful to recall. Love and pain become inexorably entwined. It is not unusual for these daughters to get involved with men who are physically menacing.

Sandra, thirty-two, went into therapy to cure her of this warped attraction. She recalls the instant she understood the reason for it, like a bubble shooting to the water's surface and bursting into the open air. She says,

> I was talking with my therapist about my crying all through my childhood, and suddenly she asked me, "What do you do to a child who's crying?" I blurted, "You hit it. You don't pick it up and say, 'Poor baby.' " It was an automatic, crazy connection: I remembered that that's what my mother used to do. The only time she ever touched me was when she was angry. If I fell and cried, she'd hit me and yell at me to shut up.

The Avenger's Origins

What causes an Avenger's callousness and insensitivity? The shop-worn adage "The bigger they are, the harder they fall" begins to offer an explanation. Of all maternal styles, she is in many ways the most frightened. And, in a sense, she is the most tragic—because she is so destructive, it's hard to care what, in her childhood, spawned her fears. It is the Avenger who is most likely to be rejected, ultimately, by her children.

The Avenger gives lie to the myth that only boys and men are bullies. According to a *New York Times* interview with Dr. Leonard Eron, a University of Illinois psychologist who has studied the life-long behavior of bullies, "One way women manifest their aggression is by punishing their children. The more aggressive little girls grew into mothers who punished their children harshly."

And in so doing, Dr. Eron found, they were repeating family patterns as they echoed down the generations: parent bullied child, child grew up and bullied his or her child. But bullies were not simply roughed up in their childhoods; often they were ignored. Their parents confused them with the mixed messages of excessive discipline and indifference; they become composites of too few controls, and too many penalties.

The majority of Avengers were once themselves physically or psychologically abused children: Such children are six times more likely to mistreat their children, when they become parents, than those who were not abused.

An example of this kind of maternal legacy was recently described in a *Newsweek* article about the emotional abuse of children. A woman punished her child for stealing by tying him to a chair in front of her house and hanging a sign around his neck that read, "I'm a dumb pig. Ugly is what you will become every time you lie and steal. . . . My hands are tied because I cannot be trusted. . . . Look. Laugh. Thief. . . ." This mother was merely repeating an identical punishment inflicted on her by her parents when she was a child.

But many mothers who were brought up in psychologically abusive circumstances—and even some who were the victims of the most harrowing brutality—are able to make the conscious choice not to repeat with their own children the vicious cycle of their histories.

The Avenger is not one of them. She fits the definition of the psychologically maltreating parent outlined by Dr. James Garbarino, a leading authority on child abuse: She rejects, isolates, terrorizes, ignores, or corrupts her child. Much of her behavior was learned by observing her own parents. Such parents, he writes, "perceive the child as being 'very bad,' 'much too demanding,' 'provocative.' . . . The child . . . is typically also perceived as eliciting and enhancing the maltreatment by his or her own behaviors and personality."

Other Avengers were "abused" in a different way—they were the centers of their parents' universe. Their parents almost never applied limits to their child's incessant demands; they gave in to her every whim, fed all her appetites, and—by absolving her of reasonable consequences for her behavior—denied her the opportunity to learn from her own mistakes. She could do no wrong.

As Dr. Louise J. Kaplan writes in *Oneness and Separateness: From Infant to Individual,*

> Such a child then grows up supposing that he will lose his identity and selfhood the moment he finds himself unable to control everything and everybody. . . . The child who is given all whenever he demands it is not a confident or courageous child. He treads his way through life perpetually haunted by the dread of being found out for what he is: an all-bad monster child whose greed and raging aggression can swallow up mothers and fathers, sisters and brothers, friends, lovers and children.

Many Avengers suffer from what is called by behavioral scientists a "narcissistic personality disorder." Such people are typically given to grandiose self-importance, behaving as though they are more important than other people by virtue of simply being alive. They are hypersensitive, but only toward imagined or real slights to themselves.

Narcissists lack one essential and extremely important quality: the ability to walk in another person's psychic shoes. If there is one piece missing from their characters, it is empathy for the feelings of others. This is why conversations with them often seem disjointed and illogical—they are masters of the non sequitur and nearly always bring any discussion back to themselves. This lack of empathy makes it extremely difficult—although not impossible— for therapists to help them.

The Avenger is all bluster and little confidence, a lost child lodged within a vain, self-seeking, emotionally ravenous adult who will do whatever she can to protect her wounded sense of self. She is like a tire with a tiny, perpetual leak: In order to remain inflated, she must constantly be filled with people's praise, flattery, servility. Without it, she inflates herself with rage—in extreme cases, murderous rage.

Somewhere within the Avenger's heart is an agonizing awareness that she is not truly lovable and that she is, in fact, a great pretender. The roots of her despair go so deep that her angry, tyrannical facade is a panicky attempt to keep those roots hidden, especially from herself.

Because the Avenger is not the perfect child she may once have tried to be—or was told she was—she passes her self-loathing on to her own child, who is an extension of herself. Keeping her child imperfect and frightened protects her from seeing her profoundly imperfect and frightened self.

When the Avenger discussed earlier said, "I have this thing inside that drives me, and I can't stop it," she was, unwittingly, close to revealing the very fear that goads her: that she will be discovered for the worthless child she believes she is.

Such parents who also beat their children, Alice Miller writes, "are struggling to regain the power they once lost to their own parents. For the first time, they see the vulnerability of their own earliest years, which they are unable to recall, reflected in their children. . . . Only now, when someone weaker than they is involved, do they finally fight back."

Profile of an Avenger

When Irene called me in response to my ad, I offered to interview her at her house. "Oh, no," she said, laughing, "we can't do that. My mother lives with me. You're not going to believe my story—I doubt if you'll find anyone who can top it." We agreed to meet for lunch in a restaurant.

Irene was already sitting in a booth when I arrived. At sixty-two, she is petite and girlish, daintily dabbing the corners of her mouth with a napkin betweens sips of tea. I suggested we wait to begin the interview until she had finished her meal, but she wanted to start immediately, eager to unburden herself of a story that, indeed, was as unique and dramatic as she had promised.

She is the youngest of three children, two girls and a boy, who were raised in a small town in Virginia. Her father was a farmer who, she says, "had a temper, just like me—he would blow up, and then it would all be over." Her mother, however, could harbor a grudge "for days, for weeks. When she got good and ready, she'd forgive you." Sometimes her mother would hit her with a belt. "She whipped me plenty," she says.

Irene describes herself as having been "a good child. I never gave her any trouble. You could take me anywhere. I would sit on a couch and never put my feet on it. I would not speak unless spoken to. But I wasn't perfect enough for my mother."

Her mother was never loving to her because, Irene explains, her grandmother died when Irene's mother was an infant, and her grandfather shipped her mother off to an aunt's house; he visited her occasionally, but Irene's mother has said very little about him— except that he used to beat her. "Anyhow," Irene adds, "she never wanted me—she wanted another son."

When she was five, Irene's older sister died of leukemia. Her parents never spoke of the child again—feelings were never discussed in the family. Irene and her brother were brought up with fundamentalist principles: rigid rules, no music, no dancing, even when they were teenagers.

Irene's brother joined the army when he was eighteen; she married at twenty, moving with her husband to Washington, D.C., where he worked in a printing plant. Her husband was, she says, very much like her mother—sometimes cold, sometimes throwing tantrums, although not violent. They produced two daughters. "I raised them like my father raised me," she says.

If I spanked them for something, five minutes later I was kissing them. The same thing I do with my grandchildren. A lot of people say to me, "You hit your grandchildren?" You're damn right I do, if they do something wrong, or they might get hurt, or if they don't listen to me. My husband could never understand it—he thought I was too strict. But this was my nature; this was my dad's nature. You might be punished, but I'm not going to hate you for weeks.

(Irene mixes her memories; her mother beat her, not her father—her disciplining of her children seems to have been a blend of both her parents.)

The fondest memory of Irene's childhood is of her great-aunt, the one who raised her mother. "She was the kindest person I ever knew—when I was five, she bought me a doll," Irene says, suddenly weeping. "It was the only doll I ever had—it had real eyelashes, glass eyes that closed, and pearl teeth."

When her father died fifteen years ago, Irene invited her mother to live with her. Irene was in the throes of divorcing her husband, whose temper had become intolerable, and, working as a receptionist, she was struggling to support her children on her modest salary. Her mother sold her house and moved to Washington.

The two women struck this agreement, which was spelled out in a document drawn up by a lawyer: Her mother would pay off Irene's small mortgage, and in return Irene would pay her a modest amount of rent. Irene kept her part of the bargain for a couple of years, but her earnings could not keep pace with the expense of supporting her mother and paying rent. So they struck another agreement, but this one was verbal: In exchange for Irene's clothing her mother and paying her medical expenses, the rent would be waived—all her mother had to do was buy her own food, using her social security payments.

Two years ago her mother instituted a lawsuit against her for the back payments of rent Irene had not paid for thirteen years. When she reminded her mother of their verbal agreement, she says, her mother replied, "Do you have that in writing? You owe me twenty-five thousand dollars. But I'll do you a favor—I'll reduce the debt to five thousand."

"I wanted to kill myself," says Irene. "I didn't have the money. I know my mother doesn't like me. But I couldn't believe she'd do this to me." Nor could she believe it when, recently, she discovered that her mother had given Irene's children varying amounts of money from the life insurance funds left to her by her husband fifteen years ago, untouched until now.

Irene suspects that one of her daughters, with whom she claims to be on good terms, is the cause of all the trouble between her and her mother. "Money is the root of all evil," Irene says. "No one wants to rub Grandma the wrong way, because she might ask for the money back. She never would have thought to sue me if somebody hadn't put the idea in her head. I'm very cautious with my daughters; I'm waiting to find out who the bad guy is, and until I do, I tell them nothing."

"I don't get mad," she continues, "I get even." And so she had her lawyer send her mother a letter saying that the rent on her room is $250 a month, and if she doesn't pay it, she has to move out.

I ask her why her mother would do such a thing as to sue her own daughter. She replies,

> I approached her once on that subject. All she would say was that I was mean and miserable, just like my father. But I've taken care of her all these years. When she was in the hospital, I was there every single day.
>
> I'm not a bitter person—I'm usually devil-may-care—but I've become so bitter. She's just so petty. She has a refrigerator up in her room and she keeps her food up there. But she comes down and steals food from me so she doesn't have to spend any of her money. Ever since I was a child, my mother has gone through my mail, gone through my drawers, my refrigerator. So I had a padlock put in my bedroom, and another on the kitchen. And she has a padlock on her bedroom door.

Today the two women are prisoners of each other in the house they share. They wait, in separate corners, for the legal machinery to settle their financial differences and define their relationship.

Here are two generations of women, each of whom is avenging the losses of her own childhood. Each is a refugee from parental perfectionism and harsh punishment, hoarding her food, her possessions, her emotional malnourishment, behind locked doors.

Before I leave, I ask Irene if she has considered getting some gratis professional help in a social services agency—she interrupts before I can add that it might provide her with some emotional support and relief from the stress in her life.

"I don't need it," she says briskly. "My mother's the one who needs it." She ducks into her car, the backseat of which is covered with legal envelopes that are bulging with documents.

They are the paper evidence of the lingering rage—if not the anguished loneliness—of one woman who is sixty-two, and another, her mother, who is eighty-five, bound together by retribution and loss.

9
The Deserter

Memories are like little rooms you go and visit. Across the door to my mother's room is the word "schizophrenic"—I don't visit it much anymore. When I learned she was mentally ill, I cried my eyes out. I had to give up all hope that she would ever be a normal mother. It would never get better, no matter what I did to try to help her. There's a lot of sadness in knowing she will never be there for me.

—Claudia, twenty-nine

For some mothers—and they are a small minority—parenting is simply beyond them. These mothers are exaggerated versions of all the mothers discussed up to now—they take dependency, criticism, smothering, and retribution beyond the breaking point.

The Deserter is a mother who, for a variety of reasons, cannot connect with her child at all.

"Silence breaks the heart," wrote poet Phyllis McGinley, and for the Deserter's children, her mothering is a sort of muteness. Parental silence has many faces—alcoholism, madness, abandonment, indifference—and feels, to a child, as though he or she has been utterly forsaken. The mother, emotionally, cannot "speak" to her children.

And sometimes she literally cannot speak. Here we add one other form of parental silence: the Bad Mommy who dies during a daughter's formative years or teens, stranding her for all time in the limbo of unfinished mother–daughter business.

The Deserter brings to her parenting a history of instability and vulnerability so damaging that it has submerged most of her sensibilities. So buried are her feelings that she renounces her children in her wounded retreat.

Unlike Avengers, these women have a compelling excuse for their "silence" that makes it possible for their daughters to make some sense of their mothers' behavior later in life—to understand, if only intellectually, that their mothers were unable to take responsibility for their actions.

If there is one characteristic that all Deserters share, it is that they are emotionally unavailable. This unavailability is expressed in four primary forms:

> The psychotic mother;
> The alcoholic or drug-addicted mother;
> The "nonattached" mother;
> The deceased Bad Mommy.

The Psychotic Mother

It wasn't until she was eighteen that Claudia, mentioned previously, had a name to attach to her mother's erratic spells.

Claudia grew up in Missouri and when she was ten, her father moved the family to California, where he got a well-paid job as a driller on an offshore oil rig near Santa Barbara. Her mother would be left for weeks at a stretch to cope with the demands of managing a family alone. It was a role for which she was not emotionally provisioned—she got married at sixteen, and by the time she was twenty, she had four children. In many ways still a child herself, she had few psychic reserves upon which to draw.

"My mom's childhood was no picnic," Claudia says, "She was one of ten kids, and there was never enough to eat. She once told me that snow used to blow through the walls of the shack she grew up in in Missouri. But her roots were there. She hated it in California—she was plucked up from everything and everyone that was familiar to her."

Her memories of her mother until that time are happy, although, Claudia adds, "I'm a great suppressor." Her mother was "Mrs. Clean—she was always buffing the floors, washing the walls. She could be a lot of fun—our happiest times were around food, when she'd make bread and roasts and wonderful cakes. Maybe that's why I have a weight problem," Claudia says, chuckling.

Two events dramatically altered the relative harmony of the family. First, her oldest brother was killed in Vietnam. Then, when Claudia was eighteen, her father was operated on for lung cancer. Says Claudia,

> My mother fell apart. She became a walking, talking zombie. She wouldn't get dressed in the morning, she wouldn't comb her hair, she wouldn't go to the hospital to see my dad, dishes would pile up in the sink. She'd sit in front of the television set watching a test pattern, like it was a poltergeist. She'd say she was being sent coded messages about my brother, that he was on a secret mission, and not really dead.

Claudia took her mother to a doctor, who said she had to be committed. "It was very frightening," she says, "because I didn't have any idea what was wrong. I didn't know if she'd come back to life. The most horrible part of signing her into a mental institution was having the doors locked behind me and being told, 'Don't visit. We'll tell you when you can come see her.' "

Claudia drove from the institution to the hospital where her father was recuperating and told him what had happened. "He cried; somehow, he knew. He'd always kept a lid on her depressions, trying to hide them from us. He was devastated that I was the one who had to deal with them now."

As she talks about her family, Claudia's mind drifts back to the early years in Missouri, and certain pieces of her off-center childhood seem to fall into place. She remembers that her mother used to go into her room, lock the door, and stay there for hours; that her mother was phobic about driving, and once a month would go shopping with her father for enormous stores of food; that in their family album, every picture of Claudia as a child shows her standing next to her mother, crying.

> My mom and I would have these off-the-wall conversations; she'd say my dad was a Communist, or having an affair. I was always walking on eggshells. In high school I failed every subject in my sophomore year. I couldn't talk to her about anything—she was in her own little world and forget it. She'd have these delusions; I didn't know she had a problem—I'd just walk away.

Today Claudia lives in Pittsburgh, where she works as a travel agent. Once a year she flies to California to visit her mother, who is too frightened ever to leave the small house where she lives with Claudia's sister. Says Claudia, "I always leave there with this sense of terrible sadness and incompletion. We don't have a relationship because there's no cure for what she's got. She can't do anything for herself. She doesn't have a life. I've read a lot about schizophrenia, but it doesn't make it better. It just makes you feel less alone."

This kind of Deserter is what authorities on resilient children describe as "psychologically unavailable." They are emotionally detached from their children, withdrawing behind their depression, unable to provide reassurance and tenderness when their children are unhappy—or even to react when their children are loving to them. They are walled up "behind a barrier of silence."

The Addicted Mother

This subgroup of Deserter is the largest, and the most complex, because it encompasses a multiplicity of people with myriad dysfunctions.

Where there is alcoholism or drug addiction in the family, it is often accompanied by battering of wives and physical and sexual abuse of children. Violence can erupt in helter-skelter torrents of substance-induced rage. But not always. In many cases, alcoholic behavior is confined to mere drunkenness and its companions, neglectfulness and melancholy.

Marion is the only child of parents who drank themselves to death. "My mother was always in a kind of haze," says Marion, a forty-year-old computer programmer. "She was just this amorphous presence—there was nothing crisp about her."

Her mother, ethereally beautiful in her youth, had moved from Maine to New York, intent on studying fine art and becoming a painter. There she met a "bohemian—my dad was an aspiring novelist, had an IQ off the charts. He fascinated her. But he was very remote, and totally undependable." They married and lived a rather eccentric life in Greenwich Village, made more precarious by her father's paltry income from the slim volumes he published, and his small salary teaching creative writing.

"I don't know how he was able to hold down a job," Marion says, "because he needed a certain alcohol content in his blood or he'd shake apart. He and my mother both put whiskey in their morning coffee."

And yet her mother was always there when she came home from school, asking how Marion's day was. "It was a lovely quality—I always felt that she waited, doing nothing, until I returned in the afternoon. I thought she wanted to be there for me—in reality, it was the other way around."

In the alcoholic family, there is often a history of excessive drinking, and this was true of Marion's family: her maternal grandmother was an alcoholic, as were her father's father and all his siblings. It was years before Marion could address their generational addiction.

The alcoholic family is bound by secrets, chief among them never to discuss with anyone what goes on within it. Says Marion, "Mom taught me the rules: Do not like anyone outside the family; do not become attached to anyone other than me, because it will crush me if you do."

And so Marion was swept into the undertow of boozy stealth and blaming—her father would berate her mother for having passed out when he came home, for being the detritus of her former self. Her mother blamed her father's alcoholism for making her so unhappy that she, too, had to drink. And Marion was caught in the middle.

> I would get up at night to go to the bathroom, and she'd be dead drunk on the couch. I would check her breathing to make sure she was alive—my dad would be upstairs, obliterated—and cover her with a blanket. From the time I was very young, I got the message that I was so wise, so mature, so good, that she never had to worry about me—she said she looked up to me. Once I asked her a typically childish question, "What would you do if I were drowning?" expecting that she would say, "Oh, darling, I would save you." What she said was, "I'd drown right along with you."

Although Marion's childhood was precarious and unbearably sad, it did not involve physical brutality. The same cannot be said of Leah, a thirty-eight-year-old social worker, whose mother was a battered wife.

The oldest of five children, Leah was raised in a mansion in a wealthy suburb of Chicago. Her father had inherited a multimillion-dollar estate, which he managed from a corner office in a Michigan Avenue skyscraper. Her mother, whom he married when she was eighteen, was from a prominent Illinois family. She was virtually raised by a housekeeper. "I'm told that at the age of six my mother didn't even know how to use a fork—she must have been horribly neglected," Leah says.

"There's a difference between social drinking and a bender," she wryly observes. "It's called money. My parents were social drinkers—from early in the morning until late at night."

She believes that her mother drank not only because she had been an unhappy child but also because she was lonely—her husband usually did not get home until 10:00 P.M., having had dinner with business associates or cronies nearly every evening. "She had all us kids for companionship," Leah adds. And so the children were nurtured until they were each around two—then, when they displayed a normal degree of contrariness, Leah's mother would lose interest. Says Leah,

> You'd be amazed what little kids can do when they have to. When I was four, my job every morning was to put up coffee and bring it to her. Once I fell down the stairs and coffee spilled all over me—I got third-degree burns. So the job went to my sister, who was three.

Her childhood wounds were only beginning. Her father wouldn't allow them to eat unless he was home, and sometimes two days would go by with the children not being fed. But occasionally he'd be in a good mood when he came home from the office. He'd "play" with the kids, making them lie on the floor while he threw lighted matches at them, promising ten dollars to the one who didn't flinch. Leah says,

> My mother would sit watching him do this and it would be fine because her husband was happy and her children were laughing—all our reactions were bizarre. Other times she'd sit and watch while he beat the hell out of us. If we weren't around, he'd slug her. If anyone ever knew about it—he was very careful not to leave marks—they never intervened. We certainly never told anyone.

Don't forget, we lived in "polite society." My mother wouldn't get help, not for us, and not for herself. She didn't want to rock the boat.

According to Sharon Wegscheider, an authority on alcoholism, the alcoholic sinks his or her anguished feelings beneath a sea of drinks, drowning feelings of loss and abandonment.

"Unfortunately," she writes in *Another Chance: Hope and Health For the Alcoholic Family*, "positive feelings like love and compassion—the feelings on which relationships are built—get buried along with the negative ones."

The "Nonattached" Mother

In *Every Child's Birthright: In Defense of Mothering*, psychologist Selma Fraiberg eloquently expresses a passionate plea for the growing population of children who are society's casualties, children who grow up in grinding emotional, economic, and psychological poverty. The parents of these children are unable to form loving bonds because they never experienced them in their own childhoods. She calls their affliction "the disease of non-attachment."

"In personal encounter with such an individual," she writes, "there is an almost perceptible feeling of intervening space, of remoteness, of 'no connection.' . . . There is no joy, no grief, no guilt, and no remorse." These people are neither clinically psychotic (although mental hospitals count them among their patients) nor neurotic, because of their total lack of ability to attach on any basis. They are morally and emotionally bankrupt.

And while many of the men and women of whom Dr. Fraiberg writes fill the slums and crowd police blotters—killers who commit random murders come from this group, she says—not all of them are beyond the social fringe. Neither Hedda Nussbaum, a former children's book editor in New York, nor her lover, disbarred lawyer Joel Steinberg—who was convicted of manslaughter for bludgeoning to death their illegally adopted daughter, Lisa—was disadvantaged. Nevertheless, their lives plummeted into a black hole of drugs, paranoia, hideous child abuse, and nightmarish savagery.

White-collar horror characterized Ilsa's childhood as well. She was brought up in a wealthy family, but her mother was not an abuser of alcohol or drugs. A different disease shattered Ilsa's youth—incest.

Her mother had been incestuously abused by her father and

grandfather, about which Ilsa's grandmother had done nothing; and in the ineluctable mimicry of emotional contagion, Ilsa's mother married a man who raped their daughter repeatedly throughout her childhood.

Somewhere along the line, Ilsa's mother lost her capacity to feel another's pain, or to believe the evidence of her own eyes and ears. It was as though any shred of normal compassion and humanity had been surgically excised in her own childhood, when she had been horribly stripped of all traces of dignity. And in its place, she became a clone of her mother. Says Ilsa,

> My mother hates her mother, because she allowed her father to get away with so much. My grandmother would make excuses for him—she never saw anything my grandfather did as wrong. She defended him whether he lied, cheated, stole, abused his child—it didn't matter. To her he was perfect; he was God.

Ilsa, as the oldest of four sisters, became her siblings' protector; as long as she was being abused, her father seemed to spare the other girls. She had kept the incest to herself because once she had told her father she'd "tell," and he had threatened to kill her. But when she went to college, her younger sister was next in line for his nighttime invasions of a daughter's bed and body. It was then that Ilsa confronted her mother with the incest she had suffered all those years.

> I told her that the only reason I was coming to her was to protect my sister, and that she had to do something about it. My mother was dressed in an evening gown, about to go to a black-tie charity ball. I was crying my eyes out, feeling rotten about having to upset her. She said in a voice so cold, I still shiver thinking about it, "Do you realize what you're doing to my marriage?" And she walked out the door. She's never been a victim of my father's violence. That's because she knows exactly how to set us up to take the heat. She just let it happen.

The Deceased Mother

For a child, the death of a parent is a loss so staggering that the empty place in the child's life remains an open wound. With only minor differences, the daughter of a mother who literally deserts her child and disappears for good suffers the same kind of loss—the abandonment is as close as one can get to actual death, as far as the child is concerned.

Nevertheless, a great many children of mothers who died prematurely eventually emerge from their terrible loss with the capacity for love and hope—providing their relationships with their mothers when they were alive were loving and supportive and steady. But if the relationship was ambivalent or unhappy, the child is wedged between grief and anger.

In this case, the daughter who loses her mother early in life is in perpetual limbo, a purgatory that is like an unfinished sentence. She has the incalculably painful legacy of trying to pattern her womanhood on a memory, and to separate from the very person who has literally, albeit unintentionally, abandoned her.

In defining herself, she has to draw upon myth and theory, fact and fantasy. And if she hates her mother for deserting her before the tension in their relationship has been tempered by time and understanding, she is in some ways always a question mark.

Felicia's childhood was studded with such losses. Before she was born, her mother suffered two miscarriages; after she was born, her mother's next three deliveries were all stillborns.

Although she adored her mother, she was, as she put it, "behind the eight ball. There was no way I wasn't going to be a disappointment, there was no way I could make up for all those children's deaths. I was doomed to failure."

Felicia's mother was a Smotherer. "She was wonderful in times of trouble. When I was sick, she'd pamper me—she was wildly protective, anxious beyond belief. When I was healthy, she was awful. If I forgot her birthday, she'd say God punished her by sending her someone so heartless and selfish. She had a really hard time when I began puberty and started coming into my own, defying her."

When Felicia was fifteen, her mother abruptly died of a brain aneurysm. Now forty-four, happily married and the mother of three grown children, Felicia jokes about her unmoored anxieties, the result, she says, of her unsettled childhood: "I've always been afraid of *everything*. I deserve credit for just being able to get up in the morning."

For when her mother died, their tangled relationship went into eternal hibernation, sealed up by Felicia's nonexistent connection with her father, who was cold, judgmental, forbidding. Says Felicia,

> My mother died much, much too young, for her and for me. When I got married, I wished she could have been there. When my daughter got into college, I wished I could have called her to tell her, it would have pleased her so.
>
> No one's ever going to love me as much as my mother did, which is a mixed blessing. She wanted to be my friend; I wanted a mother.

Felicia's mother died at the very time most mothers and daughters begin to renegotiate their relationship from the child's dependence to her fruition and separation. With one foot emotionally out the door, Felicia is still straddling the threshold of self-determination, as though the clock stopped the moment her mother died twenty-nine years ago. She says,

> Relationships have an agenda—I hadn't nearly finished mine with her. I have this ferocious anger toward her, and I miss her terribly. To everything there is a season, and it wasn't time for me to lose her. I never anticipated the implications, I always thought that when I got to a certain age I'd be able to work many things out with her. But we didn't get there. I never had the option of breaking off, I couldn't cut loose of my own accord. I never reached a place of comfort with her. And since she died, it's as though I'm on "hold." If she came back today, I'd ask, "I don't know why you were so disappointed in me, because I was a good kid. Would you explain that?"

Lilly Singer, an authority on bereavement, describes the bequest of this kind of confusion:

> If the daughter didn't resolve her ambivalence during the mother's lifetime, that's very tough, because she cannot retrieve it,

cannot redo it, cannot relive it. It's a question of not having gotten what you needed when you needed it most from the person who brought you into the world.

Resolving issues is best done when the parent is alive. If she is not, if she is only alive in your memories, your pain becomes something more—it turns into resentment, which gets spread around to everyone else in your life.

Bereavement is a matter of coming to terms with your feelings. If you had the hope that someday you'd straighten them out with your mother, that she would tell you she loves you dearly, even that is gone. The pain of not having a mother emotionally available through the years that you're growing up will stay with the daughter forever.

The Legacy of Desertion

As Drs. Michael Kerr and Murray Bowen of Georgetown University have pointed out, balance in the unstable family is often maintained when one member "absorbs" the anxiety for everyone else; the person becomes a kind of sacrificial lamb to preserve some semblance of order, even if "order" is skewed to mean keeping the family together at horrible cost. The Deserter takes the fall by being emotionally frozen, or by being a compliant sponge, shrouding herself with addictions or disintegration of the spirit.

"Adustments made by an individual in response to giving up self to the relationship system," the psychiatrists write, "can play a role in the development of physical, emotional, and social illness. . . . Chronic psychosis and depression can be thought of not just as diseases but as *symptoms* of having given up too much self."

In a sense, *all* Deserters are psychologically unavailable to their children, and in their unavailability are abusive parents, even if they never physically or sexually harmed their children, and even if they were never addicted.

If, for example, the nondrinking Deserter is married to an alcoholic, she is, as Ms. Wegscheider points out, an Enabler, covering up for the alcoholic spouse's behavior with rationalizations and denial. And in order to survive, she can take on many of her spouse's characteristics, among them, as Ms. Wegscheider writes, "delusion. The most tragic miscalculation of all is the Enabler's failure to see the very real power she has to change things." Both alcoholic and

Enabler extinguish their awareness along with their feelings, and their ability to claim their own pain.

The children of psychologically unavailable parents, according to a study of abused and neglected children by Drs. Ellen Farber and Byron Egeland, "exhibited the largest numbers of pathological behaviors . . . the effects of psychological unavailability on a child's development are as serious as the effects of physical abuse and neglect."

Profile of a Deserter

When Marla opens the door of her stately eighteenth-century colonial house in Connecticut on a bright, still July afternoon, I gasp in recognition: she is a former television news correspondent and well-known journalist whose books I have read and admired. I was put in touch with her by a friend who is an addictions counselor, and was told nothing about Marla except her married name and that she was willing to be interviewed for my book.

"I know you!" I say, and Marla laughs as we walk to the back of her house and sit beneath the heavy, protective branches of an oak tree near her patio.

Her latest book, she tells me, the one she is working on now, is about alcoholism. I cock my head in curiosity: I thought she simply had a rocky relationship with her mother. She tells me the relationship was beyond "rocky"—both her parents were alcoholics. So, she says, gazing at me evenly, is she, a detail of her highly public life that will, with her new book, be revealed to the world at large for the first time.

"*Recovering* alcoholic," she adds, correcting herself with a smile, alluding to a five-year bout of heavy drinking that ended her television career ten years ago. She is fifty.

Like most of the children of alcoholics I interviewed, Marla came from a large family—she is the youngest of four children. Marla's father, an accountant, wasn't violent; her mother was.

"I didn't know she was an alcoholic when I was growing up," Marla says. Her mother drank only at parties, the aftermath of which would never be mentioned, no matter how chaotic. One night, Marla watched her mother grab every dish out of a kitchen cabinet and smash them against the wall, then tear off the cabinet and stomp it on the floor. The event was not discussed, then or ever. "It was like it never happened."

Her mother's mood swings were like windshear. "One minute she would be sweet and loving, and the next she would be demonic." Once she tied Marla and her brother to the leg of the kitchen sink and went downstairs to bring up a neighbor to witness the hilarity of it. "My mother thought it was funny," Marla adds.

She traces her mother's addiction to her escape at nineteen from Nazi Germany, arriving alone in this country in 1936 with no friends, no money, no knowledge of English. "They say Jews don't drink," Marla says. "My mother did. I think it was to hide the devastation of having her entire family die in the Holocaust."

Like many children of alcoholics, Marla became an overachiever, fueled by her innate drive and extroversion. And she was fortunate enough to find a mentor in her elementary school, her sixth-grade teacher. "She took an interest in me—she said it was because of my writing ability; I have a hunch that she sensed what was going on in my home." Marla would stay after school nearly every afternoon, to help her teacher clean the blackboard, or to chat about schoolwork. Sometimes the teacher would take her for a soda after school, and walk her home. "I think she saved my life—she made me feel she cared.

"I have a lot of ambition, and I've spent my whole life going after things to help erase my past," Marla continues. "I had huge opportunities—then I blew it."

By the time she was twenty-five, she was a bylined reporter for a major metropolitan daily newspaper, covering the crime beat. She married a man of great heart and understanding, which could not quell the fears that lurked nearby as she pushed ahead in her hard-driving reporting. At thirty she had a daughter. At thirty-five, she was a television news correspondent.

"I was juggling all those roles—prize-winning reporter, the perfect mother, perfect wife and hostess, perfect friend," she says. "Note the word 'perfect.' People fail. We all fail. And I had more right than most, coming out of what I came out of. But I thought I had to be more perfect than anyone."

And so she began to drink, unable to meet the exalted standards she had set for herself. As the mother of a young infant, convinced that her child would die in her inept hands, she called the pediatrician twice, sometimes three times, a day. The more she drank, the more hopeless and helpless she felt; she began missing work, having other correspondents fill in for her. Eventually, too drunk to go to work at all, she was fired.

Her greatest failure, she says, was to her child.

Your own self-absorption and pain are so private and personal that it has nothing to do with the people you love. You can't make them understand that—naturally—so in a sense you leave them. In my case you leave through drinking and depression and sleeping. You're watching yourself become your mother, which is the most horrifying thing, and yet you're powerless to stop.

With her husband's help and encouragement, Marla learned to understand her mother, she says, by signing herself into a rehabilitation program and by joining Alcoholics Anonymous. Although it took several more years of therapy and agonizing introspection to get on the wagon and stay there, she has been "dry" for six years. In that time she relinquished the magical thinking that caused her to drink in the first place.

When I was a kid, I did anything to keep the peace—played the parent, made calls if Daddy couldn't go to the office. You think, "If I could be better, they would love me, they would change, everything would be nice." You could be better from now until Doomsday and nothing will change unless you decide to get help. It's exhausting to be dragging the anger of that, it's like a big suitcase you can barely lift, you lug it with you everywhere. Until someone says, "You can put this bag down now. You don't need it. All you have to do is take your hands off and let it go." My parents couldn't do that. I was lucky—I could.

Marla has discussed all this with her twenty-year-old daughter, and together they have gone for counseling—her daughter joined a support group, called Adult Children of Alcoholics (ACOA). "We have a wonderful relationship today," she says, her eyes pooling with tears. "I have tried to make amends. I have apologized to her for her lost years. I have taken full responsibility for them, and I think she's forgiven me."

Just as Marla has forgiven her mother. The last time she saw her, shortly before her death last year, she was in a nursing home, her mind having dissolved into psychosis. "She didn't know me at all," Marla says softly. "She had such a sad life, and such a sad end. It was the most complex relationship of my life. But at least I have been loved. I don't think she ever felt loved."

The day after the funeral, Marla, who was flooded with unexpected grief, went back to see her therapist. "I was stunned to be so overwhelmed by her death—I thought I'd put the past behind me. I said to him, 'Why am I in such pain? Why do I feel as if I failed her?'

"'You didn't fail her,' he said. 'She failed you. But you had the courage not to fail yourself.'"

Part Three
Rebellions

10
Balancing Acts

They say that when you pick a mast for a sailboat, it has to come from a tree that has not had strong winds from only one direction, because such a tree may grow tall, but not quite straight. It's the same with people. You grow up the best you can, but you're always struggling with something that went on at a very early time. You can come pretty far, but you never rid yourself of that struggle completely—you're always a little bent.

—Janet, forty-one

One of the great misconceptions of modern life is the assumption that by the magic age of twenty-one we are jelled, dreams in place, ready to tackle the adult world and leave childhood behind. *Here,* the world seems to say as we are nudged—or thrown—out of the parental nest, *is where your true self spreads its wings: start flying.* All we lack, according to this myth, is experience. The reality is that many of us lack quite a bit more: a psychic passport to adulthood.

Even daughters who had loving and supportive mothers can find their smooth adult passage suddenly becoming turbulent. First, our life course can begin to veer sharply from any resemblance to our mothers' when they were young adults. Second, we may become parents ourselves.

Foreign to most mothers of the senior generation are our inroads into the territories of male-only careers, and our feminist demands to be considered more than lovely adornments and breeders of babies.

163

But even if we have duplicated her domestic path, the mother who weathered our adolescence with equanimity and who learned to loosen her grip may undergo a startling change when we ourselves become parents. Our own motherhood reawakens her feelings about her now obsolete role, when she was a mother of young children. *And she wants the job back.*

Because of her friendship with you, woman-to-woman, she may have felt compensated for the loss of her indispensability. But now, as you raise children, she has an opportunity to parent again. If she cannot have you-as-child, *at least she can rekindle her mothering authority as a grandmother*, telling you how best to do your parenting job. And that's when the trouble often starts, when there may have been little, or none, before.

To be fair, there is much that daughters do to beckon her back to her traditional role. For one thing, even in our twenties we are not as grown up as we like to think. Prolonged adolescence is an inevitable by-product of the Baby Boom generation. More and more women have postponed their emancipation by attending college and graduate school, and by delaying their social coming of age by not marrying and having children.

At the same time, because of the soaring costs of self-support, growing numbers of young adults—the "boomerang" generation— are returning to the parental nest. And if they do not, they still rely on Mom and Dad to bail them out financially.

"Emotional separation takes much longer than we initially thought," says Dr. Jane B. Abramson. "Many women don't come near to resolving separation issues until they're close to forty. You see a lot of 'little girls' out there who are doing great things in terms of advancing in their careers, but who are basically not grown up."

But then there are the daughters whose mothers have *always* had trouble allowing them to grow up. For these daughters, there are huge gaps in their "flight instructions." And the biggest gap is this: Their unsuccessful efforts to separate from Mother keep them stranded in the past. For them, adulthood is not unlike being on a high wire without a safety net. They set a tentative toe into independence, drawing from the only guidelines they know: *what Mother wants them to be.*

Their adulthood is a balancing act: they inch their way toward the secure platform of their grown-up identities, trying not to be jarred by their incomplete pasts. Some make it; others scurry back to the starting point, unable to hazard the passage. Still others teeter midway, buffeted by the uneven winds of childhood, flailing to gain their balance. And a few lose their footing and fall.

The psychological cost of being an "unacceptable" child is that you do not know your own mind—you only know it in relation to your mother. You are still the "false self" personality, your interpretation of what your mother wants of you, rather than your "true self"—who you genetically and temperamentally are—living according to your own talents and needs, likes, and dislikes.

Awash in the wake of their mothers' displeasure, some daughters continue their frantic attempts to measure up. Others avoid the mother's company but remain connected in their enraged reactions to her, yanked up by invisible cords of ambivalence, suspended by the stranglehold of her manipulation.

Whether held fast, or kept at a distance, these daughters remain tied to her in their *reactions:* most of their decisions are filtered through the unconscious question of whether or not Mother would bestow her blessings upon them.

Lacking the gyroscope of Mom's belief in them, of her unconditional love, they are guided instead by the nagging sense that they *still* have not got it right—they cannot make it alone. Gnawing at even the most outwardly competent, aggressive, and powerful women, there is often a child saying, "Does anybody love me for myself alone?"

The image of the unpleasable mother is always with the unacceptable daughter. Like an ill wind, it is there in our faltering. It is there in our unsuccessful efforts to ameliorate her and in our inability to alter our expectations of her. It is there in our choices of friends, lovers, and spouses. It is there in the people with whom we work. And it is there as we mother our own children.

Unless we have had some help, or are extraordinarily resilient, our true selves have not yet replaced that image—our wings are clipped.

How we falter, of course, is a collaboration between our mother's interpretation of who we are and our own temperaments and personalities. We are not brought up in a vacuum. The variables of schoolyard victories or humiliations, kindly or punitive teachers, fortunes of health and wealth, marital mismatches or unpairings, and just plain luck are all factored into the mix of who we are.

"Surrogate Mothers." Children are extraordinarily inventive in filling in the empty places of their lives. To get a semblance of the nurturing they were not getting at home, many of the daughters I interviewed "adopted" other mothers in their childhoods. These daughters had the innate wisdom to know where to go for help.

Surrogate mothers figured heavily in many of these daughters' choices of friends—and even boyfriends.

Dierdre, thirty-two, is the daughter of a woman who reeks of rectitude. The mother of Dierdre's best friend, however, is anything but a prude. When Dierdre was in college, her friend's mother said of her never having had a boyfriend, "Why don't you have some fun, for Christ's sake? It's time, already."

Says Dierdre, "I called her 'Mom.' Whenever I had a problem, I always went to her. I vowed that if I ever had kids, I'd call her for advice. She's the kind of mother I want to be."

Rhea, twenty-four, sometimes befriends women she may feel only lukewarm about, but "if I like their mothers, boy, do I attach to them—like glue."

These "significant others" are often available within a daughter's extended family. Ingrid believes she was "saved" by her aunt. She says,

> I used to visit her all the time—I entrusted her with a lot of my feelings. She was always willing to listen, she would give me advice, give me perspective, tell me she loved me. I figured out early on that I couldn't get that from my mother—I had to deal with the fact that I had to learn to live without her, at least in terms of having someone to talk to. My aunt I could talk to.

Adopted mothers can help a severely damaged and depressed daughter envision a future of hope, and sometimes even give her a willingness to live.

Christina Crawford, whose harrowing childhood was chronicled in *Mommie Dearest,* and who has spent years championing the cause of abused children, says she had surrogate mothers in the forms of governesses and certain teachers "who were extraordinary."

> They were the ones who gave me a positive mirror of myself. Without them, I don't think I would even be here talking to you. Every child needs at least one person who in her early years believes in her, trusts her, and encourages her. If the abused child didn't get that one person, then she only sees the world through the eyes of the aggressor; she only sees the

chaos, the anger and the evil. If she *did* get that one person, she has a chance to see herself in a more benevolent way.

All these daughters talked about their "adoptive mothers" with intense feelings of gratitude and idealization. When you've been an unloved or neglected child, mere decency becomes a miracle. When someone is simply being nice to you, you idolize them because you're so used to being treated shabbily.

These women did not weep when describing the ways in which their mothers demeaned or damaged them. But when they recalled *acts of kindness* by relatives or mentors, their tears flowed. As Alice Koller writes in *An Unknown Woman: A Journey to Self-Discovery*, "What more perfect evidence can there be that I understand nothing about feelings: that I cry when someone loves me?"

But adopted mothers cannot entirely appease a child's hunger for her own mother's love and encouragement. Our mothers have an incalculable impact on how we weather the variables of our lives. Mothers pull us in one direction—so, too, do we often pull in another. The *degree* to which that struggle produces tension between mothers and daughters has everything to do with how they function together in the broader context of the family.

Family Systems

As we saw in Chapter Four, a profound influence on our self-esteem is "fit." When mother and daughter are of different temperamental tempos, their relationship is often rocky—they have a "mis-fit."

Another influence on our sense of self is how we are manipulated when there is trouble in the family. Triangling, as discussed earlier, serves to lower the heat when there is a mis-fit, or difference of opinion, or assault to family tranquillity. If Mom and Dad don't get along, for instance, a child will be drafted into the fray, soaking up the parents' irritation.

"Pick up your room!" Mom screams suddenly to her startled child as Dad, in the afterburn of a marital skirmish, storms out the door. "Thank goodness I have you," she coos later, having cooled off. Such conflicting behavior may make Mommy feel better. But the child feels worse, jolted by her mother's mood swings and having little to do with setting them in motion.

But triangling works another way—Mom may be tugged by ghosts in her *own* history.

Louise describes her upbringing in a household that included her mother's hotheaded father. She says,

> My mother had a terrible temper, and it always seemed worst when it involved my grandfather. She'd say I had insulted him because I hadn't been polite enough, or because I hadn't gone upstairs to see him the minute I got home from school.
>
> As I got older, I recognized a pattern: My grandfather would get angry at her, then my mother would get angry at me. Then my father would get angry at me because my mother was angry at him because my grandfather was angry. There was this whole chain where nobody had to be totally responsible for their behavior—they always had someone else to blame.

The "chain" Louise describes is what Dr. Murray Bowen of Georgetown University calls "Family Systems." According to Dr. Bowen's theory, the family unit is "a network of interlocking relationships." When we react to other members of the family, taking responsibility for, or finding fault with, everyone's behavior but our own, we cannot assess ourselves apart from the others. Nor can they accurately judge themselves apart from us. We all become utterly dependent upon what each other thinks.

Triangling is the root of vendettas that split families apart over what appear to be trivial slights.

Says Isabel, twenty-eight,

> My mother stopped speaking to her sister eight years ago. They were at a wedding, and my aunt walked through the room, stopping at tables to say hello to everyone, kissing people along the way before finally reaching my mother on the other side of the room and kissing her. My mother was furious that she wasn't kissed *first*. We were not allowed to have anything to do with my aunt after that.

The issue for this mother is not the pecking order of her sister's greetings at a social function—rather, it is a wound buried deep in the mother's past, when she felt that her sister was her mother's favorite. But rather than address the source of her rage, she enlarges it, hauling her family into the battle.

This vignette illustrates how we can be manipulated by triangles. The price a child pays when she is called upon to settle her mother's scores is that later in life she becomes engaged in the *same kinds of triangles*. (How we can extricate ourselves from triangles will be discussed in Chapter Seventeen.)

As family difficulties continue to be bounced around the system like a volleyball, with everyone pushing them off onto someone else, they get tossed down to the next generation, as the example of Louise and her grandfather illustrates.

Children are the next line of offense when mothers haven't resolved their relationships with their parents. Being caught in triangles is one way that the daughter's high-wire act is shaken.

Birth Order

Other childhood forces over which we have no control also play important parts in choreographing our lives. One of them is birth rank, an immutable fact of a child's life. Many social scientists take issue with generalities about the personalities of firstborns, secondborns, and only children. They argue that how the parent treats each child is more important than the child's position in the numerical scheme of things.

For instance, mothers may undergo certain stresses in their lives into which young, vulnerable children are exposed simply by virtue of chance, stresses that the older children have been spared. Says Dr. Allan Stempler, instructor of clinical psychiatry at Cornell University at Northshore University Hospital, "The timing might be wrong for some children. For example, a mother may reach a certain age where things are going wrong in her marriage."

The mother may also be going through menopause. Raging hormones can make the most circumspect mother lose her cool, figuratively and literally. If a daughter is unaware of these chemical changes, she may think her mother has gone slightly mad, or that she is mad at her. Add to this timing that, in a cosmic burst of poor planning, many mothers are going through menopause at the same time their daughters reach puberty. Both mother and daughter may, because of the revolutions going on in their bodies and the enormous stress of their changing identities, find themselves with patience and understanding in short supply.

"I wish someone had explained all this to me," said one woman. "My mother was so vain, she wanted people to think she was twenty-six, and that she was my friend rather than my mother. Menopause hit her like a ton of bricks. She couldn't accept her middle age. I just thought she didn't like me."

But birth rank is nevertheless an essential ingredient in the contouring of our personalities. It "strongly influences our way of negotiating relationships," writes Dr. Harriet Goldhor Lerner.

As she points out, firstborns—since they are first up in the junior division of the family hierarchy—tend to be natural leaders.

Secondborn siblings may be torn between a desire both to be head of the line and to be taken care of. The secondborn may like it very much, thank you, that she doesn't have to be the "point man," setting the example of what gets a kid into trouble—she profits from her older sibling's mistakes.

But if she is a middle child, she often gets lost in the shuffle, isolated between the oldest—who has for a time had her parents all to herself—and the youngest, the baby.

As for the youngest, she is often coddled and "babied."

Birth rank can lead to very different experiences of mother and very different views siblings have of themselves: the oldest child may see her mother as "demanding"; the youngest may see her as "treating me like a baby"; and to the middle, she may be "indifferent."

But the sibling connection is more than rank alone.

Sibling Rivalry. Serious trouble erupts when mother shows a clear preference for one child over another. Fit plays a part in her sometimes inevitable partiality—the laid-back mother will have a built-in shorthand of shared temperament with the child who is like her in her slower rhythms, her tendency not to leap to conclusions or to jump up and down with glee or temper.

But favoritism shows up in more sinister ways. Says psychotherapist Ann Gordon, "If a mother hasn't separated from her children, then she will 'love' the most malleable ones the most, while the troublemaker, who wants to make her own decisions, is going to get her harshest treatment."

Much rides on how the mother can tolerate her children's differences. The way she expresses her love can be very uneven, even unfair, and create enormous resentment among them.

Adele Faber tells of a television appearance she made with coauthor Elaine Mazlish to promote their book, *Siblings Without Rivalry*. Says Ms. Faber,

A woman called in during the show and said that her mother had always told her, "You're terrific, you're the best little mother in the world," because she was a surrogate mother to her two youngest sisters. The day her mother died, her sisters stopped talking to her, and she was totally bereft. She said, "When I lost my mother, I also lost my sisters. The only thing that was keeping us together was my mother."

When a mother dies, sibling struggles about her favoritism are kept alive in fights over their inheritance. If great wealth is involved, these struggles are spun out in highly publicized lawsuits, each sibling attempting to extract from the mother's estate a financial metaphor for her love. If she did not bequeath enough, they will try to *take* more, trampling each other for one last chance to get tangible proof of it.

Roles. Children are often cast into roles that are reflections of the parent's need for them to *be* a certain kind of child.

Parents can instill a trait in a child. For example, a mother may become anxious over what she *thinks* is wrong with a child, when in fact *nothing* may be wrong. If, say, she frets that her daughter does not have enough friends, the daughter will get her message and suddenly notice that her dance card is nearly empty, and that this is *tragic.*

The daughter, who may be a born loner, now tries to make Mom feel better by attempting to become popular, trailing after new friends merely because she is made to feel that she is "wrong" not to have more of them—and, since being a social sort is not her longest suit, she may well fail.

And the mother, naturally, will agonize even more.

As we saw in Chapter Three, this is one way a child develops a false self. The daughter *distorts* herself to become pleasing in her mother's eyes, rather than focusing on what is pleasing to herself. She reshapes her innate qualities, talents, instincts, and insights to fit into her mother's view of her. The child becomes uncomfortable in her own skin. (Sometimes she becomes "pleasing" by getting into trouble, as we shall see in Chapter Fourteen.)

The false self is the fulfillment of a parent's prophecy. Says psychiatrist Marianne Goodman,

There's a wonderful cartoon in *The New Yorker* of a man who goes to buy a suit, and the tailor's got him in all kinds of crazy positions to get this suit to fit. He fits the suit; the suit never fits him.

Well, that's what kids do. They walk around in distorted positions, trying to make their parents right.

In the interests of survival—acting "as if" they are what their mother wants—children take on roles that will solidify their attachment to her but erode their true sense of themselves, their true self.

Daughters often try on a variety of roles over a lifetime to strike a balance between their mothers' demands and their own skewed growth.

One woman I interviewed was in childhood a frightened, peace-at-any-price personality. In her teenage years she became her mother's competent, compulsive, demanding clone. By her twenties, she had sunk into depression, the victim of her mother's constant criticisms and expectations. By her thirties she had begun to alienate herself from the family, becoming the mother's scapegoat. Finally, her relationship to her mother became so painful that she had to cut it off entirely.

The "false self" is fluid, adapting throughout life. But not everyone runs the gamut of roles, as this woman has. Most remain a variation of their childhood role.

That role looms at family gatherings. I call this the "Thanksgiving Dinner Syndrome." You may be a perfectly competent and masterful adult in the outside world. But the minute you walk into your mother's house for a holiday dinner, all the old defenses and family arguments and patterns leap into place. The "baby" of the family is treated like, and *acts like*, the "baby" she was in childhood. The "smart aleck" of the family tries to outdo her sibling as she grabs the biggest piece of pie. How you behave when in the bosom of your *original* family often mirrors the role you adopted when you were a child.

The roles we play can last throughout our lives. Says psychotherapist Ann Gordon,

If a girl learns to survive emotionally or even physically by being "nice" when she's young, her unconscious mind will automatically have her keep on being "nice" when she grows up, even when it doesn't work. This "nice girl" behavior tends to invite abuse. When she gets into serious trouble—rape, for example—she stands a chance of waking up and realizing that something's wrong. At that point, she might get herself into therapy.

These roles keep us "bent out of shape," trying to *make* our mothers like us, rendering us unable to appreciate even our own abilities, and perverting our perceptions of them. Says a thirty-eight-year-old artist,

> My mother was over here the other day, looking at a painting I've been working on. After she left, my husband said to me, "Did you see the expression on her face? That incredible envy? The competitiveness?"
> I was stunned.
> "No," I said. "I was too busy looking for her approval."

And so the daughter who in adulthood is still performing her high-wire act to win her mother over is perpetually off-balance. Says Dr. Ann Caron, who runs mother-daughter workshops in Greenwich, Connecticut, "The mother who needs to keep her daughter close is trying to satisfy her own desire for security—but it makes the daughter *in*secure. The daughter never gets a full belief in her own ability because she never gets a chance to test it. My agenda for daughters is, 'Dream your own dreams.' "

Spillovers

In adulthood, the insecure daughter will be like a ship that is off-course. Her unresolved relationship with her mother spills over into other areas of her life. The hitch is this: The internalized mother is still at the helm.

We *say* we are wise to Mom's shenanigans, we *say* we won't allow them to continue, but many of us do—*by duplicating the past in our adult relationships*.

This phenomenon is called "the repetition compulsion." Over and over again we resurrect our childhood reactions, distorting each new relationship to fit the old patterns, just as we distorted ourselves to ingratiate ourselves to Mother. Still trying to tame the parental tiger, we bend every effort to make the new relationship look just like the mother–daughter connection, *so that we can get another chance to fix it*.

Our unconscious goal is this: Make the attachment recognizable, so I'll know exactly what to do. Even if what we duplicate is our own original pain, at least it is reliable in its familiarity, and there is no guesswork about how to behave. We have the script, and our assigned role in it, down pat.

And we play it, with co-workers, friends, lovers, even our children.

On the Job. Insecurities spawned in childhood spill over into our relationships at work. Our families often become templates for office relationships—we make a "mother" or "father" or "sibling" out of bosses and co-workers.

A comment from a boss who reminds you of Mom can register as a childhood rebuke. "It's hard for me to accept either a compliment or a criticism from my supervisor," says Diane, twenty-eight, a telephone operator. "It's like my mother showing either pleasure or displeasure with me. 'You're such a good worker' translates into, 'Oh, my God, if I don't work real hard, she'll hate me.' "

Even the people who work *for* us can cause childhood reactions to Mom to surface. Emily, thirty-nine, is a headhunter. Her new secretary, Madeline, twenty-four—whom everyone else in the office considers to be an efficient and cheerful presence—grates on Emily, who says,

> I've been trying to figure out why she bugs me, and I realized that she picks on the very thing I feel insecure about: I'm totally disorganized. So when she reminds me that I haven't gone through my mail for two days, I go berserk inside. I feel nagged, just like I did with my mother. My mom was a compulsive tidier and complainer, and when Madeline starts stacking the papers on my desk in precise piles, all my buttons get pushed.
>
> So here I am, rebelling internally against my *employee*, for God's sake. I'm too embarrassed to fire her. I can't say, "Well, dear, it's because you remind me of my mother."

Friends. "Who needs her?" the daughter may say of her mother, "I will create a new family from my friendships, people who will love and accept me, who will give me what I couldn't get from her."

But there's a booby trap: Instead of choosing friends who are her mother's antithesis, many a damaged daughter will choose her mother's clone. She will select friends who will corroborate her mother's feelings for her, people who will withhold, manipulate, demand, chastise. Or who are parasites. Or who try to possess her. Even friends who will leave her.

Many of these daughters are awkward with friends, and in social situations feel as if they have been thrown overboard without know-

ing how to swim. Forming attachments is a painful, guesswork
process for them. Says Anne, twenty-seven,

> I have trouble making female friends because I don't
> know what they expect. I figure if they don't want
> anything from me, why would they want to be my
> friend? I think that goes back to when I was a kid—my
> mother only paid attention to me if I got good grades or
> if I won a contest; she loved me conditionally. I had to
> earn her love. So I expect the same of friends.

A recurring theme for many such daughters is that they form
friendships quickly in the instant intimacy of need rather than take
the time to build relationships based on self-respect, mutual esteem,
and a sharing of interests.

Says thirty-nine-year-old Annette,

> There's no balance in my life: I'm still as needy as
> when I was a child. I'm always making new friends and
> wondering if they will reject me. I always feel I'm the
> least in their affection. I put up with a lot from people
> who, like my mother, don't treat me kindly, because I
> am so afraid of being left.

Other daughters find it hard to trust, and their friendships often
don't last. Says Gail, thirty-two,

> It's almost like clockwork. I'll make a new friend, and
> she'll do something that disappoints me, and I'll think,
> "Oh, another one." I'm always on the watch for flaws.
> In a way, I'm relieved when I find one. When I can't
> find the bad side, I feel very insecure. I can be friendly
> with people when I have their number.

Still other daughters form friendships that never cross over into true
intimacy. With Sheila, thirty-eight, the *last* thing she wants is an overly
affectionate, ebullient chum, because it reminds her of her mother who
was all charm outside the family, but a harridan within it. Says Sheila,

> A colleague recently told me, "You look like you're
> ready to scratch someone's eyes out." I said, "Yes, and

it's very off-putting, isn't it?" I know what she's talking about because I've heard it for years. I have a friend who has a million pals—everybody loves her—and it upsets me about her because I don't know how she really feels about me. It's hard to read people like that. My mother was always smiling to the world, but never at me. So I only trust the stern face, never the friendly one. It scares the hell out of me to reveal myself to people. Sometimes it's awfully nice to slip back into that guise of being off-putting and say, "To hell with everybody. Me first."

Partners and Spouses. The men in our lives are also often variations of our mothers. If our mothers were loving and nurturing, the chances are good that we will choose mates who are similarly affectionate and supportive.

But for many of the daughters I interviewed, the model of the unpleasant mother can have devastating consequences in their choice of romantic partners.

Not that this is a *conscious* choice; but it is in many ways an *inevitable* one. For if what we know of love was learned in childhood; if our lessons in devotion came from a mother who did not have the gift of giving or who gave or took too much, then, knowing no other, we apply that lesson to our love lives.

If, for instance, Mom was a Critic, the "nice" guy is perceived as a wimp. But the nitpicking braggart becomes the most desired of creatures *simply because, holding us in low esteem, he can live quite easily without us.*

This replication of Mother often seems uncanny. Says Dolores, forty-one,

> My mother never wanted kids, and she never failed to tell me so. Interestingly, I married a man just like her. He, too, never failed to tell me he didn't want children—and he never failed to tell our kids the same thing. Recognizing that similarity was one of those turning points in therapy: Of *course* you're going to attract screwed-up guys who will be mean to you and be supercritical. This is what you expect when you are used to having a mother who rued the day you were born.

Without the experience of healthy loving, we may only know how to receive—either abject devotion, or neediness, or neglect or rejection. We may not know how to sustain a loving relationship of equal give-and-take.

One twenty-seven-year-old woman told me,

> I used to date this lawyer, and he was everything my mother applauded in a man—he was gorgeous, from a wealthy family, a professional. So I got him to like me. And that was all that mattered to me—he satisfied my quest to have him fall in love with me, because I knew that's what my mother wanted. I do that a lot—I'll get a guy to commit, and after he does, good-bye. I don't go the distance. I play a lot of games.

But sometimes we may "get it right" the first time out in our choice of partner, *only to try, unconsciously, to make it wrong*—to make the man *seem* more like Mother. Says Nancy, forty,

> When I married my husband, I thought, What a strange man to be so loving, so accepting. I would constantly say things like, "How come you never express anger? Come on, let it out—you *must* be angry." I'd pick these insane fights. It's because I didn't know how to handle a relationship that was tranquil. I didn't know how to deal with being loved unconditionally.

These women are all attempting to resolve their mother–daughter relationships through a man who may have no idea that he is being asked to "correct" a problem that has nothing to do with him.

Children. The final area into which our unresolved attachment to Mother spills over is children—whether or not to have them and, if we do, what kind of mother we will become.

One question I asked all the daughters in my sample was "What were your 'foxhole promises' when you were a child? What were the things you pledged you would never, *never* do when you grew up?"

The one fear that haunted every daughter I interviewed was the terror that they would not be good mothers—that, by virtue of their emotionally incomplete childhoods, they might not be able to prevent a replay of their mother's parenting mistakes.

To avoid it, some of these women decided never to have children.

Beth, forty-two, determined in her early teens that she was never going to be a mother. She says,

> Once, during a shouting match with my mother when I was fifteen, she screamed, "I hope someday you have a daughter who gives you as much trouble as you give me." It was clear to me from everything she had ever said that motherhood was awful—kids tie you down, they make noise and dirt, they ruin your life.
>
> So I decided, "Nope. I'm not bringing a little thing into the world and inflict on her what happened to me. I'm not going to risk feeling about a child the way my mother felt about me." And I never did.

Christina Crawford says that not having children was "the best decision I ever made. You are responsible for a child forever, certainly for the relationship with that child. My life was such a struggle and my psychological problems were nowhere near straightened out for a long time. So I'm very glad I made the decision, because I do not have to take the responsibility for damaging an innocent person."

When women do decide to have children, many of them, terrified of becoming like their mothers, pray for sons. One woman, the mother of two sons, told me, "I thank God every day that I didn't have girls. My boys can identify with their father, who is much less screwed up than I am."

Other women decide that the way to avoid damaging a child is to have a *lot* of kids. One woman I interviewed has six children. She says, "I was afraid if I had only one, I'd focus too much on that one child and I'd make all these huge mistakes. I figured if I had a *bunch* of kids, I couldn't do *too* much harm because it would all be spread around."

These women swear to make elaborate reparations with their own kids for all the damage done to them when they were children. They think they're going to rewrite history—it will be better, happier, more fun, more open for the kids than it ever was for them. *They'll make happen in this new generation what they couldn't, no matter how hard they tried, make happen in their own.*

And fortunately, many daughters of sad or difficult childhoods are able to make those vows stick.

But unless we are very clear about our beginnings, our ambivalences, defenses, and lingering immaturity and how they skew us, our noble intentions can backfire: The "too nice" mother can be as damaging as the one who is a monster. The mother who only gushes in hyperbolic praise loses her credibility with her child, who feels pressure to be perfect or who knows, if only on a gut level, that her mother is not being honest.

As one woman put it,

> Where I had no love and too many rules from my mother, I was going to give all my devotion and acceptance to my daughter. I fell all over myself praising her. I kept saying, "You're so wonderful, you're the smartest, most beautiful child in the world," because nobody ever said that to me.
>
> But I made her as insecure as I am.
>
> Now her little inner voice is saying to her, "I don't think I can live up to my mother's expectations," and my little inner voice is still saying to me, "You never were worth shit." In a way, it's almost the same. I can't believe it.

This is the biggest booby trap of all: Try as we may to be the antithesis of Mom, *we often produce in our daughters a twin of Mom.* And so we are *surrounded* by Mother, as the prophecies of our childhood become generational parentheses—Mom on one side, and on the other, her echo, our daughter. Our motherhood becomes a twice-told tale.

If we are acutely aware of what our mothers did to us and have a measure of sensitivity and introspection—why do we *still* make huge mistakes? Why do we sometimes re-create the strained mother–daughter connection?

In our determination not to repeat our mothers' mistakes, we may vow to be her polar opposite. To our utter surprise, our daughters may then become very like the mothers from whom we are trying so hard to be different. The reason?

We behave toward our daughters exactly the way we behaved toward our mothers.

Frequently, this effort reproduces tensions that are identical to those we had with our mother. If, for example, you and your mother often had arguments over her inability to show up on time for anything, you may have responded by making a huge issue about punctuality with your daughter. Your daughter may then have reacted to your zealous requirement for promptness by habitually being tardy, just like your mother.

Our best intentions get turned inside out when we try to be our mother's opposite, rather than a mature woman who makes her own decisions.

But sometimes, unable to see the ways our mothers harmed us, we become *just like her.* We defend her in our insistent fantasy that she really is the All-Good Mother and that it is *we* who are bad.

Unless we are able to find a middle ground, taking only the best of our mothers and understanding the worst, these reactions—be Mom's opposite or her twin—become two sides of the same coin. The relationship with our children is as skewed as it was with our mothers. The mother–daughter estrangement, the lack of real friendship, perpetuates itself, *in spite of everything we do.* (Finding that middle ground will be discussed in Part Four.)

A Strong Defense

And so, in the interest of protecting whatever sense of identity she can salvage from her childhood, the daughter grafts her "false self" personality and childhood training onto all her adult attachments.

As we saw in the last section, there are certain patterns in the ways unpleasable mothers control their daughters. So, too, do daughters react to those mothers in general patterns of their own, patterns that we adopt to make some sense of mother–child friction, to give it a semblance of balance, however lopsided. The daughters "please"

by serving (Angel);
by being ambitious (Superachiever);
by caving in (Cipher);
by being the scapegoat. (Troublemaker);
by getting out (Defector).

Many of the woman I interviewed talked about themselves as though they were twins—the "false self" that is still trying to get her wings from her mother, and the "adult" who intellectually knows where the ambivalences are. They have not yet come into their own, haven't yet figured out which is real—the uncertain, incomplete child within or the grown-up, emancipated woman she is trying to be.

But the "false self" is safer than the unknown, and these daughters are loath to give it up, the anguishing catch-22 of feeling like an unacceptable child.

The "false self" of childhood is woven into the tapestry of the daughter's adulthood, defending *against* her past even as she unwittingly *repeats* it. If she were to relinquish those defenses—those coping mechanisms—now, she believes she would be as imperiled as she was when she was a child. *Even if they distort her, they are what got her through her childhood. For that alone, they must be respected.*

For the adult women I interviewed, the most painful part of childhood was not necessarily the unhappiness they experienced; rather, it was their sense of complicity in creating it. They wince when they recall the ways they literally bent themselves out of shape. They feel a terrible sense of shame in having groveled, or lost their tempers, or mistreated their siblings—or themselves—in order to get Mommy to love them.

But greater still is the anguish that even the false self *couldn't get Mom to accept them in the way they wanted her to.* As one woman said, "I ate all the 'dirt' and it didn't work."

This section is intended to help you recognize and even admire that false self rather than blame yourself for having relied on it. Those coping mechanisms are important because *they worked.* You made it to adulthood.

But the next step is the hardest one of all: To summon the courage to give them up, trusting that there is something to take their place—the best parts of your *real* self.

As you read the next five chapters, then, use them as a road map to identify yourself rather than as a reason to beat yourself up.

You may see parts of yourself in all these categories—some of them overlap—but one will feel the most familiar to you. You may find that some of these "roles" apply to you only in part, or to a lesser degree than to the daughters portrayed here.

Bear in mind also that these categories are *extremes.* Many a mother might read them and think, I can't win. The daughters described here, however, didn't have mothers who could take a middle parental road; nor were many of them yet able to see their mothers with any perspective. And since their mothers—as we saw in Part II, were *also* extremes, so, too, are these daughters' reactions. They are explored in great detail so that you can understand how they work and why. Even if they apply to you only somewhat, you will find information that is crucial to help you see yourself more clearly in relation to your mother.

Once you get a fix on the childhood coping skills that apply to you, and how they show up in your adult life, you can start the process of letting them go. You can begin to understand and be kind to the child in you so that she can grow up.

Understanding these coping mechanisms does not make you a disloyal daughter. These portraits are not intended to be used as a means to punish your mother. Rather, they will help you to *understand and accept her.*

For just as you needed a "false self" to get through your childhood, *so did your mother.* A profound awareness of that helps get rid of the need to blame her and be forever angry with her.

For many daughters, that understanding may pave the way to a renewed relationship with their mothers, one of mutual respect and affection. For other daughters, who have been brutalized psychologically or physically, it will enable them to reach a separate peace.

These ways of adapting to mother—these survival mechanisms—are the subjects of the next five chapters.

11
The Angel

Something always made me go back to my mother. It was like an addiction. Nothing I did to please her worked—she'd use it as a reason to attack. When I was forgiving and understanding, she'd accuse me of being holier-than-thou. But still, I dutifully called her every week. And on those rare occasions when she'd call me, I'd be so elated. I'd think, "Gee, she loves me after all."

—Ellen, thirty-eight

Every daughter starts out as an Angel. For if Mommy is happy—smiling at us, feeding and caring for us, being tender and loving and consoling—then the child will want to keep her happy. Being a good girl has enormous rewards.

And not being good has terrible consequences: If I'm *not* good, I will be abandoned. Well, perhaps not literally. But when Mommy yells, or doesn't come when a child cries, or shrugs us off when she's irritated, it is a kind of abandonment. And if Mommy *hits*, there is no doubt—the child believes she has done something terribly wrong and will pay heavily for it.

So she tries ever *harder* to be a good little girl. She may even become *angelic*.

The Angel is the best little girl of all. Partly this is a learned response to being a woman-in-training. Much of the world has always preferred its females to be submissive, to be the all-forgiving peacekeepers, to be their mother's loyal ally and mirror image.

"The 'best little girl' role is easy to learn," writes Dr. Louise J.

183

Kaplan, "if one is intelligent, if one is not too aggressive . . . if one is fairly adept at reading what one's audience wants and then mirroring it back. The rules . . . are relatively simple. One looks into the other's face and emulates what one is supposed to be."

And partly it is the Angel's natural temperament to be so very good. Generally she is an unusually empathetic sort and realizes that something is missing in her relationship with her mother. The Angel will fix it by being ideal.

That's why being the best little girl in the world, *and having it not be good enough*, is so wrenching.

Mommy's Best Friend

In most cases, the Angel is a firstborn or eldest girl, or an only child, enjoying the glory, and taking the heat, of her rank. When her mother is loving, the Angel gets the fullest, undivided measure of her devotion. And when her mother is remote, jealous, or cruel, the Angel gets her mother's unalloyed displeasure. Firstborns are often punished more severely, and at an earlier age, than their siblings.

These Angels take their "jobs" very seriously. Since they have nowhere to hide—most of them have passive fathers who seldom take their part, and all lack an older sibling's comforting arms—they have no alternative but to take up the cudgel of their mothers' expectations.

Angels are the standard-bearers of the family's younger generation and are burdened with enormous responsibilities: Do well in school, don't get into trouble, set an example for your brothers and sisters. And the biggest responsibilities are these: *Be there when Mommy needs you* and *Don't bring Mommy any bad news.*

Angels abide by these rules. Says one woman,

> I always felt that I had to hold everything together, saying to my younger sister, "Hey, be nice to Mom." The highest praise my mother ever gave me was, "You did that almost as well as I could." Once she threw away all my school papers. Anything that gave you any feeling of self or self-worth, she destroyed. But I never got mad at her. As a kid, I was convinced in my head, without ever discussing it with anyone, that mothers are allowed to do that. You didn't like it, but you would never get mad. There were many times when I asked

myself, "Why does she hate me?" But I don't think I
ever said, "Now I have to take another path." I crawled
after her trying to win her love until the day she died.

The Angel may be good, but she is never a "girl"—never even a
"child." She is a good little *grown-up*, a miniature mommy.

Psychologist Robert Wright has written that for "good" children,
the "good" part really means being adult-oriented, believing Mom's
beliefs, meeting Mom's needs, reaching Mom's standards. As long
as the Angel is mother's most dependable little helper, the daughter
is seduced into thinking that she is really being loved.

In fact, she is often merely being used.

Tina is a thirty-four-year-old music teacher. An only child, in her
youth she epitomized the Angel. When her mother had company,
Tina would give up her evenings, even on weekends, to prepare and
serve dinner. Her mother's guests—although not her mother—would
praise her for being such a good daughter.

"It never occurred to me that I was being exploited," Tina says.
"You must understand that I never resented being a good girl when
I was growing up. *Never*. It gave me pleasure, because I was happy
believing I was making my mother happy."

In ways, the Angel is the junior version of the Smotherer: she
does "the feeling work" for her mother, interpreting her moods,
anticipating what will gratify her—or at least dampen her irritation—
and providing it. The Angel tries to jolly her siblings into "making
nice"—she even runs interference for Mom with Dad. Angels
are always scurrying to keep the home fires from burning out of
control.

Erica, the twenty-eight-year-old daughter of a Doormat, felt responsible for her mother's happiness as far back as she can remember. She says,

> I felt burdened, but honored to be burdened. I remem-
> ber when I was six doing little things for her, like
> hiding bobby pins and a comb from my sister, who
> would have taken them from my mother. I didn't see
> that it was my mother's responsibility to say no to my
> sister. I saw that she couldn't do that for herself, that if
> my sister took her things, she would have to do with-
> out. She was willing to do without. I was not willing for
> her to do without.

Liz, thirty-three, recalls that her parents fought constantly, and she took it upon herself to be the Good Mommy to everyone. On Sunday mornings, her parents usually were hung over from drinking the night before. Liz would get up early and make her brothers pancakes, then take them to the park. She had chronic tonsillitis but never said anything to her mother because, she says, "I didn't want to upset her. Eventually it got so bad that I *had* to tell her. But I was more concerned about her getting angry with me for complaining than I was about the pain."

Why Does the Angel Try So Hard?

Most mothers feel a degree of ambivalence toward their daughters. In the process of helping their daughters to move out into the world, and at the same time longing to have them close, they both push and pull, and give mixed messages. But the mothers we are talking about are extremes of ambivalence, whether it is expressed by their own excessive neediness or their thunderous rage.

Their daughters' reactions are, if anything, *more* extreme; as children, they are defenseless, and their survival depends on their trying to win Mommy over.

Some daughters, as we will see in the next four chapters, ultimately decide to give up the good-girl role and instead become variations of "the bad girl." Because of family circumstances, their mothers' temperaments, and their own personalities, they take a different route from their saintly sisters.

But the Angel hangs in with her everlasting sympathy for her mother, far more often, and for far longer, than do her siblings. Because nurturing is what the Angel does best.

Some daughters become Angels because Mommy is little more than a child herself. Says the daughter of a Doormat, "My mother was too frightened to deal with life. So she left it to me to take care of everything. I was much more capable than she was. When I was a teenager, I knew all the financial problems and I handled the money. I was mother to my mother."

Other Angels are enslaved by the hope that their unpleasant mothers will appreciate their goodness, and are haunted by the gut feeling that it will never happen. Says the daughter of an Avenger,

> Sometimes my mother would be friendly. And then—
> *snap!*—she would turn it off, and I'd think, "What did I

do?" She was almost schizophrenic in the sense of her two personalities. The turn-off personality was much more prevalent than the turn-on personality. It was like a switch. *Snap.* Off it went. So I knew, from a very young age, what I was dealing with. I knew I wouldn't get anywhere. But I tried for a very long time. You don't have any choice when you're a child.

The tragic flaw in the Angel's survival mechanism is that the very thing she seeks by her good behavior—closeness—is often the very thing that makes her mother recoil. The Angel is not merely imagining that her mother doesn't love her enough. There is something about the Angel that, indeed, does turn her mother off like a switch: It is that while the mother may love *servitude,* she often hates *dependency.*

Says another Angel, "My mother will not do anything for anyone. You do not ask her for a favor. When you act needy, she runs. If anybody shows dependence on her, *anybody*—children, friends, husband—she bolts."

At the same time, if the Angel is All Good, how then can her mother be the *most* "perfect"? The mother cannot allow her daughter to outshine her in saintliness, cannot permit a comparison wherein Mommy doesn't measure up to her *child's* goodness. She must keep her daughter not good enough.

But the Angel doesn't get it: she redoubles her efforts to please, becoming her mother's most ardent supporter and feverish servant. And the more Mommy withdraws, the more effort the Angel exerts, justifying her good deeds. Otherwise, it would all be such a waste.

Protecting Mommy

For the Angel, Mother can do no wrong, or if she does, she must have a very good reason for it.

The Angel's urgent mission is to protect her mother—from upset, from pain, from anxiety. She *especially* must protect *herself* from an awareness of Mother's faults. Because if the Bad Mommy were unmasked, the Angel would feel as though she had lost her purpose. The Angel makes endless and elaborate excuses for her mother, understanding her relentlessly.

Says Dr. Marianne Goodman,

If you are concerned about your mother, if you want her to be happy, if you are distressed when she is distressed, that's normal empathy. There's nothing wrong with being concerned about somebody else—it's a question of how much you let it interfere with your own life. I saw someone recently who literally has so identified with her mother that she has systematically thwarted her own advancement. It's not because she respects her or even likes her—she really doesn't. It's because of her own guilt at being *more* than her mother.

That's neurotic.

When the Angel is growing up, she is too young to understand the bargain she has struck, or its consequences: She gives up herself to gain her mother's love.

But often she *very well understands*, if only on an instinctive level, that there is something that feels phony about her good-girl role—she feels as though she were performing a tap dance, doing her "routine." As the the daughter of a Smotherer put it, "I knew exactly what it took to get the good stuff. You become something of a liar—you're not doing what is natural to you. I became very manipulative."

Says Gloria, a thirty-nine-year-old Angel whose mother is a Critic,

> I was a virgin until I was thirty, when I got married. I had this sense that I was not going to be tainted. I kept myself—not only the sexual me, but the me in general—apart from the rest of the world. As much as I always berated myself and had terrible insecurities, at the same time I always put myself up on this pedestal where I was separate and apart and better than other people. I was Gloria the Perfect.

This is the Angel's false self in operation. She pushes the "good" button and out pops the perfect child. The trouble is, by placing her mother's needs over her own, the Angel becomes her mother's accomplice in her own servitude. And to protect herself from that awful, mortifying awareness, she buries it. She is loath to consider the possibility that being good is at her own expense. Far from blaming her mother for her inadequacies, the Angel blames herself.

There is no denial like an Angel's denial. Says psychotherapist Ann Gordon,

When a client shows up in my office with her life in a shambles, at the same time claiming she had a wonderfully happy childhood, I suspect that claim represents a strong defense against fear and guilt. She learned well and early never to criticize Mommy. It takes a strong transference of trust to the therapist to dare to admit that there was something amiss in her childhood.

As we saw earlier, the mother exploits the Angel to gain for herself what she lost in childhood—her own mother's unconditional love. Now, at last, she will extract from her Angel a sense of worth. It is a worth that needs constant attention, and the Angel is on perpetual duty. Consequently, the mother's bad behavior is reinforced.

But if Mommy can do no wrong, neither, in adulthood, can the Angel, who finds it nearly impossible to apologize, because it rekindles her childhood humiliations and reminds her of the degradation of denying her own instincts and needs.

"The one thing I cannot do is say, 'I'm sorry,'" one Angel told me, "not to my children, not to anyone. To apologize is an admission that I'm not perfect. I can't do it."

Identifying with the Aggressor

The Angel believes that the only way she can survive is to serve her mother. This coping mechanism is called "identifying with the aggressor." As we know from people who join cults as well as from victims of terrorism and prisoners of war, when your survival depends on pleasing the person who has complete power over you, it is a matter of life and death to be nice. Since you cannot fight or flee, you comply. To do this without going mad, you have to believe that the aggressor is right and has good reasons for her behavior.

Angels identify with the aggressor—Mom—to protect themselves, and everyone else, in the family: Mommy gets reassured that she is a good mommy, or at least a morally correct one.

Angels have a huge stake in keeping Mommy "right," even when Mommy is consummately "wrong." This is anguishingly true of Angels who are the firstborn children of abusive parents: it was their Angelic role that provided them with the best, and the worst, of their nightmarish childhoods.

The worst was that they took their parents' most venomous emotional and physical blows, because they were first in line for their parents' uncontrolled frustration and anger.

Says one woman, "If my brothers were fighting, I'd think, 'I have to do something to stop this because they're going to get a beating.' I was not just responsible for keeping *myself* from getting hit by being good, I was responsible for *their* being good, too."

But the "best" of these childhoods (a term used solely for its relativity in these dreadful circumstances) was that they also had an urgent mission not just to focus on their own survival but also to save their siblings. One woman, the eldest of five children of alcoholic parents, told me,

> Part of the reason I survived is that I knew I had to keep my sanity for my brothers and sisters. When my parents would have screaming fights, the kids would end up in my bed, hiding. I went to all the parent–teacher meetings, got them through religious education. When I was in high school, if one of them needed surgery, it was me who took them to the hospital.
>
> I wanted to give them attention so they could have halfway normal childhoods, so they could talk about their lives. Nurturing them kept me in this world.

But the prematurely wise Angel required more than her "mothering" to be able to sustain her role: She also had to idealize her mother in an anguishing suspension of disbelief. Said another Angel of abuse, "I took care of my mother, and she loved it. I'd have these fantasies that, deep down, she really was wonderful, that she'd come to her senses and beg my forgiveness. She'd make up for everything. That fantasy kept me going."

For some Angels, their frantic efforts to make everything right and everyone good finally tips them into emotional overload—and so they begin to rebel, but only in ways that will not unravel their ties to Mother.

"Safe" Rebellions

Some Angels see their "goodness" as their rebellion. "I could keep my mother away," says the daughter of an Avenger, "by being the perfect child. It helped me to emotionally distance myself. I'd jump up after dinner and immediately do the dishes—that way, I could stay in the kitchen, away from her."

Later in life, other Angels rebel by having extramarital affairs. One Angel I interviewed, the daughter of a Smotherer, said that being a "good girl" kept her married to her domineering husband for nineteen years. The only thing she did in all that time that made her feel any sense of autonomy was to sleep with a man she met on a business trip. She says,

> My mother didn't know about it. She certainly wouldn't have approved of it. It had a kind of flair to it. You almost had to do something illicit for it to be your own. That was one thing she couldn't take over and make hers.

But for still other Angels, their rebellions were far more damaging. Because in their need to keep Mommy All Good, they took on her "badness" and resolved it by getting sick. "I showed *her*," jokes one Angel about her mother, "I got shingles." For these Angels, their illnesses are their rebellions.

Lucy, forty-three, a dental hygienist who lives in Houston, is an only child whose parents have retired to Florida. Her mother is a Doormat, and Lucy feels the dull ache of guilt about living so far from her. It is an ache that she tolerates in her awareness of what it would mean if she lived next door, because she remembers what her childhood was like.

> When I was growing up, the overwhelming feeling was "How am I doing? How am I doing?" I felt this awful frustration of trying to be perfect and not getting there. I felt so merged with her that I thought to be less than the best would kill her. She thought of me as almost a physical extension of herself. My body was her object. I discovered how to control it—by not eating.

The conventional wisdom about eating disorders—the overwhelming majority of whose victims are female—is that the good girl is dominated by an exacting and controlling mother. The daughter responds by trying to be supergood. Unable to achieve perfection—which no person can do—in her desperation she tries to regain a measure of control over her life by tyrannizing her own body.

Kim Chernin offers another view. She writes that "the woman afflicted with this obsession cannot forgive herself for having damaged her mother in earliest childhood. Consequently, [the daughter] cannot allow herself to move into the next stages of development, to turn her back on the older woman and leave her behind to the depletion and exhaustion she believes she has inflicted upon her. . . . *An eating obsession comes into existence so that the need, rage, and violence of the mother/daughter bond can be played out in a symbolic form that spares the mother"* (emphasis added).

Other Angels "rebel" by developing mental disorders. In extreme cases, the mother is *so destructive,* and the Angel is so psychologically fragile, that the Angel will be unable to avoid the evidence of her mother's cruel behavior. So she protects herself from it by having a nervous breakdown. This was true of four of the Angels I interviewed, all of whom had Avenger mothers.

Vulnerable Angels are made more so, according to some scientific research, by an inherent chemical imbalance. Such vulnerability can be pushed past the breaking point by mothers who won't let up in their domination or who drain their highly sensitive daughters of all their emotional reserves.

The *most* vulnerable Angel can become psychotic. Indeed, it is the psychotic who most needs to keep her mother perfect, as though serving a sentence for her mother's mistakes. There is no sense of "Here's where my mother ends and I begin." In the child, this is called "symbiotic psychosis." In the adult, it is called "schizophrenia."

The mere *idea* of real separation terrifies the psychotic Angel, who needs to be almost literally attached to her mother. Rather than face her mother's destructiveness, the Angel instead disengages from reality.

Only with a lot of help can the Angel give up her idealization of her mother, taking the good parts of Mom and coming to terms with the bad. Only then can the Angel decide how far she is willing to go in her emulation, and how willing she is to become a separate individual with a mind of her own—perhaps resembling her mother in some ways, but without becoming her mother's clone.

But the Angel who has not resolved her relationship with her mother continues to need her mother to need her. By seeing the world only through her mother's eyes, she sacrifices her true self.

If she can begin to recognize how much her sacrifices have cost her, the Angel will eventually be able to forgive herself, or her children, or her friends, for being imperfect—for being human. Then she will be able to accept her mother for who she really is—neither saint nor devil but a person who is somewhere in between.

But until then, her unresolved attachment will spill over into all her other relationships. She will maintain her Angelic role with siblings, friends, lovers, spouses, business associates, and her own children, trying to be loved for being such a good girl. She will be stuck in a pattern of forever wearing her party manners.

The Angelic Sister

It is usually the firstborn Angel who profits from her mother's favoritism. She has cornered the market on whatever goodwill her mother has to dispense, which encourages her to be *righteous*. The Angel is held up as the yardstick of virtue against which her siblings must measure themselves.

And the more angelic she is, the badder they become. By her oppressive goodness, she often jeopardizes her relationships with them. At special risk is her relationship with her younger sister—her gender and generational peer. George Bernard Shaw once observed, "There is only one person [a] girl hates more than she hates her eldest sister; and that's her mother."

Because it is her job to protect Mom, and to guard her special role as ranking member of the family's junior division, she often will not allow her siblings to vent any of their own frustrations.

Hers is the great cover-up: "You mustn't say that," she will chide a younger sister who wails that her mother is mean. "Mommy really loves you." And when the sisters are older, the protective beat goes on: big sister defends Mom, little sister gets angry and increasingly in trouble.

Angels and their sisters often end up hating each other—the Angel because her sister isn't being nicer to Mom, the younger sister because the Angel will not acknowledge her angry feelings.

Phyllis, thirty-nine, and Yvonne, thirty-six, the daughters of an Avenger, have never been close. "It's because Yvonne and my mother don't get along," says Phyllis, the Angel. "She always blames Mom for everything that's gone wrong in her life. My mother's a widow, she's getting on in years, and yet Yvonne can't forgive her for her childhood. She says it was horrendous—I don't see it that way. Mom did the best she could. She never meant any harm. My mother says Yvonne isn't capable of loving *anyone*. I'm beginning to think she's right."

Ever since Phyllis's father died six years ago, the family has gathered at her house for Thanksgiving. But last fall, Phyllis called

Yvonne and said, "I think it would be better if you didn't come. It's supposed to be a happy day, and it won't be if you and Mom are together. You and I can see each other another time."

Although the two sisters have not spoken since then, Phyllis suggested that I interview Yvonne and gave me her phone number. Yvonne was eager to share her version of her mother and sister.

Unlike Phyllis, Yvonne has always been her mother's scapegoat. In her childhood her mother humilated her in front of people ("You never get *anything* right"), compared her negatively to her angelic sister ("Thank God I have Phyllis"), and rarely came to her defense ("You brought this on yourself").

Says Yvonne,

> Phyllis has always been the perfect daughter. She knows about my mother's unending criticisms of me, but she blots them out. All she can see is how "good" my mother is, not how evil she is. My mother exploits Phyllis horribly. I feel sorry for my sister—she's pathetic in her need to constantly defend my mother, who is hardly defenseless. It's screwed up all her priorities.

When Yvonne was in the hospital giving birth to her son, she required a blood transfusion, which nearly killed her because of an accident in cross-typing. But when Phyllis called her, although she knew about her sister's brush with death, she didn't ask about Yvonne or the newborn. Instead, she pleaded, "You've got to ask Mom to come help you with the baby. If you don't, she'll think you're rejecting her."

Yvonne, who has had many years of therapy, tried to form a separate relationship with Phyllis. But for Phyllis, Yvonne had to make a choice: Love mother, or you and I cannot be friends.

Says Yvonne, "I never asked my sister to choose between Mom and me; but for her own peace of mind, she has made that choice. My mother has won. And I have lost my sister."

Warring siblings often resolve their differences in their adulthood when they have both acquired enough mileage from their childhood struggles to face the true source of their friction: the manipulating parent. But many Angels persist throughout their lives, even long after their mothers' deaths, in keeping Mom's favoritism alive in their quarrels with their siblings. Anger is a powerful mortar in the mother–daughter bond (it works for "bad" siblings too, as we will see in Chapter Fourteen): in the Angel's case, anger toward a sibling keeps Mom perfect.

The Angel at Work

The "good girl" in childhood often becomes a ministering Angel in her work. Many Angels work in the helping professions—they become nurses, physicians, teachers, physical and psychological therapists. In a sense, these are professions for which Angels have always been in training.

Employers generally treasure—and often exploit—the Angel, because she will work overtime without complaint, listen to her co-worker's marital troubles, tolerate her boss's tirades, and soothe his or her nerves.

On the surface, Angels are extremely competent. But inside, they tremble. Says Ethel, "When my boss calls me into his office, my first instinctive reaction is 'What did I do wrong?' I automatically make the assumption that I'm in trouble."

Genevieve, a pediatrician, is driven by the need to do her job *perfectly*. "I'm a very good doctor," she says. "But I'm always afraid if one of my patients get worse that it *must* be my fault and that I've missed something. I lie awake nights worrying about it."

But the most insecure Angels do not want to achieve *too much*. And so they hold themselves back from professional advancement. One Angel told me, "I have always tried to make myself available to my mother in case she needed me. To be ambitious meant that I wouldn't be available to her. So I sabotaged my career, passing up promotions that would take up too much of my time."

Said another, "I always bring myself to the brink of success. But then something happens to me. I panic that I won't be able to do it. So either I turn a promotion down, or I leave."

The Angelic Friend

Angels often make wonderful friends, either because they know how to placate the "prickly" pal, or because they are drawn to people who are needier than they are.

Some Angels find themselves being manipulated by domineering women. "I get myself into these inappropriate relationships," one Angel said, "because I don't know how to set limits. I let those women get away with a lot because I'm still trying to be so nice."

But other Angels feel secure only with friends who seem to be weaker than they are. Cynthia has never looked for friends who will nurture her; she looks for friends for whom she can be the Good Mommy. "I always knew what I had to do for my mother," she says, "and I always know what I have to do for friends."

Whether docile or maternal, often the Angel will reach the point where she feels she is being used and will pull back from her attachments. Says one woman, who is in therapy,

> I used to befriend women who were terribly dependent on me, and then I would be furious when I was taken advantage of. The past couple of years I got rid of a couple of friends who were like that. I realized that I was just getting my kicks out of feeling that I was taking care of them. But I didn't really *like* them.

The good girl who has not resolved her conflicts with her mother frequently loses friends through her rigid purity, her relentless insistence that she alone is All Good.

And since her mother is usually her best—and often only—friend, she frequently is not terribly concerned when her friendships end. After all, she has her mother, and who needs her more than her mother?

The Angel in Love

The Angel often marries young, or has a steady romantic partnership, in the *illusion* of separation from mother. What she does is replicate her daughterly role in her new, intimate relationship. She may be aware of the tensions she feels with her mother, but she avoids dealing with them by putting her emotional eggs into another basket.

The Angel brings her fears of being "wrong" to her love life, trying to be the "good wife" or "good partner" so that she either will not have to relive the anguish of being a not good enough child, or lose the fantasy that she is perfect. But in those relationships she often finds her mother anew, someone who will allow her to pursue *his* happiness rather than her own.

One Angel I interviewed, the mother of three children, laments her marriage, but in terms that are couched in her Angelic, peacekeeping role, as though suffering were her heaven-ordained destiny. She says,

> My husband is a wonderful man—he has a big heart, is a good provider. But he's not good with the kids. He takes care of their wants, but not their needs. He doesn't have a lot of patience. He's like my mother in that if you rile him up—which isn't often—you run for cover. So we don't make him mad. My kids and I laugh about his tantrums. But we stay out of his way. I have to deal with everything myself—I am father and mother to my kids, like I was to my brothers when I was growing up. I love my husband, but I see a lot of things I wish I could change.
>
> You can't change someone; you have to accept them or not. And of course, as with everything else in my life, I've chosen to cope.

Alice, the daughter of a Smotherer, also married her mother's clone—but she did it deliberately.

> I adored my father—he was a sweet, gentle man. And I figured out at seventeen that if I married someone like him, I'd end up being like my mother, and that's the *last* thing I wanted to do. So I married someone *like* her so that I'd have no chance of *being* like her. My husband was so like her, he even told me what to wear. The trouble was that it continued my childhood. I went straight from living with my mother to living with him, trying to placate them both.

Seeing only the good kept Lana, a nursery school teacher, in a disastrous love affair for three years. She says,

> My boyfriend was very needy and insecure, just like my mother. He fed my need to be "mommy." He was a drug user, and I didn't want to know it. I couldn't face the fact that I had made a mistake of incalculable enormity. People like me—people who do all the "right" things—don't get involved with junkies. But I did. I

made excuses for him. I believed him when he said he was taking medicine for allergies—he was really using cocaine. I denied his addiction, until he finally got busted and I woke up—and left him.

As for those Angels who have "got it right" in their choice of partners, they are haunted by the feeling that it will all go away. "I keep waiting for it to end," says one such Angel. "I keep thinking, 'You don't get this for nothing. You're going to have to pay your dues. You're so happy now, someday you're going to lose it all.' I still have the feeling that if I'm not a good girl, I won't be loved. It's hard to keep that up all the time."

The Angel as Mother

Many Angels become Smotherers to their children, and often they are able to recognize that their need to be "good," to make their children "ideally happy," is preventing their kids from being themselves.

One Angel, the daughter of a Critic, who has gotten in touch with her angry feelings toward her mother, summed up her determination not to duplicate her mother's mistakes:

> Those of us who have always been in the service of our mothers know the pitfalls. We're afraid of falling into them. That was my big fear with my kids. Every time I found myself doing something that was faintly reminiscent of my mother, I felt like slitting my wrists. The horrifying mask before me was the mask of being that woman.

Her determination paid off—she has helped her daughters feel good about themselves as women and not, as she puts it, "for being little puppets. If nothing else, I think I've been successful at that."

But other Angels, who have not resolved their childhood legacies, try so hard to be perfect mothers that they develop a kind of maternal stage fright: they weigh every word with their children. As one woman joked, "I do a lot of opening and closing my mouth, trying to find the right words to say. I look like a guppy. And my kids shout, *'What! Say something!'* "

Other Angels fall somewhere between the Smotherer and the

Critic in their parenting. They give the impression of goodness in their mothering by being dutiful, but they are somewhat distant. To find a flaw in their child feels to them like finding a terrible flaw in themselves, so they don't get too close.

For those Angels, their denial of their own "badness," or their children's troubles, can have tragic consequences.

Two years ago, Marietta, forty, a hospital administrator, would have said that she had had the perfect childhood and that she had the perfect marriage and family. Her husband coached Little League, and she taught Sunday School. "We were all considered pillars of the community," she says.

But then her teenage daughter attempted suicide. Says Marietta,

> I never saw the signs, and *I'm in the business of seeing the signs*. I still didn't make the connection that it had anything to do with me. The only thing I thought was "This doesn't happen to people like me." It's forced me to look back at my own childhood. I was brought up in a strict home, and we were never allowed to talk about anything serious. No one was ever angry. I had this delusion that everything was wonderful. It's taken me a long time to understand how closed off I was from my own feelings, so much so that I never really could hear my daughter's pain. Being able to face her pain means that I have to face my own. I'm having a very, very hard time with it.

This is an example of triangular destinies at their most devastating. For while an Angel may be able to squelch her instincts, keeping her true self locked away, in some cases her hidden vulnerabilities will become a loose cannon in her children; hence the folk wisdom that personalities "skip a generation."

But some Angels, usually the daughters of Avengers or Deserters, are occasionally ambushed by their own repressed rage. These Angels are closet Avengers. Their denial of their humiliations creates a buildup of anger at having to be a "false self."

One Angel I talked to has a temper—a trait, she says, that is an echo of her Avenger mother. In her childhood, her mother was always threatening to abandon her if she wasn't good. She says,

> I vowed I would never say that to my kids, but I broke that vow. We were on vacation, and I yelled at my

daughter, "If you don't behave, I'm going to leave you here when we go home." As soon as the words came out of my mouth I said, "I didn't mean it. Mommy would never do that. When you see Mommy get angry, you just run away. Go to your room, or tell Mommy, 'You're acting crazy.' " But that's a lot to ask of her—she's only five. I'm a happy person. I have everything—a loving husband, a beautiful child. I have more than I ever felt I deserved. And still I can be provoked to the point of wanting to throw my kid out the window. My temper terrifies me.

Profile of an Angel

For most of her life, Judith, fifty-eight, never gave up the fantasy that her Critic mother would one day love and approve of her: hope, she says, kept her "in a kind of lockup."

An only child, she grew up in Milwaukee. Her father was a high school math teacher, and her mother a housewife. Both were observant Jews and never missed a Sabbath service. Her mother maintained a strict kosher household, and Judith was discouraged from playing with the Christian children who lived on the block.

Judith was always an obedient and hardworking child, pulling straight A's in school, helping her mother prepare special Friday night dinners, attending Hebrew school for eight years.

She went to Northwestern and graduated from the School of Journalism, returning home to work as a reporter for a local newspaper. Every Friday she had dinner and went to services with her parents. Judith's only rebellion—and it was a beaut, nearly severing her relationship with her parents—was to marry a Methodist, a lawyer whose name is Tom. But since he was attentive to Judith's parents, and agreed to bring up their children as Jews—and since Judith was their only child—her parents got over her one mistake. Still, they were always frosty to him.

Judith stayed home to raise her two sons, but kept her writing career going by becoming a novelist, work she could pursue at night and on weekends. She has written eight novels, books that always get glowing reviews, if only fair sales.

Any lingering resentment Judith's mother may have harbored about her daughter's choice of husband dissipated when, twelve years ago, Judith's father died and Tom invited her to come live with them.

Once their own children had grown, Tom and Judith had moved into a one-bedroom apartment. But it was too small for three adults, so they built a new house that was tailored to the specifications Judith's mother had listed as conditions for her living with them.

The house had a suite with its own kitchen so she "wouldn't be a burden." It was near a synagogue so she could "walk to services." It was near a bus stop, so she could have her "independence" and be able to take the short ride back to her old neighborhood to see her friends.

But life with mother didn't turn out that way.

She never did take the bus back to the old neighborhood, not once. Judith would collect her mother's friends and bring them home to an elaborate lunch, until her mother tired of seeing them. She would offer to take her mother to temple, and her mother always refused to go. She'd invite her mother to join her at her dinner parties, and her mother would say, "I'd just bore your friends."

"All she did for twelve years was sit on a chair in her living room and stare out the window," Judith says.

And then, a year ago, her mother's crippling arthritis made it necessary for her to be moved into a nursing home. Says Judith,

> My mother told me she's happier there than she's been in years. Did I resent her saying that? How could I? What had she ever done that was so terrible? "I won't bother you," she'd say, and she didn't. She just made me crazy. I think there's something *seriously* wrong with me that I never had a confrontation with her. I'm mad that I spent all those years doing everything I thought was possible, and a lot that wasn't, to make this woman comfortable and happy and unworried and carefree. Because it didn't work.

The residue of that wasted effort is that Judith has been blocked in her work ever since her mother moved out. She's certain that her talent has dried up, and with it her ability to take on new literary challenges. Learning to put herself first, as she approaches sixty, cuts against the grain of five decades of self-sacrifice. She feels as though, emotionally, she's had to learn how to walk all over again.

Two weeks after her mother left, Judith took her first baby step toward her adjustment to life without Mama: She bought an ivy plant. "It was like a debut," she says, "because my mother always said that ivy was bad luck."

What terrifies Judith most is that the anger she feels at her mother, and at herself, has begun to seep into her awareness. Her paralysis in her work is a metaphor for her emotional paralysis: holding back the anger is like holding back an ocean. These days, it's all she can do to get out of bed, after a lifetime of energy and good deeds.

Judith has never had therapy, and is not considering it. I ask her what she'll do with all that anger. "Paint the house?" she replies, smiling wanly.

Her smile dissolves and she stares at the floor. Finally, with no self-pity—just a sense of wonder—in her voice, she adds.

> I thought I would feel immense and immediate relief when she moved out, and no guilt because I had done more than my share. What I feel is empty. It was all for nothing.

12
The Superachiever

People tell me my mother brags about me, but I never hear any praise from her. My success makes her look good, but she's extremely jealous of it. Her envy drove me. I was going to show her that I could succeed in spite of her. And I have. But I also have this total, constant insecurity, which most people meeting me for the first time would be shocked to know.
— Katherine, forty-two

Go ahead. Make Mandy's day. Ask her what she does for a living. "I'm an astronaut!" she shouts. Well, she's not quite that yet—she's a physicist who is training for a future space shuttle.

Mandy got her doctorate when she was twenty-nine. That she was able to pull it off with a husband and two young children amazes her still. True to Superachiever form, she chose the most challenging goal she could find. Why?

I had to prove something to myself, that I really was worth something. It wasn't enough for me to just say that I matter as a human being. I had to have some extrinsic proof of it.

I can hold up my degree and *show* you that I'm worth something. Which, I realize, is saying that I'm not really worth a hell of a lot.

Still, everyone out there doesn't know that. I get a thrill out of going to a party and having someone say, "And what do you do, my dear?" I have to clench my jaw muscles because it's all I can do not to scream with joy when I tell them. I can't describe how much that means to me. And when *men* ask, I swoon.

For the Superachiever, being anything less than the brightest and best means being the worst. Success represents far more to her than just money: It means

- a visa out of a no-win childhood;
- a buffer from the internalized messages of her mother's disfavor;
- a hedge against emotional deflation.

Of the five categories of daughters in this book, this is the smallest. Mega-success has always exalted that minority of men who are blessed with the ability to focus, fierce tenacity, great intelligence, and even greater egos.

But for *women* who today are in their thirties and forties, being catapulted to the top is extraordinary, because they were raised with the tandem messages of traditional femininity and feminism. For them to be a success in a man's world indeed required true grit.

Superachievers are *defiant*, having blazed new trails with few female role models. It is a defiance that has smoldered since childhood. What better way to get back at the all-consuming, never-pleased, hypercritical mother than to outdo her, and to outdistance even the *father?*

And what does the Superachiever really have to lose? Most of the Superachievers I interviewed have mothers who were Critics, Avengers, or Deserters. Feminine "closeness" was not a part of their experience. If being successful meant losing the "female" goodies of intimacy and attachment, they were ahead of the game, never having had much of either.

If some Superachievers seem flinty, it is because they had to play hardball in the family to survive. These women doped out their destinies long before Betty Friedan's *The Feminine Mystique*—the instruction manual of female ambition—provided them with the cultural permission to achieve in a man's world, and long before books such as Sherry Suib Cohen's *Tender Power* extolled the value of using their innate nurturing abilities in the working world.

One woman, the daughter of a Critic, voiced the *sheer will* of her

Superachieving peers this way: "My foxhole prayer when I was a kid was simple: As God is my witness, I'll be mistress of my own fate."

Don't Tread on Me

Superachievers decide, often at a very early age, that they are not going to be outdone or trampled upon. And the greater their child-hood deprivations, the harder they struggle to reach the top and stay up there.

Sylvia grew up the eldest of four children whose mother punished their misdemeanors with terror and humiliation. But their mother saved her purest rage for Sylvia, her only daughter. She says,

> My younger brothers learned that the sooner they sobbed and begged her forgiveness, the sooner she'd leave them alone. But I couldn't. *I just couldn't.* I remember thinking at the age of six, "Don't cry. Don't let her get you down." That's why I'm a success. Nothing, *especially* not my mother, was going to get me down.

Most, but not all, Superachievers are only children, or firstborn daughters. If she has an older sister, the "good girl" role has already been staked out. Big Angel gets Mom's favoritism and allegiance, so little Achiever charts a clear path to goodies outside the family. But that usually comes later. Because, like the Angel, she spends much of her early childhood being polite and obedient.

Somewhere along the line, however, the Superachiever makes the vow to get some recognition elsewhere rather than stay close to home, close to Mom. And the way out takes hard work, guts, and brains.

Making It in a Man's World

Superachievers tend to identify with men and male measures of success rather than traditional female ones. It isn't that they wish they were men. Rather, they want to be *as good as* men in the work world, because *there* it is usually men, rather than women, who have the power to make things happen and to be in control. The Superachiever would rather die than be vulnerable or dependent.

Several of the Superachievers I talked to had fathers who took a special interest in them.

Thelma, the daughter of a Critic, is an executive vice-president of a large New York advertising agency. She traces her success to both her mother's "indifference" and her father's belief in her. She says,

> My father admired my ability to take care of myself, something my mother fostered by ignoring me. He said, "You can be anything you want, because you have the intelligence and the discipline—not everyone does." I never wondered whether or not I was able, because he said I was.
>
> Recently my mother said she wished I'd sometimes ask her for advice. I said, "You wanted me to be independent—well, I am. You can't expect me to step backward. It doesn't work that way." She knew I was right.

A daughter's alliance with Dad, as we saw in Chapter Four, is not uncommon among the daughters of unpleasable mothers. Many daughters hear expressions of "faith" ("You can do it") either as encouragement of their abilities or as an unreachable standard not even to be attempted. But for the Superachiever, her father's interest—even if it's concern over the B that "should have been an A"—carries great weight, because it may be her only source of esteem and because she tends to idealize him.

Superachievers who don't have such cheerleading fathers are challenged, rather than defeated, by their mothers' certainty that the daughters are incapable. For these daughters, to have a mother say, "You'll never amount to anything," is like a match set to a firecracker: *Superachievers will prove their mothers wrong if it's the last thing they do.*

They remain attached to their mothers by their ambition—success is fueled by the hope that one day, if they work hard enough, their mothers will notice, and admire them.

"I was a failure every day in my mother's eyes," says one woman, a dean at an Ivy League college. "It made me obsessive. I never take a day off, even in the summer."

The Great Crusade

For these women, to fail to win recognition seems life-threatening: without it, they believe, they are nothing. To seek professional recognition and to *fail* is to experience a hideous sense of inadequacy and shame, which rekindles their childhood anguish. As Andrew Morrison, a psychiatrist at the Harvard Medical School, told a reporter, "A child's sense of not being affirmed or supported in his strivings leaves him feeling the world does not respond to him at all."

What propels Superachievers is anger, which, like a jet of water holding a ball aloft, prevents their sinking from the weight of their vulnerabilities.

Arlene is the president of a large retailing firm and sits on the boards of directors of several Fortune 500 companies. To the outside world, she is the epitome of gentle, unflappable wisdom, a non-threatening persona she has deftly composed as a disarming counterpoint to her burning ambition.

Her secret, she says, is her dread of falling back into her childhood patterns of supplication.

> I love to be angry. It courses through my body, it makes me feel alive. I draw strength from it. But I know that I need to use it positively to bring me the good things in life. If I use my anger negatively—if I blow my cork—I'm not going to accomplish anything. And my need in life is to accomplish.

Bonnie, forty-one, an Emmy award–winning television producer, is angry because "deep down, I think I'm a fraud." At twenty-two, Bonnie became a secretary for a network television news division, eventually working her way up to senior producer. She says,

> After five minutes with my mother, I want to kill her. She says all the right things, but there's always a rug to be pulled. Whatever I do isn't quite enough. My first on-air piece was a five-minute cut-in for the evening news. My mother said, "That was *wonderful*. But tell the family it was a half-hour documentary." So it isn't just that I want to be a success—it's that *I gotta be.* There's this spark of having to prove myself to her that enlivens me.

Lonely at the Top

Why doesn't success make the Superachiever feel good about herself? Because the timing is wrong. The Superachiever needed to feel "successful"—that is, acceptable—long ago when she was a young child. When her mother behaved in ways that said, "You don't count," the daughter had no defenses—she never developed the inner strength that leads to real autonomy and independence.

Sharon Wegscheider cites achievement as one of the survival mechanisms of children of alcoholics. The "Hero," her term for the striving child, leaves the family early in a fireball of ambition. But she is doomed to failure because her goal is to heal an injury to the family that is beyond her capacity to cure, rather than to express her talents and drive for herself.

The Superachiever senses, if only subconsciously, that it is her trophies that are loved in the family rather than herself. For some Superachievers, that awareness can cause them to burn out. Just as the Angel cannot say no to her mother's demands for devotion, the Superachiever cannot say no to a new opportunity, even if it stretches her to the breaking point. There is the panic of "I won't be asked again—I can't pass this up." Each achievement is one more brush with disaster.

Superachievers sometimes slip into depression or develop hypertension or ulcers because their appetite for achievement never gets satisfied—their self-confidence is too fragile, their self-doubt too punishing. Such daughters often are ravenous for praise, but it appeases their hunger only temporarily. For "grandiose" people, writes Dr. Alice Miller, "self-respect is dependent on qualities, functions, and achievements that can suddenly fail."

Each of the Superachiever's successes has a caveat, the fine print of her championship: She can never be as good as her mother wants her to be. And she *might* be as *bad* as she believes her mother thinks she really is. Says one woman, "People compliment me on all facets of my life, but I never believe them. It's like a shield I put up—everything, including praise, slides off."

The Superachiever's wounds are so deep that without help, she dares not slow her pace. Like a speedboat that skims over the ocean's surface, she races across the treacherous waters of her self-doubt. "I can never let up," one woman told me, "I can't imagine even being able to coast."

It is not surprising, then, to find that the Superachiever's delicate emotional underpinnings undermine all her attachments, beginning with her brothers and sisters.

The Pace-setting Sister

If the Angel enrages her siblings by her insufferable goodness, the Superachiever does so by her "winning" ways. She is held up as an example to which her brothers and sisters are compared, and compare themselves. Her mother may try to undermine her success, but finds that success quite useful in controlling her other children.

To make matters worse, the Superachiever may feel guilty for succeeding at her siblings' expense. She will be doubly chagrined if she outdistances her brother in school and, later, on the career track. Girls are supposed to be "inferior." Her feats not only reduce his portion of parental approval, but they also threaten his masculine "superiority." She may minimize her successes, or keep them secret from him. Still, she cannot lose sight of her goals, because in achieving them, she seeks salvation.

Some Superachievers, in spite of early sibling jealousies, become role models for their brothers and sisters. This is especially true in severely dysfunctional families, where children have a common enemy—their parents. For the children, when they are grown, money and awards may not buy love, but they "buy" everything else—at the very least, a real sense of purpose and freedom from the past. The Superachiever is proof to her siblings that there is a way to wrest balm for the soul from the outside world. And there's no mood elevator like success.

Says one woman, the eldest of three children,

> I was determined not to let anything hold me back, and my sisters fed from it. Maybe it was all that negativism that forced us *all* to say, "Goddammit, they're not going to get us. We're going to live." And so we all became successful.

But most Superachievers feel ambivalent about being "better" or "smarter" than their siblings. Unless parents are unusual in their capacity to make all their children feel good about their own ways of being—even if the kids are vying for the *same* things or are utterly indifferent to coming in first—the Superachiever almost always will feel that her abilities equate with being an outsider. And being an outsider feels alien to girls, for whom "belonging" and "relationship" are integral parts of being "female."

The Superachiever at Work

This sense of isolation haunts the Superachiever in her career. Most Superachievers who are firstborns or only children are used to the loneliness that accompanies their place in the junior division of the family hierarchy, having only had grown-ups for company—if they had company at all—when they were little. Since they had a head start in talking and getting their parents' undivided attention or scrutiny, they often had trouble being a "kid" with their peers.

But their very isolation helped them concentrate on how they would survive their childhood and what, later in life, they would do to find their place in the world.

Superachievers purchase their sense of self externally, hoping that their admirable achievements will sink in, like lotion on dry flesh, and replenish their lack of confidence.

For many of them, it works—but only if they pause occasionally to take stock of how much their superficial "worth" mirrors their self-image. Some of them find, to their great surprise, that their hard work has given them something *resembling* emotional resilience, and that encourages them to go into therapy. The Superachiever can use her courage to exorcise her interior demons.

Says one Superachiever, a professor of biology,

> I was a neurotic achiever. The only thing that was acceptable in my family was doing well in school. I felt that if I got good grades and got a good job, then my mother would be proud of me.
>
> But the first time I gave a lecture, for three nights before, I couldn't sleep. I thought everyone would laugh at me, because as a kid my mother always made fun of me. I was always being judged. After the lecture, several students said, "You were *wonderful*." I walked out, got into a cab, and burst into tears because I hadn't screwed up.
>
> So I went into therapy, and since then it's been the opposite. I realized that trying to please your parents won't get them to love you. You have to succeed for

yourself. I got out of my need to constantly prove
myself to my mother. Now I work hard for me. I *know*
I'm good.

Some Superachievers got help in another way. Of the psychologically battered achievers I interviewed, the ones who fared best
instinctively knew where to find mentors.
Says a Broadway musical comedy star,

> My ambition saved me. I wanted to know everything,
> to learn everything. And I found someone to teach me
> when I was seven. She was the music teacher in my
> grade school. She was an enormous influence on my
> life because she took me under her wing. She thought
> I was exceptionally talented, and she guided my career,
> even helped me get into drama school. She just opened
> up the world for me—she was so steady, so fair, the
> mother I would like to have had. I couldn't have achieved
> anything if it hadn't been for her.

Psychiatrist Marianne Goodman believes that having a career helps
make women believe in their separate sense of merit. She says,

> To be able to let go of your anger, you have to believe in your
> own worth, and part of that comes from work. You have to see the
> products of your own labor. You need concrete reinforcement.
> Many of my patients have to find something they do well and feel
> good about in order to begin to feel better about themselves. It's
> hard to do that in a vacuum. Through work, and the admiration of
> others, they begin to feel that they are not nothing.

But many Superachievers do not fare well emotionally, for reasons
that are built into their survival mechanisms. *Because their hard-won
image of external worth serves merely as a Band-Aid for their internal
turmoil,* they are among the hardest to reach in therapy. They *must*
feel they've made it, even psychologically. Introspection is too
dangerous.

Work: All in the "Family." Superachievers are more fortunate than
their hearthbound mothers in having a professional safety valve:
their frustrations and anger get siphoned off through work.

Nevertheless, these daughters still risk being more like their mothers than different from them, for they often take "Mom" with them. They see the *enemy*—the hypercritical mother—at work: the comer who seems to threaten their position, the colleague who might stab them in the back.

The Superachiever may counteract these office betrayals with the twin barrels of her understandable outrage and her unfettered fury about her childhood humiliations. She overkills the office betrayer with an atom bomb rather than a strategic booby trap. An interoffice political squeeze play becomes, for this Superachiever, all-out war.

She may become what is called a "barracuda," that graphic term applied only—and unfairly—to ambitious women, chewing out her co-workers the way her mother once tore into her. She has trouble separating her working relationships from her own stifled memories, which often blow up in her professional face.

Other Superachievers bring to their work the feminine need for intimacy, either by seeking "good mommies," or "loyal children" in their protégées. But she often invests too great an emotional stake in them. If they are not suitably grateful—acting as unctuously toward her as she, when she was a child, acted toward her mother—they commit a "crime" that is only of her wounded imagining.

For this kind of Superachiever, ambivalence toward her working relationships echoes her own ambivalences as a child, and plagues her managerial style. Says a forty-six-year-old president of her own marketing firm,

> I was afraid of my mother. I built up such a thick wall against her that I think it's getting in my way at work. I like coming off as tough—most of my staff are afraid of me. But I also want to be loved. I'm too close to the people I mentor. I don't maintain enough distance from them because I want them to be a Good Mommy. I get hooked into the feedback of "Isn't she nice, isn't she smart." Because of their loyalty, I let their mistakes slide, until I can no longer avoid them.
>
> Right now I have to fire one of them, and I keep postponing it. There's this legacy from my childhood where, if I'm disliked, internally I crumble.

Imagine how the Superachiever must feel if *she* is fired. Having put all her emotional energies into her career, she is left with nothing—except, perhaps, the powder burns of her own rage and shame. And the worst part is that, because of her impenetrable defenses and unresolved anger, she may have brought it on herself.

"Don't ask." Once established in their careers, many Superachievers have a hard time asking for help. That's because they learned early on that it would not be forthcoming. Says one woman, "When I was a kid in school, if I didn't know something, I thought I'd die. I missed out on a lot in terms of learning, because to admit you don't know is to admit weakness. The one thing I knew intuitively not to do as a child was to admit weakness."

Some Superachievers learn the hard way that asking for help leaves them vulnerable, a vulnerability they soon regret. Says Marlene, a thirty-five-year-old vice-president of an international hotel chain:

> Success for me has always meant nothing but safety. I believed that if I had enough money in the bank, nothing could hurt me.
>
> Last year was a bummer—I was carrying two mortgages, and I was not feeling terribly secure in my job because profits abroad were down, thanks to the weak dollar. I asked a business associate to meet with me to lay out a new marketing strategy. She said, "Sure, I'd love to help you." But she kept putting the meeting off, a real passive-aggressive, just like my mother. So I never asked again.
>
> I'm a real loner. I have no expectations of other people, but I have excessive expectations of myself. It's very difficult for me to survive in a corporate structure, because it's a team effort. You have to know how to play ball.

The "Best" Friend

Among the Superachiever's handicaps is her wariness about forming close friendships. Intimacy comes hard. To let down her guard is to invite the *possibility* of harm—whispered confessions might come back as weapons of betrayal, as they may have been when she was a child. The last thing the Superachiever wants is to lose her dignity, her power, so she gives the appearance of needing no one.

Still, she is seldom free of vulnerability. A state senator told me, "I go into a room full of people and I am terrified that I am going to be rejected. I can talk to practically anyone about anything, if I have to. But that's not the way I feel inside. That fear never leaves me, and I don't think it ever will. The fact that I'm never rejected doesn't mean anything."

Consequently, many Superachievers feel like outsiders in friendship. One way they get around this is by allowing their work to eat up nights and weekends so that they have no time to be lonely.

Others befriend men rather than women, a common occurrence among Superachievers whose fathers were their role models. Says one woman, "You always know where you stand with them. There's no bullshit. I can give as good as I take with them. And since I don't feel comfortable getting too close, I do better with men, because they also like to keep their own counsel."

But in times of personal crisis, the inability to reach out can be devastating. A best-selling author told me, "The other day I had to go for a bone marrow test, because my doctor wanted to rule out leukemia. I was scared out of my mind. But as I went through my list of friends, there wasn't one I felt I could impose on. It's my craziness. I don't allow myself to count on anyone."

To avoid that terrible aloneness, some Superachievers feign intimacy with female friends, but they maintain a protective zone by holding back their deepest insecurities. Says Candy, thirty-nine, a theatrical agent,

> I have a lot of friends, and many of them think they're my best friend. I do all the "friend" things—I tell them little secrets, I make lunch dates. But only if they call me. I never call them, which is a pattern I learned from my mother. She said, "You let them pick you. Keep the best and the strongest. Keep the ones who choose you." I always walk around slightly poised for assault. When someone does a cruddy thing to me, which happens fairly often, I'm never surprised. The truth is, there is no one in this whole world I cannot live without. Except my husband. Without him, I'm dead.

Superachievers in Love

The majority of Superachievers I interviewed have an Achilles' heel: the men in their romantic lives. To a large degree, it's because they transfer their unmet childhood needs for nurturing to a loving partnership. Their husbands and lovers often are their "good mommies."

Candy, the theatrical agent, puts it this way:

> Every morning I turn to my husband and ask him, "How long do we have together?" He laughs and says, "A long, *long* time." I've totally invested in him, the way I used to with my mother when I was a child. I could not exist without him. He doesn't judge me. I can be cruel, manipulative, critical, moody, really rotten. He just laughs. And he's not a wimp—his ego is so strong that I just don't buffalo him. It's my secret of a happy marriage: one of you has to be nonjudgmental. And I'm the most judgmental person alive.

Some of these marriages are extremely sturdy because the Superachiever, since she puts all her faith in her partner, can expose to him the dark places of her insecurities. He alone gets to see her cry or reveal her terrors.

But many Superachievers are so defended against their vulnerabilities that they sabotage their love relationships. Dr. Harriet Goldhor Lerner sees that sabotage as one of the ways achieving women do penance for outdistancing their mothers and jeopardizing the mother–daughter bond. The guilt Superachievers feel is replayed with their husbands and lovers.

Dr. Lerner writes, "Feelings of depression and anxiety, as well as self-sacrificing and self-sabotaging behaviors, are common ways that women apologize for their competence and success."

That guilt comes out of their experience with mothers who could not bear to see their daughters savor the options that were denied them, as well as with mothers who pushed their daughters to be more than they ever were able to be. *Not* succeeding, for some Superachievers, means letting their mothers down; *succeeding*, for others, means losing their mothers' affection.

Either way, the daughters have trouble believing in themselves, and believing, too, that their "new" mommies—their romantic partners—will approve of their need to become all that they can be.

Every Superachiever I interviewed said that an inability to trust was the biggest legacy of their childhoods. They often cannot believe that anyone would hang in with them over the long haul—

after all, what experience did they ever have with unconditional love growing up?

Said one woman, "My inability to trust has been a real problem in my marriage. I can't express affection to my husband, and I mix it up with him all the time. It's like I'm always testing, testing."

Some Superachievers whose first marriages failed are poignantly aware of their tendency to push away the people they love. The second time around they are able to allow themselves to want, and they choose partners for whom the gift of their vulnerability is not a mistake, and whose achievements their partners applaud and support. Says a forty-one-year-old lobbyist,

> With my current husband, I learned to ask. If I'm on a deadline, he'll cook dinner or take care of the kids. When I'm angry, I don't let it build up inside me. I don't feel the rage I used to feel all the time. He's mommy and daddy and lover and best friend, all wrapped up in one.

The Superachieving Mother

If it's hard for a Superachiever to be vulnerable with a friend or a spouse, in ways it's twice as hard with her children, especially her daughters. As one woman put it, "The only two people in the world who ever make me cry are my mother and my daughter."

It is here that the terrible legacies of the Superachiever's past can be bequeathed to the next generation. When her children are frightened or anxious, the Superachiever sees herself anew and pulls out her childhood coping mechanisms, forcing them on her kids.

"When my daughter is snubbed on the school bus," says one woman, "I give her ten things to do to deal with that. And when she doesn't, I get wild, because I can't bear her pain any more than I was once able to bear my own. But what works for me may not work for her. I have a blind spot."

The Superachiever sometimes resembles the Critic in terms of her insistence that her kids be achievers, and when they are not, she does what she's always done: She dives in to fix things, using the charm and manipulation that helped her false self survive childhood.

And often her kids don't buy it—they hear her "concern" but feel her manipulation. But because of the Superachiever's stubborn tenacity, she often digs in her heels and won't allow her children to assume responsibility for their own ambivalences and mistakes.

One Superachiever told me,

> I *hated* the way my mother ran my life, but I did the same thing to my daughter. I pushed, I pulled, I lied, I read diaries because I needed to know everything. There was a lot of competition between us. Her friends would come to the house and talk to me for hours. It would infuriate her.
>
> She's never forgiven me for something I did when she was twelve. She was close to failing English, so I went to see her teacher. I thanked her for having been such a good influence; I said that my daughter often talked about how much it had meant to her to be in her class. My daughter is lousy with integrity. When I told her what I had done, she screamed, "How could you! I hate that woman!" But she got a B.
>
> I wrote her college essay and she got into an Ivy League school. I got her entrée to Xerox and she's the top-selling salesperson in her division.
>
> I've asked myself if I had it to do over, would I do it differently? The manipulating, the interference, the pulling strings, things she's wild with anger about to this day? *The answer is yes. I would do it all again.* Her life will never be dull.

The hardest thing for a Superachiever to do is to let her children fail. Since she refuses to accept defeat, she similarly cannot allow her children to lose.

As a result, many of the children of Superachievers are "underachievers," a term that is open to debate. Mothers who do not treat their children as extensions of themselves give their children the latitude to be late bloomers, to be confused, to struggle, to change their minds, to be average. Some children simply have their own timetables for readiness and change, and the understanding mother respects them.

But many Superachievers are too impatient, too controlling, and too frightened to allow for their children what they cannot allow for themselves. Since success for these women seemed like a matter of emotional life and death, their waffling children are seen to be in mortal danger. The mother's "fix-it" posture is out of all proportion to the child's real needs.

Says one woman, the daughter of a Doormat, "My daughter was never able to do the things I could do as a child. I was always pushing her, trying to change her. I overwhelmed her. And, of course, her method of dealing with it was to withdraw. Which made me crazy, because now I had a parent who was withdrawn, and a child who was withdrawn."

For most Superachievers, their children's number one beef is their mothers' unavailability. Some Superachievers recognize their culpability in that complaint. Says one of them, "I wasn't a good mother when my son was young. I didn't want to be there. He wanted more from me than I was willing to give. I'd say, 'I've got an hour for you. Let's get on with it.' "

Another feels tremendous guilt at having taken advantage of her loving husband's willingness to assume all the parenting chores. "It was too easy for me to stay in the office. I felt relieved, but I also felt that I neglected my kids. And I can never get those years back."

Many of these Superachievers, through their ability to let their children really *know* them and to share the fears that drive them, eventually form strong friendships with them. Even though it's relatively late, these mothers often ameliorate their children's losses through their candor, and their children's desire and willingness to forgive and understand.

But others are too desperate to reveal themselves to *anyone*, let alone their children. All those years of frenzied work to appease the ghosts of their past make change and soul-searching a mortification. For them, estrangement from the people they love most is almost preordained.

Profile of a Superachiever

Whenever *Forbes* magazine does a roundup article on the top female moneymakers on Wall Street, Julia's name nearly always heads the list. Her summer home in the Hamptons has been photographed for *House & Garden*. If there's a spasm in the stock market, there she is in cool close-up on the evening news, calmly ticking off facts and figures in a brilliant analysis of the nation's financial health.

Julia, forty-two, is by any measure a Superachiever. She seems remote to subordinates and slightly formal with acquaintances. Her almost machinelike energy propels her through sixty-hour work-weeks and first-class travel to speaking engagements, leaving little time for her family and friends.

I've known Julia since we were children. The slim, chic Julia I see on the television screen bears little resemblance to the pudgy kid in seventh grade who wore thick glasses, got straight A's, and had only one friend—me.

Even then there was a kind of unrepentant arrogance about her: you could hate her, but by God you had to respect her. She was the smartest kid in class, and you couldn't take that away from her.

Julia never suffered fools gladly—even the boys were afraid of her. But most people never saw her the way I did. They never watched her face drain of all color as her Avenger mother, having glanced at a theme paper that got an A-plus, said, "What book did you copy this out of?" Or, if it was a B-plus, "You *dare* to bring home a grade like this?" Most people never sat next to her at the movies, hearing her cry as she watched ideal celluloid parents cherish their kids, right or wrong, in perfect homespun Hollywood-version families.

Julia's parents were Italian immigrants, and she grew up on Manhattan's Lower East Side. Julia never had a room of her own—she and her brother slept on cots in the living room of their cramped walk-up apartment. But her family's poverty isn't what she talks about when we discuss her childhood. What she talks about is the way her mother always made her feel a harrowing sense of shame. She says,

> When I was a kid, our dentist wanted me to get braces. My mother said to him in front of me, "Why should I spend the money? There's nothing you can do to make her pretty." When I went to college, she said, "Who do you think you are—Einstein?"
>
> My mother never gave me the feeling that she cared about me. I visualize our relationship as blood flowing backward to her—maternal vampire stuff. Everything was for her. My achievements were for her—she believed they were *because* of her. The joy was for her too.

Julia wanted some joy for herself. She knew at eighteen that she had to get out. Her tickets to freedom were her 163 IQ and her single-mindedness. And the only way she was going to survive was by being so smart, so driven, so successful, so rich, that nothing could ever make her taste shame again.

She reached her breaking point with her mother when she was twenty-one.

> The day I got into graduate school my mother said, "You have disgraced the family. If you leave, I'll have a heart attack." Her goal for me was not a career—it was for me to get married and raise kids. I said to myself, "This is it." I couldn't let her get to me, or she'd sink me. So I went, over her hysterical objections.
>
> I'd get these eight-page letters telling me how terrible things were without me. Later, when I got my first job, she'd call me and say, "I'm going to tell your boss what a monster you are so he'll fire you. Then at least maybe you'll stay home and find a husband."
>
> This is going to sound terrible, but it's the God's truth: The best thing that ever happened to me is that she died when I was twenty-seven. Her death liberated me. I truly believe that the only way I've been able to make something of myself is because I have the ultimate separation from her.

Julia also believes that her staggering work load has "saved" her daughters, Lorraine, eighteen, and Leslie, fifteen. Julia's husband, Mark, is an illustrator who works at home. All through their kids' growing-up years, it was Mark who took them to the doctor and attended their plays. "He's a much better parent than I am," she says.

"I used to get furious about their middling grades," she adds. "At some point I realized that grades were too important to me, and I didn't want to do to them what my mother did to me. I want them to remember me differently. And my schedule keeps me off their backs, because the time we have together has to be quality time. I've been forced by circumstances to have a relationship with them that doesn't involve grades per se."

Still, she feels she "can't win." Not long ago Leslie said to her, "One of the reasons I have problems is because you always worked. You were never around."

And while it caused her terrible pain to hear it—her response to her daughter was, "You can't lay that guilt trip on me"—she realizes that there was a germ of truth in Leslie's angry verdict. "Whatever the reasons for my ambition, I probably spent too much time, even when I was home, being preoccupied about work when they were growing up. There was always the tug between the professional and the maternal. And I didn't walk that line very well."

I ask her what her childhood cost her. She slowly replies,.

> There's no question that I am not as wholesome and mature as I would like to be. I am not comfortable in my own skin. There are lots of emotional areas in my life that I will probably never feel complete about. I don't think I'll ever get over that sense that for all my success, all my husband's help, I'm never going to be good enough to please my mother, who is long dead. I can never accept what I have—somehow there's always an ideal I haven't reached.

And so, if there is one overwhelming legacy of her childhood, it's that she still thinks she isn't good enough. Her psychiatrist speculates that her success is a metaphor for getting good grades, the only thing she ever did that pleased her mother. "Being at the top of my profession is my way of getting good grades," she says. "And I'm still trying to get straight A's."

13

The Cipher

I've always wished I were someone else. When I was a kid, I'd idealize some girl in school. I'd think, "She's perfect. It must be wonderful to be her. I'd give anything just to jump into her skin."

It's still like that. I conform to other people's personalities, rather than having my own, so people will like me. And that's exhausting. I just don't know how to be myself.

—Marcy, twenty-seven

You know this woman. Well, maybe you don't—it could be that you've never really *noticed* her.

Perhaps you recall her from your school days. She always sat way in the back of the classroom. If a teacher called on her, she'd look up, eyes blinking, like a startled bird, or she'd seem not to have heard. During lunch hour, she'd eat by herself in the cafeteria. When the other kids played in the school yard during recess, their whoops of energetic excess piercing the air, she perched on a bench on the sidelines, ignored by all.

Today, she's the nondescript woman at a desk down the hall, out of the office mainstream, quietly drifting from one day to the next in her ho-hum job. She's often late, bringing her lunch, which she eats at her desk. She may still live at home with her parents or her widowed mother, or she's married; either way, she doesn't talk much about her private life.

One reason you may not know her, though, is that she may appear to be just an average woman, with friends and a social life, like

222

anyone else. In this case, she's timorous in one context only: Once she crosses the threshold of her mother's house—or simply hears her mother's voice on the phone—she turns into a jellyfish. It's a conditioned response, triggered by one person alone—Mom.

But whether she is meek with everyone, or only in the bosom of her original family, she keeps a low profile. Because the last thing she wants to do is call attention to herself.

This is the Cipher, defined in Webster's dictionary as "one that has no weight, worth, or influence."

Of the five types of daughters described in this book, the Cipher is least able to emerge from the prison created by her unacceptability to her mother. It is the Cipher who most absorbs the belief that she is worthless and who is least able to traverse the high wire of her adulthood.

Comedian Lily Tomlin once observed, "We're all in this alone." And no one is as alone as the Cipher.

The Cipher exists only in the perception of her mother's low opinion of her. Unable to risk separation—which is far too dangerous, as we shall see—she stays emotionally bound to her, as though strapped to the maternal mast.

Like the Angel, she is an uncritical slave to her mother. But unlike the Angel, who feels a righteous sense of superiority in her mission to be Mommy's good girl and protector, and unlike the Superachiever, who soars with the frenzied momentum of her achievement, the Cipher remains earthbound.

She longs to be a speck on the landscape. To that end, she works tirelessly, if unconsciously, to make herself invisible: she pounds her identity into a tiny kernel, reducing herself to nothing, banishing into a void any sign that she is a person to be reckoned with.

The Cipher reads a newspaper without the little red flags of opinion or intellect that could spot a contradiction or a fuzzy thought. She doesn't know what friend to like, what vacation spot to visit, what dress to wear, without someone advising her. She can't rely on her own convictions because she doesn't have any—except the certain knowledge that she is a disappointment.

As one woman put it, "When I was in my twenties, I didn't have any guidelines. I didn't know what was right and what was wrong. I could rationalize murder. I had no way of thinking about anything. I was just empty."

Where the Angel cannot apologize, the Cipher doesn't know how *not* to. The words "I'm sorry" are her mantra, the running litany of her life. In her head there is a movie with many unhappy endings, and dialogue of self-abnegation to fit each finale: a friend cancels a lunch date, and the Cipher thinks, She's mad at me. A beau calls to say he'll be late, and the Cipher wonders if there's someone else. Her boss fires her, and she says, "I deserve it."

The Cipher yields to her fate, embracing defeat without a struggle. Surrender is simply a habit she cannot, or will not, break. Minimalism is her primary coping mechanism. If I could just disappear, she subconsciously thinks, no one would harm me.

The Cipher's personality is determined more by temperament than by birth rank. She is inherently a loner, intrinsically shy.

According to Drs. Alexander Thomas and Stella Chess, who have studied temperament in children, some kids are simply "slow-to-warm-up." These children do not like new situations and people, and take some time to adjust to them, even after repeated contact. Such children give the impression of lethargy, rather than excitability or cheerfulness.

The Cipher prefers doing things at her own languid pace. She doesn't reach out for help, not as a matter of pride but because it doesn't occur to her. She may be a loner, but she is not by nature *helpless*—that part is her "as if" persona.

As we know, timidity may be an inherited trait, but there is much a compassionate parent can do to help her frightened child to overcome it. Small doses of autonomy can encourage the bashful child not to feel a constant sense of dread and can help her appreciate her own gentle, rather than flamboyant, strength.

But the Cipher doesn't have a mother like that.

If the Cipher is a conspirator in her own defeat, she has an energetic teacher—the parent who encourages weakness. Most Ciphers I interviewed were the daughters either of Avengers or of Critics, mothers whose demands for perfection were crushing.

Since her mother always made her decisions for her, and since every whiff of independence, every original thought, was criticized and ridiculed, the Cipher accommodated her by not knowing *what* to think.

The Cipher is *reacting* to her overwhelming, narcissistic, or uninvolved mother by remaining childlike and unobtrusive. Rather than flatter, or achieve, or create turmoil, or defect—as her siblings may do—she lowers her profile so that she hardly casts a shadow. The combination of the Cipher's innate reticent personality and her mother's treatment of her simply drives the Cipher farther underground. In her adulthood, the Cipher remains emotionally prostrate.

What Is the Cipher Afraid Of?

The Cipher absorbs her mother's displeasure, which distills and festers within her. She is afraid of everything, but she is terrified of one thing in particular: her own anger. "I hate fighting and arguing with people," says one Cipher. "I suffer terribly. Angry feelings make me feel so bad—they swoop down on me whenever someone confronts me. I feel abandoned, rotten, laid out."

Everything about the Cipher is reduced to a single struggle—all her energies are funneled into the one battle she is willing to mount: She wages war against her anger. For if she were to release it—if she were to *really retaliate* in response to her childhood humiliations, to her complicity in her own degradation—it would blow away the world. And then she could be motherless, a fate too horrible for her to imagine.

Within the meek, modest, delicate maiden is a time bomb, ticking away with a murderous rage. "When my mother and I argue, I'm not so afraid of how she'll react—*I'm afraid of how I'll react*. I'm terrified that I'll become uncontrollably violent," says a thirty-four-year-old Cipher who still lives with her parents.

There *is* a "self," however reduced, way down in the bottom of the Cipher's soul, a strike force straining to get out. Isolation and self-denigration don't mute her violent thoughts—they are always intruding, scaring her to death.

Most Ciphers insulate their rage by never leaving their mothers, if only the "mother" in their heads. By denying her own anger and by being her mother's willing victim, the Cipher is really protecting *both* of them. Rather than "kill" her mother, the Cipher instead kills off parts of herself. Because she is unable to believe in herself, the Cipher believes she would die right along with her mother if her mother were to die.

Ciphers are like an overripe fruit that is bruised by the slightest touch. It is too perilous for them to have a self, one that is capable of expressing outrage. And so they implode. They are chronically fatigued, or they develop eating disorders. They take drugs or drink too much. Or become depressed.

For the most delicate Cipher, like the most fragile Angel, the struggle to stifle her anger slowly engulfs her, overheating to such dangerous levels that she simply disconnects in her head. These Ciphers lose all contact with reality—all feelings, all appetites suddenly cease.

It would be different if she were a man. The Cipher's extreme male counterpart can be seen at the top of the evening news: the quiet, good boy who "never gave his parents any trouble," who one day and for no apparent reason goes to a mall, or a bell tower on a college campus, and mows down everyone in sight with a machine gun.

You seldom read about women doing such things, because to be a woman and to be a random killer are mutually exclusive. It is logical, then, that the Cipher would set about to destroy herself in anguished penance for her rage. She sabotages every good thing, every relationship, every sign that she has a self.

Hers is a bind that is as confounding as one can imagine: If I stay with my mother, I'll kill her. If I leave, I'll die. As one woman put it, "How can I love myself when I have this monster for a mother? What does that make me if I constantly try to win the approval of a monster?"

The only way to explain this paradox to herself is *by believing that she deserves the treatment she gets.* Unlike the Angel, who cannot admit her own imperfections, the Cipher makes her mother "right" and "all good" by justifying her mother's behavior: My mother would never do or say all those awful things, she reasons, if there weren't something profoundly wrong with me.

The Payoff of Invisibility

There is some debate among psychological researchers as to why this kind of woman is the way she is. One school of thought is that she has a "self-defeating personality disorder," a fairly new psychological monicker for being a "loser."

According to this view, there are rewards for being desperately insecure, chief among them that, having volunteered for blame, one never need experience the embarrassment of trying and failing.

This is the flip side, other researchers say, of narcissism as we usually think of it. We're familiar with the Avenger version—all self, all raging demand, all vanity that destroys everything in its ravenous path.

The Cipher could be construed as the Avenger's alter ego. Rather than swagger in self-glorification, the narcissist who is sheepish and self-effacing, giving credit to everyone but herself, hopes to be admired for her exaggerated humility, her excessive timidity, her unctuousness.

Another explanation for the Cipher's behavior is what is called "self-handicapping." By being habitually late, or by getting mired in no-win relationships or dead-end jobs, she gives the *illusion* of success—that is, *other things* keep her from achieving her true potential. Her abilities never get tested, so she can never "fail."

In my view, underlying these symptoms is the porous bedrock of the Cipher's self-image: for her, being an eternal victim *is her identity*. To do something well and to be admired for it *imperils that identity*.

To say that *all* her diffidence is really vanity turned inside out, or simply a problem that, if she'd just pull herself up by her bootstraps, could be solved in ten easy steps, is a way of blaming the victim. Ciphers may use their "weakness" to forestall abuse or to defang the enemy, but there is nothing pleasurable about such voluntary humiliation. *Familiar*, perhaps; rewarding, seldom.

Self-defeat may be a defense mechanism, but it is far from a good one—it is as painful as being abused.

But more painful still is recognizing the price it exacts. When the Cipher realizes to her everlasting shame that she has compounded her mother's punishments by punishing herself, and by returning to her mother for more, it is harrowing. For the very thing she is trying to prevent in her self-abnegation—her mother's rejection—she has somehow *encouraged*.

As one woman said, "It wasn't until recently that I understood my relationship with my mother: From childhood on I sensed her self-serving demands and *fed them*. Everything I did to please simply whetted her appetite for more. The more I gave her, the more she wanted."

Never having received childhood tutelage in self-confidence, the Cipher who wakes up to her terrible compromises may turn to therapy. But even if she does not, life sometimes presents its own cure for the Cipher's inner prison of inadequacy: The mother dies. With the stimulus for her abjectness removed, sometimes the Cipher is liberated by de facto permission to grow up and be whole.

In time, she may find the courage to face the ultimate cost of her humiliation and her role in it. Says a forty-year-old Cipher, "I was given above-average looks and intelligence, and I haven't done anything significant with them. I had enormous potential, and never reached it. So far, I have lived a wasted life. But I don't want to waste what's left of it."

But if she cannot summon such courage, she simply drowns herself in a sea of resignation. Other daughters, such as the Angel and Superachiever, believe (if unrealistically) that if they are good enough or smart enough, their mothers will change. The Cipher has no such hope. She simply succumbs to her loveless fate.

The Weak Sister

The Cipher is ganged up on by her parents and siblings as if she had sent them an engraved invitation. They see her as weak and treat her accordingly, either overprotecting her or becoming exasperated—even furious—by her total lack of spine. They may recognize in her their own vulnerabilities, which they try to disguise: she embodies the same insecurities that drive them on a different path.

Her Angel sister has someone to dominate with her injunctions for good deeds; her Superachiever sister has someone over whom to lord her successes. Everyone tries to change the Cipher, pushing her to set goals and shape up, but the Cipher will have none of it. She's "too dumb," "too fat," "too unpopular," she believes, even to try.

How could she dare be otherwise? If Mom has taught her that she is ineffectual, she must work constantly to prove her mother to be correct. And how better to keep the family peace than to comply with everyone's opinion that she just can't hack it?

"I never turned to my sisters for help," one Cipher told me. "I never turned to anyone. If I had a problem, I either suffered with it or ignored it."

Some Ciphers in childhood become phobic, especially about going to school. The phobia is a smokescreen that diverts the Cipher's attention away from her anger at her mother.

Her mother feeds the Cipher's phobia—as well as her loneliness and incompetence—by not *allowing* her to grow up. Such mothers are often similarly dependent on *their* mothers—inadequacy is a legacy among female members of their families.

But when the Cipher—phobic or merely afraid—is an adult, she may wield her revenge on her mother so subtly that she alone knows it: She withdraws her love. Says the thirty-year-old daughter of an Avenger,

> The one thing my mother wants more than anything is the thing she hasn't gotten from me: My devotion. I do what she asks. But I don't *care* about her. I have *deliberately* failed her, if only in this one way. I don't let her know me, I don't share my thoughts and feelings

with her. I'm still at her beck and call, but I don't give
her any part of myself. That's the worst thing you can
do to a narcissist.

The Cipher at Work

The Cipher, as we have seen, often manages to become invisible
at work. And while this may shield her from the heat of scrutiny, her
lack of distinctiveness is hardly conducive to getting on the fast
track. The Cipher's coping mechanism is anathema to the hard-
charging, competitive nature of the corporate structure.

Not that the corporate world doesn't need its followers, its loyal
rank and file, to do the tedious, unglamorous stuff; but what if the
Cipher has talents she wishes she had the nerve to test?

One of the major losses for the Cipher is that she doesn't have a
career that taps her abilities. As one woman put it, "I have never
pursued any ambitions at work because I never knew what I wanted.
Nobody ever asked me. My childhood cost me my potential, and I
can't think of anything worse. I thought that by not making waves—
not with my mother, not at my job—I'd be rewarded. Instead, I am
just overlooked."

Sometimes there is a sick attachment between boss and Cipher, a
replay of the Cipher's childhood. Where the boss "overfunctions" in
his or her tyrannical behavior, the Cipher balances the equation by
"underfunctioning" and becoming inept.

Rather than change, she makes endless and elaborate excuses for
her chronic tardiness, her forgetfulness, her failure to meet dead-
lines. It is her part in the boss–employee bargain: Her passiveness
enlivens her superior officer.

"I give the impression of incompetence at work, even though I'm
very competent," one Cipher, a waitress, confessed. "I think it's
because to achieve something, you have to have goals. You have to
prepare yourself, whether through education or pounding the pave-
ment or speaking up for yourself. You have to think you're worthy of
achievement. And I never did. So my boss takes advantage of me."

But sometimes the Cipher is simply so defeated that being reprimanded, or even fired, somehow doesn't jolt her. As a secretary I
interviewed, who is constantly being passed over for promotions, put
it, "I work very hard at not having expectations. You can't be
disappointed if you don't expect that you'll succeed."

Many Ciphers avoid corporate pressures by going into business for themselves. The Cipher has certain advantages—she likes to work alone, she often has a rich fantasy life and many interests that she has pursued, privately, since childhood. Some of these women are writers or painters or musicians, giving creative vent to their hooded introspection in poems or novels, watercolors or song. Their work "speaks" for them. Emily Dickinson was a reclusive Cipher who, through her poetry, passionately and publicly expressed her rich interior world.

But, given enough stress, the Cipher's unresolved childhood feelings can intrude even on her solitary creativity. She simply loses interest.

The Friend in Need

The one thing the Cipher can count on is being rejected. So she goes through her life making her nightmarish dreams come true. Like a needle stuck in a record groove, she keeps going round and round in a series of failed friendships, as the needle cuts deeper into her self, making the wound of her lack of ego raw and running. It is the only thing she knows. *It is the only thing she is good at.*

Susan, thirty-nine, is haunted by childhood memories of friendships gone awry, of girls who behaved cruelly to her, of being shunned by the "in" crowd and being the butt of their gossip. She says,

> I remember once in the eighth grade asking the most popular girl in my class why no one liked me. She said, "It's because you're *too* nice." I didn't understand what she was talking about. Years later I learned that being a victim puts demands on people. I was asking those girls to define me—if only they liked me, I'd be okay.
>
> But back then, I couldn't handle it. I was in tears every day. So I just shut them all out.

But for many Ciphers, old habits of ingratiation die hard. Cynthia, thirty-four, says,

> I'm always afraid of offending people. If I spend the afternoon with a girlfriend, I'll imagine that I've made a terrible gaffe, and I'll call her the minute I get home to say, "Remember when I said that? I didn't mean that, I meant this. Are you insulted?"

In *Enchantment*, Daphne Merkin writes about the indignity of perpetual atonement:

> I was begging . . . forgiveness not for any specific offense I had committed but for the general crime [of] being who I was. And if I were to say now that I cannot imagine the desperation that led me to such extremes—the lack of pride or the excess of need—that wouldn't quite be true. The truth is I *can* imagine such lack of pride. I have been capable of it since and am probably still capable of it. You can develop a taste . . . for supplication.

The Cipher's supplication can cause her to close off her feelings. Ultimately, for her own sanity, she may retreat from all relationships because—having no boundaries—she doesn't know how to set limits. As one forty-two-year-old Cipher, the veteran of years of therapy, said,

> I never wanted to be close to anybody. It's very possible to live and not experience any emotion whatsoever. Just exist without rocking the boat, do an adequate job at work, be a perfect person at home, have friends but only on the surface. It's very, very easy to do that. It's more than just getting by. If you don't allow yourself highs or lows, nothing touches you. But what happens is you forget how to love.

The Cipher in Love

It is with men, more than with friends, that the line between the Cipher's tenuous, separate identity and the urge to be enfolded becomes blurred.

Some Ciphers prefer to remain single because the prospect of *physical* merging is as dangerous as emotional domination. How can you conceal your vulnerabilities while having sex? Where is the hiding place when your lover sees you at physical and emotional close range?

The best way to solve that problem is simply not to have a romantic life. These Ciphers remain detached from loving relationships with men, because they are as threatening as the mother–daughter tie. Many of these women continue to live with their parents for much of their adulthood.

Other Ciphers *do* get involved, over and over again, with men who are emotionally, and maritally, unavailable. Says Pamela, twenty-nine,

> I'm always getting dumped, and I think it's because I'm too insecure to attract someone really healthy. My mother said so many horrible things to me that it became a way of life. I wasn't good enough for a normal relationship, I wasn't worthy, so the obvious thing was to go after married men, which I did. There's nothing in the whole world more painful than that.

Still another romantic pattern among Ciphers is to choose men who are brutal to them. Ciphers are the women who are most at risk of becoming battered and bullied. They have someone to join them in their self-blame—at the same time, on some primitive level, they *have someone to blame.*

When the Cipher does marry, in more ways than she cares to think about she often marries her "mom." What appears in matrimony to be a solution to her isolation becomes a guarantee of it. Says a thirty-nine-year-old woman,

> The first time I married I was twenty—it was to get out of the house. And although I always had a lot of boyfriends, I chose the worst of the lot, the bottom of the pit. I did it because I had no appreciation for anyone who would exhibit a lot of emotion. My conscious thought was that if a man didn't bother with me, I wouldn't be hurt. You do things for all the wrong reasons. You think you're getting out of one situation by doing something completely different, and what happens? There it is again.

Because marriage often re-creates one's childhood in another context, memories of how to behave in a family can eclipse the small gains a Cipher may have made as a single woman. "Wife" equates with "dependent child," as though stepping back into a time warp.

Several of the Ciphers I interviewed described their marriages as being caught between two "evils"—their domineering mothers and their equally domineering husbands.

"I married my mother, let's make that clear," says Linda. Whenever her Smotherer mother visits, she and Linda's husband fight constantly. Linda, trying to please two masters, is usually trapped in the middle. The stress level gets so high that she feels she's floating above the ground. It's as though she's coated in cotton batting—she doesn't hear sounds clearly.

"I protect myself in this baffling way," she says, "because the potential for an atomic blast is there the whole time she's there."

Other Ciphers cling to empty marriages because they cannot face the alternatives. One woman I interviewed says that she and her husband have a marriage that often is "pure hell." And it is the hellish parts that she cannot address because, she believes, the risk of abandonment is too great. She says,

> I have a husband who is wonderful to me some of the time. I can't give that up because if I do, what have I got? I've waited all my life to find someone—where would I be without him? I've never been able to please my mother. So I tell myself, "You've got to stick it out."

Psychotherapist Lilly Singer says that these ways of "managing" a marriage are by-products of having had a mother who made the Cipher feel "no good."

"The mother's voice is in that daughter's head continuously," Ms. Singer explains. "The daughter needs to be put down in order to function in a 'normal' way. And if she should somehow find herself in a loving partnership, she thinks of it as 'a fluke.'"

Mother Inferior

Once the Cipher is a mother, she may, inevitably, pass along her insecurities to her children.

Corrie has a nine-year-old son named Seth. One day he went outdoors to play with a bunch of kids on the block. He returned a few minutes later because one of the boys had said to him, "Go home. We don't want you here."

Seth went into the living room and started watching television; Corrie went into the kitchen and burst into tears. She called the mother of the boy who had sent her son home and asked, "Why doesn't he like my child? What's wrong with Seth?" The woman replied, "There's nothing wrong with him. He's a perfectly normal little boy. You're too involved with him—you're going to make him crazy."

"She made me realize that I was creating problems where none existed," Corrie says. So much was she walking in her son's shoes that he was going to have trouble walking in them himself, a realization that sent her into therapy.

And although she told the therapist that she had really had a *wonderful* childhood—that the only reason she was there was to help her son—she began to make a connection between her childhood and her son's.

Corrie discovered that she was not able to let go of her son because she was so tied to her Critic mother. She says,

> I still react to my mother as a child would. I want her to say, "Corrie, go lead your life. You are a separate person. You are an adult. I want you to make your dreams come true." I'm still waiting for her to tell me that it's okay for me to be independent. I'm never going to *get* permission; but maybe I can *give* it to my son.

Ciphers not only inject insecurities where none may exist, but they also don't set limits on their children's destructive behavior. These kids get away with murder—the Cipher mother can *always* find an excuse not to say no—the kid is sick, or an exam is coming up, or the mother herself is just too tired.

Eager not to bequeath their emotional tremors, some Ciphers deliberately pull away from their children, believing they will prevent a reproduction of those insecurities by keeping their maternal distance. And in some cases, they retreat too far. Says a forty-one-year-old Cipher,

> My mother was so powerful and strong that I never ventured or tried anything. So when I became a mother, I was determined not to force my kids to do anything. As a result, I was a loving parent but not a caring one. I was neglectful. I ran away from the bad things. I didn't face up to facts that were staring me in the face.
>
> A couple of years ago my teenage daughter, who was rebelling wildly and getting D's in school, brought a kid home who kept nodding off at the dinner table. My

husband knew the kid was stoned. I said, "Oh, he's just tired." It turned out the kid was a heroin addict. Why that didn't ring a thousand bells and send me off to get serious help for my daughter, I don't know, but it didn't.

Whether she is too involved with her children or too negligent of them, the Cipher often re-creates the one aspect of her relationship with her mother that she swore she'd never repeat: She and her children have little basis for friendship. And because it has happened to her *again*, the pain she feels is unbearable.

Profile of a Cipher

Kendall, thirty, is a classic Cipher. Fine-boned and tiny, her dark curls obscuring her delicate features, she seems like a blank screen. You ask her an innocuous question ("What time is it?"), and she takes several minutes to respond, as though she were under water. You ask her opinion, and she says in a voice that trails off, "Gosh, I don't know . . ."

She is an only child, the daughter of an Avenger mother and a passive father who, during her childhood, frequently was away on business. Since she was virtually without allies, there was nothing to buffer her from her mother's hostility and perfectionism.

When Kendall would come home from school, her mother would be waiting for her with a list of orders to clean the house, do the laundry, go to the store. When she practiced the piano, her mother would sit in the next room calling out the correct notes before Kendall's fingers even hit the keys.

Kendall would never get angry at her mother. She says,

> It's not that I wasn't allowed to express anger to my mother, it's that I never even tried. I just knew from Day One not to start.
>
> When my mother was yammering at me, I'd just sit there, frozen. She'd start to talk, and I'd tune out. I'd just literally lose touch. The fog would roll in.

Kendall learned to be invisible by staying in her room. She quit piano, and began painting. Artistically gifted, every afternoon she would work on her canvases in her room, listening to records. She'd surround herself with Mozart and Chopin, drowning out the sound and fury of her mother's domination.

When she was a senior in high school, Kendall had no particular goals, no academic game plan, had never thought beyond the moment. Her mother forced her to sit down and fill in college applications, and when she didn't finish them, her mother filled in the blanks—she even wrote Kendall's college essays. "I just didn't care," Kendall says.

Kendall was accepted by her mother's alma mater. It was almost preordained that she would flunk out, and she did. A year later, she went to a local community college. After graduation, she got a job in a high school cafeteria, and found a studio apartment in which she holed up at the end of the day.

When her mother called her, Kendall would hold the phone a couple of inches from her head, not listening, waiting for her mother's hour-long self-absorbed opinions and observations to wind down. Kendall remained shrouded in the fog that had protected her all her life.

Two things happened that caused the fog to begin thinning out. First, she was nearly beaten to death in a mugging and spent six weeks recovering in a hospital. "It struck me then, as I lay there, that I couldn't go on this way. I could either kill myself, or I could find work that would take me out of the tomb in which I had sealed myself."

She knew that she was a good—not great—painter, and that she liked fixing things. So she decided to become an art restorer, and to that end enrolled in a school to learn about the techniques of restoration.

Kendall didn't tell her mother about her plans until she had sent off her tuition, given up her job and apartment, and packed her bags. "I kept silent until it was etched in stone," she says. "That was the happiest year of my life. For the first time, I made a decision on my own and stuck to it. I was doing something that was mine, and I didn't want her to smash it, so I waited until it was too late for her to do anything about it."

The second thing that happened was that her father died. He had been a gentle man with whom she felt a kind of spiritual kinship. "My mother always saw fit to make me believe I couldn't make it on my own. And now that my father was dead, I lost my only ally—I knew he loved me, even if he couldn't say it. Now I'd be thrown onto her hooks. When he died, I flipped out."

Because Kendall was single and had no siblings, it fell to her to accompany her mother on a trip to Florida shortly after her father's death. Unable to say no, Kendall went along—after all, her mother was paying.

One night during their Florida vacation, she made a gesture of generosity to thank her mother for the trip: She bought a bottle of wine for the two women to drink in their room. One drink led to another, and soon they were drunk. Says Kendall,

> We started talking about my dad. I said, "Well, he and I never really had a connection, he was just so quiet." She turned to me and snarled, "I thought you loved him." Then she passed out. That was the breaking point. At that moment, I thought, "If I just went over to her bed and put a pillow to her face, with all the pills she takes and all the booze she drank, everyone would think her death was an accident."
>
> I lay awake all night thinking about it. It wasn't one of those epiphanies where suddenly everything becomes clear—just a tiny sliver of light, a sense that I had some power after all.
>
> Obviously, I didn't kill her. But for the first time I could get really angry, almost *uncontrollably* angry. And at that moment, I began to feel some hope for myself.

But change was still in the future. Terrified of her fantasy, she simply worked harder at sabotaging herself. Although her reputation as a fine restorer was attracting new clients, she began turning them away. Her debts piled up. She didn't pay her rent, and she was inches away from being evicted.

"*That's* when I woke up," Kendall says, "and went into therapy." She continues,

> When the fog lifted, behind it was more pain than I ever could have imagined. The never being aware of reality until it's pounding me over the head. The always asking to be rejected. The shaking whenever I heard my mother's voice on the phone.
>
> I finally realized that I'm never going to get love from her—it's just never going to happen. I wanted to be

able to deal with my mother, and not feel like I'm
being sucked in by this incredible cyclone. And I wanted
to stop expecting that somehow she'd change.

Kendall drew on the positive memory of going to art school, her
one victory, and she used it as a talisman. She learned to reach out
to people, to strike up conversations. She started a fitness program,
and made friends with people she met at the gym. She saw her
mother less and less.

There were setbacks: For two months she dated a bodybuilder
who would rough her up when he drank too much, until, fearing for
her life, she stopped seeing him. And from time to time she'd try
again with her mother, only to feel afterward that she'd lost all the
emotional ground she'd gained.

But she was growing, step by tenuous step.

Since then, she's stopped turning down work and joined several
professional organizations—the jobs keep pouring in. You can find
her in the evening, in the small studio she rents, working late, the
strains of classical music filling in the silence of the night. You can
find her on weekends, having dinner with the small but growing
circle of artistic friends.

She's halfway to paying off her debts. She's continuing her therapy, where she is making slow strides toward a real feeling of
identity. And she's open to a healthy, loving relationship.

Kendall's number one goal now is never to be afraid of her
mother—or anyone—ever again. She says,

> I don't want to feel menaced anymore. I've created a
> life and pushed back all the fears and all my destructive
> habits to pull it off. If I fail now, if I go back to the old
> ways, my life is essentially over—it would be the same
> as putting a gun to my head and pulling the trigger.
> And I don't intend to fail anymore.
>
> For the first time, I'm glad I'm alive.

14

The Troublemaker

I was not your patsy kid—I was confrontational. I was not going to do what my mother wanted me to do. Period. Mealtime was hand-to-hand combat.
"Eat!" she'd command.
"Force me!" I'd say.
"There are starving children in China!"
"NAME ONE!"

—Heidi, thirty-two

Not long ago a friend of mine, her cheeks flushed with delight, proudly told me that she had been mugged. Yes, *mugged*. A teenage boy had snatched her purse as she walked along Manhattan's Fifth Avenue. And although she was five months pregnant, she sprinted down the street after the thief, grabbed him by the collar, and grappled him to the sidewalk.

"By *God*," she said, pounding her fist on the table as she happily recounted the tale, "he didn't get away with it!"

My friend, who is given to such imprudent impulses, is the kind of person many less assertive people wish they had the guts to be. "I want to see the manager!" she'll bark to a surly waiter. "What's your badge number?" she'll snap to a cop who gives her a ticket she feels she doesn't deserve. And if a construction worker dares to make a lewd remark about her curvy anatomy, she'll raise her hand in an unmistakable, and obscene, gesture of defiance.

This is the Troublemaker—all sass, spoiling for a fight. And somehow, like a heat-seeking missile, she always finds one. You may not like her—she may even make you nervous—but it's hard not to admire her: *she will not be bullied.*

When you are in trouble, you want a Troublemaker on your side. In my childhood, the girl I most wanted to be was a Troublemaker named Greta. She was the ringleader of the girls in my class, and always walked down the street banked by two loyal acolytes, a sure sign of her power. Luckily she liked me—that is, I was sufficiently servile so that she didn't *dislike* me.

No one messed with Greta. If you weren't the soul of adoring unction, and sometimes even if you were, she'd cut you dead. She even made the teachers anxious; she'd put sneezing powder in their desks.

Greta kept people on their toes; they never knew when they would become targets of her unpredictable animosity.

By the time she was grown, Greta had scarcely changed—except, perhaps, for the worse. In the wake of her volatile personality floats the wreckage of two broken marriages, a string of failed jobs, and friendships that somehow never last.

Not all Troublemakers are as unregenerately angry and pugnacious as Greta. Some, having maneuvered through childhood on combat readiness, find a loving mentor or go into therapy and become more moderate Superachievers later on. They fuel their careers with the high energy that once fired their wrath. This was true of Heidi, quoted at the beginning of this chapter.

Other Troublemakers become softened by the years and recall their childhood rebelliousness with wonder, as though talking about someone else. "I can't believe some of the things I did," one of them says, shaking her head. "I don't know where I got the nerve. I certainly didn't have courage; I had *gall.* It was the only way to survive."

Still other Troublemakers may appear to the world at large to be mollified, but they haven't entirely abandoned their fighting spirit, which erupts only with their mothers. As one otherwise charming and even-tempered woman told me, "Usually, I'm pretty much under control. But with my mother, I'm another person. When I'm around her for more than a day, I'm a maniac. We fight *constantly.*"

"She can still get me," another reformed Troublemaker says of her mother. "The other day, she caught me picking my fingers and said, 'Stop that.' I shouted, 'Shut your goddamn mouth!' She's eighty, for God's sake, and I'm forty-five—and we're still going at it."

But most Troublemakers maintain their belligerent childhood stance right into adulthood and in most of their attachments. They don't know any other way to behave. What you see, however, is not—if you look closely enough—necessarily what you get.

The Hasty Heart

In her fiery trajectory, the Troublemaker gives every appearance of being the Cipher's opposite number. But in reality, she is really the Cipher's negative image. Her combative demeanor is merely a smokescreen.

"The passive, clinging three-year-old has not really changed if [she] becomes an aggressive adult," write Drs. Alexander Thomas and Stella Chess. She is displaying a "reaction formation," the psychological term for keeping an unconscious need (in this case, for dependency) under wraps by going to the opposite extreme in her behavior.

Thus, the Troublemaker could be a Cipher *in disguise*. She is as emotionally connected to her mother—if only through anger—as her slavelike peer.

Where other daughters camouflage their furies with bountiful generosity, career success, or chronic contrition, the Troublemaker does the reverse: When she feels threatened, she unsheathes her rage for all to see and lunges into battle, the one she *imagines* is about to begin.

But what protects her also isolates her. One such Troublemaker, a cop, put the paradox of her personality this way:

> Everyone thinks I'm a tough cookie. On the beat, I am—nothing gets by me. I *love* busting the bad guys. But inside, I'm a marshmallow. I'm always wondering, "Can't people see that I'm bleeding from every pore? Doesn't it show?"

In many ways, the Troublemaker is the loneliest of all five categories of daughters. Behind her tart remarks and killing one-liners—or her complexion that mottles with rage as she discusses her mother—there is a woman terrified of rejection.

She may *seem* tough, but emotionally she is brittle. For if she is quick to anger, she is equally quick to weep, a weakness she would rather die than reveal.

It's not easy for the outsider to recognize her soft underbelly—and, because of her hotheadedness and her barbs, it's even more difficult to be empathetic to it.

The problem is that when she was a child, she was always far too valued as an adversary to be inspired to modify her behavior. Her mother *encouraged* her to act the way she does. And the last thing the Troublemaker wants, prickly appearances notwithstanding, is to separate from her mother.

The Making of a Hellion

Some Troublemakers are simply unwanted children. Several of the women I interviewed knew early in life that they were an unwelcome surprise, either because they hadn't been planned or because they weren't boys.

Other Troublemakers were born at bad times in their mothers' lives. One woman told me that her mother, having had several miscarriages before she was born, was permanently embittered about motherhood. Another said that her mother had wanted a divorce, but because of her daughter's birth, she felt trapped in her hopeless marriage.

All the Troublemakers I interviewed were considered "problem children." They were, perversely, fulfilling an important family requirement. It is in the interests of the Troublemaker's mother—and often her father—to keep her in the doghouse.

While at first she may try very hard to appease them by being obedient, she quickly learns that being angelic or achieving or contrite doesn't work for her. They do not *want* her to be a "good girl." Her role as *provocateur* is too important.

So the Troublemaker lives out her mandate: in her "badness," she makes it possible for everyone in the family to feel "good" because she takes the rap for everything that goes wrong. Troublemakers serve as lightning rods for family problems.

In most cases, her parents have a cheerless marriage. Rather than face their own troubles, they turn on her—she becomes the focus of their unresolved frustrations and, at the same time, the instrument of their rare consonance.

Thanks to the Troublemaker's bad behavior, Mom and Dad can become a united front. She is the child who was angrily banished from the dinner table for being "fresh." She is the one of whom her teachers would say, in terse notes to her parents, "Disruptive in the classroom; needs discipline." She is the one who, in high school, hung out with the fast crowd, the drinkers, the druggies, the dregs.

At least where she is concerned, her parents can agree on *something*. Just as they reinforce her behavior, she—unwittingly—reinforces theirs.

By the time she is an adult, the Troublemaker's confrontational behavior is so ingrained that she may not know any other way to be. She courses through life like a stray bullet. For her, trouble is an addiction.

And when she leaves home, the Troublemaker often falls apart, bereft of a target for her behavior, and bereft, too, because she still does not have her mother's approval. Continued belligerence is the way the Troublemaker keeps the acrimonious bond with her mother— by now an indelible feature of their relationship—going.

Says psychotherapist Ann Gordon,

> A daughter who telephones her mother every day to scream and yell at her is deriving some payoff for that behavior. It may be that, using anger as a connector, she is unconsciously trying to confirm— every day—that she has a mommy. For her, a negative relation- ship with her mother is better than no relationship at all.

The only way for her to sustain a sense of purpose in the family— however misguided—is constantly to be in need of rescue. So she perpetually gets into trouble, calls for help, asks for money, pro- vokes a fight.

Like a war correspondent looking for a war, the Troublemaker doesn't know how to respond to peace—for her, it is an unnatural state. Says psychotherapist Lilly Singer,

> Anger can become a pattern that has a life of its own. A consis- tently angry daughter may have learned in childhood that the only way she could get anywhere with her mother is by being angry. But by adulthood, her anger may be only dimly related to the mother. Now she's mad at her boss, or a friend, or her husband, or her kids. Consciously, her anger has nothing to do with her mother; unconsciously, it has everything to do with her.

Because of her early training, the Troublemaker finds herself in an unending series of scrapes and scuffles. And whyever not? She has *always* gotten attention this way, ever since she was a little kid.

There are three characteristics of the Troublemaker's background that helped to shape her, any or all of which apply:

> the "mis-fit";
> Daddy's little girl;
> sibling rivalry.

The Misfit

In ways, it seems as though the Troublemaker fought her way out of the womb. To a degree, that may be true. Many are "difficult" from the moment they are born—but the term, at least when used by researchers, requires definition.

According to Drs. Thomas and Chess, the "difficult child" only becomes so when her intrinsic rhythms and sensibilities are either misunderstood or ignored. This child recoils from new or unfamiliar circumstances and frequently responds to challenges with intensity—*negative* intensity.

Parental patience and careful preparation of these children for new situations or expectations can help deflect their angry defenses. But the Troublemaker's parents interpret her behavior as insolence—she is seen by them as a "bad kid." And the more they try to coerce her, the angrier and more rebellious she gets. Mother and child will inevitably lock horns in what can become a lifelong battle between them.

Many mothers and daughters don't get along because they are so *different* from one another. But with the Troublemaker, the problem frequently is that she and her mother are *too much alike*. For them, the issue is power—the daughter wants more of it. And the mother isn't about to give an inch of her authoritarian turf.

When spirited Troublemaker meets up with Critic, Smotherer, or Avenger—three extraordinarily controlling types—the results can be volcanic: unlike the Angel and the Cipher, the Troublemaker is incapable of obsequiousness.

Maria, a thirty-two-year-old Troublemaker, says that the only way she was able to deflect the suffocation of her Smotherer mother was to rebel. "Thank God I was born with an ability to fight," she says, "or I would have been pulverized by this woman. She's an iron butterfly."

Maria's altercations with her mother began when Maria started nursery school. Her mother would insist that she wear a blue skirt and sweater to school. Maria would stonewall: she would *only* wear the *plaid* skirt with the *striped* blouse.

"We had knock-down-drag-out fights over what I would wear," says Maria, "the same fight, every day. Ultimately, I would get out of the house wearing what I wanted. I would win—but it would be worth my life."

Not all Troublemakers are similarly victorious—many "win" by losing. Several of them told me that they reacted to their mothers' pressure for perfection by *deliberately* failing. A recurring theme in these mother–Troublemaker attachments was the mothers' inability to praise their daughters.

Edna, thirty-seven, never once heard her Critic mother say, "I'm proud of you," even though she was an honors student. Her mother was always finding some flaw, some tiny mistake, to pounce on: Edna's weight, or her friends, or, in her mother's terms, her being a "know-it-all."

When she was young, Edna found a useful, albeit childish, weapon against her compulsively tidy mother—Edna became a slob. When her mother would bring Edna's laundered and folded clothes to her room, Edna would carefully mix them in with the pile of soiled clothes already scattered across the floor.

Later, Edna found bigger, more self-destructive weapons. In high school she suddenly started flunking all her tests. She says,

> My mother was always telling the neighbors about all my accomplishments. But she was so cruel to me that I decided the one thing I could do to her was to deny her any chance to take pride in me. I stopped studying. I cut school. I started hanging out with greasers and drinking with them in the afternoon.

Because she didn't want her mother to have any power over her, Edna stayed in a holding pattern of defiance until she was nearly thirty, when she got her high school equivalency rating. "By then, I could do it for me, and she couldn't make it hers."

Another self-destructive Troublemaker, Susan, forty, had an Avenger mother who couldn't allow her daughter—even when she was a young child—to have any joy. When Susan would dance around the living room, lurching clumsily to music on the radio, her mother would say, "You don't know the first thing about dancing. It takes years of practice to be proficient at it."

When she was in high school, her mother criticized Susan's choice of attire: "That color is so trashy," she'd say, or "You have no style." Says Susan, "She was always, always belittling me. And I'm very strong-willed—I always fought back."

Ultimately, Susan fought back by abusing drugs—LSD, marijuana, uppers and downers. "When I was zonked, she couldn't touch me. The trouble is, it fried my brains. Although I stopped using drugs ten years ago, I still feel as though I'm outside my body. Part of me is just gone."

In some cases, the Troublemaker's volatile relationship with her mother becomes violent.

When Sheila was born, her Critic mother was overwhelmed by the stress of mothering, financial worries, and her unhappy marriage. The stresses persisted through Sheila's turbulent childhood, during which she was always the family upstart.

Her relationship with her mother reached critical mass when Sheila dropped out of high school. She says,

> One afternoon I was in the kitchen, doing the dishes. My mother came home from work and started in on me: "Well, look who's here. The Loser." She was on my back about the fact that I wasn't doing anything with my life. I wasn't exactly proud of myself, but she made it worse.
>
> She pushed and pushed and pushed—I tried to ignore her. But my adrenaline was pumping, and when she didn't stop, I grabbed a knife and shoved it at her. I knew I was being a jerk, but I did it anyhow. She said, "Go ahead, *loser*, cut me—I'll call the cops." It was like, choose your weapons. So I said, "Okay, you bitch, have your own daughter arrested." She burst into tears and went to her room.

Such Troublemakers give the impression to family and friends of bravado and arrogant indifference. But emotionally, they care *desperately* what their mothers think of them. As Sheila, now twenty-six, told me, "I hated myself for hating my mother so much. All I feel today is guilt that I acted that way. And sadness. I still want a mother."

Daddy's Little Girl

For most of the Troublemakers I interviewed, their lack of an affectionate connection with their mothers is exacerbated by being Daddy's favorite. These women sensed that a loving bond with Mom was virtually unattainable, and they turned to their fathers instead.

Some of their aggressive behavior was a by-product of having a man as a role model, and by having a father who was all too eager to have an ally against his wife. So when Dad hollered at Mom, Troublemaker identified with *him* rather than with her.

"It was my way to survive," says one woman, who spent much of her growing-up years hunting, or fishing, or playing ball, or doing chores with her dad. Her father, she says, "treated me like a boy. We'd work together on the car, and we'd chat. It was the only attention I got."

The Troublemaker's mother, jealous of the father–daughter relationship, will often withdraw even farther from her daughter, abandoning her to the only alliance available. That alliance simply compounds her mother's jealousy.

"My mother told me I was the apple of my father's eye," one woman said. "I knew she was envious. He gave me much more attention than he ever gave her, or my sisters."

Occasionally, the Troublemaker–father bond can become extremely damaging to the daughter. The daughter of an Avenger told me that her father regularly visited prostitutes and boasted about it to her. As a child, when she and her father went on outings together, she would try to please him by pointing out pretty women passing by. And when she was grown, she continued to identify with her father by being chronically promiscuous, picking up men in bars and bragging to them about her sexual prowess.

Sibling Rivalry

The Troublemaker's personality is cemented by her experience with her siblings. As the "black sheep," she is set up for failure with them.

The overwhelming majority of Troublemakers I interviewed were secondborn or younger children. Since the jobs of Angel and/or Superachiever were already filled, the Troublemaker resolved everyone's unhappiness by becoming the repository of it. Parents and siblings needed someone to blame: the Troublemaker filled that need. This is the case also with the Troublemaker who is an only child.

The Troublemaker is made the scapegoat for a variety of reasons:

According to researchers who study sibling relationships, certain children are tacitly encouraged by their parents to act out anger that the parents feel but cannot express. When these children slug it out with their siblings, their parents excuse it as so much "horseplay," secretly delighting in any display of spirit.

Sometimes the Troublemaker is used to punish another child the parent dislikes. These parents do not attempt to curtail sibling violence; they simply let it happen.

In other cases, siblings duplicate their parents' anger toward each other; the Angel may identify with the Good Mommy, and the Troublemaker, as we saw earlier, will identify with the Bad Daddy. As long as these sisters are at war with each other, each parent has an ally in the marital battle.

Finally, the Troublemaker serves as a cautionary tale to her siblings—she is used to control them by her naughty example. Her siblings see her getting grounded, or spanked, or shunned, and avoid doing anything that will attract the same reprisals.

Everyone in the family profits from the Troublemaker's badness. She becomes a rebel without a cause of her own—except, perhaps, for *some* kind of attention, usually punitive.

The only way she can get *positive* attention is by becoming sick. A large number of Troublemakers I interviewed had numerous childhood illnesses and handicaps—chronic bronchitis and stuttering were common among these women. And each of them said, "That's the only time my mother was nice to me." Failures of health were, in a sense, one more "mistake" to be rewarded. In any case, a sick child is not a threatening one.

In the running account of parental favoritism that siblings keep in their heads, Troublemakers *know* that they are being treated unfairly—they just don't know *why*. Said one woman, "My older sisters would usually do what my mother asked; but if they didn't, it was okay with her. The only person who wasn't allowed to disobey was me. I was always punished; my sisters never were. I couldn't figure it out."

The Troublemaker's lack of a sense of worth is the legacy of parents who are in many ways as immature as she is. The provocative behavior they, perhaps unwittingly, encourage in her gets reinforced by her siblings, especially by her sisters, who, as her gender peers, know exactly how to set her up. They exaggerate their goodness and stoke her badness, so that they will get a larger chunk of the parental pie.

When Penny was growing up, her older sister, Ruth, was the "perfect" child. Ruth got good grades, kept her room neat, was the sobersided, obedient older sister who tattled about Penny's every infraction.

Penny, irked at having three "bosses"—her parents and her Angel sister—became a terror. Every day she would steal money from her mother's wallet and claim to have found it lying on the street. If she wanted something, she would throw a tantrum to get it. While Ruth took no for an answer, Penny never did. When Ruth asked for a new bike, her mother refused. But when Penny screamed for one, her mother gave in.

In her confusing partiality, the mother implied her approval of Penny's increasingly vicious treatment of her older sister by reinforcing it.

Over Ruth's outraged protests, Penny routinely invaded Ruth's room and took whatever she wanted. Finally, Ruth became so exasperated by her sister's intrusiveness that she asked her mother for a lock on her bedroom door, a request her mother granted. Rather than discipline Penny and address the source of her daughter's destructiveness, her mother merely incited Penny's enraged retaliation.

Now thirty-six, Penny says,

> I cajoled and wheedled my mother for the key; I wouldn't give in. Neither would my mother. I was so frustrated that I ran outside in a blizzard to the side of the house, broke the window to Ruth's room, and climbed in. After that, my mother took the lock off the door to Ruth's room.
>
> I was really a lousy sister. I never realized until recently that my mother engineered our rivalry by never making us sort out our differences, and by allowing me to get away with murder.

Often, these sibling vendettas never heal—they become indelibly seared into the relationship. As the sisters age, their grudges fester. Their hair may be gray, but their anger remains forever vibrant and young: the "good" sister tries to make the Troublemaker feel guilty that she wasn't a "better daughter"; the Troublemaker retorts, "You were always Mom's favorite, Miss Goody Two-Shoes."

Both sisters tirelessly feed the hostility that began long ago. They become entwined in their mutual anger, having no basis for friendship outside of it, and never realizing its choreographer: the mother who divided—and conquered—them both.

And when the mother dies, her favoritism lives on in the sisters' hatred. As Stephen Bank and Michael Kahn write in *The Sibling Bond,*

. . . if one sibling was scapegoated by a dead parent, and if the other monopolized that parent's love, there is no reason for either sibling to place family solidarity above angry self-interest. Sibling relationships that have been very negative and polarized before a parent's death, will become more negative afterward.

Because of these three influences—the daughter as "mis-fit," being Daddy's little girl, and sibling rivalry—the Troublemaker, flooded by a lifetime of cumulative rage, eventually finds it boiling over into all her other attachments.

The Troublemaker at Work

Many Troublemakers are able to control their anger by siphoning it off into challenging and rewarding careers—they become, in adulthood, Superachievers.

For most Troublemakers, however, hostility often erupts on the job. They've already been outclassed in the family, and are not at all surprised to see their siblings pull ahead of them on the career track. Success in the family translates to success in the workplace; the Troublemaker, having no familiarity with the former, has little reason to pursue it in the latter.

Troublemakers blow their stacks at the boss, overreacting to criticism. They start fights with co-workers, who they think are out to get them. They quit their jobs in uncontrollable bursts of fury, slamming the door behind them. Not surprisingly, they often get fired.

The Troublemaker continues to defeat herself, edging to the brink of achievement and then ricocheting backward into self-sabotage. As one woman told me, "I'm a starter and a quitter. I have wonderful ideas, I have brains, but I cannot bring myself to go through with projects. I hear my mother's voice: 'You can't do this, you can't do that, you're stupid.' So I just give up."

For some of these Troublemakers, failure in their work is a way of staying angrily dependent on their mothers. Says a Troublemaker who can't seem to hold a job,

> I have not become anything in my life. I may have to reach the point where it's better to risk starving to death on my own than to keep failing at everything. But I always make excuses; if it weren't for my dead-end job, or if it weren't for my screwy boss who fired me, I could just bail out of my relationship with my mother. As it is, I still need her help, which I take, even though I hate her.

Fierce Attachments

For some Troublemakers, their friendships are their salvation— with buddies, they feel accepted and loved, and they treasure these connections, which are often lifelong.

But for many Troublemakers, in becoming chronically "bad" girls, they sacrifice that which women do best: They often jettison their capacity for empathy and for intimate friendships.

One woman I interviewed said that the only friendships she has are with women who are as "stubborn" and "outspoken" as she is. She explains,

> I don't repress my feelings about anything. My mother always said so many nasty things to me that I thought that's the thing you do with people. You say exactly what's on your mind, even if it's nasty. I don't take any shit from my friends, and they don't take any shit from me. We fight about everything. I find people who aren't like that very boring. It's only in the last few years that I've been able to stifle my impulse to be mean.

For these Troublemakers, intimacy with friends is too frightening because it erodes their ability to keep their dukes up. "I'm always the first to reject someone—I do it before they can do it to me," one of them says. "I have one best friend at a time. If we get too close, I ditch her and find another friend. I've always done that, pull away, and I've always been sorry afterward."

Says another Troublemaker, who has had several years of psychoanalysis,

> I never had close friends as a kid, and the few buddies I did have I was rotten to. I mistreated them out of anger at how my mother treated me. I would call them names. If a friend slept over, I'd be terrible to her. There was a lot of anger in me. I can still feel it. Sometimes I turn into my mother because of my temper, which is exactly like hers. Sometimes you just don't know how to stop. I see the mistakes I make, but it's hard to stop when you're in a rage.

Trouble in Paradise

Troublemakers tend to have chaotic attachments with the men in their lives, and the news somehow always filters back to their mothers.

Ida, for instance, has never wanted to marry, but she has always had stormy affairs about which she tells her mother, who constantly rebukes her for them.

Ida always thought that "if you love somebody, you fight with them." So she and her lovers constantly quarrel, and many of those men let her get away with her hostile treatment of them. When they do, Ida ends the relationship; when they do not, she just fights harder.

If the Troublemaker is married, anger can become the mortar of her relationship with her husband. In fact, according to one Troublemaker, it was what *kept* her married. She could only function when she was being attacked—that's when she felt most alive. So she saw to it that her husband had plenty to complain about. She says,

> I was miserable to my husband—I had an affair two weeks after we got married. I didn't want to, but somehow I couldn't help myself. It was *exciting*. He forgave me, but I did it again. I put him through hell. He finally got fed up and divorced me.

The most troubled of these women ultimately end up with men
who terrify them. Says one woman, the daughter of an Avenger,

> When a man is really nuts about me, it turns me off.
> I'm drawn to men like my mom. I like the ones who
> scare me.
>   One guy I dated broke my nose. The fact that I
> didn't break up with him caused terrible upheaval in
> my family. Finally I realized that I was going to get
> myself killed if I kept up the life I was leading. In
> therapy I discovered that I did crazy things to get
> attention, the way I did when I was a kid. But the only
> one who got hurt was me.

This woman has dreams, she says, "that keep me going." They
are the dreams of a little girl, about Prince Charming riding up on a
white charger to rescue her from her mother, her past, herself. She
says wistfully, "I really want a normal life—a happy marriage, kids,
a house with a picket fence that I'll keep clean and filled with the
smells of pies baking in the oven. I hope I get the chance."
Of such women, psychiatrist Marianne Goodman says,

> What they are looking for is a recapitulation of the unloving
> relationship they had with their mothers. They are still willing to
> be the "bad ones." They *say* that they're looking for a loving
> relationship, but they're really looking for failure, time after time,
> because they have to prove mommy right.

The Troublemaker as Mother

Many Troublemakers start out as loving parents—here, finally, is
an opportunity for them to be rewarded for *good* behavior. When
they sing to their baby, the baby smiles; when they take their child
to the zoo, the child laughs with pleasure. It's wonderful.
Until the child begins to rebel. And at that instant, the Troublemaker is thrown back into an earlier, perhaps even forgotten, scenario: in her gut, she feels her "controlling mother" in the guise of
the child who is trying to carve out his or her own identity. It's like a
double exposure: she looks at her child's face that is crumpled with
rage, and "sees" her angry mother.
Says the daughter of a Critic,

I had a huge investment in being right with my kids. It was hard for me to acknowledge them as separate human beings with opinions of their own that might differ from mine. They've told me that I never let them in close. I didn't know how to show them love and approval. I just knew that I couldn't ever be wrong.

Many Troublemakers are extremely strict, and, obeying the internalized Bad Mommy of their childhoods, are in danger of acting as brutally as their own mothers may have acted. One woman told me, "When my son was an infant, I was sure I was going to kill him, and half the time I wanted to. I had these fantasies about smashing his head against the wall. Awful thoughts. I didn't beat him, but I came close. I was always screaming at him, feeling out of control."

One such Troublemaker, a battered child, did in fact beat her daughter. She says, "I would just strike out at her whenever she misbehaved. It's what my mother always did. If it weren't for my husband, who made me see that there are other ways to get out my frustration, I might have killed her."

Other Troublemakers remember all too well the ways in which they were "bad girls" and are determined their daughters won't be like that. Celia, twenty-nine, says, "When I was in school there were two kinds of girls: One was the cool type who wore tight jeans and smoked cigarettes and hung out on the street; I was 'cool.' The other kind was the teacher's pet, had preppy friends, and never got into trouble. I wasn't like that. But that's what I want my *daughter* to be like."

Celia recognizes herself in her daughter, but is unable to recognize her Avenger *mother* in herself. For when her daughter refuses to obey her, she erupts. "We're a lot alike. I hit her much more than I hit my son. When she digs in her heels and talks back to me, I explode."

And so the Troublemaker creates turmoil with her children, as she did with her mother, her siblings, her friends and colleagues. Unless she gets help, or has a loving counselor in a spouse or a friend whom she trusts, she cannot break the cycle of anger that gets played out before her amazed, and blazing, eyes.

Profile of a Troublemaker

When Beth, forty-six, was visiting her married daughter, her daughter gave her my ad and encouraged her to call me. "It might help you to talk about your mother," she said.

Beth's daughter is her greatest joy. She only had one child, she says, because she didn't want ever to be in the position of playing favorites. Her own mother's favoritism was the nightmare of Beth's childhood, and the anguishing coda to her otherwise relatively stable and fulfilling life.

She was raised in a poor section of Spokane, the second of two daughters. "My older sister, Cora, was the 'chosen' child," she says. "I was not, because my mother wanted a son."

Both parents were extremely religious and devoted to each other. And their firstborn was a most rewarding daughter—industrious, respectful and adoring of her mother.

"They were like Siamese twins, my mother and Cora," Beth says, her voice lowering to a growl, as it does every time she speaks of her sister. And Cora was not about to relinquish her position of honor.

During their childhood, Cora constantly squealed on her younger sister. Once, when the girls were walking home from school, Cora told Beth to carry her books, and Beth refused. When they got home, Cora ran to her mother and related her sister's "selfishness." Beth's mother fetched a razor strop from the bathroom and beat her with it. Cora looked on, smiling.

"My mother was a morally fine woman," Beth says, "but she had this determination: You did as you were told, or else. Cora always did as she was told. I was the rebellious one."

Beth was beaten regularly throughout her childhood; when she was three, it was for wetting her pants. When she was ten, it was for forgetting to make her bed. And when she wasn't beaten, her mother would terrify her with ghost stories, and by taking her to funerals and forcing her to look into the coffins. "She said she did it to cure me of my fears," Beth says.

Her mother's treatment of her sparked in Beth mutinous and vengeful fantasies. She would walk by the city courthouse and imagine turning her mother in to the authorities as a child abuser. She'd read about colleges in faraway cities, one of which she vowed someday to attend to escape from home.

But college seemed like an impossible dream, because school was torture. It wasn't because she got poor grades (they were average) or because she didn't have friends (she preferred keeping to herself)—it was because she had panic attacks whenever a teacher called on her. Occasionally, one of the boys would taunt her for being unable to speak in class, and she'd wait for him after school and beat him up.

To compensate for her feelings of isolation, Beth formed a semblance of attachment with her father, something her mother, in a curious blend of cruelty and canniness, engineered. Her mother once said to her, "Cora is my favorite child; you can be your father's favorite, if you try hard." And so Beth would help her father, who raised chickens in the backyard, to clean out their pens and to gather eggs. "He liked me," she says. "At least, he never played favorites."

When she wasn't working outside with her father, she was working inside the house. Cora, who was petite, was considered too frail to do menial work. It was left to muscular and robust Beth to scrub the floors, to do the washing and ironing and cooking, while her mother sat reading or talking on the telephone.

Beth left home at eighteen and went to the University of Florida. There she met a young man whom she married after graduation, settling in Omaha, where they raised her only child. Beth's husband died when her daughter was eleven, and Beth got a job working as a typist, and later became an office manager.

Beth gave her daughter ballet and tennis lessons, and when her daughter reached her teens, Beth helped her become independent, not taking personally her child's pubescent mood swings. "I was determined that she would feel good about herself, and that she would have a life of her own. She's had more trouble separating from me than I had separating from her."

Almost miraculously, Beth created a life of tranquillity and acceptability for her child. But the rage she felt toward her sister was never far below the surface. When there was a wedding in the family, Beth never attended. When her mother died, Beth refused to go to the funeral or take any of her mother's personal effects. Both situations would have required being in her sister's presence.

She says,

> I could disconnect from my mother, because I understood that she had a hard life. But I couldn't let go of my hatred for Cora. In a way, they are one person—I think about my mother, and my sister's face appears in my mind.

After her mother died, Beth made one attempt to reconcile with Cora. Beth invited her to visit, and the floodgates opened—all of Cora's righteous indignation spewed out at her sister.

Cora said things like "You'd think that people who let themselves get fat would go on a diet." She cited the material advantages Beth's husband had once provided—new cars, a new house, vacations in the summer—and put them down as "ostentation."

Says Beth, "After two days, I threw her out, and I haven't seen her since. I don't ever want to see her again as long as I live."

The sibling rivalry that pushed Beth and her sister into opposite corners still seethes, even though they have no contact. "Our terrible hatred for each other has become more and more intense as years have gone by," she says.

As the two women move toward the last season of their lives, they do not perceive that their enmity is the only real connection either of them ever had with their mother.

Both women are equally damaged by their childhoods. Cora, the good daughter, never tasted the freedom and affection that Beth sought for herself by rebelling against her mother. Beth is all the things Cora, the devoted child who never strayed from her mother, has not allowed herself to be. Goodness didn't pay off for Cora; hers are the regrets of an emotionally impoverished Angel.

But neither did "badness" bring Beth any real peace. "In my head, my sister will always be the 'chosen child,' " Beth says. "And I am still the child my mother never wanted. I will never forgive her for that. And I will never forgive my sister, who won't let me forget it."

Beth has no regrets. What she has—even after all these years, and in spite of the joy her daughter gives her—is an angry wound that shows no signs of healing. It defines her. She cannot give it up.

15
The Defector

My mother and I cannot have a relationship. I cannot say, "I forgive you for neglecting me, for humiliating me, for never showing me any affection." If I did that, I'd be crazier than she is. I used to have these fantasies that she'd say how sorry she was for being so cruel to me, we'd weep in each other's arms, and walk off into the sunset together. But that's not possible for me—my sanity depends on staying away from her. Most people don't understand that.

—Amy, thirty-three

Edith, thirty-nine, has not seen her mother in five years. No cards, no visits, no calls. Nothing.

Until their estrangement, Edith would occasionally visit her mother. But she always did so with a knot in the pit of her stomach, for on those occasions her mother would spend the entire time either talking about herself or—more likely—denigrating Edith.

Her mother would criticize her for how she was bringing up her child; she'd reminisce about what a "good man" her ex-son-in-law had been, and add, "Your father never ran out on *me*." Each time, Edith would vow never to see her mother again—but after a while she'd start to feel guilty, and she'd call. The cycle would begin again.

The turning point was six months after Edith's divorce. She was at her mother's house for Easter, and her daughter, then five, was having a difficult time adjusting to her new, ruptured life. During dinner, the child removed a piece of gristle from her mouth and put it on the tablecloth.

Suddenly Edith's mother launched into a tirade about the child's table manners, reducing her to tears. Says Edith,

> Something in me snapped: Appearances always came ahead of feelings when I grew up. I would be smacked if I mussed up the pillows on the living room couch. I would be spanked if I didn't say "please" and "thank you." Here was my mother doing it *again*, only this time, with my daughter—haranguing her about *etiquette* at the worst time of her life. Watching her attack my child made me wake up to the fact that our relationship was too destructive to continue.

Edith is a Defector, that category of women—psychologically or physically battered by their mothers—who bolted from their families and, with rare exceptions, never looked back.

Why did they do it? What makes them different from the faithful Angel, the workaholic Superachiever, the spongelike Cipher, the reckless Troublemaker, who may have grown up *in identical circumstances* yet stayed connected, in one way or another, to their families?

Why did the Defector, and not the others, bail out? The answer to that one is easy. They were *desperate* and believed they *had no choice.* For if they had stayed within the relationship, they say, they would have killed their mothers, killed themselves, or lost their minds.

But are they strong? The answer to that one is not so simple.

Most of the Defectors I interviewed did not begin life as mutineers. Like other children, they were eager to please their mothers. But something set them apart in their early years, something that made them feel different from their siblings.

For one thing, they were more damaged than their siblings. Stubborn Superachievers and hotheaded Troublemakers got their share of devastating punishments—but Defectors got more of them. Why? Because their mothers sensed, rightly or wrongly, that *this* child could not be broken.

Defectors quickly became self-reliant, believing that their relationships with their mothers were utterly hopeless. And the last thing they were going to allow was their own devastation. As one of them put it, "I knew when I was a little girl that I'd never be taken care of, never protected, never helped. I knew if I was going to survive, I'd have to do it on my own."

Most Defectors are firstborn children. A large minority, however, are middle-borns. Of them, a researcher wrote, "They think they notice that they matter least among the siblings. Hence they may long to leave the family earlier in life than their siblings would. They may move out, move far away."

Whatever their birth rank, as far back as most Defectors can remember they wanted out—if not at sixteen or seventeen, then when they were emotionally able to pull it off. Some spent their childhoods and early adulthoods as Angels or Ciphers, doing exactly as they were told. But inside they kept a psychic bank account: in it they made regular deposits of anger, and when they had enough "saved," they broke out of the family.

These were women who, rather than deny their anger, *drew upon it*. Anger was their ticket to freedom. One of them said, "I learned not to be vulnerable, because the minute I was, my mother would abuse me more. If I cried, she'd hit me harder. So I became hard as a rock. Once I said to her, 'You can break every bone in my body. But you're not going to break my spirit.' "

Defectors have some or all of the following characteristics in common:

They had virtually no relationship with their fathers, who were either as cruel as their mothers or failed to intervene on their daughters' behalf;
they were victims of either child abuse or incest;
they had parents who were alcoholics;
they felt like outsiders within the family.

Breaking Points

It's hard to predict when a Defector will decide to terminate her relationship with her mother.

Carol's defection occurred when she was twenty-five. The first-born of her parent's two children—her brother is six years younger than she is—she grew up in a household devoid of warmth and redolent of fear.

Her Avenger mother routinely degraded and terrorized her plain but brilliant daughter. She would tell neighbors on the stoop of their Baltimore row house, or relatives at a family event, that Carol was ugly and worthless. If a classmate called Carol on the phone to invite her over, her mother would not permit her to speak to her. "What's the point?" she'd say. "You can't go anyhow—there's too much work to do around here. Anyhow, who'd want to play with you?"

The turning point in their relationship came when she was twenty-four, working as a photographer and still living at home. Her mother, a Roman Catholic, woke her in the middle of the night to confront her angrily about a letter from a non-Catholic beau she'd found while rummaging through Carol's purse. Says Carol,

> She ranted about how ungrateful and disloyal I was. Until then, I had never talked back to her, never been less than obedient. But suddenly, I felt like my life was on the line—I couldn't take one more attack. I got up, put on my clothes, and went to a friend's house. I stayed away for three days without calling.

The final break occurred a month later, when her mother had a stroke. Carol spent every evening sitting at her mother's hospital bedside, struggling with whether or not she should quit her job and take care of her mother, which both her parents fully expected her to do. She says,

> I had to make a decision: I thought to myself, "It's her life or mine." Six weeks after she came home, I packed my things and moved out, the sounds of her screams and threats ringing in my ears. I remember standing on the street with my suitcases, looking up at the apartment and saying to myself, "If you go back into that house, you'll be swallowed up. Run for your life." I've never been sorry.

Unlike Carol, Roberta had no ambivalence about her defection. She knew from early childhood that leaving was not only necessary but would be welcome. "My mother didn't want to be a mother," says Roberta, thirty-five. "That's the whole foundation of my relationship with her."

Her mother had made it abundantly clear that Roberta was an unwelcome, even detestable, addition to the family. Once, with sadistic pride, her mother said to her, "I never had to touch you when you were a baby—I always had a maid."

Such little murders were fixtures in Roberta's childhood. When she was little, her mother would try to force her to drink her milk, and when she did not, her mother would make her sit all day at the table until she had drained the glass. She never spent a holiday with her parents—they were always traveling. She would eat Christmas or Thanksgiving turkey at a friend's house, or at the home of the servant of the moment.

Roberta frequently ran away from home when she was a teenager, and neither her mother—nor her father, who kept out of their fights—would look for her. And at seventeen, she ran away for good.

She found a job and rented a room over the garage on an estate in the suburban community where her parents lived. Roberta built for herself a split-level life; she would visit her brothers and sisters at family gatherings, but she wouldn't see her mother outside of those occasions. She read every self-help book she could find and went to college at night.

At twenty-eight, she worked her way through graduate school, earning a Master's in social work. Today, she treats women like herself—outraged emotional orphans who have learned to make lives for themselves out of the emotional rubble of their childhoods.

Of her mother, Roberta says, "She kept me an outsider all my life. I literally invented myself. I had to learn to make friends, to talk to people, to make my own way. There's nothing I need from her now; there was everything I needed from her when I was young."

This Way Out

Certain factors seem to contribute to the Defector's sense of survival—one is temperament. As psychologist Louise J. Kaplan writes, "Some babies start to separate unusually early, particularly those whose mothers had no belief in the baby's urges to grow and grab on to the world. [The mother's] continuously intrusive excitability may often prompt a baby to move into separateness as quickly as possible."

Some Defectors are so maimed by their childhoods that flight is their only coping mechanism. They think of the world as essentially inhospitable, and they never put their faith in anyone or anything— they live for themselves alone.

But other Defectors are simply "indomitable"—or, as they are also called, "invulnerable"—children. They seem to have a miraculous ability to retain their sanity, even sanguinity, in the face of parental psychosis, alcoholism, and physical and psychological brutality.

Scientists who study invulnerable children are interested not in why children become mentally ill, but rather in *why some of them appear to be strong and emotionally healthy.* These children are extraordinary in their ability to cope. They seem to adjust well to new situations, taking change in stride. They are eager and curious.

Invulnerable children seem to be insulated from the chaos that surrounds them, unlike their more vulnerable peers, who, as Freud put it, tend to undergo "too searching a fate." Some are extremely creative, cocooning themselves within their imaginations, reading voraciously, and writing stories that make some kind of logic out of the turmoil in their families.

Others are exceedingly spiritual—some believe there is a higher purpose in their misery, and that faith will ultimately save them from it.

These children do not shroud themselves forever in depression and despair—instead, they see their misfortunes as challenges to be met and overcome. They bounce back from adversity—each victory over it makes them *stronger.* As one researcher writes, "pain and suffering can have a steeling—a hardening—effect on some children, rendering them capable of mastering life with all its obstacles."

One of their special gifts is that they know where to go for help.

Invulnerable children are not unacquainted with love. Many were nurtured in their first year of life by their mothers, before those mothers abandoned them to neglect or abuse. Others got love from a grandmother or cherished aunt, or a kindly teacher or neighbor.

Amy, quoted at the beginning of this chapter, grew up in a household of horrifying abuse. She was able to keep alive a spark of self-worth by searching for tenderness outside the family. She says,

> I guess I looked like I needed adopting when I was a kid. On the block where I grew up, there was a woman in her sixties who walked her dog every day around the time I was coming home from school. She'd invite me in to have milk and cookies. My parents forbade me to see her, and I'd sneak out of the house to visit her. It was the only time I deliberately disobeyed them. That woman gave me whatever it is that children are supposed to get from parents—a pat on the head, a "How did it go today?" With her, I got to be a little girl and not be afraid.

These mentors help Defectors believe that they have value. As one Defector put it, "I guess I always knew I wasn't garbage."

The most riveting characteristic of invulnerable children is that they do not deny their experiences, good or bad, or the feelings attached to them. Somehow, they retain their humanity.

Whether invulnerable or not, memory serves the Defector. For one, it is her tool for being strong and staying sane. For another, it is her reason for never trusting anyone ever again.

Defectors may appear to be tough, but they bear permanent scars. For them, the world does not feel like a safe place, a feeling that is reinforced by the Bad Mommy Taboo. If someone asks the Defector about her parents and she says, "I don't see them," that person responds with a blank look. "How about your siblings?" such a person might press, trying another approach, searching for happy endings. "I don't see them," the Defector repeats. And so the potential friend may either rebuke the Defector ("Surely you can't mean it") or dismiss her as an oddball, and retreat.

"I've learned that most people really don't want to know," a Defector says without rancor. "They think it's catching."

And so the Defector continues to feel like a woman without a country. One Defector told me, "I stopped seeing my mother because every time I did, I always got pounded on the head. It was like walking into a fire. How can you keep doing that and expect not to get hurt? So I walked away. But I haven't found anything to walk toward."

The most damaged Defectors plummet into a lifetime of self-destructiveness. Unlike Troublemakers, they do *not* want rescue. They have internalized the message that they deserve nothing but rejection, and so they continue to place themselves into situations that keep them outcasts.

One woman I interviewed has been in and out of mental institutions for most of her adulthood. She has been an alcoholic and a drug addict. She has gambled away thousands of dollars. In her youth she married, had two children, and left them to go off with a man of no particular value—just someone who would take her away from anything that required a commitment.

Now fifty, she has not seen her parents or siblings in thirty years. A year ago she decided that she had only one choice: either she was going to die, or she was going to live. So she decided to try living. "It was that simple," she says.

She checked into a rehabilitation center, and upon her release got a job as a waitress. She found a therapist "who would not allow me to keep running away. I'd yell and scream at him, but he just never gave up on me. I've been dry for six months. Maybe I'll be able to have a life after all—but believe me, I don't count on it. I live one day at a time."

She's one of the lucky few of the most emotionally mutilated Defectors, the majority of whom leave their families and sink into oblivion.

The Price of Defection

Most of the Defectors I interviewed did not fall into the abyss. But they have retained an impulse to flee from any kind of attachment. The risk of always looking for an "out" is that they may find themselves stranded, the escape route out of the family overrun with brambles, blocking the way to *any* connection.

One woman summarized the Defector's terrible dilemma this way: "I've got suitcases of emotional baggage that stretch across the road. You keep dragging this stuff along even when you don't need it anymore. But it's very hard to give that up, because what do you have if you don't have what's in that bag? *What if it's nothing?*"

This anguish is inevitable, according to many psychotherapists, when Defectors cut off from their families of origin. To cut off from one's mother is, from the daughter's point of view, an act of desperation—she believes she has absolutely no choice. And when she defects, all the arguments she had with her mother are frozen into place. If and when she does see her mother again, even if it's years later, those heated issues resurface as though the break had just occurred.

These daughters are doing something sons have always done—men show they don't "need" their mothers anymore by getting as far away from her as possible. But for women, the issue gets muddied, because Mother represents her daughter's biological and emotional role model.

Virtually all psychotherapists agree that you cannot hate your mother and love yourself. For your own self-esteem and growth, it is necessary to reach some kind of understanding of, and resolution to, your relationship with your mother.

Says Dr. Michael Kerr, "To deal with your mother by cutting off—which is what many people tend to do—is not the answer. It relieves the anxiety of the moment, but it doesn't solve the long-term problem. Why not? Because you're vulnerable to transferring it from one relationship to another. When people focus on their new family, they argue that cutting off from the old one was the best thing they ever did. Until they run into problems in the new family. It's like being in a pressure cooker. Problems become more urgent because they have no way back to their original families."

Judith M. Fox, a psychotherapist who works with adolescents and their families, says that the child who defects still hasn't solved her difficulties. "It's an illusion that she's becoming her own person, because the daughter who runs takes her mother with her. She *seems* to function on a higher level. But the internalized mother is there and trips the process up. It gets played out later with her spouse or her child. The break is not really complete."

Defectors may bolt from their mothers to save their own lives. But if they don't resolve the relationship with the mothers *in their heads*, they never *really* grow up. For them, the unfinished business of their childhoods casts a long shadow over their adult lives.

Alone in the Family

As we have said, Defectors first become aware that they are "outsiders" in their own families—not just with their mothers, but with their fathers as well. One woman says, "My father has told me he won't see me unless I see my mother. It's a package deal: If I don't love her, he won't love me. I absolutely cannot be with her. So now I have no parents."

Defectors often become estranged from one or more of their siblings as well. Many Defectors were heroines to their brothers and sisters when they were little, shielding them from physical abuse by literally taking the blows for them, or by standing up to their parents in their siblings' defense, at great risk to themselves. Tragically, many of those Defectors are ultimately betrayed by the very siblings they fought so hard to protect.

Because they are less resilient or hardened than she is, the Defector's siblings often come to believe that they deserve the callous or barbaric treatment they received from their parents. But in their own need to survive, they often are unaware that their punishments were seldom as harsh as the Defector's punishments were. In some ways, siblings in severely dysfunctional families are unaware of each other; they are too busy putting one foot in front of the other, surviving one day at a time.

As we learned in the last four chapters, daughters who are insufficiently separated from their mothers often deny or cover up the pain of their childhoods to protect their mothers, or act out their anger to retain their place in the family.

It is natural, then, for some siblings to see the Defector as the enemy. She looms as a terrible reminder of the past in her ability to remember it, and in her ability to stand on her own. Because she refused to be scuttled in the same boat with them, she has violated a bizarre trust.

So when the Defector criticizes her mother, her siblings may say to her, "What are you talking about? We were never treated like that." In denying their own experience, they deny hers as well.

Said a thirty-eight-year-old Defector of her three sisters,

> Part of the problem is that we were all attacked separately by my mother and trained never to talk to anyone about our problems. We didn't confide even in each other. We didn't have sibling relationships. I was their substitute parent, never their sister. When I cut out of the family, I stayed away from weddings, funerals, everything, and they'd try to make me feel guilty.
>
> Once, when my mother was sick, my sisters came to see me to put pressure on me to visit her. They said, "You're being selfish." I said, "You're entitled to your version of Mother, and I'm entitled to mine. You're going to have to respect that." I refused to go. I told them that what I resent most is that I never got to be a sibling and that I didn't want to be their mother anymore. I didn't want that phone call in the middle of the night. I said, "I want to be your sister, not your savior. I don't know if that's possible for us now, after all we've been through." One sister made an effort to understand, and today we're close; the other two couldn't handle it, and we never see each other.

And so the Defector gets "isolated," not once, but fourfold—first, by her mother, who punishes her for her apparent indestructibility, trying to make her succumb; second, by her father, who is too weak, or too savage, to take her part; third, by the siblings for whom she represents a reality they cannot face; and fourth, by the Bad Mommy Taboo.

The Defector at Work

Defectors often become successful in their careers. For one thing, because they grew up under fire, they can withstand enormous stress.

"I'm really not afraid of anything," one of them says, "because nothing in my life could ever be as bad as my childhood. Domineering bosses don't scare me; I was trained by an expert. I can't be intimidated. I function well under pressure."

But they frequently become bored. Having met the challenge of one career or job, they lose interest and move on to another. Their résumés often are zigzags of experience, with no unifying theme.

Some Defectors, because they knew from childhood that they were "different," use their individuality in their work.

"I never fit the mold," an advertising copywriter told me. "My sisters felt they had to be like other kids to fit in. The difference with me is that I don't have a burning desire to fit in. So I can see things in a unique way—I guess that's why I'm a success. I come up with ideas that are for me, not ideas that I think will please. And somehow, mine are the ideas that are always used."

Many of the Defectors I interviewed became writers and artists, tapping their memories in a way that helped them to make sense of their early childhoods.

Edgar Johnson, in his biography of Charles Dickens, describes the process of artistic resolution of childhood loss. At the age of twelve, Dickens lived alone in a boardinghouse and supported himself as a bootblack, while his father and mother resided in debtors' prison. Johnson writes,

> In one sense, the grieving child in the blacking warehouse might be said to have died . . . but was continually reborn in a host of children suffering or dying young and other innocents undergoing injustice and pain; from Oliver and Smike and poor Jo to all the victims of a stony-hearted and archaic social system. . . . In a final sense, the great and successful effort of his career was to assimilate and understand . . . the kind of world in which such things could be.

Other Defectors go into the helping professions, using their familiarity with anguish as a vehicle for compassion and courage. A psychotherapist joked, "I said to myself when I was a child, 'Are you going to let all this pain go to waste?' "

But, like the Troublemaker, Defectors sometimes experience a kind of double vision in their career ascent; they run into Avengers who try to knock them down, and "see" their mothers.

A department head of a major corporation told me that her boss is "an amazingly accurate reproduction of my mother—she's verbally abusive, she puts me down in meetings, nothing I do is good enough for her. So I reenact the mother–daughter battle. I instantly put her away—but I try not to overkill. Sometimes I think she goes after me because I look like I can take it. I can. I can protect myself. But it isn't easy."

The Defector as Friend

It is in the area of intimacy that the isolation of being a Defector exacts a poignant price. For if you were raised in a hurricane, how do you relate to other people who have never experienced foul weather, or who must deny it if they did? If most people have not shared any semblance of your family history, where is the basis for understanding?

It's not that Defectors want people to feel sorry for them—they have a horror of being pitied. As one of them said,

> I learned early on that the only person I can count on is me. I don't allow myself to lean on anyone because I'm afraid I'll be consumed.
>
> The hard part—the real pain—is that when I'm getting the attention I need, I'll start to reject it because of the humiliation I felt as a child. But I also have an absolutely dire fear that I'm being pitied. I don't want anybody's pity.

The Defector merely wants to be accepted, and that is one thing that people who are trapped within their defenses and denial cannot do. So she keeps her experience and innermost feelings to herself—except, perhaps, with another Defector—because they are too painful, too *unbelievable*, for others to hear.

The Defector may be hurt by such lack of empathy, but she's used to it. It simply underscores a hard lesson learned in childhood: *Don't let the pain show.*

It's difficult, then, for her to open up. She must deal with people only on a surface level, sticking to pleasantries. Plenty of Defectors do it, of course. Often they have a wide circle of friends, and their social lives are extremely full, because the Defector asks little of others.

But few people really know her. And occasionally, her sense of isolation becomes unbearable; her frustration pops up and takes her by surprise. Says a twenty-nine-year-old Defector,

> Sometimes I get tired of being so damned strong. There's a hellhole of anger that a lifetime will not erase for me. So I'll give in to my temper. I'll fly after the guy who's blocking my car in traffic, screaming at him, "You fucking son of a bitch, get out of my way!" I feel very guilty about how my anger sometimes gets dumped on innocent people.

Another woman, an incest survivor who leads self-help groups, said,

> I'm great at helping strangers; I help them put together the pieces of their lives, I help them unblock about the past so that they aren't imprisoned by it anymore. But I have a gaping need left over from childhood that jeopardizes my friendships. When I'm getting strokes, I'll start to pull away because I don't want to be taken care of. Most of the women I work with have been horribly disabled by their need to be taken care of; I don't want to be like that. But I go too far in my being so big and strong. I have trouble letting people in, giving them permission to just love me.

Several Defectors said that they must constantly remind themselves that their friends are *not* the mothers who didn't acknowledge or care about them. Many of them have friendships that they keep on a superficial level, and when the relationship reaches a certain point, they find a flaw and flee. It's as though there is an internal measuring device that alerts them to impending rejection, whether or not that perception is real. And when the alarm sounds, they drop the friend.

Since any attachment is a leap of faith, they require constant reassurance that they are loved. If a friend does not place the Defector first in his or her affections, the Defector believes that she comes last. And this feeling proves, once again, that the Defector must never lower her guard, because the fear of rejection is too harrowing to bear.

She keeps score: I did this for you, you didn't do that for me. The trouble is that her arithmetic is skewed; she has a hard time remembering the kindnesses of friends, once she imagines that they do not *really* like her. Her good deeds count twice as much as theirs count. Balance and circumspection are not easy for her because, lacking a childhood in which tolerance had a place, she doesn't have the confidence to believe that good times follow bad in the equation of friendship. For her, worse always leads to worst.

Defectors often are initially attentive to their friends, sending birthday cards, showing up at graduations, hosting surprise parties. But when they have an event or triumph of their own to be celebrated, sometimes their friends don't return the favor in equal measure. The Defector's expectations of herself sometimes get transferred to friends, who don't value her affection and attention as urgently as she, having no "family," values theirs. And so she gets furious and disappointed.

"That's a real 'little kid' piece of me," one Defector said, smiling ruefully. "I don't think it's unreasonable to expect recognition from your friends. But I used to carry it to unreasonable lengths, dropping a friend who didn't do what I would have done, rather than telling her what I need and giving her a chance to do it. I've lost friends in my life of whom I expected too much. I don't trash people anymore. I just state my needs, and try to accept them for what they *can* give."

The Defector in Love

Most of the Defectors I interviewed are either married or living with someone. Since they often knew in childhood where to go for help, they allow themselves to be involved with someone who will *really* help—a person with whom to share their lives, someone to stabilize them when they begin to come apart at the seams.

But they hold a little in reserve. They are always packing their bags in their heads. There is the small voice inside them that says, "What if . . . ?"

What if I am left? Where are the safety exits? How do I get out of the fire? Where are the lifeboats?

One Defector, who has an extremely loving connection with her husband, says that even after fifteen years together she still keeps strict accounts of her "debts." What she earns goes into her separate checking account so she can pay her own way when they go out to dinner or on a vacation. "It's silly," she says, "because he's a millionaire. But I need to feel that I can take care of myself. He tolerates it; that's the trade-off for my staying married to him."

Some Defectors deliberately marry men who are somewhat aloof in order to get the space they require to feel independent. But these marriages often run into trouble in middle age, when the momentum of their careers levels off, and when their children are grown and on their own. When the time arrives that they are able to travel or spend more time together, the Defector may find that she is unable to allow her husband to have the closeness he now may desire.

As one such Defector says,

> When my last child moved out, I had this terrible feeling of loss. I knew I'd have to deal directly with my husband for the first time, and I hadn't been dealing with him for years. I should be able to say how I feel to the person that I have the *most* intimate relationship with. But I can't. It's too dangerous—it's like he might have something on me and will use it against me. That's how I grew up: you didn't let on how you felt. You always stood watch. At my stage of life, unless you're prepared to divorce, you have to *deal* with a spouse. I'm used to escape. I'm not used to dealing.

The Defector is adept at recovering quickly from a lover's departure or a husband's death, because she is a pro at survival. But part of her "bravery," her "courage," her "resiliency," is that *she doesn't give so much that she has a whole lot to lose.*

But in time she may begin to feel that, in spite of her caution, she *does* have a lot to lose.

A fifty-year-old Defector, who is married for the second time, finds to her horror that the older she gets, the more dependent on her husband she becomes. She is aware that as her parents—whom she never sees—edge toward the ends of their lives, she will soon be literally, irrevocably, abandoned by them. She is aware, too, that she is no longer a nymphet, and her options are narrowing, options that are the province of younger women.

And so her relationship with her husband has begun to feel altogether too *necessary*, creating a need that is anathema.

Because "love" means "dependent," and "dependent" means "pain," the three words get entangled and terrify her. She says,

> Lately I feel that my happiness is hinged to my husband, and it scares me to death. When he's cranky, intellectually I know it's usually because he's got troubles of his own. But I don't have enough inner security to feel that they have nothing to do with me. I can't say, "It'll pass, he'll get over it," and be happy with myself. I still feel just as much pain as I felt as a child.

The Defector as Mother

It is with her children that the Defector feels most vulnerable. She is acutely aware that, having never experienced a normal childhood, she is poorly trained for motherhood. More anguishing still is that she knows the terrible consequences of blowing it.

Every mother is afraid that she won't be able to spare her children the sadness she may have experienced, or, if she was lucky enough to have a loving mother, that she won't measure up to the example in her childhood.

But the Defector's own worst fears for her children are those she herself has experienced. For her, there are no dress rehearsals for motherhood and no mother to call for direction: she walks into her own maternal performance without a script—or, perhaps, the wrong one—and no prompter.

Some Defectors hover over their children in ways that are similar to the Smotherer's—vigilant against her kids' every disappointment, shielding them from the consequences of their mistakes. Every handyman is a potential molester; every teacher, a probable tyrant. In her projected fears, she stifles her children's individuality and strength.

But other Defectors veer to the opposite extreme—they push their children away in a logic they alone understand. They are afraid to get too close to their children, because they are terrified they will become like their mothers. If they keep their children at arm's length and do not get too involved with their lives, their children will be safe from the internalized mother that rages within them.

Says the thirty-three-year-old mother of two young children,

I don't consider myself verbally abusive, but the fear is that I *might* be with my children. I have to force myself to stay in the present, because when I'm tired or stressed out, I can feel myself becoming like my mother. When I feel the anger rising up, I just refuse to let it in the door. That takes constant monitoring.

The Defector does not want to create a scenario in which her own children defect, because if they did, the blame could be traced directly back to her.

She feels guiltiest when occasionally she wishes they *would* bolt. When they reach their teens and flex their psychic muscles—rebelling, talking back, defying her—sometimes she has fantasies of throwing them out. Her anger turns immediately to thoughts of escape, even from her kids.

And sometimes her anger turns to violence toward them. The burned-out Defectors described earlier see any rebellion, any back talk, as another assault. These mothers may beat their children, just as they were once beaten.

One woman said, "I thought that's what you did—you belt the kid who is bad. It was an automatic response. If it weren't for my therapist, who taught me that there is another way, I don't know what I would have done to my children. I shudder to think about it."

No one is as critical as a Defector can be of herself when it comes to her own parental performance. It is when discussing her children—*rather than her own childhood*—that the usually dry-eyed Defector is easily brought to tears.

She is never as good a mother as she would like to be. She's not the child whose life was threatened long ago; but she often feels like her, as though time had stopped. And because she is so hard on herself, so vigilant about her own internalized mother, so unforgiving of her parenting mistakes that are compounded by her anger about them, her children seldom get to know her very well. At least, not until they are much older—and not unless she learns that sometimes it's safe to be open, to risk hurt, to be vulnerable.

Profile of a Defector

Brett, forty-two, is a flight attendant. I caught her a few hours before she was to leave for Kennedy International Airport and an evening flight to Amsterdam. As she opened the door to her Long

Island home, she was beaming. "I just found out my daughter was accepted by Princeton," she said, nodding in the direction of the living room, where a lovely eighteen-year-old girl was curled up on the sofa, talking on the phone.

Brett and I went to the family room, the walls of which were covered with photographs of her husband, her daughter at varying stages of growth, and assorted friends. "I call it 'the shrine,' " she joked. But nowhere was there a picture of her parents, an omission she explained by saying, evenly, "This is my family; I don't consider my parents part of my family."

The second of three children—she has two brothers—she was brought up in Alabama, where her father owned a television repair shop. Her mother was a housewife; she was also an alcoholic.

Brett hasn't seen either one of them in eight years. That's not quite true—she did run into her father at his mother's funeral five years ago. She almost didn't go, she says, "because I was still terrified of him. Just being in his presence depleted me. We shook hands. That was it."

Today her father is in the advanced stages of senility, and wouldn't know Brett if he saw her—his illness has erased his memory. "Isn't he lucky," Brett says, her voice taking on a sharp edge. "He doesn't remember anything; I remember it all."

Brett's father was not an alcoholic—he was a child batterer. When he got into a rage, he would smash his children with his fists or feet. His rampages would be set off by the most unpredictable and innocuous things. Once when she was six, Brett went to the refrigerator to get an apple. He saw her and said, "Did I give you permission to eat?" and threw her onto the floor.

Both her brothers would cringe in his presence; but Brett would not. And so he was even more brutal to her than to them.

"No one ever knew," Brett says. "He never broke any bones, never left visible scars." Where was her mother in all this? Brett draws a deep breath and replies, "She was always too drunk and too beaten herself to help us."

When Brett was twelve, she came home from school one afternoon and heard her little brother sobbing in his room. She found him sitting on the edge of the bed, holding a towel to his legs—they were covered with angry red stripes, like hash marks on a military uniform. Her father had whipped him with an electrical cable for playing with his tennis racquet.

"My mother sat slumped on the living room couch," Brett says. "She was conscious. She saw everything. She just kept sipping her beer."

Brett ran into the living room and screamed at her father, "I hate you! I hate you!" He gave her the same punishment he had given his five-year-old son. But this time—for the first time—she didn't feel anything. "I just literally detached from my body," she says. "I kept thinking, 'Don't give him the gift of your tears.'" When he finished, she returned to her brother, cleaned him up, and took him to her room and locked the door.

Such nightmares were a daily event in Brett's childhood. From time to time her father would throw her out, and she'd go to her grandmother, a quiet, rather stiff woman who lived two blocks away. "It was so nice to sit down at the dinner table, with a placemat and a folded napkin, and have my grandmother say, 'Did you have enough to eat?' I've idealized her—she knew what was going on at home—but I can't hate her. She was my link to sanity."

Brett learned to nurture herself by burying herself in books, music, and dreams of travel. She never told her parents anything about herself or her plans of escape when she was of legal age.

When she was seventeen, her father threw her out for the last time—she never went back. She got a job working in a restaurant and rented a studio apartment that she kept virtually empty. "I never even wanted furniture," she says. "I'm still terrified of possessions. It means being an adult in the way my mother was—she only cared about her possessions, not about her children. When she was sober, she'd clean and dust like a robot, but she'd ignore us."

Having a husband and kids was also what "adults" do, and Brett vowed she'd never get married or become a mother. But when she was twenty, she met a man who was all the things her parents never were—tender, patient, steady. And so she married him, with this proviso: He would not interfere with her plan to become a stewardess and explore the world.

Her husband was prescient enough to know that if he didn't support her ambition, she'd feel fenced in and leave. He understood her restlessness and never complained about the trips that took her all over the country and, when she was senior enough for international flights, to Europe and the Far East.

During those years, she also stopped seeing her brothers. Once, when she tried to have her father arrested for battering her mother, her brothers told the police, "Our sister is out of her mind—he never hit anyone." When Brett later reminded them of the beatings their father used to give them, her younger brother—the one she helped after his father whipped him for playing with his tennis racquet—looked her in the eye and said, "It wasn't as bad as all that—I was a rotten kid. I asked for it." It was the last time she saw either of them; she's since been told that they, too, are alcoholics.

Eventually, Brett's husband persuaded her to have a child, and she gave birth to a daughter, Gineen. But her restlessness persisted. She was still resisting some of the "adult" parts of being a woman— being *a* mother meant being *her* mother.

Inside, she wanted to grab her daughter and never let go. That part scared her most of all. She says, weeping softly,

> I pushed Gineen away because I know how I am. I couldn't separate—when she had problems, I'd bleed, because I felt them as though they were my own. But when she talked back, I wanted to hit her with a two-by-four. So I let her go. She felt unloved because I couldn't stay put. I had to get out of the house as much for me as for her. I was so afraid of being smothered by her—and of smothering or hurting her—that I put her in nursery school before she was ready. She was such a sweet, concerned, loving child, and I wasn't there for her. She suffered enormously from that.

When Gineen became a teenager, she began withdrawing. She became anorexic, and spent hours alone in her room with the door closed. Brett, remembering her own childhood, saw herself behind the door that barred her from her daughter. She recognized that she was re-creating herself.

Brett went into therapy so that she could learn to become more earthbound. Her therapist helped her to see that if you use childhood survival mechanisms when you are adult, the situations that once called for them no longer apply. By running from everything— including facing her own rage—she risked losing everything that mattered to her.

Brett began repairing her relationship with her daughter in the same determined way she had once escaped her childhood. "I wanted Gineen to know me—I wanted to tell her what she means to me before it was too late."

Brett started finding ways to be with Gineen, even though, at first, they felt awkward and forced. When Gineen came down in the morning for breakfast, Brett would get up and offer to make breakfast for her, something she hadn't done in years. If Gineen was in her room, her mother would knock on her door and say, "Can I hang out?" For a time, Gineen always said no. "I just wouldn't give up," Brett says.

In Gineen's senior year of high school, she underwent "a miraculous conversion. All the sweetness, love, and honesty came back. One day she said, 'I felt you didn't love me when I was growing up. You never told me what was on your mind. You were always angry or gone.' "

Brett saw her opening and grabbed it. She told her daughter everything—about her own fears growing up, about her father, who she feared would kill her, and about her mother, who was capable of just letting it happen. She told her that it was hard for her to have a child because she was still so much a child herself. She apologized for having been unavailable to Gineen—in a way, as her mother had been unavailable to her. And she added, "You are the most wonderful thing that ever happened to me; I wish I could have said that sooner."

At the end of my interview with Brett, I asked her, "Could you ever have such a conversation with your own mother? Could you ever let her know you the way Gineen does?" The color left her face. "Never," she blurted. *"Never. I couldn't."*

Then she paused for several minutes. "I would love to," she said. "But she'd never respond the way my daughter did. I don't dream those dreams."

Part Four
A Separate Peace

16
Breaking the Cycle

I think I've made my peace with my mother. There's no blame anymore—there's occasionally some anger, still. More and more I see that she is who she is and that she did the best she could. And it wasn't good enough. And even though it wasn't, it probably gave me a lot of the tools I now use to lead a full life.

Robyn, forty-one

Priscilla, seventy-five, is still a hostage to her past, and she knows it. "Did I ever come to terms with my mother?" she asks rhetorically. "No. And it troubles me terribly. I tell myself, 'You're an old woman, your mother has been dead for thirty years. Let it go.' But when my sister says, 'Mom was a *corker*,' I'm off to the races: I love talking about how awful she was. I should have relinquished the anger by now. I haven't."

The purpose of this chapter is to help you avoid Priscilla's fate—to begin resolving your relationship with your mother so that you can be freed from the prologue of your childhood—and to prevent a repetition of the damaging patterns of your childhood with your own children. For only if you break the cycle of generational conflict, mother to daughter to grandchildren, can the ghosts of the past finally be put to rest. It is to the daughters who want to get beyond the despair of their childhoods that this chapter is chiefly addressed.

But even if you have a cordial relationship with your mother, there is much in this chapter that will be useful to you. Your relationship with your mother may not be fraught with pain and

281

destructiveness, but it's still not quite what you want it to be—you may, for example, feel that your mother still treats you like a child, and you want her to accept you as an adult.

Many daughters want to make what is already a good relationship with their mothers *even better*. For them, there is a great deal of information here that will help them reach that goal.

The good news about mothers and daughters is that by the daughters' middle adulthood, their relationship is usually better than it ever was. According to numerous studies, the majority of grown daughters, tempered by time and experience, are able to see their mothers as human beings of human proportions rather than as giants who have the power of life and death—a process one researcher calls "shrinkage."

Moreover, female Baby Boomers, because of radical social changes in their generation, often are more circumspect about their mothers than their mothers were about *their* mothers. These daughters have more sources of satisfaction outside the family than their mothers had—challenging jobs, friends who share their conflicts about work versus family, a wide range of support groups and therapies to help them resolve their problems. Consequently, they frequently are less critical of their mothers than their mothers were of them.

The bad news, however, is that many daughters—age, feminist gains, and outside support notwithstanding—have *not* been able to get beyond their childhood disappointments with their mothers. Despite all the social progress women have made, in some ways it's as hard as ever for daughters to resolve their relationships with their mothers.

For one thing, lots of people—not just your mother—have a stake in your *staying* in your old roles and behavioral patterns. They don't want to hear about your struggles to redress your childhood losses.

"Grow up, already," says a friend.

"You have to pull yourself up by your bootstraps," says an aunt.

"It could have been worse," says a sister.

"You're not discussing my private life with a stranger," says the spouse who forbids you to go into therapy.

All these statements are forms of denial and fear by people who are threatened by change. As much as they may criticize, they want you to stay as you are, incomplete and recognizable. Because if you change, the implication is they *ought* to be able to follow your gutsy example—as long as you are imperfect, the status quo is maintained. And if you skulk back into your old insecurities and coping mechanisms, you are saying, "You're right. I don't count."

Your dismay or pain regarding your mother are not relative and do not have to be justified or defended. The only criteria that matter are whether or not they are sabotaging your life, preventing you from being as whole and as alive as you can be, and whether or not you want the relationship with your mother to get better.

How you achieve a separate peace is your responsibility. Will anyone be better off if you *don't* try to break the cycle of mother –daughter disaffection? If you slam the door on your emotional growth? If you perpetuate the anguish of the past?

Does growing up, and perhaps getting help in your quest for completeness, really require *permission*? If you think it does, then you are not a grown-up yet.

Sorting out the past means holding yourself accountable for who you are today—beyond blame, beyond subjugation, beyond rage. Choosing to grow up is a leap of faith that life can be better—that faith is the beginning of belief in yourself. You cannot permit anyone to rob you of it, not a friend, not a partner, not a parent.

Such faith is difficult for women because it embraces the ability to have separate values and to live by them. The worst-case scenario— which may be subconscious—for many women is this: If I declare my emotional independence, if I state my needs, if I insist on being my best self, my mother (lover, husband, friend, child) will leave me.

They might leave you *regardless* of what you do. But many women were raised to think that they are *nothing* outside of a relationship. For them, femininity means attachment—to parents, spouse, children, friends.

If risking being a mature person means risking a relationship, then the relationship is bad for you. The people in your life who love you and who are themselves emotionally grown up will not be threatened by your growth—they will welcome and applaud it, because they profit from it as much as you do. (Even though your mother may love you, she may not welcome it, for all the reasons we explored earlier.)

If you saw yourself in any or all of the last five chapters, then you may recognize that something is missing in your life, and recognize, too, your compensating self-destructive patterns. The missing piece may be a healthy self who feels in charge of her own destiny rather than a victim of her past, and of her mother.

That recognition is the start of a journey to a fuller, richer, more rewarding existence, and a sense of full participation in it. Your awareness is the "permission" that allows you to come into your own. You are at the threshold of believing in yourself, apart from all your attachments. And the first step in that journey is knowing that *the only thing you can change is you—you cannot change your mother or anyone else.*

But change is not easy. The familiar, even though it may be damaging, *is what we know.* Change takes us to an alien place. And it surely takes us away from mother—away from our old ways of dealing with her. At the heart of our anxiety are the needs to be both close to and separate from her. We may go too far or stay too attached—both extremes are the two sides of dependency. Emotional separation can feel like being orphaned.

The irony is that our mothers often have the same anxiety—they watch us try to learn to live our own lives and become anxious that *they* will be rejected. How odd—and how sad—that often mother and daughter are both frightened of being abandoned. Perhaps it is because they haven't allowed their *relationship* to grow up, to take it to a new place where they can really see and appreciate each other—their differences as well as their similarities.

For some women, as we shall see in Chapter Twenty, a new, redefined relationship is simply not possible. But you have to *be certain* of that fact. And you cannot be certain if you don't first explore the possibility, by sorting out your own ambivalences, by no longer feeling like a child, and by really seeing your mother as a separate human being.

Getting Unstuck

Many of us are not able to do that because we are still *stuck* between our false and true selves, our desires to merge with Mom and to run from her. We are caught in the limbo of unfinished filial business—we can't seem to move on, beyond the defenses of anger or supplication, to a secure self and more rewarding attachments. So we run around in emotional circles, repeating the mistakes of the past. And, with something resembling resignation, we sigh, "My mother will never change."

How do you get *unstuck?* How do you get rid of your defenses against your mother? Those defenses took a lifetime to shore up. How do you let go of the roles that kept you going all these years—being saintly, or driven, or crushed, or in trouble, or mutinous?

You begin by examining the three things that may be *keeping* you stuck: denial, blame, and guilt.

Denial. "Mom wasn't so bad," you may say. "The problem is me, not her." Many daughters graft their mother's parenting inadequacies onto themselves and do penance for both of them. "It's my fault" is a way to assume a fragile sense of control. If I am a better person, the reasoning goes, my mother will love me, and I will be okay. The flaw in that thinking is the assumption that *your mother will love you the way you need to be loved.* If she didn't until now, she may never.

The Bad Mommy Taboo fuels our denial by saying, "Thou shalt love thy mother no matter how lousily she treateth thee." The hidden message is "Your feelings aren't important." By denying your own instincts and awareness, your filial business can never be finished.

Denial keeps us from getting in touch with our anger and pain. When you've been taught all your life not to feel, or that your feelings are wrong and even *bad*, it's not easy to turn them on. You're mired in all these rubrics: "I'm now allowed" and "That's ancient history."

Blame. Those who do not deny, blame. Your anger, however justified, about your mother's unpleasability does not mean that she is responsible for your present unhappiness. What *is* "her fault" is how she treated you when you were a child. What is *not* her fault is what you do about it in adulthood.

Blame is a trap: as long as we can pin the rap of our misery on Mom, *we keep her strong,* and we keep ourselves weak.

Blame keeps our happiness contingent on someone else.

Blame is the wall between victimization and recovery.

Blame keeps us stuck because we may not have learned how to use our anger constructively—instead, we use it to spin our emotional wheels.

To free ourselves from the past and the blaming that keeps us forever looking backward, we have to be willing to give up childhood and childish expectations. We have to stop hoping that Mother will change. What *she* does is moot. It is *we* who must change.

When we are adults, emotional "growing up" is not a package deal. Real maturity does not hinge on someone else—the contingency of our growth cannot be Mother's becoming a Good Mommy. Real maturity hinges on our ability to believe that we can stand alone, optimistic, resilient, capable of relying on ourselves for a sense of worth, and experiencing the joy of that ability. *It hinges on being a Good Mommy to ourselves.*

And until we grow up, we cannot begin to resolve our relationship with our mothers.

Guilt. Few things make us feel as guilty as believing we ought to "forgive" our mothers, the women who bore us. Does breaking the cycle of our despair require forgiveness? To many theologians, philosophers, and therapists, it does. They believe that the ultimate goal of a child's evolution is to be able to forgive her parents for their mistakes, no matter how egregious.

While Webster's definition of "forgive" is "to cease to feel resentment against (an offender)," that is not how most people interpret the word. Most people think it means turning the other cheek as if to say, "Okay, you're off the hook, you're excused for your dreadfulness."

The concept of "forgiveness" is loaded with guilt. To forgive implies that you must overlook all those assaults on your spirit, as though they never happened. And it also means "You are not entitled to your anger. You are a sinful person for being mad at your mother."

For most people, "forgiveness" occurred long ago. Children, even the most horribly abused of them, *automatically* forgive their parents. It's how they keep Mommy All Good. But forgiveness does not erase or prevent psychological and emotional wounds. You say you forgive your mother, but still you can't seem to break out of the patterns of childhood. Forgiveness isn't enough. It may not even be suitable.

The best interpretation of "forgiveness" comes from a therapist I interviewed. She says,

I'm not a believer in forgiveness as an absolute. I've known people who have been abused in such atrocious ways that forgiveness would not be appropriate. For me, *acceptance* is a much more therapeutic goal than forgiveness. When you can accept that your childhood needs didn't get met, that you didn't get what you were entitled to, that you're allowed to feel anger and sadness, then you can truly let go and move on to meeting your own needs in appropriate ways with appropriate people. The delusion most people have to give up is that their parents really were innocent.

If we leap over our authentic feelings to instant absolution of Mom—without examining the cost to ourselves of keeping her all good or all bad—we hold ourselves accountable for our childhood wounds. When we do that, our feelings, our false self, and the shame of our complicity are trivialized.

What about love? Doesn't "forgiveness" pave the way for love? The Bad Mommy Taboo relentlessly insists that it does, in this masterstroke of non sequiturs: "Of course you love your mother. She's your mother."

Accepting your mother is not the same thing as loving her. You may in fact love your mother a great deal, because she has lovable qualities. But you are not *required* to love her to achieve an accommodation with her. Your only mandate is to *understand* her and to stop expecting the stuff of which dreams are made—that she will turn into a saint.

You don't have to forgive her. You don't have to love her. You don't have to admire her. You don't have to even like her. *But you do have to know and accept her as she is.*

That may feel like letting her off the hook. Being "fair" to one's smothering, critical, neglectful, or cruel mother feels like commuting the sentence of a criminal. You may lust for retribution. But the person who is imprisoned by your need to punish her is you. You need to get *yourself* off the hook of your expectations.

Does this mean you have to fall into her arms? No. It means that you have to grow up and see her not as your savior or your archenemy but simply a person, neither idealized nor vilified, but real. Not easy. But altogether possible.

All that sounds very *like* forgiveness. I prefer to call it resolution.

Resolution

The primary goal of this chapter is to help you recognize the "as-if" child within you that keeps popping up in destructive patterns, to take her by the hand, and slowly begin leading her out of childhood. The aim is to help you rid yourself of magical thinking, destructive rage, contingent hopes, and the feeling that you are nothing without a mother who loves you.

Once you have done that, you can see your mother as she really is: a woman with good qualities and bad, a woman who is a product of her times and history, a woman who did the best she could even if, sometimes, it wasn't good enough.

If you can see her that way, so, too, can you see yourself. You will no longer be bent out of shape, trying to make Mom "right," but, rather, grow into your own true form, free of the distortions that got you through your childhood but that may now skew your adulthood.

The mother you see today may not be the woman she has *become*—she may still be the mother of your memories. She might even have changed for the better and tried to make amends—and now she says to herself, "I can't win." And, indeed, she can't, until you can be a grown-up yourself and really *see* her, apart from yourself and your unmet needs. Somehow you cannot see her as she is because *you are still a child inside, wanting to go back in time to correct the memories and fix the past.*

To resolve this disparity is not without risk. Because if you see her as she is, incapable of defining or "saving" you, you may feel stranded, bereft of all hope that you can make it alone.

Resolution means coming to terms with what is. It is a gradual process that takes courage and forbearance. For if we did not truly grow up in childhood, then we must make the effort to do it now.

Getting to that point is not a simple process of "Authenticity in Ten Easy Lessons." It takes time. It takes patience. It takes understanding of Mother and of ourselves. And, in many cases, as we will see, it takes help.

To resolve our relationship requires three steps—*not three "easy" steps*, but a painstaking progression that can lead to emotional freedom from the past:

getting at our feelings;
mourning our childhoods;
accepting reality.

Getting at Our Feelings

The hardest thing for unacceptable daughters to acknowledge is that they are entitled to their feelings. By adulthood, the as-if personality is so fixed that we are *terrified* of giving it up—the seductiveness of the familiar corrupts our ability to change. And if we have not acknowledged our feelings of having been "robbed" in childhood, we will continue to limp along in our old patterns.

As we saw in the previous section, some people have never resolved their attachments to their mothers or their conflicted feelings. They have rerouted their ambivalence to other, more manageable arenas—siblings, colleagues, friends, lovers, and children.

Such people are not stupid. They often recognize that their attachments and choices are frequently harmful to them. They may even know, intellectually, why their lives are a mess. "I know all the reasons," they testily say, "but it doesn't help."

Knowing is not the same thing as *feeling*. A thought is not resolution; working through the feelings is. And that requires experiencing these emotions fully, in all their torment.

But knowing is a beginning. One of the Ciphers described in Chapter Thirteen, who in her thirties still lives with her parents, is now in therapy. She is a work-in-progress, examining her relationship with her mother in a way that has already begun to free her. She says,

> I wanted my mother to be Donna Reed. I wanted a mother who was intelligent and bright and charming and interesting. I'm an adult, and my concerns now are for *me* to be those things. My vow was "If I ever get out of this alive, I'm going to make it all up to myself and I'm going to do all the things she never let me do." I always wanted to learn how to ice-skate. But I can't bring myself to do it. I still hear my mother's voice saying, "You'll get hurt." I just feel afraid—and that's the one thing I don't want to feel anymore.

Says another work-in-progress, a Superachiever,

> I always look at my mother with two sets of eyes. There's the side of me that wants to cut her out of every aspect of my being—I don't want to let her off scot-free. But I also want to be honest with myself and say, "Listen, jerk, you're not the terrific person you are by accident. Some of it you got from her."

When thought and feeling become one, there are those thrilling "clicks" in the head where you begin to *change*. Those clicks are the signs of growth; each click leads to another, and you build yourself, one click at a time.

There are many routes to unearthing your feelings and getting unstuck.

Soul-searching. One route is solitary introspection. Alice Koller, in her powerful memoir, *An Unknown Woman: A Journey to Self-Discovery*, describes her three-month odyssey while holed up, alone, in the chill of winter on Nantucket Island. Starting from emotional scratch, she wanted to stop her thirty-seven-year pattern of reaction to her unloving mother, and to try to find out if there was a life worth living for herself alone. She wanted to make sense of her past in order to cull from it meaning for her future. Her starting place was this:

> From now on I must stop being shocked by how much authority I have acceded to, in the unknown hope that the authority before me would magically turn into my mother, who would then open her arms to me . . . I now have to examine every opinion I've ever held, in order to see whether I'd still hold it once the authoritative voice who spoke it to me is removed.

And her resolution of her feelings, the product of stripping away all her defenses—which led her to consider, and then reject, suicide—was this:

> I can see my own outlines. *That's* why I'm able to see other people: the glass that used to reflect me is now transparent. I know where I end and where other people begin . . . How the thing all fits together! I'm no longer eyeing people as instruments for filling my needs: I fill my own needs. So I can see their needs, their purposes, as separate from mine.

A Loving Marriage. Other women uncover their feelings by marrying a Good Mommy—a compassionate and tender man who has the patience and psychic strength to help them feel at ease not only with expressing their fears and doubts but also with the giving and receiving of love. Such women somehow manage not to destroy the relationship in the course of learning that they are in fact lovable.

Spirituality. Still other women find, in such religions as born-again Christianity, or such philosophies as Zen Buddhism, or New Age thinking, a spiritual route to getting in touch with their feelings, and coming to terms with the confusion of their childhoods. One woman I know spent ten years in a Zen center, studying, teaching, and ridding herself of acrimony toward her mother. Although, at thirty-two, she finally recognized that "I will never reach nirvana," she had come sufficiently far to allow her mother to be who she is, and to find peace within herself.

Therapy. But many people need professional help in reaching the innermost feelings that made it necessary for them to deny their true selves.

The psychoanalyst, psychologist, or psychiatric social worker serves as the patient's guide, helping the patient feel safe enough to allow her feelings—good and bad, fantastic or vengeful—to emerge without fear of rebuke. The therapist is a surrogate Good Mommy who provides the patient with unqualified acceptance, teaches her to recognize and respect her feelings, and helps her to become aware of, and change, the patterns of her self-defeating behavior.

Therapy is not a substitute for living, nor is the reputable therapist a domineering and all-knowing "mother" who keeps her "daughter" forever hobbled and dependent. It is a means of learning to live in a healthy way, getting through and beyond the denial, blame, and guilt so you can let the false self go.

"It's a long process, partly because of the bond between the therapist and the patient," says Dr. Marianne Goodman. "Patients will often try to sabotage the process and seek out therapists who will fit into exactly what they want, which is a critical, unloving kind of person. But if they find someone who is responsive, who is caring, who sets limits but who is there for them, what they can begin to do is believe in their own worth."

That's what the Good Mommy was supposed to provide us. But if she couldn't, we can benefit from a therapeutic version of her.

The fundamental feeling that therapy helps us get at is the rage we feel for having had to depend on people who made us "take" whatever they dished out. You have no choice when you're a child. And unless you get angry and then resolve the anger, you *still* have no choice as an adult.

By "anger," I do not mean a license to kill—your mother or yourself. Unconstructive and unresolved rage is what we saw in the previous five chapters. The "anger" I'm talking about is the kind that allows you to say, "My rights as a child were violated. I was entitled to more and I didn't get it."

Such a statement is the beginning of an authentic self. For if we believe that the fatal flaw is not in ourselves, we can begin to see ourselves as separate from mother. We can believe in ourselves as having value and find a separate peace that is not contingent on someone else's approval.

Getting really angry feels as though you are killing off your mother. Without a mother who defines you—whether as a bad, bad girl or the *best* little girl in the whole world—you still feel what you felt as a child: that you will not survive without her.

You will survive, if you can hang on to the tiniest sliver of faith that someday—perhaps not tomorrow, not even next year—you will become yourself and not simply a constellation of *reactions* to your mother. You have to trust the fact that behind the false self is a true self worth salvaging. But if it took a long time to form a false self, it takes a long time to develop the courage to give it up.

Here's where the forbearance kicks in. "When is this ever going to end?" laments the woman who has been in therapy for five years. We are as impatient with our therapeutic "performance" as our mothers once were with our simplest tasks ("Don't *dawdle!*").

"Blocking" is the term for being therapeutically "stuck." The problem usually is that the patient or client is too frightened to lower the defenses that protected her in childhood, believing that without them, she might be destroyed, either by her own anger or by her Bad Mommy.

Depending on the damage of one's childhood, giving up that defense can be harrowing. It takes an essential, if tattered, optimism that *it will get better*, and that there's somebody—the therapist and, later, yourself—who will catch you if you fall.

It will get better, as long as you don't give up on yourself. It won't get better if you don't make an effort, if you don't gently and respectfully confront your denial, if you don't learn how to tell the real self from the false self.

This is a scary business. But fear is part of the process—it is, after all, *a feeling*. What can be scarier than unlocking one tiny prison cell of denial, and remembering—through a dream or recollection—the things that caused you, as a child, to be afraid? Better to keep them locked up, the key buried in the garden. Incest victims have the hardest time unblocking because in remembering, they relive their terrifying sexual abuse. But, as we have seen, denial doesn't work—our unresolved feelings just leak out into other areas of our lives.

The memories are there—they have but to be freed. And that is painful. But it's what I call "constructive pain." For every therapeutic session in which you sob uncontrollably, there is a moment in which those feelings are validated simply because someone is there to listen and to care. And, step by tiny step, in time the fear begins to melt, and the tears stop. *Denying the feelings keeps us imprisoned; accepting the feelings frees us.*

Many people bail out of therapy the moment the memories become too hot. Why else would we develop a false self except to feel less agony? To reduce the anxiety? But the real pain doesn't go away—it just gets camouflaged. Resurrecting the deepest pain of our most profound childhood wounds, in all its anguish, is the beginning of recovery.

"I used to have this recurring dream that I killed my mother," one woman told me. "In my dream I was driving my car, I aimed it at my mother, I felt it slam into her and I watched her body fly through the air. The dream haunted me. As soon as I went into therapy and told the therapist about it, the dream went away. I never had it again."

Such is the power of being able to trust the therapist, and only the most compassionate and skilled professionals are able to help us dive back into the emotional waters and begin to redress *for ourselves* the deprivations of our childhoods.

But some people get stuck in the anger part—they feel a temporary sense of autonomy, a rush of excitement in finally unleashing their rage. These people find real "benefits" to their anger, among them, a thirst for revenge. Staying angry at someone allows you not to think about who you are and where you're going. All your energy is focused elsewhere, rather than on making changes in yourself.

By the time you are an adult, your problems are your own. No parent—even if she has changed for the better—or partner or friend can make them all go away; many weary of even hearing them. Only you can redress your past. And only you can preclude the possibility of becoming a Bad Mommy yourself.

Getting professional help may be essential to prevent the duplication of your mother's parenting inadequacies with your children. In spite of all your vows to the contrary, if you don't resolve your own conflicts with your mother, such repetition is often inevitable.

Mourning Our Childhoods

Exhuming the pain and reliving it is what makes us able to get beyond it. Many a patient has spent weeks, or months, or even years weeping in therapy sessions, addressing the terrible compromises and emotional cost of their childhoods. This is the mourning process at work.

Mourning the child you were, the child who tried so hard to make your mother smile at you, or who worked tirelessly to be your mother's "Mommy," is essential to resolution.

Many daughters have had glimpses of the mourning process, although they may not be aware of it. Those moments when we cry at the recollection of the kindnesses of others—rather than over the losses of our childhoods—are moments of mourning what we never got from our mothers.

The mourning period will pass. Once you really see your pain, taste it, touch it, *feel* it, a time comes when you know that *nothing will ever be that bad again*. The worst is behind you.

A fifty-year-old woman said,

> Looking at the pain was terribly hard for me—the anger would intrude so I wouldn't have to feel it. But when I finally focused on *just* the pain, I realized how little there really was between my mother and me. And while it made me terribly sad, it became more and more ridiculous to make a big deal over what she did or didn't do.

Alice Miller writes,

> If a person is able . . . to experience that he was never "loved" as a child for what he was . . . and that he sacrificed his childhood for this "love," this will shake him very deeply but one day he will feel the desire to end this courtship. He will discover in himself a need to live according to his "true self" and no longer be forced to earn love, a love that . . . leaves him empty-handed since it is given to the "false self," which he has begun to relinquish.

Healing cannot take place without mourning what never was.

Accepting the Reality

Once you've mourned the child you were never allowed to be, you can begin to accept the adult that you are or are becoming. One piece of acceptance is understanding that your pain will never entirely disappear—it will simply be in smaller, more manageable doses.

Accepting what wasn't helps you to accept what is. Says psychotherapist Lilly Singer,

Resolution is an issue of coming to terms with your own feelings, accepting either that your mother never really loved you or she didn't know how. The pain of not having a mother emotionally available through the years will stay with the daughter forever. My concern is not to take the pain away, but to moderate it to a level on which the person can build and not live with constant resentment. Are you going to spend the rest of your life kicking everyone around you for what your mother did to you? Conflict and ambivalence is something we have to live with every day of our lives—if we can learn to do that, that's personal growth. Once you give up the dream that your mother will be a perfect person, you accept the reality, and the dream can be set aside. You can just give it up.

Pain is a part of your history—and it is part of your *strength*, the key to your compassion. You do not want to deny, or ever forget, the sadness and confusion you experienced growing up, because it helps you to recognize it when it resurfaces and not run from it.

When you are a veteran of pain *and the resolution of it*, you are, better than most people, able to understand it in others, the people you love and care about. And if you can understand *their* anguish, perhaps, eventually, you can understand your mother's.

17
Redefining the Mother–Daughter Relationship

My relationship with my mother has improved immeasurably since I stopped expecting so much of her. When I started to recognize that there are times she can't come through for me because she isn't able to—and not because she doesn't love me—I stopped being so disappointed in her. I used to call her and discuss problems I knew she couldn't respond to. Now maybe I'll talk to a friend about them, and go to my mother only for what she can give me. I like her a whole lot more since I accepted her.

—Sandra, thirty-two

Once you have dug up your feelings, mourned the little girl who felt unloved, and accepted the fact that nothing you can do or could have done will ever alter your childhood, you are able to reexamine and redefine your relationship with your mother through the prism of your new maturity.

Redefinition is the last piece of growth, the last step on the high wire that takes you from childhood to your adult self. Now you have the inner strength to see her as who she is, not who she wasn't or who you wish she could be. When you can establish healthy boundaries, visualizing yourself and your mother as two separate, individual women, you can begin to set limits on how she may still try to hobble you, and set the stage for her to begin to *recognize and accept that you are a grown-up.*

She may not like it. She may, as she always has, redouble her efforts to put you back into the box of childhood. Only now, you won't fit. *You're too big.* It simply cannot be done, as long as you stand firm on your own beliefs.

Here's where many women begin to clutch: "Oh, God," they say, "do I *have* to spend a lot of time with her? Do I have to reveal myself to her? She'll just dump on me. What's the point?"

It is not that you must become intimate with her to achieve peace. Rather, it is that by *knowing* her, you learn a great deal about yourself, and about the family patterns, passed down through the generations, that are an integral part of who you are and how you came to be.

Detriangling

The process by which all this can happen is called "detriangling," a technique developed in Family Systems therapy by its creator, Dr. Murray Bowen, and considered the most important part of it.

The basis of detriangling is a way of thinking rather than a way of feeling. Instead of blaming your mother for all your problems, you focus on the emotional process that explains the behavior of, and events in, your family. You try to be emotionally neutral so that you don't get drawn into other people's quarrels by taking sides on issues that are really not your province to repair or assuage.

"Getting beyond blame," write Drs. Michael Kerr and Bowen, "does not mean exonerating people from the part they play or played in the creation of a problem. It means seeing the total picture, acquiring a balanced view—not feeling compelled to either approve or disapprove of the nature of one's own [family]."

The goal is to define yourself *within the mother–daughter relationship,* rather than simply react to it. Your mother may not accept you any more than she ever did. But if you can learn not to become snared by reactions to her, you find that you have the capacity to avoid being trapped by emotional overreaction to other people as well.

Here's an example. A forty-five-year-old woman I know recently went to visit her mother, who asked her to bring a pizza for dinner. The daughter, who doesn't like pizza, also brought along some chicken for herself. When she took the chicken out of the bag, explaining that she preferred it, her mother cried, "How can you not like pizza!"

"We got into a huge fight," the daughter recalls. "It was stupid. But I got caught up in feeling judged, and I reacted badly. I should have said, 'I don't know, I just don't like it.' My mother felt rejected because I didn't want what she wants. But at the time, I couldn't see it. I just felt criticized, like a ten-year-old, so I blew up. Over *pizza.*"

To really know your mother, according to the Family Systems approach, you need to find out more about her, about her mother's mother, and so on, as far back as possible. As you do this research you will see stunning similarities through the generations—your mother's actions begin to be part of a family pattern rather than a deliberate attempt to "get" you.

For example: Your grandmother and her brother may never have gotten along. Your mother may have always been drawn into their fights—she may have been fond of her uncle, which made her mother furious, and consequently was forbidden to see him.

How does that play out between your mother and you? She always applied a great deal of pressure on you to be "nicer" to your brother, which looked like favoritism. It may be that consciously or unconsciously, your mother was simply trying to prevent a repetition of the sister–brother friction that caused her mother, and her, so much grief. She may be trying to right a wrong that is two generations old.

In order to get a fix on triangles in the family, Bowen and Kerr recommend gathering the following data about your relatives: date of birth, date and cause of death, education, work history, health history (including emotional problems), marital history, and where they grew up and later lived.

You can collect this information not only about your mother and your grandmother and great-grandmother on her side of the family, but also about their spouses, siblings, and extended families. You repeat the process with your father's side of the family.

If your mother will cooperate, you can begin the research process with her. Having gathered hard facts about her history, you might then ask her these kinds of questions:

"Did you like your mother and father?"

"Did your mother like her mother and father?"

"When you were a child, what got you into trouble, and how were you punished?"

"What did you do to be 'good'? What pleased your mother? Did she praise you?"

"How did she express affection for you?"

"Did you like your sister (brother)? Did you like one more than another? What did you fight about? How did you help each other?"

"Did your parents play favorites?"

"Did you like school? How did you feel about your teachers, or the other students?"

"Who was your best friend growing up? What was she like?"

"Who was your first boyfriend and what was he like? How did your parents feel about your dating?"

"What did your mother tell you about sex?"

"Did you ever consider marrying someone besides Dad?"

"Were you scared of having kids?"

"What was the hardest part of raising a family?"

"What was the most difficult part of marriage? The best part?"

"If you had it to do over again, would you work, or work in another field? What work would you really like to have done?"

"What were some of your successes at work? What were some of your disappointments?"

"When did you first feel 'old'? Was reaching forty hard for you?"

"How did you feel when you began menopause?"

"How old was your mother when she began menopause? Did she tell you about it? How did she feel?"

"Did all your dreams come true? Which did, and which didn't?"

"Was I a planned child? Did I come at a good time or bad time?"

These are compassionate and blame-free questions. They show more interest than bias, more empathy than censure.

Most daughters, I've discovered, don't know their mothers—or fathers—very well. And most mothers also don't know their daughters very well. As you pose these questions, you might begin volunteering to your mother some information of your own, even answering your own questions.

By now, you are probably having a heart attack even *imagining* such a conversation with your mother. There is the chance—especially with Critics, Avengers, and Deserters—that she will say, "Well, nosy, what's all this? Since when were you interested?"

Whatever her personality, your mother may not want to answer all, or any, of these questions; she may feel prodded more than is comfortable for her. But she *might* be beguiled by your interest—most people love to talk about themselves, and for mothers of Baby Boomers, these kinds of questions were seldom asked, seldom even considered. The conflicts and ambivalences of the senior generation were rarely on anyone's agenda.

If she is hesitant, you could say, "I'm really trying to find out about our family so I can get an idea of who I am, and I need your help. And I'd like us to get to know each other better."

There is *no* chance that you will get the answers to these questions if you don't try to pose them. And if your mother doesn't want to participate, even after your patient and repeated attempts to glean such information from her, you can pose them to your father, or aunts and uncles, or grandparents or cousins. Whatever the source, all this information helps you see your mother in a three-dimensional way rather than simply as the "mother" to the "child" in you.

Among the nuggets of information you might gather are these:

The mandates of her childhood may have become her mandates for you—she may have an inherited internal calendar of expectations. A mother recalls events in her own life at a certain age, and filters her view of her child at the same age through her memory. If, say, her mother married at twenty-two, and she married at twenty-two, when you were twenty-two she may have begun making comparisons: "I was married at your age, and you aren't even *dating*!"

Her sister may have developed polio at fifteen, so when you turned fifteen, your mother may have been particularly protective. She may or may not have made the connection that this sudden gearing up of nervousness had more to do with her experience than anything you were doing. Still, you were left only with the feeling of her craziness.

Your mother's mother may have died when she was twenty-eight. When you turned twenty-eight, she may have started to be distant in a way that she never was before. It may be that, unconsciously, she was afraid of losing you, too.

Perhaps she had a miscarriage when you were seven and you never knew it—all you knew was that she suddenly was irritable all the time. Maybe that was the year you started having real problems in school. Being aware of concrete reasons for a change in her behavior will go a long way toward explaining that she may not have been angry with you, even though that's how it looked.

You might discover that she was *never* punished or even reprimanded as a child. As a consequence, she never knew how to curb her own appetites, her own need for constant gratification. Her narcissism may have been forged in childhood—that she is incapable of giving you love may have everything to do with how her mother treated her—and nothing to do with you.

You might even uncover acts of extraordinary courage—such as your mother's donating a kidney to her sister—that she, in her reticence, never discussed before. Such a discovery might make you see her with more respect and admiration.

Lots of mysteries, ones that caused you to feel that it was *your fault* that she couldn't show you affection when you needed it, can be cleared up by such information.

"Researching one's own family sufficiently to formulate impressions about the multigenerational process makes it possible to see the emotional 'script' in one's multigenerational family and, as a consequence, to *be less preoccupied with the actions and inactions of any one family member,*" write Drs. Kerr and Bowen (emphasis added).

Your own experience and emotional maturity will contribute to your understanding of the facts of your family. Sometimes you'll hear a story you've heard a hundred times, and it "clicks" for you because of your own experience. This is particularly true for daughters when they become mothers. As one woman said,

> When you're a kid, you think your mother should make parenthood her top priority. But when you become a parent, you realize that you can't always put motherhood first. If I have a fight with my husband, or if I'm worried about something with another child, I can't put that aside and totally be a parent to *this* child. I'm affected by what goes on in my life. So I've begun to see my mother as a person. I've been able to stop blaming her for many of the things she did when I was a child. My father was a tyrant. That explains a whole lot about my mother as a mother.

There is much in the Family Systems approach that is extremely valuable. I agree, for instance, that it is *imperative* that you require people in your family to solve their own problems and not allow them to manipulate you into taking sides. As we will see in the last three chapters, many daughters have learned how to "detriangle"—to extricate themselves from being dumping grounds for their mother's frustrations.

This "dumping" usually begins with such statements as "Wait'll you hear what your father did *this* time!" By staying out of the middle, you can love both people for themselves alone, and not as contingent on what they perceive as your "loyalty."

The most valuable part of Family Systems is that it teaches you to know your mother as a person so that you can understand and accept her. You won't be indifferent to her future actions and inactions; but at least they won't be as loaded. You may find that she is merely as human as you are.

There are some aspects of the Systems approach, however, with which I disagree. The notion of total emotional neutrality is, I think, an impossible and questionable ideal—people are not robots. In addition, all the fact-finding and history-gathering in the world may not fill the huge hole of having felt unloved as a child (that is the work of therapy and introspection, as we have seen). The Family Systems approach is only one tool of many that are available to you in defining yourself.

Still, by looking at family patterns and by getting to know your mother, woman-to-woman, you can find areas in which you agree, or have much in common, so that you can abide and respect your differences.

One tool that might help you do that is to make two lists: First, a catalogue of the qualities in your mother that you admire, and a list of those you don't admire. This will help you appreciate her strengths and see them as separate from the things that make you crazy. You can admire the former and learn to deflect the latter.

The second list would be a catalogue of your *own* "good" and "bad" qualities. Some of them may echo your mother's, others will be all your own. The point is to be able to see that you are *separate* from her, an individual with your own beliefs, values, strengths, and weaknesses. This is extremely important for women who lament, "Oh, God, I'm just like my mother." You may be similar in some ways, perhaps, but *you are not identical.*

A comparison of the two lists will be extremely helpful in seeing where you and your mother can learn from and enjoy each other, and where you need to accommodate each other's individuality. "Same" and "different" are not necessarily bad. It's what is.

Whatever route you have taken to work through your feelings, your history, and your ambivalence about your mother, now it may be possible for you to achieve some compassion for and understanding of her.

As we have said, this won't necessarily make her a soul mate. You may, even after all your efforts, still dislike her, as you would any person who you decide, after a period of examination, is not friendship material. She may even be utterly *unredeemable.* But at least you will be able to accept her for who she is—the product of her parents, her genes, her times, her experiences, her demons, her marriage, all the things that make up the whole of who anyone is. She will be defused, no longer able to annihilate you.

You will probably never reach emotional neutrality—to do that, you have to be devoid, I think, of all passion—but you can make your mother more third person and less "you versus me."

Reconnection

Achieving redefinition of your relationship with your mother may require a period of transition as your mother adjusts to you, and you to her. For women who have had stormy relationships with their mothers, or who have cut off from them, it may be an act of extraordinary courage simply to write or call the mother you may not have seen in weeks, or months, or even years, and say, "I'd like to see you." And, if she ignores your letter, gives you a hard time, or hangs up on you, to write or call again.

You can't reconnect if you haven't done the work we discussed above and in the previous chapter. When cut-off or seldom available daughter and mother get back together again, what often happens is that all the old arguments fall back into place.

Reconnection is not possible if you haven't gotten rid of your anger, or most of it, first. You don't want to go back into the attachment expecting your mother's remorse, or prepared to slug it out if she makes you sore, or if you are unable to stand your ground and not become the supplicant you once were.

Much depends on how you implement your new maturity and awareness in the relationship. You have to learn to talk to her in a new way, even a new vocabulary. When you do that, most mothers will try to get you to "change back" to the old patterns—but eventually they will adjust. (For those mothers who can't, or who are too psychotic, addicted, or destructive to be reached, see Chapter Twenty).

Let's say your mother can't seem to talk to you without criticizing. You can deflect those criticisms by not overreacting to them—by reacting, in fact, in a new way. If she says, for instance, "I can't believe that you feed your family TV dinners," you could joke, "Well, Mom, you know I never was a very good cook." Or you could say, "I don't want to get into that right now—I'd much rather talk about the movie I saw last night." The point is not to allow the conversation to get to the level at which it will erupt. You keep off those heated areas about which you always seem to disagree.

Another example. Let's say your mother never lets you get a word in edgewise. All she does is moan about her aches and pains and you never get a chance to tell her about your job promotion. Again, you can change the pattern in which you and your mother typically interact. After listening to her for a few minutes, you can interrupt by saying, "Excuse me, but I have terrific news," and then telling her in detail what that news is.

She may interrupt you, but you keep returning to the subject so that you have an opportunity to participate equally—without anger or sullenness—in the conversation.

At first, these techniques may feel altogether artificial and make you extremely nervous. Nevertheless, they have a very important purpose: to change the lifelong ways in which you and your mother respond to one another. In time, your new way of behaving may become automatic and the relationship more spontaneous.

The basic rule is this: When she attacks you, you don't counter-attack. When she attempts to make you feel guilty, you don't take the bait. "My back is killing me," your mother says, "I wouldn't feel so crummy if I saw you once in a while." You could say, "Gee, I'm sorry to hear that," and ignore the second half of her comment.

You stay within yourself—or, as Dr. Harriet Goldhor Lerner puts it in *The Dance of Intimacy*, you "self-focus." By that she means you become an expert *only on yourself*, and not on your mother. "She's selfish, she's a wimp, she's psychotic, anal-compulsive, a rat" is being an expert on your mother.

Redefining our attachments, and shifting the ways we behave in those attachments, are the subject of another of Dr. Lerner's books, *The Dance of Anger: A Woman's Guide to Changing the Patterns of Intimate Relationships*. In it, she offers guidelines on how to keep ourselves from being engulfed by our anger, among them,

- speaking up about issues that are important to you;
- avoiding blame and "analyzing" the other person;
- respecting people's differences;
- being responsible only for your own behavior;
- speaking only for yourself and not through a third party.

Dr. Lerner explains three "essential ingredients" of detriangling: First, "staying calm." This is self-explanatory—you don't want to overreact when you're feeling angry or anxious.

Second, "staying out." By this she meant that you don't inject yourself in other people's disagreements—that is, "no advising, no helping, no criticizing, no blaming, no fixing, no lecturing, no analyzing, and no taking sides in their problems."

Third, "hanging in." This is the hard part—staying in touch with two sides of a triangle—say, your mother and your father, with whom your mother is furious—without taking sides. If you don't get caught in the middle, thereby absorbing some of the heat between them, the other two sides are forced to keep the problem where it belongs—between themselves. Even if they won't or can't deal with it, your relationship with them is not contingent on your side-taking "loyalty."

When we self-focus and stay out of triangles, we can state who we are and what is important to us. We can *share ourselves* rather than get snared in other people's unresolved issues and *lose ourselves*. By being responsible only for our own actions and reactions, we can salvage and strengthen our relationships.

Part of self-focusing and sharing is the ability to say to your mother, for example, "I always felt you didn't love me," and *not* "You were unable to love." You can reveal without condemning or angrily confronting. She may hear only criticism in your statement. But she *might* take it as an opportunity to reveal something about herself. She might say in response, "I was always afraid of expressing my feelings; it wasn't allowed in my family when I was growing up. I just never learned how."

Learning how to be separate within the mother–daughter relationship is harder, it seems, than climbing Mount Everest barefoot. Because there are *all those buttons*. The idea is to *disconnect the buttons*.

You cannot change who your mother is and why she does what she does. But you might change her behavior. When your mother discovers that you will no longer play in her ballpark, she has no choice but to learn how to "play" in yours. And if she decides not to "play" at all, it won't be because you haven't been true to yourself or because you blew her away. The barometer of your growth is not *her* changing, but the way in which *you* have changed.

If you can stop reacting in an angry or supplicating way, your mother will, in time, probably respond differently toward you. The point of all this effort on your part is to become more mature *within the mother-daughter relationship*, rather than running from it. If your only interest is the ways in which your mother did not live up to your expectations, you won't be grown up enough to see that she is a separate person who had her own life, her own joys and stresses.

Ideal mothers, "perfect" mothers, are the stuff of immature fantasy. And if we insist that our mothers fit the fantasy, we won't be able to recognize that we have unrealistic and impossible standards: we want them to be superhuman.

The goal in all this work is to see your mother as a separate human being who has her own experience, and, like all of us, her own good and not-so-good qualities.

If you can see your mother in this way, and be with her without jeopardizing your true self or reverting to old patterns, then nobody in any of your relationships can cause you to give up your true self again. Attempting to reconnect with your mother is the proving ground for all your other attachments. By declaring who you are, without asking other people to change who they are, forces them to take you seriously; but even if they do not, you have not compromised who you are.

It cannot be overstated that this process of reconnection, wherein you find out who you are in relation to your mother and her history, takes a tremendous amount of effort and courage. As Dr. Lerner told me, "I've worked with people for three years before they can go to their mothers and raise painful issues. This is not easy stuff."

In time, however, you find that the old fears, the old reactions, the old automatic responses, simply wither away. Eventually, you can see your mother, and yourself, with more generosity and more acceptance.

The danger in seeing mom as either angel or devil, says Dr. Marianne Goodman, is that "she's not a real person. And if she's not, you can't be. You can only be who you are if you allow Mom to be who she is. It's really that simple."

When you understand your mother in this way, and stop pressuring her to change, your other relationships do not become so life-or-death, so urgent, so intense, so desperate. In a way, you can't "live" with your mother until you learn to live without her. Once you release your fantasy about your mother, and with it your unrealistic expectations of her, so, too, do you release the fantasy and the unrealistic expectations you have of yourself, your friends, your co-workers, your partner, and your children.

That is what true healing is all about.

Interdependence, Not Independence

The purpose of all this work is not for you to be stoically independent or resolutely uncommitted, refusing ever to need or to feel or to be vulnerable. The goal is to learn how to be a part of the world, to allow yourself the risk of joy and love and pain in your attachments—to recognize the healthy and altogether *human* desire for loving connections—and at the same time to be a whole, separate individual. This is mature interdependence. Those women who have come to terms with their mothers, one way or another, achieve it.

But just as some mothers dare not be pleased with their daughters, so, too, do some adult daughters refuse to see their mothers as anything but evil. Some mothers are, indeed, evil. But if we have the capacity to stay within our boundaries, to limit our mothers' intrusions or criticisms or inappropriate demands, a redefined relationship with them is possible. And if such a relationship is *not* possible—for reasons we shall explore in Chapter Twenty—we can at least examine the forces that formed her and glean *something* from our knowledge of her, and of the family that molded her, and ourselves.

Friendship, Truce, or Divorce

Breaking the cycle of the unresolved mother–daughter relationship and redefining it begins with one metaphorical grain of sand, the thought of "I can't go on like this." One grain becomes two, then a handful, then a tiny island of self-worth on which to stand and build a life. Slowly, self-esteem gleaned from accomplishment, from seeing your mother as she is, and from understanding yourself and therefore her, becomes a continent of your new separate, worthy, human, fallible self.

Once that self-esteem is solidified, and once you know all you can know about your mother and your shared history, *then* you can decide what in your relationship with your mother is best for you, a decision that is freed of fantasy, ambivalence, anger, denial, and blame.

These are the options that now are open to you:

Friendship. You may love your mother very much, but your relationship doesn't seem to get out of the category of "mother–child." In this instance, you want to make a good relationship even better. Mostly, you want to be treated like an adult. You want greater closeness, more honesty and open communication, woman-to-woman.

Perhaps you have never had a good relationship with your mother. Now you want what has been a lousy relationship to break into friendship, because you have changed—or you *and* your mother have matured—and the timing is right for both of you.

Truce. Your mother may not be capable of real friendship, but she is not necessarily evil—she is merely trapped in her own defenses, her own "false self." You discover that there are some very good qualities about her that you do not want to lose, but you are aware that she is simply unable to allow you to be who you are. In this instance, you resolve to see her for the sake of those good qualities, for the sake of her attachment to your children, and for the sake of a realistic sense of "family" without compromising yourself. You and your mother may not be intimates, but you can, by setting limits on her insecure behavior and your own emotional reactivity, be friendly.

Divorce. In this rare instance, a relationship with your mother holds nothing but her uncontrolled disdain and rage, no matter how good you are at self-focusing. Reconnection with such a mother is like walking into a propellor. There are some mothers who are so destructive that a relationship with them is an exercise in masochism. In these instances, you still must resolve the relationship, but you have to do so on your own. You have to deal with the mother in your head, by yourself, or with outside help, so that your childhood losses will not infect your other attachments. You have to accept that you are an emotional orphan. But that doesn't mean you cannot live a full and rewarding life, or that you cannot create a loving family with your husband and children, or simply a "family" of affectionate friends.

These options are the subjects of the next three chapters. Only you can decide which category is best for you, which form of redefinition is possible. There is no single "right" way.

18
Friendship

"The greatest tribute I can pay you is this: You helped me to become myself. I know how much you struggled against your need to keep me close—you felt I was all you had in life. I have come to believe that you let me go at tremendous expense to yourself. Toward the end, you worried so that you had not been a good enough mother—you needn't have worried. I'm really okay. I can take care of myself. I believe in myself—I have you to thank for that. But I will always miss you."

So spoke Sophie, forty-five, at her mother's funeral. It was the bittersweet coda to her mother's last, agonizing weeks when she lay dying of cancer in her daughter's house. During those weeks, Sophie served as her mother's nurse and constant companion, meeting her most basic bodily needs and trying to comfort her about her terror of dying.

In that time, difficult as it was for both of them, Sophie and her mother talked for hours about the sum of her mother's life and the sum of their bond. Each woman spoke of her doubts about herself and of their good times and bad. They put to rest any unanswered questions, knowing that their time together was nearly over, and savoring, as best they could, what was left of it.

In recalling her mother's final days, what struck Sophie most was her mother's dignity, and especially how her mother fought her helplessness. "Isn't this too much for you?" her mother asked, over and over. "Shouldn't I be in a nursing home?"

"Being a mother was my mother's finest effort," Sophie told me with awe. "This was a woman who was frightened all her life. My father left her when she was twenty-seven. She never had many friends. And yet she hated being a burden to me. Mind you, I know all my mother's faults. I do not idealize her. But the crowning achievement of her life was that she refused to allow her insecurities to destroy me. Her childhood had been a gothic horror, and she had had no choice about what kind of parents she had. But she made a conscious choice about what kind of parent she would be."

I met Sophie a year after her mother's death. Her lingering grief was not over what had never been—rather, it was the inexplicable sadness and joy at having had so much to lose. Her mother not only loved her unconditionally but also gave her encouragement and support in everything she did—her work, her marriage, her children. Sophie's mother made it possible for her daughter to live without her, and left her with memories of a friendship of unique depth and richness.

Their attachment was wonderous in this specific way: Both mother and daughter were able to respect and even celebrate each other's strengths and weaknesses—they could certainly talk about them—and just let each other *be who they are.*

It sounds so simple. After all, many of us are able to do that with friends. But to end up forming a friendship with the woman who once embarrassed or spanked or rebuked or even humiliated us is extraordinary. For if what we know of love we learned from our mother, what we know of hate we learned from her as well. Love and hate are the tandem cadences of the mother–daughter connection, and ultimately to find harmony between them is a stunning accomplishment.

Those women who have managed it have cleared several hurdles:

- the mother's parenting mistakes and the daughter's rebellions;
- the Bad Mommy Taboo;
- the Myth of Motherhood.

By the time the daughter is an adult, it is this last that is the most difficult to transcend.

The Myth of Motherhood

One reason so many mothers and daughters aren't friends is this: *Every woman's relationship with her mother comes close to, or falls far from, the Myth of Motherhood.*

In infancy and childhood, we see our mothers as All Good because we must; our survival depends on it. But in adulthood, we often still see them with the eyes of a child, filtering our view of them through the fantasy of long-suffering, all-sacrificing maternal perfection.

The "mother" of our dreams—the inspiration for millions of Mother's Day cards and their poetic and often incredible messages—is, indeed, dreamlike. She is an ideal—she is not real, so even our dream of her is in some way suspect, not to be trusted. Still, we cling to it. There are all those high hopes of our magic years—the years in childhood when we idealized her because we had no choice—hopes that linger in the aftertaste of childhood. And if she never measured up to that ideal, we feel cheated.

So, too, does Mother feel cheated if we do not behave according to the Myth, that we cherish her and sanctify her, abiding by the Bad Mommy Taboo.

Most adult daughters still want their mothers to love them no matter what, and most mothers want to continue to be adored as they were in their daughters' childhoods. But love can be a sometime thing. Is "love" on your mind when your husband is in a foul mood? When your child screams, "Get out of my face"?

The answer, if one is honest, is that you love the people who mean most to you most of the time, but you don't always *like* them. A component of friendship is the ability to tolerate the bad stuff in order to get the good stuff, and to see the person as real.

But we don't want our mothers to have *any* bad stuff, yet we want them to love us in spite of *our* bad stuff, just as they want us to love them. It may be too much to ask—perhaps not in childhood, when we have a right to unconditional love, because we are so utterly dependent—but certainly now that we are both, allegedly, grown-ups.

When we are adults, we are no more bound to love our mothers unconditionally than they are to love us unconditionally. As daughters who have children quickly learn, motherhood is an exercise in ambivalence. Where once we felt "I can't win" with our mothers, now often we feel "I can't win" with our *own* children—that no matter how hard we try to be good enough mothers, there is no way we *can* be. Look at the evidence: Our kids want to leave us. How good can we really be?

We need to pull out the single strand that will untangle the knot of the Myth: as long as maternal perfection serves as our yardstick—

whether or not we have children—true friendship between mothers and daughters is not possible.

To have friendship with our mothers, we have to let go of the Myth.

What Do We Mean by "Friendship"?

"The absence of war is not peace," Amrita Pritam, one of India's best-known writers, has said. "Peace is when life flowers."

By friendship I do not mean the symbiotic mother–daughter attachment that is the goal of Smotherers, Doormats, Angels, and Ciphers. These are relationships in which the mothers and daughters have not yet separated—they may have an absence of war, but they do not have peace. Nor do I mean *"best"* friend. As we will see, that may be both impossible and even unhealthy.

By friendship, I mean something quite different: an affectionate relationship that is based on mutual likes, and respect—sometimes even admiration—for each other's differences as adults.

And where is there a greater *potential* for peaceful friendship than with one's mother? After all, we share the same biology and history. We know each other's best and worst qualities. We've shared the best and worst of times. We've seen each other without makeup. We do not feel compelled to fill up the silences between us with nervous chatter, because we are not constrained by rules of non-kin sociability. Theoretically, we don't have to *prove* anything.

Mother–daughter friendship has been tested by the fires of the daughter's claim to her own identity, and the mother's parental choices. If they can accept each other's flaws and terrible bargains, and if at the same time they *really like each other*, allowing themselves to appreciate each other's strengths and lovable qualities, they have a treasured gift.

Some friendships blossom when both mother and adult daughter take what was a good relationship and refine it—they are both able to relinquish the expectations of long ago, expectations that no longer apply when the daughter is an adult. Out of that acceptance of who they *are*—not a fantasy of who they *were*—they form a much closer bond that is based on their humanness and their similarities as women. These women become friends because they choose to continue their affectionate attachment—not because they "ought" to. Their friendship flourishes because the *affection* of their past is augmented by the *autonomy* of their present, when they each have healthy boundaries.

Other friendships with mothers are formed out of the ashes of the daughter's horrendous beginnings—both mother and daughter recover from their false start together and learn to accommodate and love each other on a new basis.

Every daughter I interviewed longed for such friendship.

Is Mother–Daughter "Friendship" an Impossible Ideal?

Numerous social scientists think that "friendship" with one's mother is an inappropriate and unrealistic goal. One of them is Dr. Bruno Bettelheim. He writes,

Friendship requires a different type of relationship than does parenting. When a parent hopes that his child will become a close friend, the result is a relationship based on relative immaturity. The parent is seeking friendship from a person who is immature when compared to him; the child is led to seek friendship from a person who is poorly suited to offer it in a satisfactory manner, because of the constellation of parent–child emotional experiences that have taken place during the child's formative years.

To the extent that every parent–child attachment bears some inevitable scars, I would agree. And to the extent that a mother cannot be a "pal" to her children—as many of the children of perpetually adolescent hippies of the 1970s discovered, to their dismay—I also agree. (However, I cannot help adding my own grain of salt: Dr. Bettelheim, much as I admire and respect him and his work, is not a woman.)

When we are children, friendship—as opposed to friendliness—with our mothers *is* inappropriate. Psychologist Louise J. Kaplan explains why: "The toddler must say 'no' in order to find out who she is. The adolescent says 'no' to assert who she is not. She does not belong to her parents; she belongs to her own generation. To pave the way for her own generational possibilities the adolescent must first undermine the utopia of childhood."

But what is true for the toddler and the adolescent is no longer true for the mature daughter of thirty or forty or fifty who has laid to rest her utopian needs. A daughter's chronology and seasoning—to say nothing of the mother's—do more to ameliorate generational differences than any other single component. As we begin to feel better about ourselves in the big bad world—facing challenges and surmounting them—our grudges against our mothers seem increasingly petty, and we see the ways the loose ends of our relationship trip us up. Age differences alone need not eclipse friendship with one's mother.

We often have friends who are much younger, or much older, than we are because of *an affinity of the spirit*. Age plays *a* part in friendship, it's true. For example, you refer to "the war," and, because you are forty-five, you mean the Second World War—but a twenty-two-year-old might think you mean the latest Third World dustup.

A disparity of historical contexts can enrich members of different generations as they explore each other's worlds—we are, after all, eyewitnesses to our own, and have much to share about it. How we feel has *something* to do with our chronological context; it does not have *everything* to do with it. Age has for too long been a barrier between the generations and a source of the most horrendous bias— "too old" or "too young" are phrases that arbitrarily keep people apart in ways that are tragic for the culture, and impoverishing individually.

Nevertheless, some aspects of mother–daughter affection are forever a one-way street, because, unlike other attachments, your mother is always your mother, and you are always her child. You probably have a key to your mother's house—and she probably does *not* have a key to yours. I am reminded of a fifty-year-old friend of mine who, in a voice heavy with concern, told me,

> My daughter phoned last night to say that yesterday was the worst day of her life: her boss bawled her out and her boyfriend broke up with her. So I went to her apartment with a care package of take-out Chinese food and flowers from my garden.
> Here's my question: *Am I infantilizing her?*

It is a question only a mother would ask. "No," I replied, shaking with laughter and more than a bit envious of her daughter. "You're just being a mother—and a friend."

With all these caveats, there is still plenty of room for you to find real friendship with your mother, filial privacy—the cornerstone of your distance from childhood—notwithstanding.

The Contours of Mother–Daughter Friendship

Many social scientists have researched this question: *Can*—not "should"—mothers and daughters really be friends? The answer is a resounding yes, but with several asides.

One question that has been studied is whether or not a daughter's own motherhood is a prerequisite for friendship with her mother. A wonderful homily in that regard is this: "When you have kids, you stop picking on your mother so much." But is that the only requirement?

Jane B. Abramson, who conducted a study of mothers and daughters, concluded that motherhood does *not* guarantee either friendship with your mother or even your own maturity. She writes that "psychological well-being in later life hinges less on parental status than on development of a full and unique personality, the result of having been 'well mothered' to begin with."

The most important finding in her study was this: Adult daughters who were the most "successful"—meaning those who were leading rich lives—were both "maternal" and "achieving." That is, they drew self-esteem from their own competence at work and *also* had the capacity for nurturing and empathy. They had both a sense of mastery and a talent for loving, for being concerned about another person's feelings and caring about their happiness. *But they weren't necessarily mothers themselves.*

Grace Baruch and Rosalind Barnett, in their study of mothers and daughters, found that a daughter's motherhood *dilutes* her ties to her own mother, and that the daughter without children is more closely connected to her mother.

The researchers write, "The mother–daughter bond was especially important to women who were not themselves mothers. [They were] affected more strongly by relationships with their mothers than are women who have children. . . . So being a mother seems to reduce the significance of one's own mother in one's life." The more sources of support a woman has, they found, the less urgent any one relationship becomes. Nevertheless, "most women derive a sense of well-being through rewarding relationships with their mothers. . . ."

As to whether or not having children per se helps a woman feel better about *herself*, the researchers concluded that it does not—the most important finding in their study was that "whether a woman did or did not have children had no significant impact on her well-being."

Lucy Rose Fischer conducted two studies of the mother–daughter attachment—one among young adult women twenty-one to thirty-one, and a later study of middle-aged daughters and their elderly mothers. Dr. Fischer corroborated the view that unmarried daughters, because they had not reached their mother's "social age" by becoming wives and mothers, tended to be more dependent on their mothers than daughters who were married with families of their own—although that didn't necessarily mean they were friends. Single daughters, she found, "did *not know* what their mothers' lives were like."

But she also found that a daughter's motherhood made it possible for her to reconnect with her mother in one way that childless daughters cannot. Once daughters had children, they were their mothers' "role colleagues" and could create a bond out of their very specific shared experience.

It was married daughters with children who were more likely to have "peerlike relationships" with their mothers. Still, if a daughter's motherhood allowed her to tear down one barrier between herself and her mother, the daughter's marriage—and changed allegiance (or at least divided loyalty)—erected another.

So the jury appears to be out on the question of whether or not having kids automatically fosters friendship with one's mother. Friendship ultimately seems to depend on qualities having little to do with the replication of the mother's role.

It also depends on the daughter's age—as we have said, this is perhaps the most important variable in mother–daughter friendship. By thirty-five or so, most women are beyond their rebellions. And it is the daughters in midlife who seem to have the best relationship with their mothers.

In the Baruch–Barnett study, approximately half the daughters—who were between the ages of thirty-five and fifty-five—reported "high maternal rapport" with their mothers. These daughters felt great warmth for their mothers and enjoyed their company.

Dr. Fischer called the kind of friendship I am talking about "mothers and daughters with peerlike friendships." According to her research, such friendships are rare among young adult daughters who have not developed the circumspection that comes with seasoning and maturity. Still, the characteristics of their attachments apply to all mother–daughter friendships.

Three qualities prevailed in these peerlike relationships. First, the mothers and daughters were realistic and objective about each other.

Second, they were highly involved in each other's lives. Third, they each maintained their boundaries, valuing their own independence and respecting it in the other.

These women made a concerted effort not to be too dependent on each other. They struck a middle ground of closeness that did not jeopardize their individuality. The strength of their attachment was both their love *and* their separate sense of self.

In my own interviews, I found that many of the daughters who have children are indeed able to enlarge their perspective of their mothers by virtue of their own ambivalences about, and the pressures of, *being* mothers. As one woman said, "When my two toddlers are eating dinner, I worry that they'll choke on their food, so I cut it in tiny pieces, just as my mother did for me when I was a kid. If *I* get crazy over such things, imagine how my mother must have felt—she had *seven* kids."

But even such maternal insight didn't guarantee friendship among these daughters and their mothers. While it is true that our being mothers provides—arguably—the most profound awareness we can have of *what it means to be a mother*, it does not necessarily provide us with an awareness of *what it means to be a friend*.

Many of the unmarried and childless daughters I interviewed were *also* able to paint a more sympathetic picture of their mothers, by knowing that they share the stresses of simply being women and having adult responsibilities. If a daughter is at all sensitive, and if she has resolved her own childhood, she can identify with her mother simply because of her own *humanness*.

When Mothers and Daughters Can Be Friends

We know by now all the ways mothers and daughters *aren't* friends and why. What of those who are? How did they pull it off?

The daughters I interviewed who are friends with their mothers fell into two categories: those who were *always* close to their mothers in a healthy way, and who in adulthood redefined the relationship; and those who at some point in their adulthood decided to turn around their relationship from one of open warfare to profound affection.

A Good Thing Made Better. In this category, it was the mothers who set the tone for friendship. These mothers and daughters cared about each other from the daughter's early childhood on. The love they felt for each other was never questioned on either side, not by the mother when her daughter was buried in an avalanche of raging pubescent hormones, nor by the teenage daughter when she was energetically trying to carve out her own separate identity—attempting to be *different*, whatever that meant, from her mother.

The daughter's adolescence was the Rubicon for these women— these were the years that strained the composure of even the most even-tempered mothers. But they managed to treat their daughters' teens with loving resignation, as though it were a squall that would blow over. And whenever the mothers found their pulses racing with anger or anxiety about their daughters, they took their own *emotional* pulses.

It is at this point that some mother–daughter attachments can permanently derail, because the teenager's "badness" becomes a self-fulfilling prophecy. *All* teenagers need something to push against, even if they have to create a problem, so that they can get permission to separate. Some mothers do not navigate that separation well. They assume that they will be locked into an adversarial relationship with their teenager *forever*—and when the adolescent begins to give up her need to make her mother the enemy, the mother stays in her angry, hurt, self-protective role.

Says Judith M. Fox, a psychotherapist who is an authority on adolescence, "When something stressful happens between mothers and daughters, it's important for a mother to look at her own feelings, and not simply react. If she's not happy with her own response, or the outcome of a disagreement, that's the time these mothers can stop and say 'What's going on?' and try to figure it out."

In this way—this *very difficult* but important way—the mothers who have always had good relationships with their daughters were able to "self-correct," to keep themselves from losing control, and to maintain the long view. They doped out the difference between a "button" from the past and the reality of the daughter's continuing efforts to separate, however awkwardly or even hurtfully. These mothers had more successes than failures in lovingly letting their daughters go. They knew that by so doing, *their daughters would be able to come back, of their own accord, into a renewed and redefined, adult mother–daughter relationship.*

This is not to say that it was *easy* for those mothers to hang in with the belief that once the "storm" had passed, their relationships with their daughters would right themselves on a new course.

Sophie, described at the beginning of this chapter, believes that the very nurturing and unconditional love her mother gave her made separation much more painful than it is for daughters who have always hated their mothers' guts. She says,

> The only way I could separate was to *tear* myself away. Between the ages of fourteen and twenty-one, I didn't confide in my mother at all. She didn't like it that I was out late with boys, and yet she wanted me to be free, as she had not been. She was amazingly liberal with me. When I was in high school, my boyfriend—the man I later married—was allowed to spend the night in my room. This was *not* done in those days—I'm not even sure how much it's done today. But she figured I'd be safer at home than staying out all hours, or having sex in the backseat of a car. Her messages were often mixed: Do what you want, have a good life, but I'm scared you're going to hurt yourself. Still, I always had a secure feeling that she was there for me.

Once the adolescent years are behind them, loving mothers and daughters find a new and enriching middle ground that draws on what was always an affectionate—if not trouble-free—relationship.

One woman I know weathered her daughter's adolescence—during which the girl experimented with drugs and had a worrisome romance with an unemployed rock singer—and when the clouds lifted, found a closeness with her daughter that corroborated the mother's ultimate faith in her.

Their friendship today is constantly deepening because they do not let patterns and reactions from the past corrupt the present. Recently the woman's daughter, now twenty-seven and the mother of Tim, a two-year-old, said, "I have the feeling sometimes that I do things with Tim that you disapprove of," and cited an example. My friend thought about the example and replied, "I promise you, that didn't even register. The next time you have a question, just raise a flag on the spot and we'll talk about it. If I give out those messages, let's look at that, because I don't mean to. And if I do disapprove, I'll tell you—even if I'm wrong!"

Says Judith Fox of her own relationship with her grown daughter,

> I'm quite connected to her, and she's quite connected to me, in, I believe, healthy ways. There's a lot of space between us, the ability to listen to one another and to accept each other's different

positions. When I'm being "mother," I very often phrase it as, "I need to say this, I need you to hear it, but you don't have to do anything with it." She asks for my input because I don't insist that she has to follow it—she just sticks it into her "computer" and retrieves what she needs. But I do the same with *her* input—she teaches me a lot.

I enjoy her enormously. It's a wonderful, wonderful relationship. She doesn't have to keep fighting for her own space anymore. She knows she has it.

The "Turnaround" Friendship. In this latter category of mother–daughter friendship, the turnaround from distance to closeness was initiated by the daughters. This was usually because their mothers were still flooded by their own defenses and emotional legacies, and didn't know how to move their relationship with their adult daughters to higher ground. At the same time, the daughters had worked very hard on their own—either in therapy or solitary introspection—to come to terms with their ambivalence about their mothers, and had the tools for resolution.

These "turnaround" daughters were Superachievers, Troublemakers, or Defectors. Wanting to form a friendship with their mothers had something to do with their extreme bitterness and anger—the *intensity* of their feelings. They wanted to find a peace with their mothers that they had never had.

In these cases, *both* mother and daughter wanted something better between them—but the daughter had to make it happen. She had to break through her own, and her mother's, defenses. In ways, she had to be more mature than her mother.

Cristina, described in Chapter Four, had a childhood that was scarred by eternal battles with her Italian mother about food. Her Critic mother, who lived by old-country values and whose female role was defined by the kitchen, believed that her maternal success depended on how much she was able to get her daughter to eat. "Fat Daughter" meant "Good Mommy."

When she was grown, Cristina, a Superachiever, spent many years churning up the fast track, hurtling away from her mother, fueled by her rage at having been so dominated. Armed with a doctorate in marine biology, she spent half her life beneath the sea, observing dangerous creatures, in keeping with her daring personality and fierce curiosity. But in her early thirties, she found her anger to be a burden that was interfering with her work and her relationships. She says,

I had refused to have anything to do with my mother—so, naturally, she was constantly on my mind. My anger was so great that it was paralyzing me. I knew I could not accomplish all the things I wanted to accomplish if she was that paramount. I knew I had to learn to accept her—I didn't want *anybody* taking over my life. So I had several years of therapy, and I did a tremendous amount of healing. Eventually I could see that she had never meant any real harm—she was simply a product of her times, doing what she was trained to do. Once I came to that conclusion, it was incredible—I just stopped running from her.

If there was one moment—and there were many—when their relationship turned around, it was when Cristina decided to try using her mother's fixation on food, the very thing that had enraged her, as the road back to her mother. Cristina wanted to lose five pounds, and she asked her mother, "the master of diets, the nutrition and caloric expert of the world," to help her accomplish her task during a week-long visit to her mother's home. Says Cristina,

> I put her in total charge of what went into my body. She fed me only what she thought I needed to lose weight. She said, "Today we're going to have three apples and eight ounces of rice." Sure enough, I lost weight. She felt needed, as she was, and we could connect in a way that was bliss for her, and nonthreatening for me.

Since then, her mother has come full circle. She has said all the things Cristina always wanted to hear, such as "I wish I could have been a better mother for you. I literally starved you of affection." Cristina, too, has come full circle, and has allowed herself to recognize enormous good in her mother.

> For all her craziness about food when I was growing up, she gave me huge permissions in other parts of my life. She urged me to get a graduate degree. She urged me to have a profession. She urged me to be a pioneer. I was a very provocative kid, and we had a personality conflict—we don't anymore. Every so often she'll say

something critical about my work and we'll have a blowout on the phone. I'll scream, "This is out of bounds, you don't know what the hell you're talking about, shut your mouth," and hang up on her. I'll sulk for three days. Then I'll call her back and say, "Listen, we're both grown-ups. You just triggered a kid thing in me." And she'll say, "I guess I was just feeling left out." We have a phenomenal relationship.

The turnaround for Marilyn, a Deserter, occurred when she was forty-five, and her Doormat mother was seventy-two. Marilyn had spent five years in therapy, sorting out why being with her mother—a twice-a-year obligatory get-together, usually because of a wedding or christening—always resulted in gastritis, and why she exploded whenever her mother said anything mildly critical or remotely guilt-inducing. Her mother's sighs and wounded silences drove Marilyn berserk. But then she had a breakthrough in her therapy, one of those "clicks" after which nothing is ever the same.

Marilyn's father was an alcoholic—not an all-day-falling-down drunk, but an evening-sitting-down drunk, when he would suddenly change from his cheerful public personality to a dark and roiling fury. Evenings were hell for the family—Marilyn would flee to her bedroom, her mother would hide in hers—and Marilyn felt abandoned.

Marilyn did a lot of reading about the adult children of alcoholics and figured out that her mother's father had also been an alcoholic, although her mother had always denied it. Some pieces began to fall into place as a result of that research. She realized that her mother was dealing with two generations of men around whom she had to tiptoe and become invisible—there was nothing left over for Marilyn. Once Marilyn learned how alcoholism infects every member of the family, she was able to begin—step by step—repairing her relationship with her mother.

The first turning point came when the two women were driving to the funeral of her mother's brother, a five-hour trip (Marilyn's husband had gone in another car with other relatives). Says Marilyn,

I wanted to find out more about her. I got her to admit that her father was an alcoholic. She told me in great detail what it was like living in fear of him and how she had to shut down to survive. She said she'd been afraid of me, too, because I was an aggressive kid, very like her father.

She told me about marrying my father and living in a strange city with no friends and no supports, stuff I was too young to remember. I worked up the courage to ask her why she never left him. She said, "Where could I go? What could I do?"

Suddenly, recalling those years she got really furious, not at me, but at how they had damaged her. It absolutely threw me that she was able to get so angry, because all I knew about her when I was growing up was that she was a wimp and a blank wall and had no emotions, no strength, nothing. Here was a side of her I had never seen. That talk animated her so much—she loved it. So did I.

The second turning point was when Marilyn had to have a hysterectomy. Marilyn had rehearsed with her therapist how she'd break the news to her mother, a woman who had always fallen apart under stress. She says,

When I told her, she was rational and reasonable and supportive. There was no hysteria. She said she would stay with me and take care of me. She told me about her own menopause. She didn't respond like a "mother" —it was more the way a friend would respond. She did exactly what I had hoped she would do.

I thought, Was I talking to some other woman? Or does the woman I thought she was no longer exist, and this is the woman she has become? Maybe the way I dealt with her allowed her to approach me in a different way. Then it all just cracked open in my head. I thought, Wait a minute. *I'm not the same person anymore either.* I'm not the insecure fifteen-year-old living in an alcoholic house, desperate for approval. We've *both* changed.

Cristina and Marilyn both needed therapy as a precursor for their newfound friendship with their mothers. Trudy, thirty-one, also a Defector, was able to manage it by hitting the emotional skids and building from there—*with* her mother.

Trudy's turnaround began in college, when she started to see that she was treating her friends as she had been treated by her Avenger mother. When her roommates would have friends in for pizza, Trudy would get annoyed and ask them to leave. If a boyfriend became too ardent, she'd dump him in an angry public scene.

In her childhood, Trudy's mother had been the epitome of patrician elegance to the world at large, but a sadistic presence to her daughter. When Trudy was little, her mother would slap her for not curtsying when someone came to visit. When Trudy was in high school, her mother would force her to leave parties and come home to clean the attic. Or she'd fill Trudy with terror for wearing an "unsuitable" or "vulgar" outfit.

It was enough to make most daughters flee for their lives forever. But at twenty-five, Trudy, an only child whose parents divorced when she was five, decided she had to figure out who she was within her relationship to her mother. Trudy says,

> Because I was no longer a kid, I began to get sick of my self-pitying ways. I realized that I was becoming my mother. And I realized that I was not the only person in the whole world who had a wicked mother. I had to find another way to live, and I couldn't as long as I was so angry. I decided I wanted to be happy, and if I could be happy with her—if I could find some reason why she's alive and why she was my mother—then I could learn to live in a better world. So I tried to find the good things about her and focus on them, and set limits on the bad things. It was like behavior modification. If she gave me positives, I'd spend time with her. If she gave me too many negatives, I'd say, "Okay, I have to go now."

Three things made their reconnection possible: First, Trudy made the first move, a fact that her face-saving mother appreciated and even admired, since she had been unable to do it herself. Second, Trudy, a travel agent, looked for areas in her own life where her mother could be of help. For example, her mother, a tax attorney, set up a new file system for Trudy and organized her office. "She did a fantastic job," Trudy says. "My work is so much easier now that I can find things."

Third—and most important—she was able to express how she felt when her mother became critical and judgmental. Once, for instance, her mother wanted to know why Trudy's boyfriend hadn't given Trudy an expensive birthday present. Trudy replied, "Do you know how rotten that makes me feel? It makes me feel as though the only way he could love me is to spend a lot of money on me. It makes me feel that I've somehow failed. I don't want to think that I'm a failure because I don't live up to your dreams."

Since those reentry years, when Trudy and her mother learned to reach each other in new and honest—not confrontational—ways, they have become extremely close. Her mother still has lapses, particularly in her vigorous denial of Trudy's perceptions about her own childhood. "It wasn't like that," her mother archly states. But Trudy says,

> Whenever I've talked about the past, and how I'm trying to grow up, she always changes afterward—she makes an effort. Do I understand her? I understand that she was desperately insecure when I was a child. I understand that she did all those hurtful things not out of a need to destroy me but out of a need to feel better about herself.

Trudy's mother has learned what *not* to say, because her daughter has explained it to her in a way that she can hear, rather than as an accusation. And since she has stepped back a bit, Trudy feels free to step *in* and show her mother that she loves and appreciates her.

When I asked Trudy what her childhood cost her, she replied,

> I prefer to think about what it gained me. I know the cost was tremendous—I still am slightly paranoid about what people think of me, for instance. Still, I've faced something very ugly that seemed to have absolutely no possibility of working out, and it did work out. It's sort of a tenacity that says, "There are ways of creating better relationships that are worth the effort, that are worth digging for." I made a definite decision that I am the master of my own fate. And I got a good friend out of all this—my mother.

Friendship with our mothers, like friendship with anyone, requires a certain rare kinship of the soul. You cannot expect it to be any less rare with your mother, who for very real reasons may not touch something in you that leads to true intimacy. She may be an entirely different kind of person—a good person, maybe, but not the stuff of which close friendships are made.

If you and your mother have a loving affinity, and *if* you are both open to change in yourselves and in each other, and *if* you truly want your mother's friendship, a deep and lasting bond can be created.

Many mothers and daughters are not able to find that intimacy together, and may not require it. However, they often *do* arrive at an affectionate truce. This may be the best that you can ask or hope for, and it is the subject of the next chapter.

19
Truce

A big change in my relationship with my mother is that I realize she didn't wake up every morning of my childhood and plan how she was going to hurt me. I think she loves me, even if it's not the way I want her to. I can laugh about how ridiculous our arguments are—I'm getting to the point where it just doesn't matter anymore. It's no longer the "terrible parent" issue. Now I can speak to her on the level of two adults. She's not somebody I'd choose for a friend, but we're capable of having some good times together.

—Hannah, forty

Not long ago, Linda, her husband, and her widowed mother, Grace, went to a barbecue at Linda's in-laws' house. All afternoon, Grace sat glumly on the edge of the group, making little effort to participate. Occasionally, someone tried to draw her into conversation, asking her questions about herself or her family. Grace replied in monosyllables and retreated into sullenness.

The "silent treatment" was always Grace's way of expressing displeasure or discomfort. It usually worked, at least with her children. Sulking caused her kids to jump to attention, especially Linda, the Angel, who eagerly tried to cheer her mother up. But as Linda got older it began to dawn on her that her mother's happiness seemed to depend on her, and required the sacrifice of Linda's own feelings and needs.

Linda, now thirty-two, was tired of being her mother's savior and of feeling like a puppet. So at the barbecue on that hot, still July afternoon, she silently observed her mother from the other side of the garden and, for the first time, she did not try to "save" her. Says Linda,

> Ordinarily I would have finagled the situation to make my mother feel more part of what was going on. But this time, I allowed things to take their natural course. I felt that if she was uncomfortable, she'd have to do something about it herself. And if she couldn't, she'd have to survive on her own. This was not a threatening situation, even though she may have perceived it as such. I stopped being her caretaker. The sadness of my relationship with my mother is that I have always been her "parent," and I don't want to be that anymore.

This may sound very like heartlessness on the part of a stubborn daughter toward her "helpless" mother. In fact, it was a healthy move toward a a more evenhanded and honest relationship. For Linda, this meant not so much leaving her mother in the social lurch as it did extricating herself from the old pattern of Doormat mother—rescuing Angel. If Linda was going to approach her mother on a woman-to-woman basis, she had to step out of her former "fix-it" role. If she was going to grow up, *she would have to allow her mother to grow up as well.*

Linda called a truce to the mother–daughter relationship as it had been. She began to establish healthy boundaries between herself and her mother, so that their ways of dealing with each other could get unstuck and be redirected toward something more equal, more real—even more affectionate.

"Truce, n. 1: a suspension of fighting esp. of considerable duration by agreement of opposing forces 2: a respite esp. from a disagreeable or painful state or action"

The relationships most of the women I interviewed have with their mothers fall into this category. A truce is not true comradeship, but neither is it open combat—it is a broad territory somewhere between the two. A truce feels like a definite "maybe": it's a lot easier to either totally adore your mother or thoroughly hate her than it is to tolerate her mixed blessings and your mixed emotions. But while there is enormous latitude for ambiguity and resentment in a truce, there is also enormous potential for mother–daughter resolution.

A truce can take one of three forms:

> righteous obligation;
> holding pattern;
> peaceful coexistence.

Righteous Obligation. Perhaps your relationship with your mother cruises along on automatic pilot, splitting the difference between your guilt and your mother's demands. You do your daughterly duty, calling her once a week, springing for lunch on Mother's Day, taking the kids to see her every now and then. The most meaningful topics of conversation you've had with her in years—in which you listen with half an ear—are the state of the weather or her health, which seem to be her favorite subjects.

You wouldn't dream of renouncing your relationship, but it doesn't give you any real pleasure except, perhaps, the amorphous and altogether tenuous sense of being a "good daughter." Indeed, such a relationship may give you a good deal of pain, as you listen to her many complaints and defend your choices and decisions.

The problem is that you both try to exert inappropriate control over each other. In the name of filial obligation, you allow her too great a role in your life. You are too influenced by her judgments about your work or friends or decisions—feeling you must take her on vacation with you when you'd really rather spend it alone with your partner or a chum, for example, or letting her discipline your children.

And you have too great a role in *her* life—letting her call you at work when her microwave conks out, paying her bills for her, or accompanying her every time she sees her doctor, even though she's perfectly capable of getting there under her own steam.

This category is what Dr. Lucy Rose Fischer calls "Mutual Mothering." Mother and daughter are entwined in a web of commitments that do not lead to real friendship but that, rather, make them feel uneasily beholden to each other.

Your connection seems to have calcified into place, like an improperly knit bone. This certainly applies to Dorothy, a Superachiever who, at forty-three, has her sense of obligation calibrated to a precise and grudging science. I asked her if she had ever tried to resolve her relationship with her Critic mother. She replied,

It's impossible—you simply can't get through to her. The way I deal with her is to acquiesce to certain responsibilities, such as inviting her for dinner, and just getting through it. I go through the motions. She gets under my skin the minute she walks in the door, so I avoid her as much as possible. Do I wish it were otherwise? Nah. At this point, I really, honestly don't—it's too late and life's too short to open it all up now. I will never forgive her for how deeply, and often, she has hurt me all my life. But I accept her for what she is. I do what I have to so I won't get the guilts—the absolute minimum.

Holding Pattern. Linda, the rescuing Angel mentioned above, falls into this category and so, maybe, do you. Perhaps you've decided that you and your mother aren't friends, even though you've given her that impression through the years, telling her all your secrets, listening to all her problems, and giving her unending advice. Now you want to pull back from what has been a surfeit of devotion you don't really feel. You don't want to defect, but you realize that you've neglected too many of your own needs in order to win her approval and affection. Now you've declared a truce to decide how to redefine the relationship—and yourself.

This is true of Terry, twenty-nine, a Cipher who realizes that whatever sense of self-worth she ever had automatically got drained off into constantly trying to appease her mother. Today Terry is dealing with the emotional vacuum that is the residue of their unsatisfying bond. She says,

I used to delude myself into thinking there was the possibility for something more with my mother, and now I know there really isn't—I'm facing the fact that there never was. It all came to a head recently, when I told her that I wanted us to have a relationship where I could talk to her about anything without being put down. It took a lot for me to say that—I was crying. And for a minute there, I thought she was going to show some emotion, some response—but then the moment passed. She didn't say anything. It was the biggest non-event of the year. At that moment, I knew I'd have to start accepting that this is as good as it's ever going to get—but I'm left with such an emptiness.

On the other hand, perhaps you've gone to the other extreme. You may have been cut off from your mother for years, put some emotional distance between the present and the past, and done your psychic stint at the shrink. Now you're ready to move up from defection to something that is not so emotionally loaded, because you no longer feel perpetual and self-destructive hatred for your mother, and you believe there is the possibility for *some* sort of relationship.

Laura, a thirty-two-year-old Defector, recently reconnected with her Avenger mother after a five-year silence. Of their renewed relationship, Laura says,

> I understand now why she always tried to belittle me: a woman who doesn't like her daughter in some ways is saying that she doesn't like herself. It's one of the great paradoxes of my life to discover that my mother, a woman who is extremely aggressive, domineering, and manipulative, a woman who used to fill me with terror, is basically horribly insecure. I work very hard to get past all her bluster to the frightened woman inside. It takes time, and a whole lot of patience on my part. Sometimes it works. Sometimes, we can actually have fun together.

Today, Laura and her mother are still in the process of adjusting to each other on neutral ground, learning how to trust each other, to simply *be* with each other without squaring off into their former combativeness.

Peaceful Coexistence. This category is the most stable and rewarding of the three forms of mother–daughter truce. You have exorcised your psychic demons and you've broken down the defensive walls of your false-self personality. You want a relationship in which you are neither servile nor hotheaded—a bond that is free of constant tension and animosity.

Peaceful coexistence doesn't necessarily mean a *loving* connection. It means a relationship that is no longer mined with unresolved and unrealistic expectations. But such coexistence can, in fact, be amicable—particularly when grandchildren are involved, as we shall see later in this chapter.

In this instance, you want to improve your relationship, keeping the good in it and deflecting the bad. You appreciate the things you and your mother have in common, and that's enough to forge a connection that is cordial, if not really intimate.

One daughter I interviewed has achieved such a relationship. She says,

> My mother and I are altogether different kinds of people. Where she's dramatic and tends to be hysterical, I am more low-key and deliberate. Once I got rid of my anger about our differences, I was able to see the positive things about her. Instead of going in exactly the opposite direction from her, which I'd always done in the past, what I've done is make a quarter-turn, because I have much stronger boundaries. Now I learn from her, rather than throwing the whole package away—which is what I did for a long, long time.

Acceptance that you and your mother will never be soul mates—that your childhood foxhole prayers will never be answered, and that they belong in the past—is not achieved without some sadness. But by giving up the impossible dream that your mother will change, you allow the dust between you to settle so that you can really *see* each other and, perhaps, find a middle ground of affable, realistic potential.

As Vivian Gornick writes in *Fierce Attachments,* her memoir of her relationship with her mother,

> Flux is now our daily truth. The instability is an astonishment, shot through with mystery and promise. We are no longer nose to nose, she and I. A degree of distance has been permanently achieved. I glimpse the joys of detachment. This little bit of space provides me with the intermittent but useful excitement that comes of believing I begin and end with myself.

Claire, forty-eight, has acquired that kind of distance. Because of it, she was able to recognize a window of opportunity with her mother when it recently came her way, a window that helped them make peace with each other. Her mother, Dinah, who is eighty, called her and, in an anxious voice, told her about a dream she had about her own mother. In it, Dinah is a little girl who has been naughty, and her mother says to her, "Honey, do you love me?" In the dream, Dinah replies, "Of course, Mother, but you don't love me, you don't even like me."

Says Claire,

The dream scared the hell out of her. And suddenly, I finally understood her. She's an old woman who *still* feels she was never a good enough daughter. Just as I had suffered so many years of my life trying to work out my abortive, crazy expectations of her, trying to make myself whole, she had her own struggles. But there's a big difference—*she has not resolved any of this for herself.* The end of her life is a continuation of longing and feelings of deprivation. She will never know how it feels to be loved, because she never got over her childhood.

Starting in the Middle

How do you get to peaceful coexistence? If your mother is such a pain, why bother? Isn't it better to just let the relationship coast as it is? *Why rock the boat?* Because, as we have seen, a "definite maybe" puts all your other relationships into the same kind of watery limbo. As a thirty-nine-year-old woman put it,

> Back in the sixties, there was a Broadway comedy revue called *Beyond the Fringe.* In it there was a sketch where a guy is talking about making tunafish salad, and he refers to "the itty bit left in the corner of the can that you just can't quite get at." That's the way it used to be with my mother—I was holding out for something from her I could never quite reach. I found myself doing that with other people, too, particularly with emotionally unavailable men. But I've grown up a lot—for me the glass is now half full, instead of half empty. I'll always have that little bit in the corner of the can, but I can live with it, because I can enjoy my mother for what she is able to give me, instead of being angry over what she can't.

Your relationship with your mother may be far from ideal, but—assuming she is not altogether evil—it doesn't mean that your connection is worthless, or that it can't be made better. Says Dr. Jane B. Abramson, "If daughters view their mothers as all negative, that comes from the daughters' needs. Sometimes the very negativeness is the beginning of moving toward greater closeness, because it is a way of preserving the connection; you can build from there because you *are* connected. In my study, I never came across a single woman who had received absolutely no love from her mother. There are very few mothers who have nothing to give."

Reaching peaceful coexistence often requires a *constructive* limbo in which mother and daughter give each other the space to see each other as separate adults so the relationship can mature. Both mother and daughter need to try to hang in during the transition from "mother–child" to an enriching connection between two adult women.

How Mothers Can Hang In. A mother can do a great deal to help her adult daughter stay a "child"—or to become more mature. Many mothers maintain the status quo by not allowing their daughters to grow up. They may understand the concept of "truce" as it applied to their daughters' adolescence, but, understandably, they have a much harder time of it if their adult daughters are going through *delayed* adolescence, a by-product of the Baby Boom generation.

Dr. Lucy Rose Fischer calls this kind of attachment "Responsible Mothers/Dependent Daughters," during which the daughter's adult status is still in transition. If a daughter requires her mother's advice on every decision and makes childish demands for attention and rescue, some mothers interpret the daughter's behavior as a cue to take over. This delayed adolescence can be prolonged if the mother doesn't let go and permit her daughter to make her own decisions, or gently insist that she do so.

If a mother couldn't let her daughter learn from her mistakes as a child, she needs to do so now. And if she cannot, the daughter must come to understand that her own maturity is seriously jeopardized by her own continued and inappropriate dependence.

Often this dependence takes the form of financial obligation—the daughter dare not strike out on her own because she literally "owes" her mother so much. In this case, the daughter needs to take financial responsibility for herself. This means she passes up her parents' offer of a hefty loan for a condo or a new car—she does without the money in order to profit from her separate identity. She may be cash poor for a while, but she'll be rich in an independence that allows her to find her boundaries.

This kind of independence is difficult for many Baby Boomers who rely on instant gratification for a sense of security, a gratification for which they pay dearly. By remaining emotionally or financially dependent, their separation, and their relationships with their parents, are stalled.

How Daughters Can Hang In. Other daughters maintain an unsatisfying status quo by being overprotective of their mothers and by revealing little about their own lives. Dr. Harriet Goldhor Lerner gives an example of how this works:

> I ask a patient, "How's your relationship with your mother?"
> "Fine, it's great."
> "How often do you see her?"
> "Once a year, at Christmas."
> "What's your mother's reaction to the fact that you're in therapy?"
> "Oh, I'd never tell her—she'd be too upset. She'd feel guilty and blame herself."

These are the daughters whose filial litany is *"Don't tell Mom. It'll upset her."* In this way, daughters often maintain an unhealthy connection with their mothers in a kind of role reversal. This uneven attachment is what Dr. Fischer calls "Responsible Daughters/ Dependent Mothers."

The danger in these relationships is that the mother may be a lot stronger than her daughter thinks. By "overfunctioning," the daughter can't allow her mother to do more than "underfunction." There is a supreme irony in this kind of relationship, Dr. Fischer discovered in her study: Most daughters perceived their mothers as having more problems than the mothers, in separate interviews, claimed actually to have.

One daughter I interviewed said that for years she tried to be a kind of therapist to her Doormat mother, attempting to draw her out so she could analyze her mother's feelings and "cure" her. The daughter went into therapy and realized that, instead, she had been *encouraging* her mother's manipulation, neediness, and inappropriate demands. She says,

> The last time I tried to play "shrink" with my mother, I was visiting with my two teenage kids. I said to her, "So, you're really depressed these days, right?" She started to cry. I said, "Tell me why you're so sad." She looked at my kids and said, *"Because they never come to visit me."* So I said, "Gee, Ma, I'm really sorry I asked you that."
> I can't stand that look in her eye—a look that says, "Help me, help me, fill my needs, forget about you"—

because it's what she used to do to me when I was a kid. Now when I visit her, I go through this process of centering myself. I say to myself, "When she looks at you like that, there's nothing you can do about it. That's her, not you. Take care of yourself."

Your mother is probably not as weak as you imagine, or as she may once have been. In any case, it is not your job to make her fit into your perception of what a "strong mother" should be. Nor can you be who you are with her if you believe you must "spare" her any bad news about yourself. Such censorship precludes openness and honesty.

Breaking the Pattern

Breaking the pattern of your unsettling attachment occurs when you can set limits with your mother—which includes knowing her *limitations*, as well as your own—and when you can control your own reactions, rather than try to change hers.

Setting Limits. Sometimes you must forcefully draw a firm line between your mother and yourself in order to shatter the status quo. This is especially true for the daughters of Avengers, Critics, and Deserters.

Here's an example. Last year, Georgia, a Superachiever who is a high school principal with three young children, decided to do her Christmas shopping by mail order. She says,

> I gave all the women in my family the same gift—nightgowns. My mother was offended because I didn't take the time to go to a store and get her something different. My father wrote me a letter bawling me out. Then she called me at school and started screaming, "Why couldn't you have given it more time and thought?" I did what I always do—I got defensive and said, "Mom, I have to buy forty Christmas gifts for my brother, sister, all their kids, friends, people I work for, my baby-sitter. Do you know that the one thing I don't have is time to shop for presents?"
>
> Suddenly I realized that I was talking to a child, and I was *acting* like one. I thought, Why am I defending myself? Why should I have to be saying this? Finally, I

said, "This is unacceptable behavior and I never want to have a conversation like this with you again," and hung up. I looked up, and the office staff—who know all about my mother—was standing there cheering, "Yea, Georgia!"

Notice that Georgia did *not* say to her Avenger mother, "Drop dead and get out of my life." She began setting limits on her mother's out-of-control behavior and establishing new ground rules for their attachment. In time, her mother began to see that if she and Georgia were to have any connection, she would have to curb her chronic impulse to attack.

You can only set limits if you can stand securely on your own beliefs and needs, neither fighting nor fleeing. At the same time, you need to be extremely realistic about what you can and cannot expect of your mother, and of yourself.

Setting limits includes staying out of family triangles, as Ethel, an Angel, learned with her Critic mother. Their relationship has improved ever since Ethel got out of the middle of a three-way split between her sister, Sylvia, her mother, and herself.

For years Ethel listened to her mother's complaints about Sylvia—a Troublemaker—during which her mother said, "You've got to talk to your sister." Says Ethel,

> I used to fall into that trap, and Sylvia and I fought constantly—I never should have let myself be the mediator. Now I'm very direct with my mother. I won't tolerate her bad-mouthing Sylvia, and I tell her that if she's got a problem with her, she's got to handle it herself.
>
> My anger at my mother used to eat me up—not anymore. I don't get caught up in problems that have nothing to do with me. When she starts to yell, I just say, "We'll talk about this another time when you're calm. But I won't talk to you about it now."

You can also set limits on your mother's guilt-giving criticisms about how much time you do or do not devote to her. The area in which this kind of maternal string-pulling most frequently occurs is the issue of how often you call. Typically, your mother wants you to call her every day, or once a week, according to some arbitrary timetable that makes you feel crowded, irritable, and guilty.

Your heated conversations with her on this issue can be retired for good if you address the subject squarely and stay within yourself. It could work like this:

Your mother: "Your brother calls me every day, you only call every other day."

You: "Yup. That's right."

Your mother may be so startled by your "acquiescence" that she'll change the subject. Repeating your line enough times may discourage her from ever bringing up the subject again.

Let us say, however, that she pursues it—she tells you you're "selfish," rebuking you as though you were a misbehaving child. You can reply, "If you're going to speak to me that way, I'm not going to call you for a while. I feel you're being rude. I don't like your tone. I won't allow anyone to speak to me that way."

Sometimes "the phone call" is not a question of frequency— it's a matter of tone. You don't call your mother according to a schedule, but when you *do* talk, the conversation—like clockwork—degenerates into an argument. Frances, a thirty-five-year-old Cipher, solved that problem by knowing her mother's limitations. Frances likes talking to her mother on the phone—for exactly twenty minutes. She says,

> My mother is always pleasant when our phone calls begin, but I have to keep from getting lulled into thinking, "Isn't this nice? We're going to have a normal conversation." Because in twenty minutes, she'll pick a fight. She'll bring up my husband's religion, for instance, out of left field. So after fifteen minutes, I start winding up the conversation. I say to myself, "Keep your eye on the clock, because if you let this go on too long, it'll get ugly." By watching the time, I find that I can enjoy her.

Says psychotherapist Judith M. Fox,

> You have to be in a place where you feel you are an adult, and can respect your own needs. That's very important: in order to limit someone else you have to know your *own* limits. If you want to call your mother every day, and if you really like talking to her, that's fine. If it doesn't give you pleasure, you do what you need

to do for yourself. Your mother's need is hers—how you respond is your department. You have to have the mental space to be able to say, "That's her, and this is me." When there's guilt and entanglement, there can't be healthy separateness.

The same advice applies to the frequency with which you visit your mother. She may expect you for Sunday dinner—*every* Sunday. If you can pay more attention to your needs, and visit when you feel like seeing her, the relationship moves beyond "oughts" and "shoulds" to "wants."

Making the transition from obligation to amicability isn't easy. Having set limits on time, you may also have to set limits on your mother's behavior so that you can achieve that amicability. Resisting the impulse to storm out of your mother's house—or banishing her from yours—is not for the fainthearted.

Let us say that every time your mother sees you she feels free to be tactless, spraying you with insults. Here's how one woman I interviewed put a stop to that kind of treatment:

> When my daughter graduated from college, I threw a huge party for her. When my mother arrived, she looked at me and said, "I hate your hairdo." Then she walked into the dining room and said, "Where'd you get that ugly flower arrangement?" I calmly replied, "If you're going to talk to me like that, I don't want you here." She was shocked. But she didn't say another critical word. There was a time I wouldn't have invited her at all—now I can include her in my life, but on my terms, without wanting to murder her.

Controlling Your Reactions. In reaching a peaceful settlement of differences, much depends not only on setting limits but also on not overreacting, and staying within yourself.

Let's say your mother is a guilt-giving Doormat or Smotherer. The bait for your angry or unctuous entanglement is her "weakness" and "fragility." This is how one daughter stopped allowing herself to be manipulated by her mother's sweet suffering:

> My mother's way of punishing me is to weep and say, "I'll never understand you." I've learned to speak to her without screaming. I can say to her, "It's okay, you

don't have to understand me—I understand you, and that's good enough for me." And of course, that throws her into a tizzy, and she cries. When she does that, I say, "Go ahead, cry. It's all right. I know you feel sad, but I don't, so it's okay." *I never thought I'd be able to do that*—to just not get sucked in. She doesn't do that so much anymore, because she knows it doesn't work. She can't make me feel guilty.

But let us say that your mother is a Critic or Avenger, and you are always trying to fend off her coercive efforts to control you, or to get you to adopt her point of view. In fact, you fight with her all the time.

Gwen, a Superachiever, learned to disarm her high-powered Critic mother by simply agreeing with her on subjects that were meaningless to her, which kept their disagreements from escalating. Gwen's change in behavior did not occur overnight—it took years for her to feel strong enough to disengage her "buttons."

Gwen did *not* "sell out"—rather, she no longer had an emotional stake in trying to talk her mother out of her rigid opinions. Says Gwen,

> If I take her to lunch and she says, "This food is inedible," I'll agree with her. Whatever outrageous things my mother says, I reply, "You're absolutely right." All I care about is what's going on in my own head, and as long as I know I'm not crazy, I don't care if she's crazy. Once I've agreed with her, we have a perfectly pleasant time.
>
> I treat her as a person I've recently met who's very interesting, because my mother has led a fascinating life. Who wouldn't want to talk to her about her experiences? I can have as good a time with her as I can have with you, as long as we don't get into personal stuff. Certain subjects are out of bounds—I won't let her criticize my husband or kids, for instance. And if she tries, I just say, "I don't want to talk about that. I want to hear about your trip." I've done it so many times that she seldom brings those subjects up anymore.

The first step in reaching this rapprochement was the validation of Gwen's feelings about her mother. Early in their marriage, her husband said, "Your mother is off-the-wall," and Gwen realized that her mother's belligerent personality was neither her imagination nor her fault. "Once he said that," says Gwen, "I stopped worrying about my perceptions."

The second step was for Gwen to solidify her boundaries and to understand that she couldn't spend too much time alone with her mother. So when Gwen's mother comes for dinner, Gwen usually invites other guests so that her mother can be her fascinating self, socially constrained from provoking an argument with her daughter.

The third—and most important—step was for Gwen to stop overreacting to her mother and instead to change her own behavior. Her turnaround occurred during a visit to her mother's house several years ago. Gwen recalls,

> I walked into the living room and within three seconds we were arguing. So I turned around and walked out again. I went to a store down the street, bought a bunch of flowers, walked back into the house, and said, "Let's start over."
>
> I think the way to disentangle yourself from problems with your mother is to eliminate conflict, even if at first it feels artificial. I don't have to get into a power struggle with her, because she's never going to say she's wrong. I've come to terms with her in that I've stopped blaming her for everything that happened to me as a child, because I'm no longer a child. I've tried very hard to change our relationship to adult–adult, and not get seduced into stupid arguments. And it's happened. We get along extremely well.

Bad Mommy, Good Granny

If you have children, one of the confounding aspects of your relationship with your mother—and a big incentive for you to reach a healthy truce with her—may be that she's entirely different with her grandchildren from how she is, or was, with you. This does not hold true for all mothers—many are as critical, even cruel, to their grandchildren as they are to their daughters. In those cases, as we shall see in the next chapter, their daughters simply do not allow their children to be subjected to such treatment.

But many mothers are able to be loving to their grandchildren in ways they never could with their own children. It is here that you can see evidence that your mother—even though she would rather die than say to you, "I was terrible to you"—may have changed. While she may be too proud to tell you so, she may indeed feel real remorse about her inability to have been more loving to you when you needed it most. Now she has a chance to make up for it—to "get it right" with your kids.

Kitty, a thirty-four-year-old Cipher, often vows that she'll never see her Avenger mother again, but stifles the thought when she sees how tender and playful her mother can be with Kitty's five-year-old daughter, Julie. Says Kitty,

> Julie is the only person my mother has ever loved unconditionally—they have a wonderful relationship. My mother is able to see how terrifying her behavior can be to a child. Once Julie dropped a glass of milk, and my mother screamed at her, just as she used to scream at me, and Julie burst into tears. My mother dropped to her knees and said, "Oh, Julie, I'm so sorry, I didn't mean to frighten you, please forgive me." My mother could never see *my* terror when I was a kid, but she's able to see Julie's, whom she adores and whose adoration she wants.

Your mother's attempts to do for your children what she couldn't do for you may make you feel understandably confused and even jealous. But since you are no longer a child, you may be able to accept that your mother might not be the same person she was when you were young. Watching her be loving to your children can even help you to begin to understand her, because you can learn from the contrast between her former and current "mothering." As one daughter told me,

> My mother is definitely trying to make up for what she couldn't do when I was young. She has said to me, "I hated myself for losing my temper so much. But I was so unhappy with your father." She makes a point of coming to take care of my kids when my husband and I need a vacation. Last time she did that, she said, "It's so important for you to get away together." I said, "How did you manage with us? Daddy never gave you

even an afternoon off–you never got away even by yourself." And she said, "Now you understand. It was very
hard."

By understanding your mother, you can give your children the gift
of her love, which not only will be a source of self-esteem for them
but will acquaint them with age. Children who don't have loving
grandparents frequently are afraid of "old folks," and, later, of their
own advancing years.

If you avoid making comparisons, you can reap the tangential
benefits of your mother's ability to love your child. Some daughters
can't do that—they use their children as leverage, threatening to
withhold them if their mothers don't "shape up." All this does is
exploit your children, as you were once exploited. Daughters who
have resolved their relationships with their mothers don't hold their
children hostages to their own maternal vendettas—they don't make
their kids part of a hostile triangle. If you are tempted to use your
children in this way, and if your mother is truly kind to them, it's a
clear signal that you still have a lot of emotional sorting out to do.

Still, some grandmothers cannot always be loving—their angry
and automatic responses erupt when an unresolved feeling or long-
buried memory is triggered, inadvertently, by your child. Other
grandmothers try to ingratiate themselves with their grandchildren in
the divide-and-conquer tactics they used when you were growing
up. There may be times when you have to set limits on your
mother's behavior toward your children, just as you set limits on her
behavior toward you.

It could be that your mother can be on her "good granny" behavior only for a relatively short period of time. Some grandmothers do
not do well, for instance, when grandchildren stay a few days. If you
know your mother's limitations, your children can still enjoy her, if
only for abbreviated visits, and only in your presence.

It could also be that your mother is a "good granny" when she's
alone with you and your child, but when your father—with whom
she fights constantly—is with her, she's angry and volatile. One
daughter I interviewed solved that problem by stating flatly that her
parents could not visit at the same time. She says, "When my
mother comes alone, it's quite pleasant—we go out with the kids and
have a pretty good time. It's a shame that I can't have both my parents
here together, but that's life. It's the only way my kids can have a
good relationship with them, so that's how we've worked it out."

The point is that you can stop the cycle of mother–daughter blame from being passed on to your children—not simply in terms of your own parenting, but also in terms of how they perceive your mother. They need not experience her as you did—indeed, she may not even *be* the same person with them that she was with you. When you can accept her, and allow her a healthy role—of *your* choosing—with your children, the family triangles that have haunted your family for generations may disappear for good.

While a truce with your mother may fall short of your childhood wishes, it can be a rewarding fulfillment of realistic adult expectations, because it taps the best of what is in your mother and in yourself. You don't have to be imprisoned by overreaction, keeping your dukes up, or running from occasional bad times, or being enslaved by inappropriate feelings of obligation. When you can retain a healthy detachment within a sometimes cordial, sometimes troublesome connection with your mother, you will indeed have achieved a separate peace, and a satisfying sense of family.

20
Divorce

All mothers and daughters have some friction, and I believe in keeping families together. But only up to a point. If your mother's a psychic killer and you'll die a psychic death unless you get away, that's when you know you can't have a relationship. Otherwise, you'll be in constant emotional danger. My mother was that kind of killer. I see her as disabled and helpless and I feel sympathy for her, but not a lot. I had to break off with her permanently in order to save my life.

—Lisel, forty-eight

Odile, thirty-nine, hasn't seen her mother in seven years. Although they both live in Boston, somehow their paths never cross. Partly it's because her mother doesn't want to see *her*. "She won't even go to a restaurant if she knows it's one I like," says Odile. Mostly, however, it's because Odile believes that any effort to reconcile will be met with venom.

Not that she hasn't *tried* to salvage her relationship with her mother. She's had years of therapy. She knows all about her family history—her mother's feelings of impermanence and unacceptability to *her* mother, her thwarted dreams, her unanswered prayers. Odile has asked her father and her aunt to intercede on her behalf, to no avail. She's written letters entreating her mother to meet, letters that get no response.

When Odile was a child, her mother never laid a hand on her— that was the problem. She couldn't express physical or verbal affection, nothing except the cruelest criticisms. Once, when Odile was fourteen, her mother said, "I have never loved you." It took Odile fifteen more years to really *believe* it. She says,

> When you have a mother who's always been devastating to you, you'll continue to function as a child unless you can confront it and realize she'll never stop punching you. I can't go on trying to get something that is beyond her. I've finally come to the conclusion that I am much better off never seeing her again. She's just not good for my mental health.
>
> I've gotten to the point where I can live my own life without her. Still, there will always be a void, something missing inside. It's like having an injury that can't be fixed by surgery; you have to live with that wound. I've learned to live with it.

Dorothy, thirty-six, hasn't seen her mother in five years. Like Odile, she made elaborate efforts to find a middle ground where she and her mother could have some kind of cordial, or at least civil, relationship. But Dorothy had a deck that was stacked against her—her mother is an alcoholic. Dorothy would visit or call her mother in the mornings, when she was temporarily sober, trying to find *something* about her mother that she could admire, *some* memory of tenderness that would provide the impetus for at least a sympathetic connection. Those sober moments were few. Most of their meetings would be in the middle of the night, when her mother would appear unannounced at her apartment, so drunk she could barely stand.

Ultimately, Dorothy reached a profound and painful resignation. Nothing she could do would ever change her mother. The only way she could complete her own recovery from her childhood was to disengage from her. Dorothy had to sort out for herself, with the help of a therapist, the horrors of her beginnings in order to find an oasis of peace in her future. She says,

> I had to stop letting my mother in the door, literally, and stop taking care of her. She wouldn't do anything to help herself. I finally realized that I couldn't make anything right, at least not for her. I can only make something right for myself.
>
> I want to be able to forgive and accept her. But I

can't forgive her actions. I don't buy the notion that alcoholism is a disease that you can't help. She made a *choice* not to function as a mother to her children, to neglect us and fail to provide any nurturing, any protection—even, much of the time, a meal. I'd be crazier than she is to form a relationship with her. My survival and my mental health depend on not being with her. I die the minute I do that. I have to learn to take care of myself.

These two women have divorced their mothers as an act of self-preservation rather than one of punishment. For them, and for women like them, there are some situations—and they are, mercifully, extremely rare—when you simply cannot go home again.

Divorcing your mother is to do the unthinkable, as the Bad Mommy Taboo has taught us. It is seen by many people as a fit of adolescent pique, an act of the most selfish and spiteful sort. In the all-American, love-your-mother-no-matter-what scheme of things, the filial road less traveled is a sure path to social censure. To turn your back on your mother strikes at the very core of what we think family should be: loyal, loving, forgiving.

For that reason, to divorce your mother is a desperate last resort. Of the women I interviewed who have divorced their mothers, there isn't one who wouldn't gladly have sacrificed just about anything to avoid the harrowing conclusion that it was the only alternative.

What most people fail to realize is that a daughter makes so heretical a move only after years of trying to make it unnecessary. Determining not to see your mother again is never a snap decision, as all those "false self" convolutions described in Part Three make abundantly clear.

To divorce your mother is, by any yardstick, an unpopular and, for most people, unimaginable option. Nevertheless, there are some cases in which divorcing your mother is not simply your only choice— there are times when it may be your healthiest choice.

To be a mature adult is to accept the good and bad in your mother and in yourself. It requires resolving the Bad Mommy in your head, in your memories, in your self-destructive coping mechanisms, so that you can have a life of hope on your own terms.

And that life—that healthy adulthood—may not include your mother.

Beyond Family Systems. As we know, the Family Systems approach to mother–daughter resolution endorses the idea that if you go back into the family and trace its branches and roots, you'll find reasons for how and why your mother behaved as she did. By understanding the context that spawned her, and family currents that pulled and pushed her, you can gain a deeper awareness of, and even sympathy for, why she became the person she is. That understanding, the theory goes, makes it possible for you to reconnect with your mother and redefine your relationship.

Says Dr. Michael Kerr of Georgetown University,

People get driven apart because they feel neglected or angry. They say to someone, "You don't give me the approval I need— why don't you?" The minute anyone says, "Why don't you?"— that's part of the problem they've been living with all their life. They have to get free of that and realize they're having as much trouble accepting the other person as the person is having accepting them.

Let us say, however, that you *do* accept your mother and do *not* apply pressure on her to change; nor do you have unrealistic expectations of her. You have plowed through therapy, vented and explored your rage, and have come to terms with your own and your mother's emotions and choices and family legacies.

You've followed the Family Systems approach as far as it will go—you *understand* your mother's childhood poverty, her father's drinking problem, her own troubled marriage, her lack of feminist advantages. You may even pity her, particularly her inability to defeat her own demons rather than deputize them in a battle against you. Moreover, you recognize your part in any problems between you.

But now, your newfound maturity and circumspection may enable you to see your mother in a way the Family Systems approach generally does *not* endorse: you may decide that your mother is as cruel and unfeeling as any person you have ever met, and that there is no more point in pursuing the relationship with her than there would be with anyone who treats you as she does.

For what is left—after you have done all the work of emotional resolution, set all the limits and self-focused—if your mother still insists on attacking, belittling, demeaning? Why continue to see a woman who cannot bear your happiness, and who is imprisoned by her inability to show you any kind of love or affection? You may feel there is nothing left for you to do but build a life for yourself apart from her—to let her, and the relationship, go.

"Yes, but she's your mother," someone says. That may not be enough for a relationship on any basis. If you are truly free from your past, from your need to blame her, *then you are also free not to volunteer any longer for mistreatment.*

Proceed with Caution. The danger, of course, is that some daughters interpret "permission" to divorce as a reason to avoid addressing their emotional problems and the conflicts that spill over into their other relationships. Emotionally battered daughters often bolt when their relationships get uncomfortable— too heated or too intimate. They have trouble giving peace a chance because the concept of peace is too abstract—for them, it is an amorphous ideal. They spin dizzily in the same angry orbit. Bailing out is a permanent fixture in all their attachments, because it is seen as a solution.

Consider the dilemma of this seventy-year-old mother who yearns to repair her relationship with her daughter, and whose daughter will have none of it. Cutting her mother off hasn't solved the daughter's many problems. She hasn't done the internal work that would prevent an ongoing series of destructive relationships that are echoes of her "solution" to her conflicts about her mother. She won't go into therapy. She blames all her problems on her mother—and on everyone else. And even though her mother has asked how she can help salvage their relationship, the daughter continues to "punish" her mother by refusing to have any contact with her. Says the mother,

> My daughter may have very good reasons for wanting to have nothing to do with me. But she won't tell me what they are. I don't minimize the validity of what she feels is the cause of her anger at me—all I feel is the effect. She won't allow me to understand what I have done so that perhaps I can change. I'd give ten years of my life for that to happen, and I don't have a whole lot of time left. If I could just get some communication from her, I'd be satisfied. I don't look for warmth, I don't look for friendship. If there's something new for me to learn, I'd like to know what it is. I feel I've been robbed—but I'm sure she feels she's been robbed, too.

When you divorce your mother without resolving your feelings about her and about yourself, your problems go with you. The kid in the playground who walks away from the bully may avoid the bully of the moment but must learn how to deal with the "bullies" of life by standing her emotional ground. So it is, in some few tragic cases, that you may have to terminate your relationship with your bullying mother—but you still need to confront the issues that caused you to run for your life.

Divorcing your mother per se is not a resolution. Resolving your relationship with your mother does *not* mean walking away from the emotional consequences of that attachment, or your responsibility for your own reactions. Nor does it mean nailing shut the door on any possibility of reconciliation—if, say, your mother gets help or recovers from addiction and is able at least to make the attempt to repair her relationship with you. Any discussion of divorce must include these vital caveats.

Nor is the ultimate "divorce"—your mother's death—the end of your troubles with her. For daughters who have come to terms with their childhoods and their mothers, there frequently is enormous relief in never again having to tough out their visits with their abusive mothers, trying to avoid getting "hooked" into arguments. No matter how well the daughter has resolved her feelings, being with a vicious or unkind mother is never pleasant. Her mother's death can come as a welcome respite—even an anticlimax, because the daughter has already "mourned" the relationship she never had.

Any tears these daughters may shed are those of regret over what never was, and what never could be, and not for what they could never make happen. Their mother's death is merely a punctuation, the absolute end of a "dead" relationship.

But for those daughters who have not resolved their filial conflicts, the death of their mothers may have painful psychological consequences. As Lilly Singer, an authority on bereavement told me, "If a daughter is truly ambivalent about her mother, and she didn't resolve that ambivalence during her mother's lifetime, it's going to be very difficult, because the chance to repair the relationship and work it through while her mother was alive is permanently gone."

What Therapists Say About "Divorce"

Virtually all therapists believe that getting beyond blame and anger toward one's mother is necessary for healing to begin. Most would also agree that certain rare and extreme *circumstances* about the attachment may never change. Such circumstances might include your mother's acute and chronic drug or alcohol addiction, psychosis, or brutal narcissism and emotional battering of you.

None of the therapists I talked to at any time suggested that trying to repair a ruptured relationship requires sitting still for sadistic behavior—their aim is to help people get beyond the over-reaction that leads to being enmeshed by anger, supplication, or victimization.

Where the therapeutic community falls into separate camps is on the subject of divorcing one's mother. Some therapists believe that resolution can *only* be accomplished within the mother–daughter attachment, although it may entail a temporary break—a trial separation—in order to clear the way for healthy reattachment. Other therapists believe that in some instances, divorce is therapeutically valid, even necessary.

Trial Separation. "There are times," says Dr. Harriet Goldhor Lerner of the Menninger Clinic, "when you have to take a 'vacation' from your mother and stay away because things are too intense, and any contact isn't productive. I never advise people to reconnect until they've got a much more objective perspective on their mother and what happened that caused things to get so intense. There's some groundwork that has to be done first."

Nellie, twenty-seven, is in the middle of such a trial separation. Still caught between the fantasy of a "perfect" mother and the reality that she and her Critic mother can't seem to get along, she is in therapy, trying to decide how she will come to terms with her conflicts. I asked her if she could imagine a time when she could accept her mother as she is. She replied,

> I'm way too angry and too confused—I feel divided between two worlds. I guess it's because part of me feels I should love her—the child in me wants to see her as a perfect parent. But I don't think I'm really going to change my feelings about her unless she changes. Every time I visit her it takes me about a week to

recuperate. I always get pounded on the head. I always feel like a child again, and I just don't need that.

But I feel guilty—I think, Gosh, I only have one mother, so why not try to make the best of it? I wish I could say wonderful things about my mother, but I don't feel them. If it were up to me, my mother and I would be living next door to each other. I would love to have a good relationship. But it's not possible when two people aren't working together to make it happen.

I haven't made a decision about whether I'll cut all ties or not, but I'm working on it. Whatever decision I make, it'll be from the heart. I feel I have to be born again with no one and try to be here for myself. You come into this world alone and you leave it alone. If I'm going to rely on my mother—or anyone—for my happiness, I'll be waiting my whole life.

Harriet, forty-two, took a "vacation" at the suggestion of her therapist, who made her promise that for six months she make no contact at all with her extremely narcissistic and hostile mother. Says Harriet,

In those six months I learned that I had rights, too, that I didn't owe my mother anything. I realized that she loved me the best she could, but that she really was handicapped. I also learned that I could be connected to my mother on my terms, and not hers. That was a huge breakthrough for me. When my therapist gave me permission to take some time off, it was an enormous relief. I found out you can change and be in control of yourself, and give up the hope that she will change. That's the hardest thing to accept. And I've accepted it. Now I can be with my mother occasionally, but I don't *have* to. When I see her, it's with no expectations at all, and no anger. Don't get me wrong—there will always be some sadness. But it doesn't destroy me anymore.

For Ginger, forty, a trial separation of considerably longer duration—twelve years—was necessary for her to heal and grow so that she could re-connect with her mother in a healthy way. Two years ago, she took a human potential course that trains people to take responsibility for the unhappiness in their lives, to rid themselves of magical thinking and the urge to exact retribution, and to communicate their needs. Because of that training, Ginger has moved her relationship with her mother up from divorce to truce. Says Ginger,

> I knew I had to educate my mother about what I wanted from her. I called her and she was glad to hear from me, but the words I was waiting for—"How are you?"—she didn't say. After about half an hour I said, "Listen, I hate to interrupt, but I was curious to know if it matters to you how I am." She said, "Of course it matters." I said, "Then do you think you might be able to ask me?" I told her I was eager to reconnect and asked her if that's something she wanted, too. I went very, very slowly.
>
> Every so often I realize how dependent the process is on me, and I resent it. But it was important to me to prove that I don't have to give her so much power. By obliterating her from my life I didn't kill her off. By my not dealing with her, the pain festered and got worse. I just wanted that thorn removed from my side. It's a conscious programming of myself to let go of the anger and stop focusing on all the negative stuff.

Permanent Separation. Other therapists go beyond the idea of "trial separation" to address the reality that in a few cases, reconnection may be masochistic. They believe that in very rare circumstances, it is too damaging for a daughter's mental health to go back into the mother–daughter relationship.

But the suggestion to divorce one's mother almost never comes from the therapist. That idea should come from the patient herself. When the patient expresses it, generally the therapist will then ask her how she feels about the possibility, about the consequences of such a decision, and help her to make a choice that is ultimately a mature one, rather than simply reactive or vengeful.

In a very few extreme instances, however, the therapist may recommend divorce—but only if the patient's life is in danger, or if she is in real physical jeopardy, or if her own sanity hangs in the balance.

Says Dr. Marianne Goodman,

I think you owe it to yourself to try to repair the relationship. But if you have tried, and if you know that you have tried, then you also know you can't control her reactions, you can only control your own. If your controlled reactions do not improve the situation, then you have to let it go.

I recently said to a patient, "You have to get rid of your mother and put her to rest—you cannot make peace with her. She's too psychotic and dangerous." In such a situation, you regret that your mother is your parent. You regret that she couldn't be other than what she is. You've done all you can do, and you just say good-bye. You form a healthy bond with yourself and leave her behind. Then you can start getting involved with people who are not like her.

Jessica, forty-six, was able to begin resolving her rage toward her mother with these words from her therapist: "Your mother's treatment of you is the most adversarial I've ever heard. She's an extremely destructive and dangerous woman." Says Jessica,

> No one had ever said that to me. It was as though the waters parted, and I could see how harmful my relationship with my mother really was. I suddenly realized that I could be free of a nasty web of humiliation and torture. My mother is a woman who sent me to boarding school when I was five because she didn't want me around. This is a woman who when I was in high school grabbed my hair and pounded my head over and over against a bed frame. I had to face the rage I felt and get past it. Through therapy, I found I could just walk away from that kind of treatment. So I just did it. I stopped seeing my mother. But I also built up a "self" so I wouldn't feel abandoned, and wouldn't repeat the mistakes in my own life that she had made in hers.

Another woman, Toni, thirty-two, told me that she, too, had to stop seeing her mother, and that her therapist helped her to make peace with that decision. Today happily married and the mother of two young children, Toni says,

> There are people whose mothers are horrible but nevertheless have *some* redeeming qualities about them. With

my mother, there aren't *any* redeeming qualities. It took me a long time to realize that. The idea of divorcing her first occurred when I saw how she treated my kids. She has an uncontrollable temper. She was always yelling and screaming at them, and I just couldn't let them be with her. When I saw how damaging she is to them, I began to see how damaging she is *to me*. Isn't it odd that I had to have someone else to protect before I could protect myself? I have one of those mothers that you can't be alone with. She's sick. She's defective. There's nothing I can do about it. She can't help herself; I can help myself. I've had to repair my own life. I wasn't taught to be happy—it was something I had to learn on my own, and that's okay. I think I finally have the capacity to be happy.

Recovering Outside the Mother–Daughter Attachment

While divorce may include cutting off contact with your mother, it does not mean "cutting off" from *relating* to another human being. To really heal, you have to learn how to form healthy attachments—if not with your mother, then with the people you love and care about. That is not easy to do. One-sided resolution of the mother–daughter relationship feels like lingering death. Without the example of any kind of love, however brief, from your mother, or of reaching a truce with her, happiness and even mental health can seem like so much pie-in-the-sky theory. But it can be achieved. As a survivor of child abuse told me,

> Traditionally, therapeutic closure comes from going through the whole cycle of blame and self-destruction until you finally get enough emotional detachment to go back and reconnect with your parents. That's the true therapeutic model. I'd love to have that kind of closure. But in my case, it's never going to happen. They're too psychotic.
>
> I finally got closure when I gave up the ghost and said to myself, "You do not have parents." And then I realized something else: I don't need them. What I need is good care, and I have found it in other adults who give me the kinds of things everyone needs—love and attention and acceptance.

Women who divorce their mothers have to learn how to have healthy relationships with *someone*. It's possible to work on the same issues in those attachments that you would with your mother: expressing your feelings, setting limits, staying within yourself, allowing the other person to be who they are without risk to your own sense of self, having boundaries so you are not perpetually overreacting. You still define yourself *within a relationship*, but it's not within the mother–daughter connection.

There are ways other than through the mother–daughter relationship to recover from your childhood. Some women simply can't accomplish it in the parental attachment. But it does not mean that they *cannot heal*.

Those adult daughters who are still treated savagely by their mothers—or whose mothers are too defeated by illness or addiction to be reached—and who deeply wish to recover from their childhoods, can still learn how to stop the cycle of generational blame and unhappiness. Many of the women I interviewed who have achieved mature "autonomy" without their mothers did it by staying "connected"—either to a therapist until all the poisons were gone, or to the lifesaving awareness that they had to resolve the relationship emotionally in order to avoid overloading their other attachments with expectations of unmet needs from the past.

Many daughters have healed through the trials and efforts and blessings of relationships with friends, lovers, and extended family. But their recovery is not seamless; often these daughters hit an emotional plateau when they wonder if they'll *ever* resolve their pain. And then suddenly, or so it seems, a significant relationship with someone they love and admire will trigger a growth spurt, or will give them a new insight about themselves.

Resolution of deep anguish doesn't occur solely within one relationship. Life is a collaboration—we learn and grow from a variety of sources. So when we are able to glean from a loving, concerned friend or partner or mentor a new awareness about ourselves, it is then possible to apply that awareness to the mother–daughter relationship, and to see it in larger perspective.

The women who have healed in these maverick ways have enormous courage and spiritual strength. They accept and understand their mothers. They acknowledge that their mothers did the best they could, and recognize and sometimes even appreciate their family legacies. They have stopped passing the emotional buck in their relationships with friends, partners, and children. They have taken responsibility for their parts in their own unhappiness.

But they do not see their mothers.

You have not flunked psychological and spiritual health if you find another path—outside the mother–daughter attachment—to your own growth and resolution.

Dealing with the Bad Mommy Taboo

Sorting out your emotional conflicts with your mother and deciding to divorce her may be the end of one set of problems—and the beginning of another. Like any "unpopular" position, the daughter who chooses to divorce her mother will have to deal with people who cannot fathom her choice. Such a daughter will run into four kinds of bias:

- the bias of the "damned";
- the bias of the denier;
- the bias of the ignorant;
- the bias of relatives.

The Bias of the "Damned." Some people have been so maimed by their childhoods that they never recover from them. They go about their lives duplicating the past in all their attachments. When you reveal to them your childhood, they fixate on your "horror stories" with a curious zeal, savoring every grim detail.

These people, because they are still so suffused with rage, can be as harmful to you as your mother may have been. They may resent your recovery, wanting you to share their own bed of pain. They may particularly resent you if you do not actively and hungrily hate your mother. In their bitterness, they will say such things as, "Aw, you don't really mean she was just a 'victim'—she was a *bitch*, right?" and get angry with you if you don't agree.

If you feel you must defend yourself and your decision, and find yourself cornered by anger at these people, you may have some unfinished emotional business. Such defensiveness is a form of enmeshment and indicates a lack of firm emotional boundaries. When you are really whole, you don't have to engage in such discussions. You can simply say, "You have your opinion, I have mine." Or better yet, "I'd rather not discuss it."

The Bias of the Denier. These are the people who spread the gospel of Bad Mommy Taboo. They cannot believe that you feel as you do, and will try to proselytize you, through guilt or reprimand, into "making nice on" the woman who caused you such self-doubt and anguish. By denying their own unresolved feelings and conflicts about their mothers, they denigrate your resolution of your problems.

The Bias of the Ignorant. Still other people, who have not had your terrible experience but are not insensitive or mean-spirited, simply cannot absorb the concept of filial divorce. Many daughters have difficulty helping loving spouses, friends, and adult children understand the decision to divorce their mothers.

Blissfully, there are those people who were truly loved by their parents, and who are entirely at home in their own adult skins, who can allow you to be who you are and accept you at face value. These people, while they did not share your experience, *do not dismiss it.* Of such people Dr. Alice Miller writes, "Those who actually had the privilege of growing up in an empathetic environment . . . are more likely to be open to the suffering of others, or at least will not deny its existence."

The Bias of Relatives. Divorce is seldom an issue that is confined only to the mother–daughter relationship, *even though it ought to be.* But families are social units. It's hard enough for *you* to separate, particularly if you come from a family that is severely dysfunctional. To ask relatives to be as clear as you are may be asking for a miracle.

As a result, you may have to come to terms with your feelings not only about your mother but about the rest of your original family as well. Unless you are prepared to hold on to your beliefs and your right and need to find your own way alone, you may be shaken by the enormous pressure that is brought to bear on your decision to divorce your mother. But you still have to do what's best for you. Your acceptance of your mother, and your resolution of your attachment to her, will require acceptance of your relatives as well.

As one woman put it, "I can't explain a concept that they are constitutionally incapable of hearing. I hope in time they'll understand why I had to stop seeing my mother. I'm here when they do. But I'm not counting on it. It makes me very sad, but not as sad as the feelings that led me to make this decision in the first place. There was nothing sudden or hostile about it—it took years."

In the family, the Bad Mommy Taboo is more heavily invoked

with "divorcing" daughters than sons. Sons who withdraw are more frequently exempt from family censure in a kind of automatic, boys-will-be-boys forgiveness of—or at least grudging tolerance for—their defecting highjinks. And, as we saw in Chapter One, the mother–son relationship is entirely different from that between mothers and daughters. Consequently, many brothers have a hard time digesting a move as radical as a sister's divorcing her mother.

Sheila, thirty-four, recently made a painful declaration of her own filial and sibling independence to her younger brother, who feels she is being "selfish" in her unwillingness to have her mother visit her. Says Sheila,

> I told him, "Listen, if you want to see her, I respect that—that's your need. The difference between us is that I don't have that desire." He doesn't get it, because we come from a tightly knit ethnic clan. Women in our family would *die* rather than have nothing to do with their mothers. So that makes me something of a pariah.

It's hard enough to get brothers to come to terms with your maverick resolution of your relationship with your mother. To get a sister to accept—or sympathize with—your decision is much more complex, because she is your gender as well as generational peer.

The only person who gives better guilt than a mother is a sister. And often, what's behind it is the real anger she may feel for believing she has no choice about carrying the mother–daughter load all by herself. Sometimes she's not even aware of her inability to consider healthy options for herself because she's still trapped in a symbiotic relationship with her mother, and hasn't yet separated.

Joanna, a woman I know who has divorced her mother, was told by her Angel sister, "How could you do this to me? How could you be so self-centered?" Joanna replied, "No one is forcing you to be at her beck and call. If you want to do it, that's what you have to do. But don't ask me share your need."

Of her relationship with her sister, Joanna says,

> It's only this year, and only after a lot of therapy, that I've gotten it clear that I'm never going to get what I want from my family. I will never have it. Ever. A lot of the pain from that reality is gone because I've done so

much work on myself. I'm at an age where that's the way it's got to be. I'm fifty years old—the rest of my life is for me. Not for my mother, and not for my sister.

The result of your decision to divorce your mother may be a package deal: Daughter divorces mother and loses sister—or brother or aunt or uncle—in the bargain. Consequently, one or more members of your family may divorce you.

This occurred when Margaret, thirty-five, stopped seeing her mother, a widow. Margaret's sister, Joyce, thirty-two, moved up in "family" rank and into her mother's undivided affection—she was able, at last, to be her mother's number one child, her loyal lieutenant. To protect her seniority, she felt she had to reject Margaret.

The estrangement between the sisters persisted for ten years, during which time their mother died. Margaret learned that Joyce had got her mother to change her will so that Joyce would be the sole beneficiary of her mother's estate, including her house. What troubled Margaret was not a loss of money or property, something she had long ago accepted as a fait accompli. Rather, it was the discovery of how deeply her sister hated her, and the lengths to which she would go to try to punish her for divorcing their mother.

Then Margaret got cancer, which galvanized her into a reassessment of her life. She says,

> I literally became a different person—a better person. I wanted to have a relationship with my sister because suddenly our old fights didn't matter anymore. I wanted to see what makes her tick, to get into her skin, to find out what makes her love and what makes her hate.

After her recovery from her illness, Margaret called her sister and arranged to meet with her. During that meeting, which led to many meetings, she discovered that the only connection of any importance in her sister's life had been with their mother. The mother's house was a metaphor for that connection and for her need to be perceived as the "favorite" daughter. "It was her heart," Margaret says, "and she thought I'd try to take it from her."

Their most painful, and cleansing, talk included Margaret's declaration of her feelings—all of them. She says,

I told Joyce that one of the reasons I got sick was because of this estrangement between us, and our hatred of each other. I told her that she'd never given me the chance to try to help her or understand her—all she'd done was shut me out. I told her I understood that Mom couldn't love me, and what that had done to me and how hard my life had been trying to accept that fact. She was devastated. She cried and cried. And then slowly, very cautiously, we got back together. Now we're very close.

Such reconciliations between siblings are not always possible, just as they are not always possible with your mother. But—as with your mother—it's important to try to bridge your differences, so you can contain the sibling fallout of mother–daughter disaffection and even find a friend in your family.

The Last Resort: Making Sense of the Unthinkable

Those daughters who were unable to reconnect with their mothers, and who had to relinquish their dreams of family in the conventional sense, still had to find something good in themselves and in their experiences in order to be part of any "family"—be it with husband and children or with cherished friends. They had to discover some purpose for living, a reason to create a loving legacy for themselves in all their relationships.

Many of these women were able to chart new emotional territories, guided only by a vague sense of hope. They invented themselves with few, or no, supports from their original families. They grew beyond their false selves and forged a bond with their true selves. But they did not entirely turn their backs on their histories. Instead, they drew strength from them.

Nancy, thirty-six:

I feel very, very cheated by not having a mother who loves me. When I'm with friends and their mothers who love each other, I am reminded of what I don't have. But if you can live with that reality, you can live with anything. I am so grateful to have the love I *do* have from my husband, my children, and my friends. I consider it the triumph of my life that I am healthy today in spite of my childhood.

Dana, forty:

> I think I had to learn something in some cosmic way by having a mother who couldn't help herself, who couldn't stop brutalizing and humiliating me. Somehow, it didn't destroy me. Nothing in my life has ever been as bad as my childhood was.
>
> What my experience taught me—and I don't mean to romanticize it—is that as bad as things were, some good came of it. There was a gift in there somewhere. I learned that I had amazing strength. If you ask me to *thank* my mother for that strength, the day will never come. But unlike my mother, I'm not alone. When I think of all the joy in my life today—my friends, the people I work with who admire me, the people I care about—I treasure the fact that I am capable of giving and receiving trust and love. My mother never knew peace—all she knew was war. I'm acquainted with war. So I know how sweet peace can be.

Marlene, forty-six:

> There are no easy answers. The hardest thing to accept is that you can only change yourself, not your mother. All you can do is keep working on yourself and be as full of optimism and as much a part of life as you can be, and not get in your own way.
>
> That's the best one can do. And it's enough for me.

Final Thoughts: Some Guidelines on Divorcing Your Mother

Don't do it to punish her. Some women reject their mothers in a kind of "I'll show *her*!" attitude, a form of filial machismo. As we have seen, such divorces are really pyrrhic victories—you've declared war, and you're in for a long and bloody struggle. This stance could ultimately destroy all your attachments.

Do focus on your own needs and feelings. If you do see your mother occasionally, you need to stay within yourself, setting limits on her behavior and being very clear about your own beliefs and values.

Try a temporary separation. As we saw, sometimes a "vacation" can help lower your anger and anxiety long enough to sort out your highly charged reactions. Some daughters are able to find enough of value in their mothers to want to reconnect and redirect their relationships. Tell your mother, without adopting a punitive tone or precondition, what you are doing—sometimes, it may be enough to jolt her into at least examining her part in your estrangement. If she knows exactly what the consequences are of her destructive behavior, she might begin to make an effort to correct it.

Be utterly convinced that you have absolutely no alternative. If you believe that your mother will never be able to make an effort to behave in a way that is anything but systematically and deliberately hurtful to you, it may be necessary for you to stop seeing her. There is no point in throwing good love after bad, expending emotional effort in a relationship that probably is never going to get better.

If you find you must let go, know that your mother is more to be pitied, and *it isn't your fault* that she can't be loving to you on any level. Your lovability is not contingent on whether or not *she* loves you. Mourn your loss and you will be able to develop your own talent for loving, for being friends with your children when they are grown, and for creating out of your desperate history a whole and optimistic future.

Part Five
Closing the Circle

Epilogue
Five Generations,
One Family Album

*When my daughter, Jenny, was sixteen, I had a dream. In it,
I am on one side of a river, a strand of silver that splits a
vast, hushed valley. The deepening greens of lush fir trees
behind me recede to black in the waning afternoon. Far below,
flecks of gold sparkle on the river, as though the sun were
caught inside it.*

*On the other side, Jenny is walking along a trail with some
people I don't know. I call to her, but she doesn't hear me.
She talks easily with her companions, her lovely face softened
by a smile. Watching her, I am damp with sweat, terrified for
her, because she is beyond me, beyond my protection.*

*I can't get the two images, the two feelings, to fit together:
on my side of the river, now plunged in shadows, I am chilled
with fear. On Jenny's side of the river, she is serene, bathed in
the pastels of the last light of day, warmed by the afterglow of
the astonishing sky, as though the sun were now inside her. I
am stunned by the contrast. How can it be that I am cold and
afraid, and she is warm and content? Is it because I cannot
accept that she is happy without me?*

*No, that isn't it. I am frightened for myself because I have
been left by the person who means more to me than the world,
the same feeling I had as a child when I was "left" by my
mother. Jenny is gone and has taken the sunlight with her. And
I am alone in the dark.*

"Congratulations. It's a girl!" the doctor announced when Jenny was
born on a spring day twenty years ago. I nearly swooned with

joy—relieved that I wouldn't have to confront my ambivalence about men, ecstatic to have a gender partner.

With my daughter—*my daughter*, the words felt odd and wonderful in my mouth, like exotic fruit—I could start fresh. I could begin life again, in a kind of spiritual rebirth of my own. I would have a real family.

With Jenny, I would redress the failures of my childhood.

When I recall my beginnings, certain memories loom, casting everything else in shade. I seem to have been noticed only when I made a mistake, a chronic condition, it appeared. Punishments and tongue lashings were swift, and I could never figure out what would set my mother off. The worst thing was to be punished with silence. "You should be able to figure it out," she would say when I asked what was the matter.

I learned early on to apologize even when I had done nothing wrong, to keep my mother's displeasure below the flash point by volunteering for blame. It was an unwritten game we played in which I could participate only by being consummately contrite. Ours was then, and for much of my adulthood, a fearful connection.

But with Jenny, I vowed, it would be different. I would be to her all the things that my mother had not been to me. Where I had felt humiliated and ridiculed, she would feel cherished. Where I had been neglected, she would be nurtured. Where I had been terrified, she would be utterly secure.

I did not realize, because I couldn't know it yet, that at the moment of her birth, Jenny inherited not only my joy but all my convoluted history and curious emotional legacies, all the unfinished sentences of my childhood.

Jenny embarked on her life burdened by the highest expectation a mother can bequeath: *You will make up for everything.* And in ways beyond counting, she did, because she enabled me to see the world through her young eyes. When she was an infant, I—a city girl, raised in Manhattan—took her on long walks through the woods near my suburban house, pointing out birds and butterflies and worms and insects. Creatures that once sent me scampering with screams of "Kill it! Kill it!" now became gifts to give her as we explored the world together. Thunderstorms that used to send me burrowing under the covers became fables about clouds clapping their hands. Life was full of miracles that I had never before noticed. Where had I been for the previous thirty years?

Suddenly I could tame the skies, befriend the fauna, make the world safe and gentle and inviting, because I had someone to protect. The only thing I couldn't shield her from was my all-consuming love.

If Jenny's infancy brought me newborn wonder and beauty, it was a temporary, blissful hiatus in the chaos of my life, because it was contingent on her unfettered adoration of me. I was going to be the first mother since the beginning of time to have a seamless bond of love with my daughter. We would be innocents *together*, our relationship so special, so solid, that nothing would ever shake it.

When she was eleven, I remarked to her that the only difference between grown-ups and children is that grown-ups come in bigger packages. Inside, we still feel like little kids. "That's the best-kept secret of adulthood," I said, chuckling.

My adulthood, I should have said. For most of my life, I felt as vulnerable as I had ever felt—the trick was not to let it show. I thought having a child would eclipse my childhood, a theory that would be trashed by my maternal experience.

By the time of her adolescence, which exploded like a cork out of a champagne bottle, I began to see up close the consequences of my loving control and anxieties. I thought I had walled Jenny safely from my past, but somehow I had imprisoned both of us within it. I was living her life for her and not letting her live it for herself.

As she grew up our relationship often felt like a duet in which I sang both parts. One part sang the maxims of parenthood: eat your spinach, tell me your troubles, go to your room. The other part was a countermelody of second-guessing: I should have said that, I shouldn't have said this, I picked a bad time, she didn't mean it, she's a selfish bitch, she's tired, who could blame her, I am afraid of my own child, what's the *matter* with me?

I weighed every word with her, as though on a jeweler's scale. But I longed for a time when we could be easy with each other, when every utterance would not be so heavy with import, when the tone of our conversations would not feel to me as though I had either ruined her day or made my own.

Until her adolescence, Jenny was afraid to do anything without me—go to the ladies' room in a restaurant, run an errand, talk to salespeople. She didn't know how to do anything for herself because I did everything for her—even doing the feeling for her, telling her what to say and how to react. She had no identity. She had no idea how to relate to her peers. All my emotional eggs were in the one basket of my only child—she alone was responsible for making me happy. And she had no one with whom to share the stress of my love and sadness.

I know all this, because she told me—right around the time she became anorexic. Now fully recovered, she recently said of those years, "My body was the only thing over which I had total control."

Jenny's adolescence blew our relationship apart. As her hormones ignited her fiery flight from me, she scrambled for room to breathe, room to be herself without my interpretations of her experiences, my everlasting editing, ameliorating, manipulating of the painful realities of life.

At fifteen, she made a break for it. She ran for her life through self-destructive behavior, which included indifference to her health, indifference to the consequences of her angry and unpredictable outbursts, indifference to everybody's feelings but her own. Jenny's teenage rebellion was such that I felt surrounded by two hurricanes —my roiling feelings about my mother on one side, my volatile and confused teenager on the other.

Because of the terrible effect my maternal enmeshment was having on her, and the pain that her frightening behavior was causing me, I took cover in therapy. Jenny's adolescence forced me to finish growing up—to *pay attention* to the fact that I could not see her as a person apart, and to see that I was still thrashing about in the undertow of unfinished filial business.

With my therapist's help, I learned, finally, to set limits, to establish boundaries, to separate *myself* from Jenny. She asked me to let her assume more responsibility for her life, especially her grades and schoolwork, and I agreed. I did more than that—I also let her assume responsibility for her room, her laundry, and the budgeting of a small clothing allowance. If she ran out of money, she would have to get a job.

I withdrew behind a protective emotional wall that kept her punches from landing, but I did not disengage. I expressed both my love and my refusal to be bullied. Her successes, her failures— except for crises that absolutely required parental intervention—were hers alone to create and to handle. When it came to such decisions as when and where to apply to college, I kept quiet (I admit it—I had to bite the inside of my mouth to make my new resolve stick).

For a long time she didn't like it—pushing buttons that were now disconnected, having a mother who would no longer take her abuse or carry out her orders. Mostly, she didn't like me, or herself.

Without abandoning her, I let her go. The revolution in my

behavior ended up being the best thing I could have done for either of us. When I stopped making Jenny the center of my life, she moved into the center of her own. It was an enormous relief to both of us.

But none of this could have occurred had I not mounted a second front in my battles with my maternal demons. At the same time that I began redirecting and salvaging my relationship with my daughter, I also came to terms with my mother.

How could Jenny know, when she was born, that she was the newest cast member of an ongoing play? How, indeed, could I? Only when Jenny began her angry retreat was I able to take center stage of my own life and begin to figure out the plot. I started tracing my family's history to fill in the holes of my own erratic experience, to make some sense of how I came to be the person I was—a woman who had flunked childhood and was failing motherhood.

I began interviewing my mother, on the rare occasions that we were together, about her life and that of her family. I wanted to know her better. I wanted to find out what shaped her, why she made the choices she did, so that I might understand her, and our relationship.

Some of my mother's answers to my questions resonated like half-remembered snatches of a song—others were entirely new to me. The rest I already knew from stories I had heard since childhood. All this research and my own memories began to coalesce into a recognizable whole.

My maternal grandmother's birth in 1887 and her mother's death were simultaneous, an event that was to reverberate down through the next three generations. Grandma was given a proper, if not loving, upbringing by her cold, rigid, and exacting father, and his spinster sisters. The circumstances of her birth were the genesis of her lifelong estrangement from her older brother—she had "killed" their mother. Her birth must have dealt no less mortal a blow to her relationship with her father. He never displayed any warmth for my grandmother, no emotion, really, except disdain.

She was an enormously talented pianist and had a rich, wonderful voice, gifts that earned her a chance to study at the London Conservatory of Music, which her father forbade her to take. It was a lost opportunity that she never forgot, although she would eventually use her talents to support herself as an organist in pretalkie movie houses.

My grandmother married a man who was in many ways as remote as her father—he was indifferent to passion, she longed for it, she once told me. He was greatly respected for his character and integrity, but he was aloof. My mother was his adored and indulged only child, the sweetness of his life.

My grandparents divorced when my mother was a young girl, a decision that my grandmother abruptly announced in a taxi in front of her, with no preamble. My grandfather had just returned from a business trip to Europe. "I remember the gloves," my mother wistfully recalled of his homecoming gift to her. "They were doe-skin, embroidered with little roses." Their divorce caused a scandal among their pedigreed and morally upright social circle. Many of my mother's schoolmates were forbidden to talk to her.

My grandmother never remarried and for the remaining years of her life lived alone. One of her dying wishes was to be cremated and her ashes buried in her mother's grave, united with her mother in death, if not in life. At the cemetery, the gravediggers opened her father's grave by mistake. My mother became hysterical. "My mother *hated* her father!" she said.

What puzzled me most about all this was the one question I could not ask my mother: How could my grandmother produce a child who seemed so unlike her? Was the grandmother of my fond remembering—who patiently taught me to sew, who tirelessly accompanied me when I was a voice student, who sympathetically listened to all my troubles, who stayed up with me half the night as we devoured old movies on TV and chocolate ice cream—the same woman to her daughter that she was to me?

The answer is that she was not. My grandmother's childhood wounds were still raw when she was a bride and new mother. Among those wounds was that she was not pretty—"handsome," people observed, but not a beauty. In fact, she bore a startling resemblance to her malevolent father. These two facts, taken together with the most important fact of all—her mother's death when she was born—set the scene for the drama into which my mother was born.

I can only imagine the jealousy my grandmother felt toward her daughter. As a child and as a woman, my mother was a staggering beauty, the kind that stopped conversation the minute she walked into a room. "A head-turner," my father once remarked. Grandma must have viewed her child, her female, *beautiful* child—as the chief competitor for her husband's affections. It was happening to her *again:* just as her father had withdrawn from her, so too did her husband. In reaction, she became a strict disciplinarian to my mother, not unlike the way her own father had behaved toward her; once, she made my mother come home from school because she had neglected to make her bed.

In later years, my grandmother tried to make up for her emotionally impoverishing young maternity by being supportive of my mother during her own marital crises, by being loving and understanding to her, by gently defending her to her children. But I don't think their relationship ever fully recovered from my mother's difficult childhood.

My mother carried her troubling history into her first marriage in her early twenties, an unhappy union that produced one daughter and that ended in divorce. Her second marriage was to my father, a man who, like her, was an indulged, beautiful only child. They were wholly miscast for each other, in part because they each had no siblings with whom they had ever had to share the spotlight.

In addition, my father was a dilettante, anathema to the heritage of my industrious Puritan forebears. Because he inherited a fortune sufficient to support him for life, he never had a real career. Rather, he produced self-published poems and essays of unfathomable literary complexity. And, true to his narcissism, he was chronically unfaithful.

After a four-year series of bitter court cases in which they fought for custody of my younger brother and me, they divorced when I was ten, my mother emerging the exhausted victor. (After their divorce, and until my father's death in 1973, I seldom saw him.)

I took this data and factored it into the mix of my own experience, as I examined how my unresolved feelings and lingering fear of my mother were endangering my relationship with my daughter. I knew much of this family lore as it echoed over five generations, beginning with my great-grandmother's tragically premature death. But only in my forties was I sufficiently removed from my childhood to use these facts to help me see my mother as more human, with good qualities and bad, and less as someone intent on harming me.

Still, the facts alone weren't enough to make sense of our relationship; there was an emotional dossier I had to construct, one that even she did not consciously know and so could not give me. It would provide the last piece in the puzzle of our unhappy connection. When I discovered that piece, it was a quantum leap in my understanding of her.

The piece was this: I was her rival for my father's affections. Like my mother, I was a beautiful child. And like my mother with *her* father, I was—at least when I was little—the apple of my father's eye. Just as my mother had "stolen" her father from my grandmother, I unwittingly "stole" my father from my mother—the emotional legacies of her childhood marched inexorably right into my own.

I realize now the enormous threat that my existence posed to my mother. Being so winning was exactly the wrong way to go about getting her to love me, because it made me more appealing to my father. My efforts to woo her were the very thing that made her recoil from me, just as her mother recoiled from her. I don't think she was ever aware of how her history was repeating itself with me.

Only when I was well into adulthood could I understand the cost to me of her anguishing childhood losses. When at twenty-three I began my first round of therapy, I started to recognize that for much of my life I had operated on automatic pilot on a flight path away from my childhood, fueled by my need to punish her. That flight often got hijacked by unhealthy attachments and, ultimately, by neurotic maternal choices, chief of which was the binding of my daughter to me with hoops of steel.

With Jenny's adolescence, I saw that an estrangement similar to mine from my mother was looming, unless, in renewed therapy, I dove back into the emotional waters of my childhood and finally laid it to rest.

I looked at the facts of my history and my feelings about them—felt them, tasted them, grieved for them. And after four more years of help, I got beyond them. Only when I reached the perimeter of my daughter's emancipation and my own middle age could I take the random pieces of my family history and make sense of my role in it.

Once Jenny emerged from her stormy rebellion and the gale-force gusts of adolescence—hers and my own—died down, she and I met on calmer seas. In her twentieth year I told her about my, and my family's, history.

I told her that I had married her father, even though we were unsuited for one another, because with him I could be safe from vulnerability, from intimacy, from choice. By allowing him to treat me like a child, I could keep the real world at bay—until the child in me began to rebel. We divorced when Jenny was seven.

I told her that, appearances notwithstanding, my mother's parenting of me was simply a variation of my parenting of Jenny, because in both cases a child's identity was endangered. By hovering over her every waking and sleeping moment, sweeping the path before her, removing the stumbling blocks, paving the way to a perfect life that required my constant vigilance, I had tried to purchase my indispensability at her expense.

I told her that it wasn't until I was in my forties that I could stand up to my mother. Before then, I had merely been terrified of her—of everything—trembling at the mere sound of her voice saying hello on the telephone, at simply seeing her handwriting on an envelope.

I told her that once I got angry, I couldn't stop. I couldn't relinquish the rage. It enlivened me, animated me, emboldened me. I, who had been so exquisitely polite to rude cashiers in the supermarket, now couldn't *wait* for them to give me a hard time. I could defend myself.

I told her that in all my frenzied childhood and adult coping mechanisms, I was walking backward through my own life, unable to see my mother as she is—a woman who is the sum of her history, her strengths and weaknesses, and, perhaps, regrets.

I told Jenny that therapy had made it possible for me finally to extinguish the anger that had defined me for so long. I no longer required my mother's disapproval or approval—or, for that matter, Jenny's—to feel alive. The life I had built for myself—through therapy, through a rewarding career and enriching friendships, through a loving second marriage, and through allowing my daughter the room to grow and separate—now defined me. Where once I had no boundaries as a child, as a friend, as a wife and mother, now I did.

Finally, I told her that it is painful learning how to grow up, but not as painful as always feeling like a terrified, unmoored child.

When I told all this to Jennifer, she said, "Thank you. You've just explained my life."

When I look at my daughter today, at how she has come to terms with my mothering mistakes, and how she straightforwardly addresses her own ambivalence, which is so different from my own, I see that the awful imperatives of one's history do not need to be passed on, like a sinister, irrevocable trust.

The differences between my daughter and me please me as much as the similarities. Where I was handicapped in ways that will always ache, like an old scar that twinges in damp weather, she has her own separate wounds that no longer paralyze her. Where I wondered if I would ever be happy, she looks forward to her future. Where I had no one—except, periodically, my grandmother—when I was a child, she has the me that I have become, she has a loving stepfather, and a loving family of aunts, uncles, cousins, and our friends.

The most important difference is that she has a true self that she did not have to spend over half her life trying to unearth.

Jenny does not have to try to be something—someone—she is not. She has a vibrant spirit, the curiosity of the artist that she is, a whimsical tolerance for ambiguity. She is now in her own orbit, separate from mine.

The best thing about our relationship is that there is little we cannot talk about, whether painful or joyous. When she was fifteen, I was convinced that she and I could never be friends. Now that she is twenty, I am convinced that we will always be friends. Not best friends. But loving friends who care deeply about each other.

We like each other. We respect each other's privacy. We have learned to let each other be who we are, all our flaws, all our fears, all our blessings, all the things that make us collapse with laughter. We are no longer attached at the hip—when she is hurt, I no longer hemorrhage. When I am irritable, she no longer arms for battle.

We love and admire and abide each other. I can think of no greater gift between a mother and a child.

And what of my mother?

As I was finishing the manuscript for this book, an acquaintance asked me about it, and when I described it—without mentioning my childhood—she said, "You really loathe your mother, don't you?"

There was a time when such a question would have galvanized me into an angry defense, protecting myself from the Bad Mommy Taboo.

Now I gave the question serious consideration. I replied, "No, I don't loathe her. Not anymore. What I do feel, sometimes, is a certain sadness."

I would be lying if I didn't tell you the rest of it. The question haunted me for days. I chewed on it, and took it a step further: Could I now give my mother credit as easily as I once blamed her?

These are the answers I came up with:

The truth is that she gave me these gifts—a love of literature, music, and art; a fine education; an appreciation for men and women of courage and character; a brother and two half sisters with whom I have finally found a sense of biological family after decades of being wary of each other.

The truth is that her greatest gift to me was her mother, who provided the rest of the good things in my childhood: a belief that I have value; hugs and kisses and a lap to crawl into when I was in pain; music to drown out my unhappiness; warmth and unconditional, undemanding, wondrous love that made it possible for me to find the courage to embark on the long journey of emotional healing. The happiest memories of my youth.

The truth is that my mother is generous and loyal to her friends; she is brilliant; and she is utterly dependable.

The truth is that my mother loved me to the best of her ability. If I did not "ask" to have her for a mother, neither did she "ask" to have me for a daughter. I believe that she did the best she could.

The truth is that I will probably always feel some anguish at how she treated me in my childhood. But she is not at all responsible for the mistakes I have made since then. Much of my childhood was her doing. All of my adulthood is my doing.

But there is an X factor in these answers that has nothing, I believe, to do with family legacies. There was some spark within me—fanned, to be sure, by my grandmother—that allowed me to believe that my future life could be better than my childhood. It was the vaguest of dreams, the most unprovable of theorems. But it guided me, even though I would from time to time lose sight of it.

The difference between my mother and me is that where she was trapped by her emotional demons, I could face mine and banish them. The unhappy forces and ill winds that tormented her sadden me. But more than anything, I am sad that she and I could not have what I now have with my daughter. It is the only regret of my life.

I wish my mother well, and I am grateful for the advantages she gave me. I think I understand her, and there is much in her I admire. She did what she could do—had she been able to do otherwise, I know she would have. That's all there is.

Today's mothers are a transitional generation. We are often tentative with our children, especially with our daughters, because we had few role models of how to be with *them* as we wish our mothers—however well-meaning—could have been with *us*. As we adjust to the changing faces of motherhood and family, it is with awkward steps. We feel off-balance, because what we learned as children was all we knew when we became mothers.

But it isn't all we can know. Unlike our mothers, we have the advantage of a social climate that sanctions candor and does not always insist that we keep our feelings and fears quarantined. There are still terrible, dark secrets aplenty lurking in the shadows of families across the country. But when we have the courage to face our fears and mistakes and change, at least now we have someone, something, somewhere—either in books or support groups or in therapy—to give us the help our mothers rarely got in tackling the most complex, challenging, and crucial job there is: raising a child.

Still, there is one unnegotiable fact that transcends all the generalities about social change, about generational conflicts, about historical imperatives, about psychological extradition from maternal "blame": A child's future turns on how his or her mother or father treats her or him in the privacy of a family. There is no mitigation, no excuse for the mutilation of the human spirit that some parents inflict on their children.

Some things are not relative, no matter what one's emotional legacies have been, or how dreadful has been the luck of the parental draw. When it comes to being a parent, either mother or father, we have the power and responsibility to get beyond our childhood losses, our defenses, and our false selves.

Some of the daughters I interviewed are permanently wounded casualties of their childhoods. These handicapped daughters couldn't make it past their own childhood injuries, and their children are the inheritors of their unresolved pain.

But many other daughters want to stop the historical imperative of their parents' mistreatment of them. These daughters, who do not hold their children hostage to their pasts, feel that they *do* have choices: They choose not to humiliate their children. They choose not to degrade them. They choose not to crush their children's innate spirits and optimism, not to punish them for their intrinsic goodness and abilities.

These courageous daughters are rewriting their children's histories where they were helpless to rewrite their own. They are beyond blaming their mothers. They are breaking the cycle of mother–daughter anguish. They are the real heroines of this book. And they are the role models for the next generation.

Notes

Unattributed quotations are from interviews conducted by the author.

Epigraph Alice Miller. *For Your Own Good: Hidden Cruelty in Child-rearing and the Roots of Violence* (New York: Farrar, Straus & Giroux, 1983), p. xi.

Chapter 1: Natural Allies, Natural Enemies

p. xxii " '. . . nothing, ever, wipes out . . .' " Simone de Beauvoir. *A Very Easy Death* (New York: Pantheon Books, 1965), p. 34.

p. 5 " 'natural allies [and] natural enemies . . .' " Liz Smith, *The Mother Book* (New York: Crown, 1984), p. 82.

p. 6 "Women may define themselves . . ." Jane B. Abramson, Ph.D., *Mother-mania: A Psychological Study of Mother–Daughter Conflict* (Lexington, Mass.: Lexington Books, 1987), p. xii.

p. 7 "Infancy is a time . . ." For discussion of early infancy, see Louise J. Kaplan, Ph.D., *Oneness and Separateness: From Infant to Individual* (New York: Simon & Schuster/Touchstone, 1978), pp. 27–28. For discussion of separation and individuation see Margaret Mahler, Fred Pine, and Anni Bergman, *The Psychological Birth of the Human Infant* (New York: Basic Books), 1976.

p. 8 "And if the mother does *not* . . ." Nancy Chodorow, *The Reproduction of Mothering: Psychoanalysis and the Sociology of Gender* (Berkeley: University of California Press, 1978), p. 78.

p. 9 "false self" described in D. W. Winnicott, *The Maturational Processes and the Facilitating Environment* (New York: International Universities Press, 1965).

p. 9 "But once the baby reaches the age . . ." Judith Viorst, *Necessary Losses: The Loves, Illusions, Dependencies and Impossible Expectations That All of Us Have to Give Up in Order to Grow* (New York: Fawcett Gold Medal, 1986), p. 121.

p. 10 " 'The daughter's process . . .' " Lucy Rose Fischer, Ph.D. *Linked Lives: Adult Daughters and Their Mothers* (New York: Harper & Row, 1986), p. 24.

p. 10 "During adolescence . . ." Louise J. Kaplan, Ph.D., *Adolescence: The Farewell to Childhood* (New York: Simon & Schuster/Touchstone, 1985), p. 169.

p. 11   "A boy, in order to . . ." Chodorow, *The Reproduction of Mothering*, p. 174; see also pp. 90–110 for a discussion of difference in the mother–daughter relationship from mother–son, and the father–daughter and father–son relationships.

p. 11   " 'As for daughters . . .' " Ibid., pp. 208–9.

p. 13   "His primary psychological value . . ." Kaplan, *Oneness and Separateness*, p. 138.

p. 13   " 'begin to experience the possibilities . . .' " Ibid., p. 221.

p. 15   "According to Dr. Louise J. Kaplan . . ." Kaplan, *Oneness and Separateness*, pp. 18–19.

Chapter 2: Good Mommy/Bad Mommy

p. 18   "According to a study . . ." Grace Baruch and Rosalind Barnett (with Caryl Rivers), *Lifeprints: New Patterns of Love and Work for Today's Women* (New York: New American Library/Plume, 1984), p. 193.

p. 18   " 'She could not see . . .' " Vivian Gornick, *Fierce Attachments: A Memoir* (New York: Simon & Schuster/Touchstone, 1987), p. 126.

p. 20   "One definition of a good mother . . ." James Garbarino, Edna Guttmann, and Janis Wilson Seeley, *The Psychologically Battered Child: Strategies for Identification, Assessment and Intervention* (San Francisco: Jossey-Bass, 1986), p. 231.

p. 20   "Another is that the good mother . . ." Alice Miller, *The Drama of the Gifted Child: The Search for the True Self* (New York: Basic Books, 1981), p. 33.

p. 20   " 'Her less-than-perfect . . .' " Kaplan, Ph.D., *Oneness and Separateness*, p. 197.

p. 24   "As one authority puts it, 'In almost all cases . . .' " Garbarino et al., *The Psychologically Battered Child*, p. 7.

p. 24   "A child who believes . . ." Ibid., p. 62.

p. 24   "Even though it does not draw blood . . ." Ibid., p. 9.

p. 25   "Dr. Garbarino and his coauthors . . ." Ibid., p. 8.

p. 25   " '*Rejecting* . . . normal social experience . . .' " Ibid.

p. 25   "Some authorities consider emotional . . ." John Crewdson, *By Silence Betrayed: The Sexual Abuse of Children in America* (Boston: Little, Brown, 1988), p. 67.

p. 26   "Such children often become narcissists . . ." Ibid., p. 67.

p. 26   "*But it is profoundly harmful* . . ." Garbarino et al., *The Psychologically Battered Child*, p. 8.

p. 29   " 'Parents . . . drive sisters . . .' " Elizabeth Fishel, *Sisters: Love and Rivalry Inside the Family and Beyond* (New York: William Morrow, 1979), pp. 108–9, 159.

p. 37   " 'We punish our children . . .' " Miller, *For Your Own Good*, p. xi.

p. 37   " 'Those who are permitted . . .' " Ibid., p. 65.

p. 37   "According to a study . . ." "Sad Legacy of Abuse: The Search for Remedies," by Daniel Goleman, *The New York Times*, January 24, 1989, p. C1.

Chapter 3: The Bad Mommy Taboo

p. 41   " 'There is one taboo . . .' " Miller, *The Drama of the Gifted Child*, p. 4.

p. 42   "According to a 1989 article in *People* . . ." "Running for Their Lives," by Jane Sims Podesta and David Van Biema, *People*, January 23, 1989, p. 72.

p. 42   "As journalist John Crewdson . . ." Crewdson, *By Silence Betrayed*, p. 81.

p. 43   "According to anthropologist Maxine L. Margolis . . ." Maxine L. Margolis, *Mothers and Such: Views of American Women and Why They Changed* (Berkeley: University of California Press, 1984), p. 12.

p. 43   " 'As for the mother, her very name . . .' " Ibid., p. 49, citing President Theodore Roosevelt's address, "The American Woman as Mother," before the National Congress of Mothers, reprinted in *Ladies' Home Journal*, July 22, 1905.

p. 44   "in the laws in thirty-one states that allow corporal punishment . . ." *The New York Times*, August 16, 1989, p. B10.

p. 44   "What is considered appropriate . . ." Garbarino et al., *The Psychologically Battered Child*, p. 10.

p. 44   " 'Even truly Christian pedagogy . . .' " Miller, *For Your Own Good*, p. 44, citing Katharina Rutschky, *Schwarze Padagogik* [Black Pedagogy] (Berlin, 1977).

p. 44   " 'willfulness must be broken . . .' " Ibid., p. 47, also citing Rutschky.

p. 44   "In a 1987 *New York Times* article . . ." "Shame Steps Out of Hiding and into Sharper Focus," by Daniel Goleman, *The New York Times*, September 15, 1987, p. C1.

p. 45   "Family therapist Marilyn Mason . . ." Ibid., p. C6.

p. 45   "Sigmund Freud's 'oedipal theory' . . ." For discussion of the damaging consequences—for women—of this theory, see Crewdson, *By Silence Betrayed*, pp. 39–42; also Miller, *For Your Own Good*, p. 60.

p. 45   "According to John Crewdson . . ." Crewdson, *By Silence Betrayed*, p. 91.

p. 45   " 'When incest victims . . .' " Ibid.

p. 48   "The child cannot afford . . ." For discussion of "splitting," see Viorst, *Necessary Losses*, pp. 36–43; also Kaplan, *Oneness and Separateness*, pp. 42–45.

p. 48   "But even if the mother . . ." Kaplan, *Oneness and Separateness*, p. 204.

p. 51   " '[The child] cannot develop and differentiate . . .' " Miller, *The Drama of the Gifted Child*, p. 12.

p. 51   " '[The child] cannot rely on his own emotions . . .' " Ibid., p. 14.

p. 51   " 'Instead, he develops . . .' " Ibid., pp. 34–35.

p. 54   " 'I haven't really lived this life . . .' " Alice Koller, *An Unknown Woman: A Journey to Self-Discovery* (New York: Bantam Books, 1983), p. 166.

p. 54   " 'I failed because the things I set . . .' " Ibid., p. 211.

Chapter 4: Evolution of the Unpleasable Mother

p. 60   " 'She had appetites in plenty . . .' " Simone de Beauvoir, *A Very Easy Death* (New York: Pantheon, 1965), pp. 42–43.

p. 61   "The Baby Boom Generation . . ." See Landon Y. Jones, *Great Expectations: America and the Baby Boom Generation* (New York: Ballantine 1986).

p. 61   " 'We ain't never, never gonna grow up!' . . ." "Growing Pains at 40," by Evan Thomas, *Time*, May 19, 1986, p. 24.

p. 62   "by 1989, this family constellation . . ." "Work and Family Responsibilities: Achieving a Balance," A Program Paper of the Ford Foundation, March 1989, p. 3.

p. 62   "In 1940, only 9 percent . . . by 1987, 64 percent . . ." Ibid., p. 10.

p. 62   "In 1960, 13 percent of women . . . more than doubled." *Newsweek*, September 1, 1986, p. 68.

p. 62   "half of all marriages end in divorce . . ." "Work and Family Responsibilities," p. 3.

p. 62   "60 percent of all children born in 1984 . . . women headed 11.5 percent . . ." Ibid.

p. 63   "The preference for male progeny . . ." Barbara Kay Greenleaf, *Children Through the Ages: A History of Childhood* (New York: McGraw-Hill, 1978), p. 7.

p. 63   "As recently as 1976, when women were asked . . ." Fishel, *Sisters*, p. 79, citing *Ms.*, May 1978, p. 20.

p. 65   "The record for the lowest fertility rate . . ." *Time*, May 19, 1986, p. 35.

p. 65   "Mother as madonna . . ." Margolis, *Mothers and Such*, p. 44.

p. 66   "The leading child-rearing guru of the 1920s . . ." " 'Give Me a Dozen Healthy Infants . . .' John B. Watson's Popular Advice on Childrearing, Women, and the Family," by Ben Harris, in Miriam Lewin, ed., *In the Shadow of the Past: Psychology Portrays the Sexes* (New York: Columbia University Press, 1984), p. 127.

p. 66   "Mothers, in their unsullied adoration . . ." Margolis, *Mothers and Such*, p. 44.

p. 66   "At risk were their children . . ." Ibid., p. 52.

p. 66   " 'Never hug and kiss them . . .' " Ibid.

p. 66   "Most children of this period . . ." "Mother: Social Sculptor and Trustee of Faith," by Susan Contratto, in Lewin, ed., *In the Shadow of the Past*, p. 237.

p. 67–68   "Stella Chess, M.D., and Alexander Thomas, M.D. . . ." Alexander Thomas, M.D., and Stella Chess, M.D., *The Dynamics of Psychological Development* (New York: Brunner/Mazel, 1980), pp. 71–72.

p. 68   "According to studies of twins . . ." "Major Personality Study Finds That Traits Are Mostly Inherited," by Daniel Goleman, *The New York Times*, December 2, 1986, C1, citing study of twins at the University of Minnesota.

p. 68   " '[The need for intimacy] is one trait . . .' " Ibid., p. C2.

p. 68   "How they 'fit' together . . ." Thomas and Chess, *The Dynamics of Psychological Development*, p. 75.

p. 71   " 'This mother unconsciously fears . . .' " Bruno Bettelheim, *A Good Enough Parent: A Book on Child Rearing* (New York: Alfred A. Knopf, 1987), p. 294.

p. 71   " 'Focusing on a "problem child" . . .' " Harriet Goldhor Lerner, Ph.D., *The Dance of Anger: A Woman's Guide to Changing the Patterns of Intimate Relationships* (New York: Harper & Row/Perennial Library, 1985), p. 188.

p. 71   "The mechanics of this dynamic is called 'triangling'. . ." For a detailed discussion of "triangling," see Michael E. Kerr and Murray Bowen, *Family Evaluation: An Approach Based on Bowen Theory* (New York: W. W. Norton, 1988), pp. 134–62.

p. 72   " 'The unending adoration lavished . . .' " "The Stolen Birthright: The Adult Sibling in Individual Therapy," by Stephen P. Bank, in Michael D. Kahn and Karen Gail Lewis, eds., *Siblings in Therapy: Life Span and Clinical Issues* (New York: W. W. Norton, 1988), pp. 351–52.

p. 72   "Triangling is also used to *exploit* . . ." For a discussion of triangling vis-à-vis marriage and children, see Kerr and Bowen, *Family Evaluation*, pp. 167–68.

p. 78   " 'An ordinary devoted mother . . . subtly undermine her ambitions.' " Kaplan, *Oneness and Separateness*, pp. 230–31.

p. 78   " 'as long as an object is devalued . . .' " Harriet Goldhor Lerner, Ph.D., *Women in Therapy* (Northvale, N. J.: Jason Aronson, 1988), p. 10.

p. 79   " 'The development of self-esteem . . .' " Thomas and Chess, *The Dynamics of Psychological Development*, p. 190.

Chapter 5: The Doormat

p. 84   "These women are what Dr. Murray Bowen describes as 'deselfed' . . ." Lerner, *Women in Therapy*, p. 182, citing Murray Bowen, *Family Therapy in Clinical Practice* (Northvale, N.J.: Jason Aronson, 1978).

p. 84   " 'The partner who is doing the most sacrificing . . .' " Lerner, *The Dance of Anger*, p. 20.

p. 85   " 'underfunctioning . . .' " Kerr and Bowen, *Family Evaluation*, p. 56.

p. 85   " 'If . . . I were a "never angry" . . .' " Maggie Scarf, *Intimate Partners: Patterns in Love and Marriage* (New York: Random House, 1987), p. 23.

p. 85   "coined the term 'Enabler' . . ." Sharon Wegscheider, *Another Chance: Hope and Health for the Alcoholic Family* (Palo Alto, Calif.: Science and Behavior Books, 1980), p. 101.

p. 86   "One characteristic . . ." Garbarino, et al., *The Psychologically Battered Child*, p. 58.

p. 86   " 'with heads firmly stuck in the sand . . .' " Stephen P. Bank and Michael D. Kahn, *The Sibling Bond* (New York: Basic Books, 1982), p. 204.

p. 87   " 'feeding the hungry heart' . . ." Gineen Roth, *Feeding the Hungry Heart: The Experience of Compulsive Eating* (Indianapolis: Bobbs-Merrill, 1982).

p. 88   " 'I am describing generations . . .' " Kim Chernin, *The Hungry Self: Women, Eating and Identity* (New York: Times Books, 1985), p. 92.

p. 88   "Many of those daughters—as Lucy Rose Fischer . . ." Fischer, *Linked Lives*, p. 166.

Chapter 6: The Critic

p. 97   "A child's winning ways . . ." Miller, *The Drama of the Gifted Child*, p. 67.

p. 102   "She cannot risk a peer relationship . . ." Abramson, *Mothermania*, pp. 17–18.

p. 102   For a discussion of the "rejecting" parent, see Garbarino et al., *The Psychologically Battered Child*, pp. 25, 53.

p. 105   " 'If they had always insisted . . .' " Malcolm Cowley, *The View from 80* (New York: Viking Press, 1980), p. 56.

p. 106   "the Critic, was probably raised *exactly the same way.*" Abramson, *Mothermania*, p. 21.

p. 107   "This behavior is symptomatic . . ." Garbarino et al., *The Psychologically Battered Child*, pp. 53–55.

p. 107   "She hides her dependency . . ." Abramson, *Mothermania*, p. 22.

Chapter 7: The Smotherer

p. 114   " 'In their study of mother–daughter relationships . . .' " Baruch, Barnett, and Rivers, *Lifeprints*, p. 84.

p. 114   " 'focused on the children as separate . . .' " Ibid., p. 83.

p. 115   " 'pursuers'—they do the "feeling" work . . .' " Lerner, *The Dance of Anger*, p. 191.

p. 116   " 'The child who is emotionally "smothered" . . .' " Crewdson, *By Silence Betrayed*, p. 67.

p. 119   " 'People become overinvolved in trying to fix . . .' " Kerr and Bowen, *Family Evaluation*, p. 109.

p. 120   " 'These daughters . . . "listen" to their mothers' advice . . .' " Fischer, *Linked Lives*, p. 59.

p. 120   " '[The mother] falls apart . . .' " Kaplan, *Oneness and Separateness*, p. 196.

p. 122   " 'For those of us who believe . . .' " Lerner, *The Dance of Anger*, p. 142.

Chapter 8: The Avenger

p. 129   " 'The safer course is to make sure . . .' " Kaplan, *Oneness and Separateness*, p. 43.

p. 130   "that child is usually in for her cruelest treatment." Chodorow, *The Reproduction of Mothering*, pp. 99–104.

p. 138   " 'One way women manifest their aggression . . .' " "The Bully: New Research Depicts a Paranoid, Lifelong Loser" by Daniel Goleman, *The New York Times*, April 7, 1987, p. C4.

p. 138   "Such children are six times more likely . . ." "And Thousands More," by Barbara Kantrowitz, *Newsweek*, December 12, 1988, p. 59.

p. 138   "An example of this kind of maternal legacy . . ." "Emotional Child Abuse" by Jean Seligmann, *Newsweek*, October 3, 1988, p. 48.

p. 139   "She rejects, isolates, terrorizes . . ." Garbarino et al., *The Psychologically Battered Child*, p. 8.

p. 139   "Such parents, he writes, 'perceive the child . . .' " Ibid., p. 57.

p. 139   " 'Such a child then grows up . . .' " Kaplan, *Oneness and Separateness*, p. 203.

p. 139   " 'narcissistic personality disorder.' " *The Diagnostic and Statistical Manual of Mental Disorders*, third edition, revised (Washington, D.C.: the American Psychiatric Association, 1987), p. 349.

p. 140   "This lack of empathy makes it extremely difficult . . ." "Narcissism Looming Larger as Root of Personality Woes," by Daniel Goleman, *The New York Times*, November 1, 1988, p. C1.

p. 140   "The Avenger is all bluster and little confidence . . ." Christopher Lasch, *The Culture of Narcissism: American Life in an Age of Diminishing Expectations* (New York: Warner Books, 1979), pp. 74–83.

p. 140   "Keeping her child imperfect . . ." Kaplan, *Oneness and Separateness*, p. 48.

p. 140   " 'are struggling to regain . . .' " Miller, *For Your Own Good*, p. 16.

Chapter 9: The Deserter

p. 145   "Silence breaks the heart." "A Choice of Weapons," Phyllis McGinley, *Times Three* (New York Viking, 1960), p. 159.

p. 148   "This kind of Deserter is what authorities . . . describe as 'psychologically unavailable' " . . . "Invulnerability among Abused and Neglected Children," Farber and Egeland in Anthony and Cohler, eds., *The Invulnerable Child*, p. 263.

p. 148   " 'barrier of silence.' " Garbarino et al., *The Psychologically Battered Child*, p. 26.

p. 149   "In the alcoholic family, there is often a history . . ." Wegscheider, *Another Chance*, from foreword by Kenneth E. Williams, M.D., p. 21.

p. 149   "The alcoholic family is bound by secrets . . ." Ibid., p. 83.

p. 151   " 'Unfortunately,' she writes in *Another Chance* . . ." Ibid., p. 66.

p. 151   " 'the disease of non-attachment.' " Selma Fraiberg, *Every Child's Birthright: In Defense of Mothering* (New York: Bantam Books, 1977), pp. 51, 133.

p. 151   " 'In personal encounter with such an individual . . .' " Ibid., p. 53.

p. 151   "These people are neither clinically . . ." Ibid., p. 51.

p. 151   "killers who commit random murders . . ." Ibid., pp. 54–55.

p. 155   "As Drs. Michael Kerr and Murray Bowen . . ." Kerr and Bowen, *Family Evaluation*, p. 85.

p. 155   " 'Adjustments made by an individual . . .' " Ibid.

p. 155   " 'Chronic psychosis and depression . . .' " Ibid., p. 87.

p. 155   " 'delusion. The most tragic miscalculation . . .' " Wegscheider, *Another Chance*, p. 98.

p. 156   " 'exhibited the largest numbers of pathological . . .' " "Invulnerability among Abused and Neglected Children," Farber and Egeland, in Anthony and Cohler, eds., *The Invulnerable Child*, p. 266.

p. 156   " 'the effects of psychological unavailability . . .' " Ibid.

Chapter 10: Balancing Acts

p. 167   " 'What more perfect evidence can there be . . .' " Koller, *An Unknown Woman*, p. 207.

p. 168   " 'a network of interlocking relationships.' " Kerr and Bowen, *Family Evaluation*, p. ix

p. 168   "When we react to other members of the family . . ." Ibid., p. 66.

p. 168   "the *same kinds of triangles*." Ibid., p. 135.

p. 169   "Many social scientists take issue . . ." For a discussion of the "myths" of birth order, see "Enchantment of Siblings: Effects of Birth Order and Trance on Family Myth" by Morton Perlmutter, in Kahn and Lewis, eds., *Siblings in Therapy*, pp. 26–34.

p. 170   "It 'strongly influences our way of negotiating . . .' " Lerner, *The Dance of Anger*, p. 129.

p. 170   "firstborns—since they are first up . . ." Ibid.

p. 170   "But if she is a middle child . . ." Maggie Scarf, *Intimate Partners*, p. 117, citing Walter Toman, *Family Constellation: Its Effect on Personality and Social Behavior* (New York: Springer, 1961).

p. 171   "Parents can instill a trait in a child . . ." Kerr and Bowen, *Family Evaluation*, pp. 210–11.

p. 171   "a mother may become anxious over what she *thinks* is wrong . . ." Ibid., p. 7.

p. 172   "In the interests of survival . . ." Miller, *The Drama of the Gifted Child*, p. 22.

p. 173   "Over and over again we resurrect our childhood reactions . . ." Ibid., pp. 78–83.

p. 174   "Our families often become templates for office . . ." See Paula Bernstein, *Family Ties, Corporate Bonds* (New York: Doubleday, 1985).

p. 176   "The men in our lives are also often variations . . ." Chodorow, *The Reproduction of Mothering*, p. 195.

Chapter 11: The Angel

p. 183   " 'The "best little girl" role . . .' " Kaplan, *Adolescence*, p. 270.

p. 184   "Firstborns are often punished . . ." Bank and Kahn, *The Sibling Bond*, p. 205.

p. 185   "Psychologist Robert Wright has written . . ." Elizabeth Fishel, *Sisters*, p. 7, citing Robert Wright, *The Enterprise of Living* (New York: Holt, Rinehart & Winston, 1976), p. 95.

p. 186   "In the process of helping their daughters . . ." Chodorow, *The Reproduction of Mothering*, p. 135.

p. 187   "The tragic flaw in the Angel's survival mechanism . . ." Abramson, *Mothermania*, p. 17.

p. 189   "the mother exploits the Angel to gain for herself . . ." Miller, *The Drama of the Gifted Child*, p. 35.

p. 189   " 'identification with the aggressor.' " Anna Freud, *The Ego and the Mechanisms of Defense* (New York: International Universities Press, 1946), pp. 109–122.

p. 191   "For these Angels, their illnesses are their rebellions." For a discussion of the connection between physical or mental illness and human adaptiveness and levels of differentiation, see Kerr and Bowen, *Family Evaluation*, pp. 221–81.

p. 191   " 'the woman afflicted with this obsession . . . inflicted upon her.' " Chernin, *The Hungry Self*, p. 125.

p. 192   " '*An eating obsession comes into existence* . . .' " Ibid., p. 130.

p. 192   "In the child, this is called 'symbiotic psychosis' . . . 'schizophrenia.' " Viorst, *Necessary Losses*, p. 29.

p. 193   " 'there is only one person [a] girl hates more . . .' " George Bernard
          Shaw, *Man and Superman*, Act II, in *Nine Plays* (Dodd, Mead, 1935),
          p. 570.
p. 194   "But many Angels persist . . ." Bank and Kahn, *The Sibling Bond*, pp.
          225–26, 231.
p. 195   "But the most insecure Angels . . ." For a discussion of "fear of success"
          in women, see Lerner, *Women in Therapy*, pp. 195ff.

Chapter 12: The Superachiever

p. 204
          Betty Friedan, *The Feminine Mystique* (New York: Dell, 1963).
p. 204   Sherry Suib Cohen, *Tender Power: A Revolutionary Approach to Work and
          Intimacy* (Reading, Mass.: Addison-Wesley, 1988).
p. 205   "Rather, they want to be as *good* as men . . ." Sylvia Ann Hewlett, *A Lesser
          Life: The Myth of Women's Liberation in America* (New York: William Morrow,
          1986), p. 138.
p. 207   " 'A child's sense of not being affirmed . . .' " "Shame Steps Out of
          Hiding and into Sharper Focus," by Daniel Goleman, *The New York Times*,
          September 15, 1987, p. C6.
p. 208   " 'the Hero . . .' " Wegscheider, *Another Chance*, pp. 104–15.
p. 208   "hypertension and ulcers . . ." Ibid., p. 109.
p. 208   " 'self-respect is dependent on qualities . . .' " Miller, *The Drama of the
          Gifted Child*, p. 42.
p. 209   "She will be doubly chagrined . . ." Bank and Kahn, *The Sibling Bond*,
          p. 221.
p. 211   "they are among the hardest to reach in therapy." Wegscheider, *Another
          Chance*, p. 104.
p. 214   "they transfer their unmet childhood needs . . ." For a discussion of how
          many women balance the "independence" of achievement with the "de-
          pendence" of relationships, see Lerner, *Women in Therapy*, p. 207.
p. 215   " 'Feelings of depression and anxiety . . .' " Ibid., p. 196.
p. 216   "She dives in to fix things . . ." For a discussion of "overfunctioning"
          women, see Lerner, *The Dance of Anger*, p. 138.

Chapter 13: The Cipher

p. 224   "The Cipher's personality . . ." For a discussion of "The Lost Child," see
          Wegscheider, *Another Chance*, p. 87.
p. 224   "some kids are simply 'slow-to-warm-up.' " Thomas and Chess, *The Dy-
          namics of Psychological Development*, pp. 71–72.
p. 225   "The Cipher absorbs her mother's displeasure . . ." "The Rotten Core: A
          Defect in the Formation of the Self During the Rapprochement Subphase"
          by Ruth F. Lax, Ph.D., in Ruth F. Lax, Sheldon Bach, and J. Alexis
          Burland, eds., *Rapprochement: The Critical Subphase of Separation-Individuation*,
          (Northvale, N.J.: Jason Aronson, Inc., 1980), p. 441.
p. 225   "She wages war against her anger." Chernin, *The Hungry Self*, p. 93.

p. 226   " 'self-defeating personality disorder' . . ." "New Research Illuminates Self-Defeating Behavior," by Daniel Goleman, *The New York Times*, September 1, 1988, p. C1.

p. 226–7   " 'self-handicapping.' " Ibid., p. C10.

p. 227   "life sometimes presents its own cure . . ." Kerr and Bowen, *Family Evaluation*, p. 56.

p. 228   "They may recognize in her their own . . ." Bank and Kahn, *The Sibling Bond*, p. 203.

p. 228   "Her mother feeds the Cipher's phobia . . ." "Facing Up to School Phobia and Dealing with It," by Joseph Berger, *The New York Times*, October 5, 1988, p. B12.

p. 230   "The Cipher has certain advantages . . ." Wegscheider, *Another Chance*, p. 128.

p. 230   "Some of these women are writers or painters . . ." For a discussion of psychological vulnerability of artists and writers, see E. James Anthony,

p. 230   "Risk, Vulnerability, and Resilience: An Overview," in Anthony and Cohler, eds., *The Invulnerable Child*, pp. 24–27.

p. 231   " 'I was begging . . . forgiveness . . .' " Daphne Merkin, *Enchantment* (New York: Fawcett Crest, 1986), p. 261.

p. 234   "These kids get away with murder . . ." For a discussion of the "infantilizing" of children by needy parents, see Garbarino et al., *The Psychologically Battered Child*, p. 54.

Chapter 14: The Troublemaker

p. 241   " 'The passive, clinging three-year-old . . .' " Thomas and Chess, *The Dynamics of Psychological Development*, pp. 98–99.

p. 241   "She is as emotionally connected . . ." For a discussion of how "troublemakers" function in the family, see Kerr and Bowen, *Family Evaluation*, p. 137.

p. 242   "They were, perversely, fulfilling an important . . ." For a discussion of how parents encourage a child's troublemaking behavior, see Maggie Scarf, *Intimate Partners*, pp. 143–145.

p. 244   "According to Drs. Thomas and Chess . . ." Thomas and Chess, *The Dynamics of Psychological Development*, pp. 72–74.

p. 248   "certain children are tacitly encouraged . . ." Bank and Kahn, *The Sibling Bond*, p. 204.

p. 248   "the Angel may identify with the Good Mommy . . ." For a discussion of how parents each ally with a different child, see Elizabeth Fishel, *Sisters*, p. 186.

p. 248   "the Troublemaker serves as a cautionary tale . . ." "There's a Black Sheep in Every Family Fold," by Margo Kaufman, *The New York Times*, November 23, 1988, p. C5.

p. 250   " 'if one sibling was scapegoated . . .' " Bank and Kahn, *The Sibling Bond*, pp. 225–26.

p. 250   "Success in the family . . ." For a discussion of feelings of shame as the root of irrational anger, see "Shame Steps Out of Hiding and into Sharper Focus," by Daniel Goleman, *The New York Times*, September 15, 1987, p. C6.

p. 253   "Troublemakers tend to have chaotic attachments . . ." Kerr and Bowen, *Family Evaluation*, p. 97.

p. 253   "And at that instant, the Troublemaker is thrown back . . ." Bruno Bettelheim, *A Good Enough Parent*, pp. 292–93.

Chapter 15: The Defector

p. 260   " 'they think they notice that they matter least . . .' " Walter Toman, *Family Constellation: Its Effect on Personality and Social Behavior* (New York: Springer, 1961), cited in Maggie Scarf, *Intimate Partners*, p. 117.

p. 262   " 'some babies start to separate . . .' " Kaplan, *Oneness and Separateness*, p. 122.

p. 262   "They think of the world as essentially inhospitable . . ." Garbarino et al., *The Psychologically Battered Child*, pp. 62–63.

p. 263   For a discussion of invulnerable children, see "Risk, Vulnerability, and Resilience: An Overview," by E. James Anthony, and "Adversity, Resilience, and the Study of Lives," by Bertram J. Cohler, in Anthony and Cohler, eds., *The Invulnerable Child*, pp. 3–48 and 363–424.

p. 263   " 'pain and suffering can have a steeling . . .' " Ibid., p. 180, citing M. Bleuler, *The Schizophrenic Disorders* (New Haven, Conn.: Yale University Press, 1978), p. 409.

p. 266   "But if they don't resolve the relationship . . ." For a discussion of the psychological consequences of "cutting off" from one's mother, see Kerr and Bowen, *Family Evaluation*, pp. 271–76, 324–26.

p. 268   " 'In one sense, the grieving child . . .' " Edgar Johnson, *Charles Dickens: His Tragedy and Triumph* (New York: Penguin, 1977), p. 40.

p. 270   "they require constant reassurance that they are loved." For a discussion of "fear of intimacy," see Abramson, *Mothermania*, pp. 17, 39.

p. 271   For a discussion of the "avoidance" of love, see Chodorow, *The Reproduction of Mothering*, p. 79.

p. 273   "they push their children away in a logic they alone . . ." For a discussion of maternal reaction to a child's moves toward independence, see Kaplan, *Oneness and Separateness*, p. 34.

Chapter 16: Breaking the Cycle

p. 282   "According to numerous studies . . . 'shrinkage.' " Baruch, Barnett, and Rivers, *Lifeprints*, pp. 194–95.

p. 283   "If I declare my emotional independence . . ." For a discussion of female "guilt" vis-à-vis autonomy, see Lerner, *Women in Therapy*, pp. 185–86.

p. 290   " 'From now on . . . spoke it to me is removed.' " Koller, *An Unknown Woman*, p. 108.

p. 290   " 'I can see my own outlines . . . as separate from mine.' " Ibid., p. 240.

p. 293   *"Denying the feelings keeps us imprisoned . . ."* Miller, *The Drama of the Gifted Child*, pp. 83–101.

p. 294   "Mourning the child you were . . ." Ibid., pp. 56–57.

p. 294   "Those moments when we cry . . ." Judith S. Seixas and Geraldine

Youcha, *Children of Alcoholism: A Survivor's Manual* (New York: Crown, 1985), p. 59.

p. 294   "If a person is able . . . begun to relinquish.' " Miller, *The Drama of the Gifted Child*, p. 57.

Chapter 17: Redefining the Mother–Daughter Relationship

p. 297
          " 'detriangling . . .' " Kerr and Bowen, *Family Evaluation*, pp. 149–162.
p. 297   " 'Getting beyond blame . . .' " Ibid., p. 255.
p. 298   "Bowen and Kerr recommend gathering . . ." Ibid., p. 301.
p. 301   " 'Researching one's own family . . .' " Ibid., p. 308.
p. 304   "as Dr. Harriet Goldher Lerner puts it . . . you 'self-focus.' " Harriet Goldhor Lerner, *The Dance of Intimacy: A Woman's Guide to Courageous Acts of Change in Key Relationships* (New York: Harper & Row, 1989), pp. 209–14.
p. 304   "speaking up about issues . . . not through a third party." Lerner, *The Dance of Anger*, pp. 199–201.
p. 304   " 'staying calm . . . staying out . . . hanging in . . .' " Ibid., p. 183.
p. 304–5 " 'no advising, no helping . . .' " Ibid.

Chapter 18: Friendship

p. 312   " 'The absence of war is not peace . . .' " *The New York Times*, October 15, 1988, p. A14.
p. 313   " 'Friendship requires a different type . . .' " Bruno Bettelheim, *A Good Enough Parent*, p. 297.
p. 313   " 'The toddler must say "no" . . .' " Kaplan, *Adolescence*, p. 239.
p. 315   " 'psychological well-being in later life hinges . . .' " *Mothermania*, p. 107.
p. 315   "The most important finding in her study . . ." Ibid.
p. 315   " 'The mother–daughter bond was especially important . . .' " Baruch, Barnett, Rivers, *Lifeprints*, pp. 196–97.
p. 315   " 'whether a woman did or did not have children . . .' " Ibid., p. 80.
p. 316   "Dr. Fischer corroborated the view that . . ." Fischer, *Linked Lives*, p. 64.
p. 316   " '*did not* know what their mothers' lives . . .' " Ibid., p. 67.
p. 316   " 'role colleagues' . . ." Ibid., p. 73.
p. 316   "It was married daughters with children . . . peerlike relationships' . . ." Ibid., p. 64.
p. 316   "the daughter's marriage—and changed allegiance . . ." Ibid., p. 8.
p. 316   "By thirty-five or so . . . ." Baruch et al., *Lifeprints*, p. 195.
p. 316   "In the Baruch–Barnett study, approximately half . . ." Ibid., p. 193.
p. 316   "Three qualities prevailed . . ." Fischer, *Linked Lives*, pp. 55–58.

Chapter 19: Truce

p. 329   " 'Mutual Mothering.' " Fischer, *Linked Lives*, p. 58.
p. 332   " 'Flux is now our daily truth . . .' " Gornick, *Fierce Attachments*, pp. 199–200.
p. 334   " 'Responsible Mothers/Dependent Daughters' . . ." Fischer, *Linked Lives*, p. 49.

p. 335   " 'Responsible Daughters/Dependent Mothers.' " Ibid., p. 53.

p. 335   "There is a supreme irony . . ." Ibid., p. 55.

Chapter 20: Divorce

p. 358   " 'Those who actually had the privilege . . .' " Miller, *For Your Own Good*, pp. 62–63.

Bibliography

Abramson, Jane B. *Mothermania: A Psychological Study of Mother–Daughter Conflict*, Lexington, Mass.: Lexington Books, 1987.

Anthony, E. James, and Bertram J. Cohler, eds. *The Invulnerable Child*. New York: Guilford Press, 1987.

Bank, Stephen P., and Michael D. Kahn, *The Sibling Bond*. New York: Basic Books, 1982.

Baruch, Grace, and Rosalind Barnett (with Caryl Rivers). *Lifeprints: New Patterns of Love and Work for Today's Woman*. New York: New American Library, 1984.

Bernstein, Paula. *Family Ties, Corporate Bonds: How We Act Out Family Roles in the Office*. New York: Doubleday, 1985.

Bettelheim, Bruno. *A Good Enough Parent: A Book on Child Rearing*. New York: Alfred A. Knopf, 1987.

Bleuler, M. *The Schizophrenia Disorders*. New Haven, Conn.: Yale University Press, 1978.

Bowen, Murray. *Family Therapy in Clinical Practice*. Northvale, N.J.: Jason Aronson, 1978.

Cahill, Susan, ed. *Mothers: Memories, Dreams and Reflections by Literary Daughters*. New York: New American Library, 1988.

Chernin, Kim. *The Hungry Self: Women, Eating and Identity*. New York: Times Books, 1985.

Chodorow, Nancy. *The Reproduction of Mothering: Psychoanalysis and the Sociology of Gender*. Berkeley: University of California Press, 1978.

Cohen, Sherry Suib. *Tender Power: A Revolutionary Approach to Work and Intimacy*. Reading, Mass.: Addison-Wesley, 1988.

Cowley, Malcolm. *The View from 80*. New York: Viking Press, 1980.

392

Crawford, Christina. *Mommie Dearest.* New York: William Morrow, 1978. (Paper: Berkley, 1984.)

Crewdson, John. *By Silence Betrayed: The Sexual Abuse of Children in America.* Boston: Little, Brown, 1988.

de Beauvoir, Simone. *A Very Easy Death.* New York: Pantheon, 1965.

Faber, Adele, and Elaine Mazlish. *Siblings Without Rivalry: How to Help Your Children Live Together So You Can Live Too.* New York: Norton, 1987.

Fischer, Lucy Rose. *Linked Lives: Adult Daughters and Their Mothers.* New York: Harper & Row, 1986.

Fishel, Elizabeth. *Sisters: Love and Rivalry Inside the Family and Beyond.* New York: William Morrow, 1979.

Fraiberg, Selma. *Every Child's Birthright: In Defense of Mothering.* New York: Bantam Books, 1977.

Freud, Anna. *The Ego and the Mechanisms of Defense.* New York: International Universities Press, 1946.

Friday Nancy. *My Mother/My Self: The Daughter's Search for Identity.* New York: Delacorte Press, 1977.

Friedan, Betty. *The Feminine Mystique.* New York: Dell, 1963.

Garbarino, James, Edna Guttmann, and Janis Wilson Seeley. *The Psychologically Battered Child: Strategies for Identification, Assessment and Intervention.* San Francisco: Jossey-Bass, 1986.

Gaylin, Willard. *Rediscovering Love.* New York: Viking/Penguin, 1987.

Gilligan, Carol. *In a Different Voice: Psychological Theory and Women's Development.* Cambridge, Mass.: Harvard University Press, 1982.

Gornick, Vivian. *Fierce Attachments: A Memoir.* New York: Simon & Schuster/Touchstone, 1987.

Greenleaf, Barbara Kay. *Children Through the Ages: A History of Childhood.* New York: McGraw-Hill, 1978.

Hewlett, Sylvia Ann. *A Lesser Life: The Myth of Women's Liberation in America.* New York: William Morrow, 1986.

Johnson, Edgar. *Charles Dickens: His Tragedy and Triumph.* New York: Penguin, 1977.

Jones, Landon Y. *Great Expectations: America and the Baby Boom Generation.* New York: Ballantine, 1986.

Kahn, Michael D., and Karen Gail Lewis, eds. *Siblings in Therapy: Life Span and Clinical Issues.* New York: W. W. Norton, 1988.

Kaplan, Louise J. *Adolescence: The Farewell to Childhood* (New York: Simon & Schuster/Touchstone, 1985).

————. *Oneness and Separateness: From Infant to Individual*. New York: Simon & Schuster/Touchstone, 1978.

Kerr, Michael E., and Murray Bowen. *Family Evaluation: An Approach Based on Bowen Theory*, New York: W. W. Norton, 1988.

Koller, Alice. *An Unknown Woman: A Journey to Self-Discovery*, New York: Bantam Books, 1983.

Lasch Christopher. *The Culture of Narcissism: American Life in an Age of Diminishing Expectations*. New York: Warner Books, 1979.

Lax, Ruth F., Sheldon Bach, and J. Alexis Burland, eds. *Rapprochement: The Critical Subphase of Separation-Individuation*. Northvale, N.J.: Jason Aronson, 1980.

Lerner, Harriet Goldhor. *The Dance of Anger: A Woman's Guide to Changing the Patterns of Intimate Relationships*. New York: Harper & Row/Perennial Library, 1985.

————. *The Dance of Intimacy: A Woman's Guide to Courageous Acts of Change in Key Relationships*. New York: Harper & Row, 1989.

————. *Women in Therapy*. Northvale, N.J.: Jason Aronson, 1988.

Lewin, Miriam, ed. *In the Shadow of the Past: Psychology Portrays the Sexes*. New York: Columbia University Press, 1984.

Mahler, Margaret, Fred Pine, and Anni Bergman. *The Psychological Birth of the Human Infant*. New York: Basic Books, 1976.

Margolis, Maxine L. *Mothers and Such: Views of American Women and Why They Changed*. Berkeley: University of California Press, 1984.

Marlin, Emily. *Hope: New Choices and Recovery Strategies for Adult Children of Alcoholics*. New York: Harper & Row, 1987.

Merkin, Daphne. *Enchantment*. New York: Fawcett Crest, 1986.

Miller Alice. *The Drama of the Gifted Child: The Search for the True Self*. Basic Books, 1981.

————. *For Your Own Good: Hidden Cruelty in Child-rearing and the Roots of Violence*. New York: Farrar, Straus & Giroux, 1983.

————. *Thou Shalt Not Be Aware: Society's Betrayal of the Child*, Trans. H&H Hannum. New York: Farrar, Straus & Giroux, Inc., 1984

Roth, Gineen. *Feeding the Hungry Heart*. Indianapolis: Bobbs-Merrill, 1982.

Satir, Virginia. *The New Peoplemaking*. Mountain View, Calif.: Science and Behavior Books, 1988.

Scarf, Maggie. *Intimate Partners: Patterns in Love and Marriage*. New York: Random House, 1987.

————. *Unfinished Business: Pressure Points in the Lives of Women*. New York: Doubleday, 1980.

Secunda, Victoria. *By Youth Possessed: The Denial of Age in America*. New York: Bobbs-Merrill, 1984.

Seixas, Judith S., and Geraldine Youcha. *Children of Alcoholism: A Survivor's Manual.* New York: Crown, 1985.

Singer, Lilly, Margaret Sirot, and Susan Rodd. *Beyond Loss: A Practical Guide Through Grief to a Meaningful Life.* New York: E. P. Dutton, 1988.

Smith, Liz. *The Mother Book: A Compendium of Trivia and Grandeur Concerning Mothers, Motherhood and Maternity.* Abridged. New York: Crown, 1984.

Thomas, Alexander, and Stella Chess. *The Dynamics of Psychological Development.* New York: Brunner/Mazel, 1980.

Toman, Walter. *Family Constellation: Its Effects on Personality and Social Behavior.* New York: Springer, 1961.

Towle, Alexandra, ed. *Mothers: A Celebration in Prose, Poetry, and Photographs of Mothers and Motherhood,* New York: Simon & Schuster, 1988.

Viorst, Judith. *Necessary Losses: The Loves, Illusions, Dependencies and Impossible Expectations That All of Us Have to Give Up in Order to Grow.* New York: Fawcett Gold Medal, 1986.

Wegscheider, Sharon. *Another Chance: Hope and Health for the Alcoholic Family.* Palo Alto, Calif.: Science and Behavior Books, 1980.

Winnicott, D. W. *The Maturational Processes and the Facilitating Environment.* New York: International Universities Press, 1965.

Wright, Robert. *The Enterprise of Living.* New York: Holt, Rinehart & Winston, 1976.

Index